MW00650812

Praise for *Business Forecasting: Practical Problems and Solutions*

This book is the survivor's guide for business forecasters. It covers a wide range of need-to-know topics from "what is demand" to "why should I trust your forecast."

—Scott Roy, Collaboration Planning Manager, Wells Enterprises Inc.

This is a wonderful resource for anyone in the field of forecasting, covering all of the major areas that a practitioner would need in order to be successful. This book covers the key areas of concern for most folks dealing with forecast, from basics such as forecastability and benchmarking to more advanced topics like dealing with politics in forecast. I would definitely recommend this reader as a key resource for those looking to learn more or to have knowledge at their fingertips for that moment when they need a refresher.

—Curtis Brewer, Forecasting Manager, Bayer CropScience

An essential reading on business forecasting indeed! Every article is in its place, and every one is worth reading. In spite of my many years in forecasting and planning, the reading was so captivating that I could not stop before it was over. Absolutely a "must read" for every person working in business forecasting.

—Igor Gusakov, Consulting Director, Goodsforecast

The science of forecasting has existed for centuries and continues to evolve. However, while it asymptotically approaches better methods of prediction, it will always have its limits. Forecasting must be recognized as a science and an art. *Business Forecasting: Practical Problems and Solutions* is an honest and true look at the craft of forecasting. This is a tremendous compilation from some of the best forecasting analytics and business minds of today. A reference that should be on the shelf of anyone whose job is to develop forecasts.

—Jim Ferris, Director of Supply Chain Analytics, Clarkston Consulting

The editors do an excellent job of introducing a broad set of topics critical for deploying and maintaining a successful forecasting process within an organization.

—Sam Iosevich, Managing Principal, Prognos

In this age when "big data," "machine learning," and "data science" are attracting all of the attention, the art and science of forecasting is often neglected. Since many forecasting methods and practices date back decades, the temptation is to conclude that "there is nothing new there." This terrific compilation of writings—from virtually all of the big names in the forecasting community—proves that innovation in forecasting is vibrant. More accurate forecasts can be one of the most effective drivers of a firm's financial performance, and the learnings gleaned from this book are sure to help any organization improve.

—Rob Stevens, Vice President, First Analytics

This book is a wonderful compendium of demand planning and S&OP insights drawn from some of the best minds and practitioners in the industry.

—Patrick Bower, Sr. Director, Global Supply Chain Planning & Customer Service, Combe Incorporated

Finally, a book tailored to business forecasting that is comprehensive for everything from data gathering to the art and politics of explaining why we are wrong!

—Eric Wilson, Director Demand Planning and S&OP, Tempur Sealy International

Business Forecasting: Practical Problems and Solutions gathers knowledge from around the globe some 60 years after computer-era forecasting research began by pioneers such as Robert G. Brown (the "father of exponential smoothing"). As a protégé of Brown's, I appreciate the content as it reflects his aptitude for capturing "lots of good ole logic."

—Donald Parent, CPF, CFPIM, CSCP, LOGOLville.com

The editors of this book of essential readings for the business forecaster have achieved their objective to "assemble a mix of the most interesting, important and influential authors and their writings in applied forecasting since 2001." Practitioners as well as forecasting managers will find this volume well-organized in these four general areas: fundamental considerations, methods of statistical forecasting, performance evaluation and reporting, and process and politics, which, along with the summaries beginning each section, make it easy for the reader to find the appropriate selection addressing the real-world forecasting challenge being faced. I predict that this volume will prove vital as a reference to all those who seek "to generate forecasts as accurate and unbiased as can be reasonably expected—and to do this as efficiently as possible."

—Carolyn I. Allmon, Detector Electronics Corporation

Business Forecasting

Wiley & SAS Business Series

The Wiley & SAS Business Series presents books that help senior-level managers with their critical management decisions.

Titles in the Wiley & SAS Business Series include:

Agile by Design: An Implementation Guide to Analytic Lifecycle Management by Rachel Alt-Simmons

Analytics in a Big Data World: The Essential Guide to Data Science and Its Applications by Bart Baesens

Bank Fraud: Using Technology to Combat Losses by Revathi Subramanian

Big Data Analytics: Turning Big Data into Big Money by Frank Ohlhorst

Big Data, Big Innovation: Enabling Competitive Differentiation through Business Analytics by Evan Stubbs

Business Analytics for Customer Intelligence by Gert Laursen

Business Forecasting: Practical Problems and Solutions edited by Michael Gilliland, Len Tashman, and Udo Sglavo

The Business Forecasting Deal: Exposing Myths, Eliminating Bad Practices, Providing Practical Solutions by Michael Gilliland

Business Intelligence Applied: Implementing an Effective Information and Communications Technology Infrastructure by Michael Gendron

Business Intelligence and the Cloud: Strategic Implementation Guide by Michael S. Gendron

Business Transformation: A Roadmap for Maximizing Organizational Insights by Aiman Zeid

Connecting Organizational Silos: Taking Knowledge Flow Management to the Next Level with Social Media by Frank Leistner

Data-Driven Healthcare: How Analytics and BI Are Transforming the Industry by Laura Madsen

Delivering Business Analytics: Practical Guidelines for Best Practice by Evan Stubbs

Demand-Driven Forecasting: A Structured Approach to Forecasting, Second Edition by Charles Chase

Demand-Driven Inventory Optimization and Replenishment: Creating a More Efficient Supply Chain by Robert A. Davis

Developing Human Capital: Using Analytics to Plan and Optimize Your Learning and Development Investments by Gene Pease, Barbara Beresford, and Lew Walker

The Executive's Guide to Enterprise Social Media Strategy: How Social Networks Are Radically Transforming Your Business by David Thomas and Mike Barlow

Economic and Business Forecasting: Analyzing and Interpreting Econometric Results by John Silvia, Azhar Iqbal, Kaylyn Swankoski, Sarah Watt, and Sam Bullard

Financial Institution Advantage and the Optimization of Information Processing by Sean C. Keenan

Financial Risk Management: Applications in Market, Credit, Asset, and Liability Management and Firmwide Risk by Jimmy Skoglund and Wei Chen

Foreign Currency Financial Reporting from Euros to Yen to Yuan: A Guide to Fundamental Concepts and Practical Applications by Robert Rowan

Fraud Analytics Using Descriptive, Predictive, and Social Network Techniques: A Guide to Data Science for Fraud Detection by Bart Baesens, Veronique Van Vlasselaer, and Wouter Verbeke

Harness Oil and Gas Big Data with Analytics: Optimize Exploration and Production with Data Driven Models by Keith Holdaway

Health Analytics: Gaining the Insights to Transform Health Care by Jason Burke

Heuristics in Analytics: A Practical Perspective of What Influences Our Analytical World by Carlos Andre, Reis Pinheiro, and Fiona McNeill

Hotel Pricing in a Social World: Driving Value in the Digital Economy by Kelly McGuire

Human Capital Analytics: How to Harness the Potential of Your Organization's Greatest Asset by Gene Pease, Boyce Byerly, and Jac Fitz-enz

Implement, Improve and Expand Your Statewide Longitudinal Data System: Creating a Culture of Data in Education by Jamie McQuiggan and Armistead Sapp

Killer Analytics: Top 20 Metrics Missing from your Balance Sheet by Mark Brown

Mobile Learning: A Handbook for Developers, Educators, and Learners by Scott McQuiggan, Lucy Kosturko, Jamie McQuiggan, and Jennifer Sabourin

The Patient Revolution: How Big Data and Analytics Are Transforming the Healthcare Experience by Krisa Tailor

Predictive Analytics for Human Resources by Jac Fitz-enz and John Mattox II

Predictive Business Analytics: Forward-Looking Capabilities to Improve Business Performance by Lawrence Maisel and Gary Cokins

Retail Analytics: The Secret Weapon by Emmett Cox

Social Network Analysis in Telecommunications by Carlos Andre Reis Pinheiro

Statistical Thinking: Improving Business Performance, Second Edition by Roger W. Hoerl and Ronald D. Snee

Taming the Big Data Tidal Wave: Finding Opportunities in Huge Data Streams with Advanced Analytics by Bill Franks

Too Big to Ignore: The Business Case for Big Data by Phil Simon

The Value of Business Analytics: Identifying the Path to Profitability by Evan Stubbs

The Visual Organization: Data Visualization, Big Data, and the Quest for Better Decisions by Phil Simon

Trade-Based Money Laundering: The Next Frontier in International Money Laundering Enforcement by John Cassara

Understanding the Predictive Analytics Lifecycle by Al Cordoba

Unleashing Your Inner Leader: An Executive Coach Tells All by Vickie Bevenour

Using Big Data Analytics: Turning Big Data into Big Money by Jared Dean

Visual Six Sigma, Second Edition by Ian Cox, Marie Gaudard, Philip Ramsey, Mia Stephens, and Leo Wright

Win with Advanced Business Analytics: Creating Business Value from Your Data by Jean Paul Isson and Jesse Harriott

For more information on any of the above titles, please visit www.wiley .com.

Business Forecasting

Practical Problems and Solutions

Edited by
Michael Gilliland
Len Tashman
Udo Sglavo

Cover design: Wiley

Published by John Wiley & Sons, Inc., Hoboken, New Jersey.

Published simultaneously in Canada.

For general information on our other products and services or for technical support, please contact our Customer Care Department within the United States at (800) 762-2974, outside the United States at (317) 572-3993 or fax (317) 572-4002.

Wiley publishes in a variety of print and electronic formats and by print-on-demand. Some material included with standard print versions of this book may not be included in e-books or in print-on-demand. If this book refers to media such as a CD or DVD that is not included in the version you purchased, you may download this material at http://booksupport.wiley.com. For more information about Wiley products, visit www.wiley.com.

Library of Congress Cataloging-in-Publication Data:

Names: Gilliland, Michael, editor. | Sglavo, Udo, 1968 – editor. | Tashman, Len, 1942 – editor.
Title: Business forecasting : practical problems and solutions / edited by Michael Gilliland, Udo Sglavo, Len Tashman.
Description: Hoboken : Wiley, 2015. | Series: Wiley and SAS business series | Includes bibliographical references and index.
Identifiers: LCCN 2015039621| ISBN 978-1-119-22456-3 (hardback) | ISBN 978-1-119-22829-5 (ePDF) | ISBN 978-1-119-22827-1 (ePub) | ISBN 978-1-119-19988-5 (obook)
Subjects: LCSH: Business forecasting. | BISAC: BUSINESS & ECONOMICS / Forecasting.
Classification: LCC HD30.27 .B874 2015 | DDC 658.4/0355—dc23 LC record available at http://lccn.loc.gov/2015039621

10 9 8 7 6 5 4 3 2 1

Contents

Foreword

Vice Admiral Robert FitzRoy is a man whom most people will not have heard of, but should have—for at least two reasons.

Readers would likely fail to name FitzRoy as the captain of *HMS Beagle*, the ship on which Charles Darwin sailed when Darwin was formulating his thinking on evolution through natural selection, thoughts that eventually saw the light of day in *The Origin of Species*.

What is even less well known is that FitzRoy was the man who founded what was later to become the British Meteorological Office. Furthermore, he was the one to coin the term *forecast* to describe his pioneering work. In *The Weather Book*, published in 1863, he wrote: "[P]rophesies or predications they are not; the term "forecast" is strictly applicable to such an opinion as is the result of a scientific combination and calculation."

A century and a half later, the Met Office is still around and still involved in "scientific combination and calculation." The intervening years have seen enormous advances in the understanding of the physics of weather systems, in the speed, quality, and quantity of data collection, in mathematical techniques, and in computational power. Today, organizations like the Met Office own some of the most powerful computers on the planet. As a result, weather forecasts are significantly more accurate than they were even 10 years ago.

Despite these advances, it is still not possible to forecast the weather with any degree of confidence more than a week or so into the future—and it almost certainly never will be. This is because there are practical limits to what it is possible to predict using any approach known to man.

Our everyday experience of weather forecasts serves as a salutary lesson to those working in the messy and complex world of business who might be tempted to believe that the path to better forecasting lies in using ever more sophisticated mathematics. However, despite what we know about our ability to predict the weather, people with a naïve faith in the power of mathematics are not hard to find. This is good news for some software vendors who make a handsome living from selling exotic black-box forecasting solutions to clients who want to believe that a fancy system will somehow make their forecasting problems disappear.

Happily, the editors of this book do not share any of these shortcomings. This is not because they lack technical expertise—far from it—nor is it because of a lack of faith in the value of forecasting to business. It is because they have the intellectual self-confidence to recognize the limits as well as the value of mathematical computation, the humility to be open to new ideas, and the honesty to let results be the judge of what is right and good. I respect and admire these qualities, so I was happy to write this foreword.

But if more math is not the "silver bullet" for forecasting, what is?

I cannot improve on the analysis advanced by David Orrell in his excellent book, *The Future of Everything*. He argues:

- Mathematical models interpret the world in simple mechanical terms, which have limited applicability in the context of complex systems such as living systems or systems that contain living systems, such as economies and organizations.
- Such living systems have properties that elude prediction. This is not just because such systems are complex; it is because they adapt and evolve. Their very nature involves making the future different from the past, which limits our ability to forecast the future by extrapolating from what has gone before.
- Forecasting has a large psychological component. Human beings are not automata; we can be rational, but we are also passionate, intuitive, and impulsive, and the way our brains are wired makes our judgment prone to bias and hopeless at understanding probability. This is compounded by the fact that, in organizations, forecasts are often embedded in a political process where many stakeholders—such as those in sales, finance, and general management—have vested interests that can skew the outcome.
- Some predictions (forecasts) are still possible. The future is never the same as the past, but neither does it completely differ. So approaches that involve mathematical modeling based on what has gone before are an essential part of the forecasting process, not least because our brains need their help to deal with the complexity of the world.

Orrell concludes that we fall short of what is possible—and to get better, we need to change our approach to making predictions. His prescription involves a more eclectic approach, using multiple perspectives rather than having blind faith in a single algorithm. We should draw on different mathematical methodologies and supplement them with judgment and intuition.

This doesn't mean abandoning rigor. We should aim to develop a deeper understanding of the mechanics of the systems we are forecasting, rather than treating them as a black box. We need to improve by testing our predictions against reality and learning from what our errors are telling us about the shortcomings of our methods. And forecasting should be embedded in a properly specified business process, run by appropriately trained and equipped professionals.

As practitioners, we should never lose sight of the fact that forecasting is only of value if it helps us deal with the real world. This means that we need to be able to explain and convince our colleagues, recognizing that not everyone will share our knowledge or perspective on the world or our motivation to expose the objective "truth." It also means that we need to be able to balance the aesthetic pleasure we derive from an elegant piece of mathematics or a beautifully designed process with the usefulness of the results and the degree of effort required to produce them.

I believe that forecasting in business should be regarded as a craft. Good craftspeople understand the materials they are working with and know that their work will only be as good as the tools they use. But they understand equally that real skill comes from knowing how and when to use those tools. So we need craftspeople who are eclectic but rigorous, professional, and pragmatic.

Acquiring such knowledge from personal experience can take a lifetime, which is longer than most of us are prepared to give. What we can learn from others is worth a high price.

I don't know of a better source of forecasting craft than this book—and I commend it to you.

Steve Morlidge
CatchBull Ltd.
London, UK

Preface

Anthologies are only as good as the material compiled, and 2001 saw publication of a seminal anthology in the forecasting field, J. Scott Armstrong's *Principles of Forecasting*. That broad collection, along with the Armstrong and Kesten Green website www.forecastingprinciples.com, has been a standard reference for academics, forecasting software developers, and a subset of forecasting practitioners. And yet, the principles and evidence behind them remain largely unpracticed by the great majority of business forecasters.

Now, in 2015, the editors of this volume sought to assemble a mix of the most interesting, important, and influential authors and their writings in applied forecasting since 2001. Our objective was to provide material that is both thought-provoking and of great practical value to everyone involved in the business forecasting function. Our intended audience includes forecast analysts, demand planners, and other participants in the forecasting process, as well as the managers and executives overseeing the process and utilizing the forecasts produced.

Several articles highlight findings of recent research, and many reveal areas still subject to discussion and dispute. The common message, however, is that enlightened forecasting management (not just fancy new algorithms) may be the best way to improve forecasting practice.

This book could be subtitled: *What Management Must Know about Forecasting*. Forecasting is an inherently politicized process within organizations, and the self-interests of process participants are frequently at odds. This is an issue that only management can solve, but to do so, management must first be cognizant of the problem.

One thing every business executive does know is the harm of *error* in an organization's forecasting. Harms include customer service failures, revenue shortfalls, and other public embarrassments. But what is the solution? The standard quick fixes—implementing fancy-sounding forecasting algorithms or elaborate collaborative processes—have generally failed to effect improvement. What is needed, we contend, is something less familiar—a critical understanding of the capabilities, and *limitations*, of what forecasting can realistically deliver.

The material is organized into four chapters:

Chapter 1: Fundamental Considerations in Business Forecasting

Chapter 2: Methods of Statistical Forecasting

Chapter 3: Forecasting Performance Evaluation and Reporting

Chapter 4: Process and Politics of Business Forecasting

We provide a brief introduction to each chapter, along with commentary on the significance and implications of each article.

Much of this book's content first appeared in *Foresight: The International Journal of Applied Forecasting,* and appears with permission from the International Institute of Forecasters. Len Tashman, co-editor of this compilation and *Foresight*'s editor in chief, extends special thanks to his staff: Liza Woodruff, Kim Leonard, Mary Ellen Bridge, Ralph Culver, and Stacey Hilliard.

We include several articles from the *Journal of Business Forecasting,* with permission graciously provided by its editor-in-chief, Dr. Chaman Jain. Thanks also to our longtime friends at the Institute of Business Forecasting: Anish Jain, Stephanie Murray, and Latosha Staton.

In addition, we incorporate various book, blog, and newsletter adaptations, as well as some original material, with thanks to Elizabeth Proctor of APICS, Rob Hyndman of Monash University, Andrey Davydenko and Robert Fildes of Lancaster University, Eric Stellwagen of Business Forecast Systems, Shaun Snapp of SCM Focus, Tim Rey of Steelcase, and Chip Wells of SAS.

The authors wish to thank SAS Press and Wiley for accepting the manuscript into the Wiley and SAS Business Series. We were assisted at SAS by Julie Platt, Shelley Sessoms, and Karen Day with the book contract and administration, by Brenna Leath as our managing editor, and by Jeff Alford and Denise Lange in many of the nuts and bolts of book production. Deborah Blackburn of BB&T reviewed and commented on the manuscript.

A special debt of gratitude is owed to Steve Morlidge of CatchBull Ltd., who wrote the foreword in addition to providing four of the articles.

Last, and most important, the editors wish to acknowledge all the authors whose work has been included in this book. We thank them for their tremendous contributions to the understanding, and better practice, of business forecasting.

Michael Gilliland
SAS Institute
Cary, North Carolina

Len Tashman
Foresight
Golden, Colorado

Udo Sglavo
SAS Institute
Cary, North Carolina

CHAPTER 1

Fundamental Considerations in Business Forecasting

Challenges in business forecasting, such as increasing accuracy and reducing bias, are best met through effective management of the forecasting process. Effective management, we believe, requires an understanding of the realities, limitations, and principles fundamental to the process. When management lacks a grasp of basic concepts like *randomness, variation, uncertainty,* and *forecastability,* the organization is apt to squander time and resources on expensive and unsuccessful fixes: There are few other endeavors where so much money has been spent, with so little payback.

This chapter provides general guidance on important considerations in the practice of business forecasting. The authors deal with:

- Recognition of uncertainty and the need for probabilistic forecasts
- The essential elements of a useful forecast
- Measurement of forecastability and bounds of forecast accuracy
- Establishing appropriate benchmarks of forecast accuracy
- The importance of precisely defining *demand* when making demand forecasts
- Guidelines for improving forecast accuracy and managing the forecasting function

■ ■ ■

Although we were unable to secure rights to include it in this book, Makridakis and Taleb's "Living in a World of Low Levels of Predictability" from the *International Journal of Forecasting* is an important piece worth mentioning in any consideration of fundamental issues.

Spyros Makridakis is very well recognized as lead author of the standard forecasting text, *Forecasting: Methods and Applications,* and of the M-series forecasting competitions. Through his books, *Fooled by Randomness* and *The Black Swan,* Nassim Nicholas Taleb has drawn popular attention to the issue of unforecastability of complex systems, and made "black swan" a part of the vernacular. Their article, published in the *International Journal of Forecasting* (2009), speaks to the sometimes disastrous consequences of our *illusion of control*—believing that accurate forecasting is possible.

While referring to the (mostly unforeseen) global financial collapse of 2008 as a prime example of the serious limits of predictability, this brief and nontechnical article summarizes the empirical findings for why accurate forecasting is often not possible, and provides several practical approaches for dealing with this uncertainty. For example, you can't predict when your house is going to burn down. But you can still manage under the uncertainty by buying fire insurance.

So why are the editors of a *forecasting* book so adamant about mentioning an article telling us the world is largely unforecastable? Because Makridakis and Taleb are correct. We should not have high expectations for forecast accuracy, and we should not expend heroic efforts trying to achieve unrealistic levels of accuracy.

Instead, by accepting the reality that forecast accuracy is ultimately limited by the *nature* of what we are trying to forecast, we can instead focus on the efficiency of our forecasting processes, and seek alternative (nonforecasting) solutions to our underlying business problems. The method of forecast value added (FVA) analysis (discussed in several articles in Chapter 4) can be used to identify and eliminate forecasting process activities that do not improve the forecast (or may even be making it worse). And in many situations, large-scale automated software can now deliver forecasts about as accurate and unbiased as anyone can reasonably expect. Plus, automated software can do this at relatively low cost, without elaborate processes or significant management intervention.

For business forecasting, the objective should be:

> *To generate forecasts as accurate and unbiased as can reasonably be expected*—and to do this as efficiently as possible.

The goal is not 100% accurate forecasts—that is wildly impossible. The goal is to try to get your forecast in the ballpark, good enough to help you make *better decisions*. You can then plan and manage your organization effectively, and not squander resources doing it.

1.1 GETTING REAL ABOUT UNCERTAINTY*

Paul Goodwin

Business forecasters tend to rely on the familiar "point" forecast—a single number representing the best estimate of the result. But point forecasts provide no indication of the uncertainty in the number, and uncertainty is an important consideration in decision making. For example, a forecast of 100 ± 10 units may lead to a much different planning decision than a forecast of 100 ± 100 units.

In this opening article, Paul Goodwin explores the types of "probabilistic" forecasts, the academic research behind them, and the numerical and graphical displays afforded through prediction intervals, fan charts, and probability density charts. Providing uncertainty information, he explains, can result in better decisions; however, probabilistic forecasts may be subject to misinterpretation and may be difficult to sell to managers. There is also an unfortunate tendency we have to seriously underestimate the uncertainty we face and hence overstate our forecast accuracy.

Goodwin's article provides practical recommendations and additional sources of guidance on how to estimate and convey the uncertainty in forecasts.

---

* This article originally appeared in *Foresight: The International Journal of Applied Forecasting* (Spring 2014), and appears here courtesy of the International Institute of Forecasters.

Avoiding Jail

In October 2012, the scientific world was shocked when seven people (engineers, scientists, and a civil servant) were jailed in Italy following an earthquake in the city of L'Aquila in which 309 people died. They had been involved in a meeting of the National Commission for Forecasting and Preventing Major Risks following a seismic swarm in the region. At their trial, it was alleged that they had failed in their duty by not properly assessing and communicating the risk that an earthquake in the area was imminent. Their mistake had been that they had simply conveyed the most likely outcome—no earthquake—rather than a probabilistic forecast that might have alerted people to the small chance of a strong earthquake (Mazzotti, 2013).

Point versus Probabilistic Forecasts

This case dramatically highlights the problem with forecasts that are presented in the form of a single event or a single number (the latter are called *point forecasts*). They give no information on how much uncertainty is associated with the forecast. As such, they provide no guidance on what contingency plans you should make to cope with errors in the forecasts. Is the risk of an earthquake sufficient to evacuate an entire town? How much safety stock should we hold in case demand is higher than the forecast of 240 units?

But incorporating uncertainty into forecasts is not straightforward. Probabilistic forecasts need to be presented so that they are credible, understandable, and useful to decision makers—otherwise, we are wasting our time. And, as we shall see, getting reliable estimates of uncertainty in the first place poses its own challenges.

Prediction Intervals

Prediction intervals are a common way of representing uncertainty when we are forecasting variables like sales or costs. The forecast is presented as a range of values, and the probability that the range will enclose the actual outcome is also provided. For example, a 90% prediction interval for next month's demand for a product might be given as 211 to 271 units (or 241 ± 30 units). Clearly, the wider the interval, the greater uncertainty we have about the demand we will experience next month.

Fan Charts

More information about uncertainty is provided by a fan chart (see Figure 1.1). Here, the darkest band represents the 50% prediction interval, while the wider ranges show the 75% and 95% intervals.

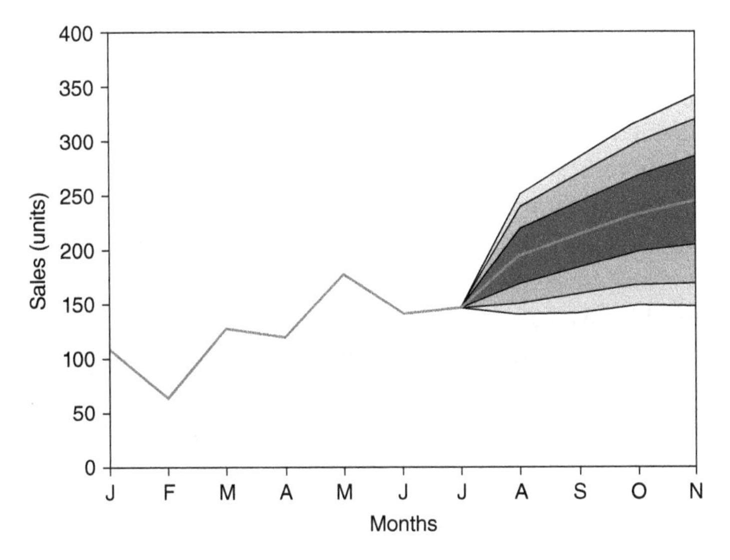

Figure 1.1 A Fan Chart

Probability Density Chart

Lastly, the forecast can be presented as an estimate of an entire probability distribution. For example, we might forecast a 10% probability of snow, a 20% probability of rain, and a 70% chance of fine weather for noon tomorrow. Estimates of probability distributions for variables like sales, costs, or inflation are usually referred to as density forecasts. Figure 1.2 provides an example. It can be seen that sales should almost certainly fall between 200 and 1,200 units, but sales around 500 units are most probable.

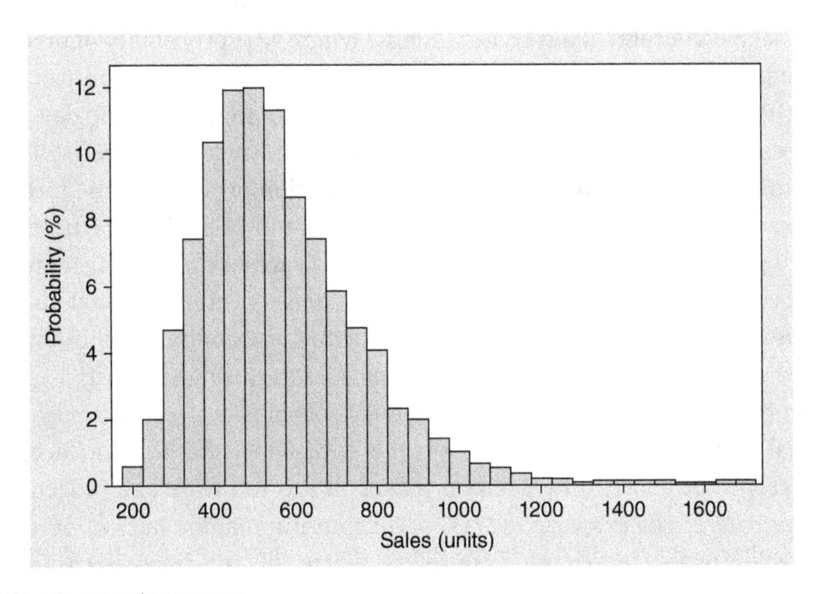

Figure 1.2 A Density Forecast

Is it Worth Communicating Uncertainty?

Does communicating uncertainty in forecasts lead to better decisions? In a recent experiment conducted by Ramos and coauthors (2013), people received forecasts of a river's level and had to make decisions on whether to open a floodgate to protect a town. Opening the gate would cause flooding of agricultural land downstream and liability for compensation payments from farmers. The decision makers received either a single-figure (point) forecast, or they were additionally given a prediction interval (e.g., 3.52 ± 0.51 meters), together with a forecast of the probability that the town would be flooded. Providing uncertainty information resulted in better decisions in that, over a series of trials, more money was lost when no uncertainty information was available.

Clear advantages of providing prediction intervals are also evident in research carried out by Savelli and Joslyn (2013). Participants provided with 80% prediction intervals for high and low temperatures in Seattle were more decisive when faced with the dilemma of whether to issue temperature warnings about freezing or very hot conditions than those provided only with point forecasts. They were also better at identifying unreliable forecasts and expected a narrower range of outcomes—so they had a more precise idea of what temperatures to expect.

Limitations of Probabilistic Forecasts

However, probabilistic forecasts are not without their limitations. In particular, they may be prone to people misinterpreting them. For example, a study carried out more than 30 years ago by Alan Murphy and coauthors (1980) found that some people interpreted a weather forecast where "the probability of precipitation today is 30%" as meaning that only 30% of the relevant region would see rain. Others thought that it meant that it would rain for 30% of the day.

Second, with interval forecasts there is often a mismatch between what you need to know for your decision and the information provided in the forecasts. For example, a 90% prediction interval for demand of 211 to 271 units does not tell you what your safety stock needs to be to achieve a 98% customer service level (Goodwin and coauthors, 2010). A density forecast would give you this information because it would present the full probability distribution—but these are not regularly available in commercial forecasting software.

Third, there can be a problem in selling probabilistic forecasts to users. An interval forecast may accurately reflect the uncertainty that is being faced, but it is likely to be spurned by decision makers if it is too wide and judged to be uninformative. For example, a 90% prediction interval for sales of 50 to 900 units will probably be regarded as useless. Worse still, it is likely to cast doubts on the competence of the forecaster who produced it.

Sometimes, the reactions of users may be more nuanced. Ning Du and coauthors (2011), in a study of earnings forecasts, found that when people recognized there was significant uncertainty in what was being predicted, interval forecasts carried more credibility than point forecasts. However, only a limited interval width was tolerated. Wider intervals that were judged to be uninformative had less credibility.

What Is the Best Way to Convey Uncertainty?

All of this indicates that we need to know more about how to convey uncertainty to forecast users. Some recent studies offer a few pointers. One of these (Kreye and coauthors, 2012) provided experts on cost estimation with graphical forecasts of the monthly price of a raw material that were given in three different forms: a line graph showing minimum, maximum, and medium estimates; a bar chart showing the same information; and a fan chart. Fan charts were found to be the most effective method for raising awareness of the uncertainty that was present.

Another study, this by David Budescu and coauthors (2012), found that the uncertainty associated with forecasts produced by the Intergovernmental Panel on Climate Change (IPCC) were best communicated to the public using both words and numerical probabilities together. For example, an event might be referred to in a report as "likely, that is having a probability of 67% to 90%" or "very unlikely, that is having a probability of 2% to 10%." Supplying valuations of uncertainty using only words, such as "likely" or "virtually certain," was less effective. People seeing both words and numerical probabilities were more consistent in interpreting the messages, and—importantly—their interpretations were closer to what the authors of the report intended.

When prediction intervals are provided, it appears that users trust them more (in the sense that they make smaller judgmental adjustments to them) if their bounds are expressed in everyday language like "worst-case forecast" and "best-case forecast" (Goodwin and coauthors, 2013). Trust can also be increased by supporting prediction intervals with scenarios or narratives that provide a justification for their two bounds (Önkal and coauthors, 2013).

Estimating Uncertainty

Even if we can provide meaningful probabilistic forecasts to users, we still have to estimate the level of uncertainty. The main problem with prediction intervals, fan charts, and density forecasts is that they tend to underestimate uncertainty. This is particularly true when the forecasts are based on managerial judgment. Research has repeatedly shown that people produce prediction intervals that are far too narrow, and thus outcomes occur outside the interval more often than they should according to the stated probability. For example, Itzhak Ben-David and coauthors (2013) reported recently that a large sample of senior U.S. financial executives produced 80% prediction intervals of one-year-ahead stock market returns that included the actual returns only 36.3% of the time.

Spyros Makridakis and coauthors (2009) suggest a simple remedy for this problem: Once you've estimated a prediction interval, double its range! However, if you need a full density forecast, other methods might help. For example, estimating probabilities for the different factors that will influence sales, rather than estimating probabilities for sales themselves, may make the judgment task easier. Monte Carlo simulation can then be used to combine these separate estimates to generate a density forecast for sales, as shown in the *Foresight* article, "Assessing Uncertainty in New-Product Forecasts" (Guthrie and Markland, 2010).

Many past studies have found that statistical methods also tend to produce overly narrow ranges for possible outcomes, although new algorithms are faring better. George Athanasopoulos and coauthors (2011) compared the performance of different forecasting methods on over 1,300 tourism time series, and found that both an automated algorithm embedded in a commercial software package and an automated algorithm for implementing exponential smoothing produced prediction intervals that were very well calibrated when the data were monthly or quarterly. For example, 95% prediction intervals contained the actual outcome around 95% of the time. Researchers are also working to enhance statistical methods for producing density forecasts (e.g., Machete, 2013).

Conclusions

Psychologists tell us that our brains seek certainty in the same way that we crave food and other basic rewards. Uncertainty is often experienced as anxiety, and can even be felt as a form of pain. But this doesn't mean that it's sensible or even advisable to ignore or underestimate the uncertainty we face, since there is evidence that accurate information on uncertainty can lead to better decisions. Probabilistic forecasts can provide this information, and researchers are making progress in finding the best ways to estimate and convey uncertainty so that these forecasts are more reliable, understandable, credible, and useful to decision makers.

REFERENCES

Athanasopoulos, G., R. J. Hyndman, H. Song and D. C. Wu (2011). The tourism forecasting competition. *International Journal of Forecasting* 27, 822–844.

Ben-David, I., J. R. Graham, and C. R. Harvey (2013). Managerial miscalibration, *Quarterly Journal of Economics* 128, 1547–1584.

Budescu, D. V., H-H Por, and S. B. Broomell (2012). Effective communication of uncertainty in the IPCC Reports. *Climatic Change* 113, 181–200.

Du, N., D. V. Budescu, M. K. Shelly, and T. C. Omer (2011). The appeal of vague financial forecasts. *Organizational Behavior and Human Decision Processes* 114, 179–189.

Goodwin, P., M. S. Gönül, and D. Önkal (2013). Antecedents and effects of trust in forecasting advice. *International Journal of Forecasting* 29, 354–366.

Goodwin, P., D. Önkal, and M. Thomson (2010). Do forecasts expressed as prediction intervals improve production planning decisions? *European Journal of Operational Research* 205, 195–201.

Guthrie, N., and D. Markland (2010). Assessing uncertainty in new-product forecasts. *Foresight*, Issue 16 (Winter), 32–39.

Kreye, M., Y. M. Goh, L. B. Newnes, and P. Goodwin (2012). Approaches to displaying information to assist decisions under uncertainty. *Omega* 40, 682–692.

Machete, R. L. (2013). Early warning with calibrated and sharper probabilistic forecasts. *Journal of Forecasting* 32, 452–468.

Makridakis, S., R. Hogarth, and A. Gaba (2009). *Dance with Chance*. Oxford: Oneworld Publications.

Mazzotti, M. (2013). Seismic shift. *Times Higher Education* 2121, 38–43.

Murphy, A. H., S. Lichtenstein, B. Fischhoff, and R. L. Winkler (1980). Misinterpretations of precipitation probability forecasts. *Bulletin of the American Meteorological Society* 61, 695–701.

Önkal, D., K. D. Sayım, and M. S. Gönül (2013). Scenarios as channels of forecast advice. *Technological Forecasting and Social Change* 80, 772–788.

Ramos, M. H., S. J. van Andel, and F. Pappenberger (2013). Do probabilistic forecasts lead to better decisions? *Hydrology and Earth Systems Sciences* 17, 2219–2232.

Savelli, S., and S. Joslyn (2013). The advantages of predictive interval forecasts for non-expert users and the impact of visualizations. *Applied Cognitive Psychology* 27, 527–541.

1.2 WHAT DEMAND PLANNERS CAN LEARN FROM THE STOCK MARKET*

Charles K. Re Corr

The value of conveying uncertainty and other considerations for what makes a forecast useful to investors is the subject addressed by Charles Re Corr of Merrill Lynch. Wall Street, he observes, is generally averse to providing specific numerical forecasts, not only because accurate forecasting is difficult, but also because negative forecasts can be bad for business.

Forecasts are still necessary, however, because they are the basis for making investment decisions. But financial forecasting differs fundamentally from demand forecasting in that new

* This article originally appeared in *Journal of Business Forecasting* (Fall 2012), and appears here courtesy of Dr. Chaman Jain, editor in chief.

information can be immediately integrated into market valuations. A demand planner, on the other hand, is forced to move more slowly in reaction to new information—having to work around production and inventory schedules and human resource policies.

Acknowledging the difficulty of accurate financial forecasting, Re Corr lists seven characteristics that make a forecast useful for decision making. These are time frame (a specific period or date at which to compare forecasts to actuals), direction (up or down), magnitude (a specific number, although a distribution about that number is more valuable), probability (assigning probabilities to the distribution of possible outcomes), range (highest and lowest possible outcome), confidence (statistical or subjective), and historical forecast error. Ultimately, he concludes, a "perfect forecast" need not be 100% accurate, but should provide enough information to improve management's decisions under conditions of uncertainty.

If you think forecasting product demand is hard, try forecasting the future values of the Standard and Poor's 500 Stock Index (S&P500)! Dissimilar as they might be, there are lessons to be learned for demand forecasting from stock market forecasts.

Despite much popular evidence to the contrary, Wall Street collectively has an aversion to putting a number on the future value of the stock market. This is primarily due to three reasons:

1. It is very difficult to forecast accurately.
2. A cynic would point out that a negative forecast is not good for business.
3. The market in the past has trended upward; so is the naïve forecast, "It will go higher," calling for more of the same, which has been on average fairly correct. The statistics support the viability of a naïve forecast over the past 86 years, from 1925 to 2011. During these years, Large Cap Stocks, as represented by the S&P500, have been up over the previous year 62 times, a little better than 70%. The naïve forecast, therefore, isn't so bad even if it is woefully incomplete.

Why Forecast the Future Market

We all forecast because all decisions we make require some expectations about the future. Accurate forecasts improve our chances of making the right decision. The problem for stock market predictions is that even though the trend bias is upward, the magnitude of downward markets in any year can wipe out successes of many years.

Telling the investor that market history will repeat itself evokes the basic question, "Will it happen in my remaining lifetime?" Generally, Wall Street encourages a long-term horizon, which is termed *strategic*. Since it may take years before the forecast can be proven accurate, the more vague the forecast, the better. Ironically, any allocation decisions among different asset classes—stocks, bonds, cash, real estate, and so forth—are based on forecasts, even if not acknowledged.

Allocation percentages represent confidence levels about expected returns, risks, and correlations. Even if I weigh all classes equally (because I have no opinion or information), I am in fact expressing a forecast.

The fact is that even the gold standard certification of Wall Street analysts, the coveted designation of Chartered Financial Analyst (CFA), encourages candidates not to forecast. In one study on behavioral finance, James Moniter, a Visiting Fellow at the University of Durham and a Fellow of the Royal Society of Arts, wrote a whole section titled "The Folly of Forecasting: Ignore all Economists, Strategists, and Analysts."

Why is it so difficult? The primary reason is that the market is itself a leading economic indicator. It has been used by the government as part of its Leading Indicator Index for years, and now is reported by the Conference Board monthly. Essentially, the market predicts the economy; therefore, you are trying to "predict the predictor."

Historical analysis of the S&P500 suggests that the market moves in anticipation of economic activity, up or down, about six to nine months in advance. It also sometimes signals a change in the economic activity that does not occur. The question you might ask is this: Why is the S&P500 index such a sensitive indicator? The answer is that new information is integrated into market valuations almost immediately.

This is very different than what happens in demand forecasting. The response time for a company to react to, for example, the hint of slowing sales is not the same as that of an institutional investor receiving the same information. A company has to work around production issues, inventory levels, human resource policies, and the like before it can respond to changing markets; whereas an institutional portfolio manager, within minutes of his or her decision, only has to call the trading desk and sell/buy millions of dollars of that company's stocks or bonds, virtually instantaneously in response to new information.

What Makes Any Forecast Useful?

As difficult as it is, we have to forecast. Clients expect it, and all decisions are made based on assumptions about the future. The prize for being more successful than your competitor is worth the effort.

So, what would make up a valuable forecast? Here is a famous quote:

"All forecasts are wrong, some are useful."

Although this may seem like an escape clause for forecasters, if we accept the first part of the quote as true ("All forecasts are wrong"), then we are left with the question, "What makes some of them useful?" It is the descriptive elements of a forecast provided to decision-makers that prove to be useful.

Some of these seven elements are more obvious than others, depending on the industry, but all are worth reflecting upon. They are: time frame, direction, magnitude, probability, range, confidence, and historical forecast error for similar forecasts.

Time frame: What date, or period, are you using for your ending forecast? "Soon" is not a date—you need a close of business date to compare the forecast with actual results. The time frame depends on the decision makers' cycle. Even if not requested it can be very helpful to provide a series of forecasts up to the requested end-forecast date. For example, management might want a one-year-out number, yet it would be valuable for them to see the trend in three-, six-, and nine-month forecasts. This can help them understand the forecasted trend, and possibly seasonality. This can relieve anxiety if management knows the intermediate forecast numbers may be temporarily trending in the wrong direction.

Direction: Very simply, the forecast is compared to a baseline: Will it be up or down from that on the forecasted date? As with time frame, trend and seasonality may create an intermediate point where the end forecast looks like it will be wrong because it goes down before it goes up.

Magnitude: "Up" is not an amount—you need a specific amount. Although most managers like one number because it makes it easier to make a decision, they need to be reminded that the number will be wrong. Distribution around the number is the gold standard of a forecast, which is expressed in terms of probability.

Probability: A single-number forecast is called a point forecast, and by definition is assumed to be a mid-point of the possible outcomes. Therefore, 50% of the outcomes will fall on either side of the number. You can, however, provide a higher probability of meeting or exceeding the forecast by simply reducing your forecast magnitude. Here is an example using the stock market: If you provide a point forecast that the stock market will be up 10% by the end of the next 12 months (a 50% probability), you can increase the probability of beating the target by reducing the forecast magnitude. In other words, if you believe there is a 50/50 chance that the market will rise by 10%, then there is an even higher probability it will rise by 5% (the probability depends on the distribution of possible outcomes). You may do this on your own or at the management's request to help them understand the forecast.

Range: Providing a high and a low number can be very valuable to management for decision making. Low may take you to a different direction, down versus up. This is useful because management can decide if it can live with the potentially downward outcome.

Confidence: Use statistical confidence levels if available. If necessary, provide a subjective confidence level; it is, after all, part of the forecasting job. If the confidence level is subjective, make sure to tell the decision maker. This approach can at least allow you to put a probability on a positive outcome.

Historical forecast error: In most cases the forecast you are doing is repetitive and, therefore, you have the past data. Past accuracy is informational, but past consistency is also useful. Being consistently wrong, although embarrassing, can be very valuable to decision makers, depending on the range of errors.

Some Errors Are More Forgiving than Others

It is important to recognize which components of your forecast are critical—for instance, magnitude, time frame, or direction. What about market shocks (stock market and economic conditions), natural disasters, terrorist acts, and so on? Obviously, if we could predict such things, we would be in extremely high demand. There are those who continually predict such events; we usually consider them Cassandras. If they turn out to be right, people will hold them in great esteem and ask you why you did not see that coming. But for the most part, shocks are shocks because they are not generally expected.

We can treat market shocks in a similar manner as new product launches that do not go as planned. Here we look at history to find similar events and try to draw some inferences with respect to production or inventory adjustments and how long it might take to recover.

In addition to the seven components described above, there is one more point that could also be of value to any professional forecaster. The finance industry has created a wide variety of exchange-traded funds whose movements can be helpful in forecasting a wide variety of product categories. These funds represent economic sectors and industries, and, like the S&P500, they tend to move in advance of their representative sector or industry. They are baskets of stocks that are believed to fairly represent the underlying sector such as Materials, Energy, or Healthcare sectors, which could serve as a leading indicator for industries such as North American natural resources, home construction, and pharmaceuticals.

Although attributed to many, I believe it was Yogi Berra who once said,

"Forecasting is difficult, particularly about the future."

Providing complete data and continually finding ways to improve forecasts can increase your value as a professional. Ultimately, the "perfect forecast" is the one that has enough information to improve management's decisions under conditions of uncertainty.

1.3 TOWARD A MORE PRECISE DEFINITION OF FORECASTABILITY*

John Boylan

One challenge that is poorly understood, difficult to resolve, and, as a consequence, often ignored is the determination of forecastability, the potential forecasting accuracy of an item, product, or revenue flow. Forecastability is the basis of benchmarking: If we can know the best accuracy we can hope to achieve, we would have a benchmark to judge how effective our current efforts are and how much room remains for improvement. This is the subject of the next three articles.

By *forecastability,* John Boylan refers to the range of forecast errors that are achievable, on average. But, he points out, the concept of forecastability needs sharpening. Boylan shows that forecastability is not the same as stability, the degree of variation in demand over time. He argues that forecastability should be measured by a band or interval in which the lower bound is the lowest error we can hope to achieve and the upper bound is the maximal error that should occur. With such a band, we could know how far we've come (reducing error from the upper bound) and how far we can still hope to go (to reduce error to the lower bound).

Clearly, any forecasting method producing greater errors (less accurate forecasts) on average than the upper bound should be discontinued. The main difficulty, of course, lies in calculating a lower bound—how can we know the potential for forecasting accuracy?

In general, we can't pin down this lower bound. But Boylan explains that we can frequently make useful approximations of the lower bound of forecast error by relating the product to be forecast to its position in the product hierarchy, by combining forecasts from different methods, and by identifying more forecastable series.

Stability versus Forecastability

The idea of forecastability has been championed by Kenneth Kahn (2006). In fact, the term *forecastability* can be interpreted in various ways. It can relate to an assessment of the stability of a data series, as in Peter Catt's (2009) usage. It can also refer to the degree of accuracy when forecasting a time series and can indicate the precision with which we estimate an expected range for the mean absolute percentage error (MAPE) when employing a time-series method.

It's clear that the concepts of stability and forecast accuracy are related. We expect forecast accuracy to deteriorate as a series becomes less stable (more volatile). We anticipate that it is harder to estimate the expected range of any error measure as a series becomes less stable. Nonetheless, stability and forecast accuracy are distinct concepts. We should remember this in order to avoid confusions that arise from using forecastability to refer to different things.

* This article originally appeared in *Foresight: The International Journal of Applied Forecasting* (Spring 2009), and appears here courtesy of the International Institute of Forecasters.

The definition of forecastability as stability makes no reference to forecasting methods or forecast-error measures. This is a strength, as the definition then relates to the data series alone and is not restricted to any particular forecast method or error measure. But it is also a weakness, as the link between stability and forecastability isn't always apparent.

In some cases, stability and forecast accuracy align nicely. The sine wave is an example of a perfectly stable time series, with no random components. If we know the phase and amplitude of the sine series, then we can forecast the series precisely. For any sensible error measure, in this case, the forecast error will be zero.

In the Hénon map example, it is assumed that the data-generating process is known to be chaotic. If we base our assessment of its forecastability on the approximate entropy metric, we would say that the series is stable. It is only forecastable, however, in the sense of forecast accuracy if the process can be identified and the parameters estimated accurately. It is doubtful if a forecaster, presented with a short Hénon time plot, would be able to deduce the dynamical system it is based upon. If the forecaster mis-specifies the data generating process, forecast errors may be large and difficult to determine. So stability of a series does not automatically imply good forecast accuracy.

This raises the question: Is stability a necessary condition for good forecast accuracy? When a series is considered in isolation, without contextual information or accompanying series, this may be the case. A volatile series cannot be extrapolated with great accuracy. However, a volatile series may have a time-lag relationship to another series, enabling good forecast accuracy to be obtained.

Alternatively, qualitative information about the business environment may enable accurate forecasts of a volatile series using judgmental forecasting methods. So taking a perspective broader than extrapolation, we can see that stability is not a necessary condition for good forecast accuracy.

Stability is important but should be distinguished from forecastability. The term *forecastability* has been used in various ways, making the concept rather slippery. A sharper definition is required, one leaving stability out of the picture.

Defining Forecastability in Terms of Forecast Error

Tentatively, I offer this definition: "Forecastability is the smallest level of forecast error that is achievable." One series is more forecastable than another, with respect to a particular error measure, if it has a smaller achievable forecast error. To avoid technical difficulties, the word *smallest* must be interpreted sensibly, according to the forecasting error metric being used.

Three examples will show that caution is needed with this interpretation. For the mean absolute error, "smallest" simply means the "lowest." For the mean error, "smallest" means "closest to zero" (e.g., a mean error of +1 is "smaller" than a mean error of –2). For the Accumulated Forecast to Actual Ratio (Valentin, 2007), "smallest" means closest to 100 (e.g., a value of 102% is "smaller" than a value of 96%).

This definition does suffer from some problems.

The first problem is that, if we take the error measure over just one period (say, the next period), we may be lucky and forecast the value exactly, giving a forecast error of zero. Clearly, such luck is not sustainable over the long term. To overcome this difficulty, we can amend the definition of forecastability to "the lowest level of forecast error that is achievable, on average, in the long run."

This definition of forecastability is not restricted to one particular error measure but can be applied to any forecast error metric for which the word *smallest* is interpreted appropriately. Nor is this definition of forecastability restricted to a "basic time-series method" (as suggested by Kahn, 2006).

Rather, it can refer to any forecasting method. In doing so, it addresses Peter Catt's objection to the use of the coefficient of variation of a series after decomposition (removal of linear trend and seasonality). Classical decomposition, which may be considered a "basic time-series method," is just one method that can be applied to detrending and deseasonalizing the series. Perhaps, after taking into account autocorrelation based on the more complex ARIMA modeling, we may be left with a smaller coefficient of variation. My definition of forecastability overcomes this difficulty by not limiting the scope of forecasting methods that may be applied.

A second problem: The definition depends on the achievement of the smallest forecast error. It is possible that a series is difficult to forecast and will yield high forecast errors unless a particular method is identified, in which case the forecast errors are small. In cases such as these, it would be helpful to specify both a lower bound and an upper bound on forecast errors. Methods for estimating these upper bounds are discussed in the following sections.

Our definition is now broadened accordingly: "Forecastability refers to the range of forecast errors that are achievable on average, in the long run. The lower value of the range represents the lowest forecast error achievable. The upper value of the range represents an upper bound based on a benchmark forecasting method."

Upper Bound of a Forecasting Error Metric

If we could find an upper bound for forecasting error, based on a simple benchmark method, then any method producing greater errors (less accurate forecasts), on average, should be discontinued and an alternative sought. An upper bound can also be used to generate exception reports, to inform corrective actions by a forecasting analyst.

Many relative error metrics use the naïve as the benchmark method. The naïve method predicts no change from the present to the next future period. Metrics that incorporate the naïve baseline include the relative absolute error, the Theil coefficient, and the mean absolute scaled error (Hyndman and Koehler, 2006). For all of these metrics, results above 100% show that we could do better by using the naïve, the last actual observation as the forecast. Relative error measures with the naïve as the baseline are provided in most forecasting software packages.

One disadvantage of using the naïve as the upper bound is that it may set too low a bar. Often, it is obvious that better alternatives are available, especially when the data are trended or seasonal. The M1 and M3 forecasting competitions (Makridakis et al., 1982; Makridakis and Hibon, 2000) confirm that the naïve is generally inferior to other simple forecasting methods. This research evidence matches the experience of practitioners, who would be unlikely to view the naïve as a viable forecasting method.

Two alternatives may be considered. For nonseasonal data, the simple moving average or simple exponential smoothing may be used as a baseline. For trended or seasonal data, a baseline that takes trend and seasonality into account (such as classical decomposition or Winters' exponential smoothing) may be more sensible. These alternatives take the approach suggested by Kahn (2006) but use it as an upper bound, rather than as a lower bound. As Peter Catt argues, methods based on decomposition of trends and seasonal components can often be improved upon; while not appropriate as lower bounds, they can be used as upper bounds. These upper bounds should be sharper than the naïve method, meaning that analysts will be able to detect problems with current forecasting methods earlier, as they are being compared with better alternative methods.

Lower Bound of a Forecasting Error Measure

The previous section has indicated some methods for determining an upper bound on forecast accuracy. How about the lower bounds? If the data-generating process (DGP) is known, and the time series does not deviate from the DGP in the future, then it may be possible to set the lower bound exactly. This is done by determining mathematical expressions for the long-run averages (expectations) of the error measure. This approach has been adopted in studies of seasonal DGPs and is discussed later.

When we do not know the data generating process, or when the DGP is changing over time, the lower bound must be estimated. This is the situation facing the practitioner working without the luxury of well-specified, well-behaved data.

At first, the estimation of a lower bound for forecasting error may seem an impossible task. After all, there are endless forecasting methods, weighted averages (combinations) of methods, and judgmental approaches that may be used.

One approach is to estimate the lower bound of a set of methods $M_1, M_2, \ldots, M_m$. For example, M_1, M_2 may represent two methods currently used by an organization. The other methods may not be used presently but may be under consideration for implementation. But we can't be sure that we've included the ideal or optimal method in this set. So we should expect that the lower bound from our set of methods will not be the ultimate lower bound.

In Figure 1.3, I have assumed that the ultimate lower bound is unknown. We have reordered the methods so that method M_1 has the largest error, and method M_m has the smallest error. The error induced by method M_m is a measure of forecastability, when the methods are restricted to the set of methods $M_1, M_2, \ldots, M_m$.

From a more practical perspective, users of forecasting software may wish to examine the forecastability of series by using automatic model-selection procedures. Automatic forecasting is based on a set of methods built into the software, and an error measure is used to pick the best method. This approach can be applied to give an immediate lower bound, based on the software being used and an error measure of the user's choosing (not necessarily the same as the one used by the software to "pick best"). It also serves as a very useful benchmark for assessing judgmental adjustments to software-generated forecasts. If forecasts are consistently improved by the application of judgment, then the lower bound can be reduced further, giving a more accurate indication of the forecastability of the series. For example, Syntetos et al. (2009) found that a pharmaceutical company was able to improve the accuracy of its intermittent demand forecasts, based on company software, by incorporating judgmental adjustments. Thus, the lower bound had been reduced.

An alternative approach to the comparison of a set of methods is to look at combinations of those methods. For example, suppose we are considering

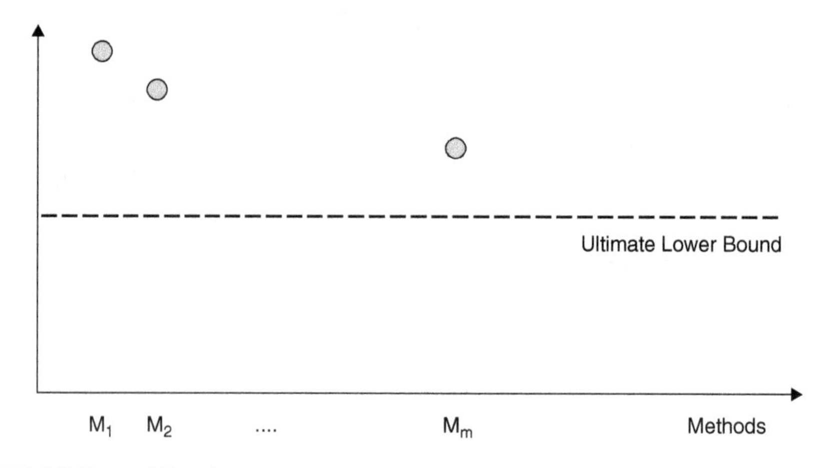

Figure 1.3 Forecast Error Lower

five methods, $M_1, M_2, \ldots, M_5$. We can also examine the simple averages of all subsets of these methods, starting with all pairs, then moving on to all triplets and so on, until we finish with the average of all five methods. The best combination can be used as our lower bound if it produces lower forecast errors than each of the methods used individually.

Armstrong (2001) argued that such combinations are particularly valuable if you use methods that differ substantially and are drawn from different sources of information. Graefe and his colleagues (Graefe et al., 2009) found that simple averaging of four components of U.S. election forecasts improved accuracy of poll share forecasts. Goodwin (2009) summarized evidence from three studies on economic forecasting, all of which showed that combining forecasts is likely to improve accuracy. The M1 and M3 competitions also showed combination methods to perform well, making them a natural choice to include in estimating the lower bound of forecast error.

In some cases, such as new-product launches, it is not possible to compare methods, or combinations of methods, based on historical data. In this situation, the best we can do is to conduct such analyses for analogous series (e.g., launch of a similar product some time ago). When more data become available, our lower (and upper) bound estimates can be refined.

Finding More Forecastable Series

One strategy for improving forecasting error has received much attention, namely working to improve statistical forecasting methods (or linear combinations of methods). A second strategy is to take advantage of judgmental forecasts or judgmental revisions to statistical forecasts. Increased attention is now being given to this important aspect of forecasting. A third strategy is to identify more forecastable series to forecast. This strategy has received less attention in the forecasting literature but has great potential to reduce forecasting errors.

Hau Lee and colleagues (Lee, 2000) studied demand at a retailer that follows a particular type of model, known as an autoregressive model of order one. In this model, the current demand is related to the demand in the previous period by a multiplicative factor, plus a random disturbance term. If the multiplicative factor is positive, then the series is said to be "positively autocorrelated."

Lee and his coauthors supposed that the retailer uses an "order-up-to" ordering policy on the manufacturer. At each review period, the retailer places an order to bring the stock up to a predefined level. In these circumstances, if demand is positively autocorrelated at the retailer, and optimal forecasting methods are used, then the orders on the manufacturer will have greater variability than the demand at the retailer. This is an example where one series (orders on the manufacturer) is inherently less forecastable than another series (demand at the retailer). It makes sense, in this case, to share information so that the wholesaler can base orders on the more forecastable demand at the retailer. There have been recent case studies showing that this strategy can reduce costs significantly in practice (Boone and Ganeshan, 2008).

Lee's model was developed by assuming that the DGP followed an autoregressive structure. In real-world applications, demand may not follow this autoregressive process, or an optimal forecasting method may not be used, or the inventory policy may not be "order-up-to." In such cases, a range of forecasting methods can be applied on retailer demand and on orders to the manufacturer. As indicated in the previous section, the errors induced by the best methods may be compared, to assess which series is more forecastable. This is a pragmatic policy, since the range of potential forecasting methods employed by many organizations is limited by considerations such as forecasting software and familiarity by forecasting analysts. Of course, we may be missing a method that would reverse our decision about which series is more forecastable. This can be addressed only by a more exhaustive method search.

Another example of finding a more forecastable series relates to seasonality. Estimation of seasonal indices is often difficult, particularly if there are few years of data and the series are noisy. In many practical situations, there is a wealth of associated data that could prove helpful. The same product may be sold at many different locations, for example. If it is reasonable to assume that the same seasonal patterns prevail at all locations, then the seasonality of the total demand may be more forecastable than the seasonality of the individual series (at the different locations). If we use a multiplicative index, then seasonal indices found at the aggregate level can be applied directly at the individual level. A similar argument applies for product families, where it is reasonable to assume that the same seasonal indices apply to all products in a family.

Leonard (2007) discusses the use of hierarchical models for seasonality, incorporating many individual time series and their aggregates. It should be noted that the aggregate series are not always more forecastable. Chen and Boylan (2007) present rules for the use of aggregate series for seasonal models, based on comparisons of expressions for the lower bound of forecast error (based on mean squared error). Suppose one series is very noisy, but its seasonality conforms to the group. Then it can "borrow strength" from the other series, and an aggregate seasonal index should be used. Suppose a second series also has seasonality that conforms to the group, but its data are very well behaved, with little noise. Then it will only "borrow weakness" from the group, and it is better to use its own individual seasonal index. In a subsequent paper, Chen and Boylan (2008) applied their rules to real data from a manufacturer of light bulbs, showing that accuracy gains can be achieved.

Conclusions

The idea of forecastability is valuable; it allows the focus of attention to shift from forecasting methods to the very series that are being forecasted. The concept of forecastability requires sharpening, however. I proposed this definition: "Forecastability refers to the range of forecast errors that are achievable on average, in the long run. The lower value of the range represents the lowest forecast error achievable. The upper value of the range represents an upper bound based on a benchmark forecasting method."

By not restricting the concept to a particular forecasting method or forecast error measure, there are two benefits. First, the concept is more general, allowing for error measures from a very broad class of error metrics. It is not restricted to basic time-series methods. Secondly, it may be applied to both theoretically generated series and to real-data series. The former may give some indication of the circumstances under which one series is more forecastable than another. The latter can be used to test such insights on real data, using forecasting methods and error measures that are relevant to the organization. This approach is well worth examining in practice, as substantial gains in forecasting accuracy may be attained.

REFERENCES

Armstrong, J. S. (2001). Combining forecasts. In J. S. Armstrong (Ed.): *Principles of Forecasting: A Handbook for Researchers and Practitioners*. Norwell, MA: Kluwer Academic Publishers, 413–439.

Boone, P., and R. Ganeshan (2008). The value of information sharing in the retail supply chain: Two case studies. *Foresight: International Journal of Applied Forecasting* 9, 12–17.

Catt, P. (2009). Forecastability: Some insights from physics, graphical decomposition, and information theory. *Foresight: International Journal of Applied Forecasting* 13, 24–33.

Chen, H., and J. E. Boylan (2008). Empirical evidence on individual and group seasonal indices. *International Journal of Forecasting* 24, 525–534.

Chen, H., and J. E. Boylan (2007). Use of individual and group seasonal indices in subaggregate demand forecasting. *Journal of the Operational Research Society* 58, 1660–1671.

Goodwin, P. (2009). New evidence on the value of combining forecasts. *Foresight: International Journal of Applied Forecasting* 12, 33–38.

Graefe, A., J. S., Armstrong, A. G. Cuzán, and R. J. Jones (2009). Combined forecasts of the 2008 election: The Pollyvote. *Foresight: International Journal of Applied Forecasting* 12, 41–42.

Hyndman, R. J., and A. B. Koehler (2006). Another look at measures of forecast accuracy. *International Journal of Forecasting* 23, 679–688.

Kahn, K. B. (2006). In search of forecastability. Forecasting Summit 2006, Orlando, Florida.

Lee, H. L., S. K. So, and C. S. Tang (2000). The value of information sharing in a two-level supply chain. *Management Science* 46, 626–643.

Leonard, M. (2007). Forecasting short seasonal time series using aggregate and analogous series. *Foresight: International Journal of Applied Forecasting* 6, 16–20.

Makridakis, S., A. Andersen, R. Carbone, R. Fildes, M. Hibon, R. Lewandoski, J. Newton, E. Parzen, and R. Winkler (1982). The accuracy of extrapolation (time series) methods: Results of a forecasting competition. *Journal of Forecasting* 1, 111–153.

Makridakis S., and M. Hibon (2000). The M3 Competition: Results, conclusions and implications. *International Journal of Forecasting* 16, 451–476.

Syntetos, A. A., K. Nikolopoulos, J. E. Boylan, R. Fildes, and P. Goodwin (2009). The effects of integrating management judgment into intermittent demand forecasts. *International Journal of Production Economics* 118, 72–81.

Valentin, L. (2007). Use scaled errors instead of percentage errors in forecast evaluations. *Foresight: The International Journal of Applied Forecasting* 7, 17–22.

1.4 FORECASTABLITY: A NEW METHOD FOR BENCHMARKING AND DRIVING IMPROVEMENT*

Sean Schubert

Extending this discussion of forecastablity, Sean Schubert shows how to create internal benchmarks based on product-specific attributes, such as product volume, product stability, and company and market characteristics. Schubert calls these characteristics the forecastability DNA of the product, and his approach attempts to supply a prediction of the forecast error we should expect based on the item's DNA, hence providing internal benchmarks for forecast accuracy.

As a practical consequence, the forecastability model can help identify items that are "uncharacteristic" and therefore require special attention. It also allows comparison across different businesses, and determines suitably customized targets for forecast accuracy.

Introduction: Establishing Comparability

Whenever the topic of forecasting comes up in polite company, one of the first questions asked—after the complaints about bad forecasts have died down—is, "Well, what should my forecast accuracy be?" Since few seasoned business professionals believe that a target of 100% forecast accuracy is realistic, the question then becomes, "What forecast accuracy is achievable?"

When we talk about a metric or key performance indicator (KPI), we typically ask, "How are other companies doing?" Benchmarking competitors in similar businesses is certainly a relatively simple way to see how we compare.

---

* This article originally appeared in *Foresight: The International Journal of Applied Forecasting* (Summer 2012), and appears here courtesy of the International Institute of Forecasters.

If our competitors are at 70% accuracy (30% error on average) while we're at 50%, we know we have some work to do. If we're at 75% and similar businesses are at 65%, then we can feel confident that we're holding our own and getting results.

The devil is in the details of how these metrics are calculated in different companies, or even in different business units within a single company. Stephan Kolassa stresses this point in his *Foresight* article (Kolassa, 2008) on the usefulness of benchmarking surveys: "In benchmarking, comparability is the key!"

To establish comparability of forecasting metrics, we need to ask, among other things:

- What is the forecast lead time?
- What time buckets are we forecasting (monthly, weekly, or daily)?
- What level in the product hierarchy are we looking at (SKU, SKU × Distribution Center, SKU × Customer × Location, etc.)?
- Is anything scrubbed out of the accuracy metric?
- How is the metric weighted?
- Are direct-import or make-to-order SKUs included?

We might also question how hard a business is to forecast. Generally, it's easier to forecast sales for a nonseasonal consumer staple like diapers than the latest short-lived fad aimed at tweens. We try to neutralize this by benchmarking competitors in similar businesses, but even if we're calculating the metric consistently and the companies are in the same sector, can we say everything else—strategy, supply chain, product makeup, customer behavior, and so on—is also equal, or even reasonably similar? Without reasonable comparability on all the relevant dimensions, we agree with Stephan Kolassa that "the quest for external forecasting benchmarks is futile" (Kolassa, p. 13).

Since scratching the surface of benchmarking creates as many new questions as it answers, where does that leave us when we think about assessing forecastability?

What Is Forecastability?

Some researchers define forecastability as the ability to improve on a simple forecast, such as the naïve method (forecast is the same as the last actual). Such a definition treats the naïve method as the benchmark and hence may be an indicator of the minimum forecast accuracy to be expected. It is uninformative, however, about the best achievable forecast accuracy.

More generally, Ken Kahn (2006) called forecastability "an assessment of a data pattern's stability." The presumption here is that the more stable (less volatile) the series is, the more accurately it can be forecast. Still, it does not tell us what forecast accuracy improvement is achievable.

Looking still more broadly into data patterns, Peter Catt (2009) defines forecastability as the complexity of the underlying data-generating process, along a continuum from deterministic (can be forecast without error) through random (cannot be forecast any better than predicting "no change"). Catt's definition, like Kahn's, helps us to determine the relative forecastability of different products, but again does not readily translate into a metric that reveals what our accuracy aspirations should be.

All these definitions illuminate the problem at hand. How can we tell if we could be doing a better job forecasting a specific item? What is the reasonably achievable degree of forecast accuracy for a given SKU, group of SKUs, customer, or business?

These are not simple questions. Whatever the method we put in play, we won't know if we can do better until we try to do better—perhaps by using a more sophisticated method. And if a new forecasting algorithm is invented tomorrow, then maybe we'll get even better forecast accuracy. John Boylan's discussion in an earlier *Foresight* feature on forecastability (Boylan, 2009) examines these challenges in more detail, and offers some general guidelines for determining the lower bound to achievable forecast error. His suggestions include relating the time series to its position in the hierarchy, combining forecasts from different methods, and identifying more forecastable series with similar data characteristics.

But our objective here is to stay focused on where there are opportunities for improvement, how large those opportunities are, and how forecastability varies by business, region, customer, and item.

Forecastability DNA

Searching for answers to the question of what degree of forecast accuracy is reasonably achievable, we can think about the types of things that might affect the forecastability of a particular product. Table 1.1 offers a list of possible candidates for consideration. Most relate to the product itself, others to broader company policy, still others to the markets in which the product is sold.

While the list in Table 1.1 is not exhaustive, it can give us some insight into why certain products are easier to forecast than others. We can think of these factors as the forecastability DNA of each item. Once we understand an item's DNA, then we'll understand what drives its forecastability, and why it's different or similar to other items in the same or different businesses.

Let's walk through an example using just one DNA factor—the variability of the SOH, which is frequently measured (see Kahn, 2006, for example) by a statistic called the coefficient of variation (CoV). The CoV is traditionally

Table 1.1 Attributes of a Product's Forecastability

Yearly volume of Sales Order History (SOH)
Length of the SOH
Variability of the SOH
Intermittency of the SOH
Promotions (frequency, magnitude, repetitiveness)
Trend and seasonality
Forecast error from a naïve model
Number of customers and concentration of sales in the largest customers
Supply-chain and inventory strategies
Lead time required for the forecasts

defined as the ratio of the standard deviation of the series to the mean, and, as such, measures the percentage degree of variation in the series around the average.

The usual argument is that the higher the CoV—that is, the more a series fluctuates—the more difficult the series is to forecast. One notable exception is that series with seasonal sales patterns could be more forecastable despite their additional variation over the seasons.

Figure 1.4 plots the mean absolute percent error (MAPE) vs. the CoV for all the SKUs in a particular region for a business. This mix of SKUs includes both seasonal and nonseasonal, steady runners, and highly intermittent items. The forecasts were "automatically" generated using statistical software.

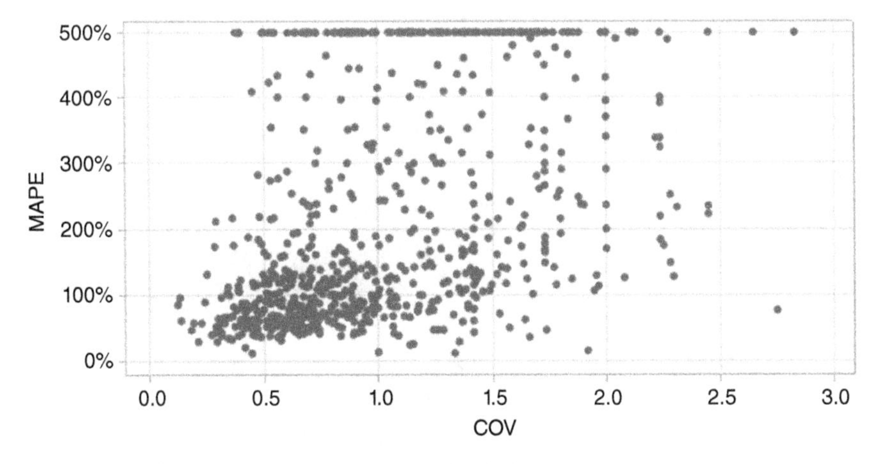

Figure 1.4 Forecast Error (MAPE) vs. Coefficient of Variation (CoV)
All SKUs for Business 2 Region 4. Forecast Error (MAPE) @ 60-day lead time. MAPEs above 500% were set to 500% to keep the graph to a manageable scale. CoV measured over recent 12 months.

In Figure 1.4, there is an apparent correlation (R^2 = 30%) that suggests that the SKUs with greater variability were forecast with greater error (less accuracy). Clearly, the CoV doesn't tell the whole story, but it can help us identify items that are "uncharacteristic" and therefore require special attention. For one thing, we see numerous items that have low CoVs (less than 0.5, for example), but still suffer high errors.

It's also logical that higher volume SKUs are easier to forecast than lower volume SKUs. Figure 1.5 shows such a correspondence (R^2 = 38%). In the same manner, we could walk through the rest of the genes in the forecastability DNA (Length of SOH, Intermittency of Sales, etc.) and select the factors that best predict forecast accuracy. However, we should use the more powerful multivariate approach that combines all that information in the DNA into a single model.

Building a Model of Forecastability

Form of the Model

Following advice from Einstein and William of Ockham, we should construct the simplest model that helps us understand forecastability, but no simpler. Once we've completed the analysis, we will get a relationship of the general form:

$$\text{Forecast Accuracy Metric} = \beta_0 + \beta_1 * \text{DNAFactor1} + \beta_2 * \text{DNAFactor2} + \beta_3 * \text{DNAFactor3} + \ldots$$

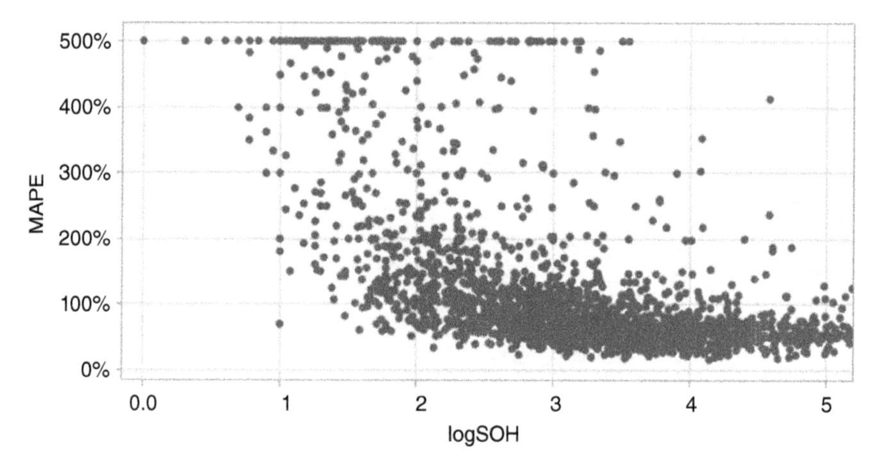

Figure 1.5 Forecast Error (MAPE) vs. Yearly SOH Volume
All SKUs for Business 3 Region 3. Forecast Error (MAPE) @ 60-day lead time. MAPEs above 500% were set to 500% to keep the graph to a reasonable scale. Yearly SOH Volume measured over recent 12 months.

With this model customized for our own unique businesses, we can proceed to benchmark ourselves against ourselves. Internal benchmarking in this way automatically adjusts the benchmark based on the specifics of each item, which addresses the comparability question as well as the common reaction to benchmarking comparisons, i.e., "My business is harder to forecast because of *x*, *y*, and *z*." By including the effects of each gene in the forecastability DNA, we address and compensate for each of those *x*s, *y*s, and *z*s, thereby developing a relevant benchmark for that business. Again, there is the caveat that while no metric is perfect, a metric is useful if it helps us improve the performance of our forecasting process.

For example, if one particular business introduces a large number of new products every year, we can compensate for that in our benchmark by including length of sales history as part of the DNA, which means we are truly comparing "like to like" across our many items, regions, customers, and businesses.

Pulling the Data Together

As presented above, an item's forecastability DNA can include quite a few genes, which implies that we need a reasonable amount of data to estimate the forecastability model. How much data is enough? A statistician would say that "more is better"—as long as it's all relevant and representative. It's best if we can get the full history, as well as additional information on customers and promotions at the SKU level; but at minimum we'll need the last 12 months of actual sales and forecasts at the item level (at key lead times of interest) with information on business, brand, product family, item, and all other details of interest. Remember, we're pulling this data together not to generate forecasts from the history but to judge and learn more about what drives the effectiveness of our forecasting process.

Internal Benchmarking

Once estimated with the available data (more is better!), the forecastability model will supply a prediction for the forecast error to be expected for each item based on its particular DNA. This prediction is our internal benchmark, which can help sound an alarm for cases where the forecasts for an item are performing significantly worse than their benchmark. In those cases we would ask questions like: "Are you using statistical forecasting?" "Are you using best practices to select and manage your forecasting models?" "Are you making inappropriate judgmental adjustments to your forecasts?" And so on.

This approach to internal benchmarking also avoids the assumption that sophisticated methods are automatically good performers: that just because a business is using advanced forecasting techniques (e.g., ARIMAX, neural nets, etc.), there is little room for improvement. Of course, we would generally expect regions or businesses using more advanced tools to beat the benchmark when compared to forecasts generated from Microsoft Excel or other "primitive" methods, but we will let the analysis tell the tale of what works.

While pulling the data together to build our internal benchmarking model, we may find there are some data missing. Even if that's the case, we may still be able to create a model by using robust modeling techniques like neural nets, ensemble methods like decision trees, or other data-mining techniques, or, in the case of a regression model, by substituting the average value of any predictor where values are missing.

Another common recommendation in the modeling literature (Gelman, 2006) is to center and normalize each of the predictor variables (*x*s) to help us create more easily interpretable model coefficients. This means for each potential predictor like CoV, we subtract the mean from all the values and divide by the standard deviation of all the values. Once we've done this for all the potentially predictive factors in the forecastability DNA, we will be ready to build our multivariate model.

Defining the Forecast-Accuracy Metric

A key decision in building the model is the definition of the forecast-accuracy metric. Should the metric measure forecast *accuracy* or forecast *error*? (See the note by David Hawitt in the Summer 2010 issue of *Foresight* for more discussion.) In addition, we must decide whether the metric should assess the absolute forecast errors (expressed in volume units) or percentage forecast errors. A problem with percentages is that, while they allow easy comparisons between SKUs, they can disguise the true impact of forecast error on the supply chain. After all, the business is much less concerned about a 50% forecast error for a SKU that sells 100 units than for a SKU that sells 1,000,000 units (assuming similar pricing, of course).

We have chosen here to express the metric using absolute forecast errors, which allows us to more directly see the impact and cost of forecast error on the supply chain. Moreover, once we have the model output in terms of absolute errors, we can readily convert the results to percentage errors (MAPEs), forecast accuracy percentage (100% minus the MAPE), or any other version of the metric (symmetric MAPE and so on) that we could choose to present our forecasting performance to the business.

Transforming the Variables

As a final "trick" in building the model, we used a log transformation for the variables that are expressed in units, have a large range of values, or a highly skewed distribution. The log transformation helps ensure that the model satisfies certain key regression assumptions, reduces the influence of the very largest values, guarantees positive values for absolute error, and facilitates interpretations of the statistical results (Gelman and Hill, 2006; sections 3.4 and 4.4 explain the role of the log transformation in more detail).

Now our forecastability model will have the general form:

$$\log(\text{absolute Forecast error}) = \beta_0 + \beta_1 * \log(\text{DNAFactor1}) + \beta_2 * \log(\text{DNAFactor2}) + \beta_3 * \text{DNAFactor3} + \ldots$$

Certain predictors, such as the CoV, are not transformed into logs since they are ratios or percentages to begin with.

The Forecastability Model in Action

In Table 1.2, we show a portion of the regression results obtained by fitting a forecastability model to 12 months of data on all items (70,000+) in a company's global product hierarchy.

Because the list of potential drivers is long, it is likely there will be some overlap (collinearity) between and among some factors. So the final forecastability model may use only a subset of these factors.

In our illustration, the dominant factors were the Yearly SOH Volume, Naïve Error, and CoV. The #Customers and Length of History, while statistically significant, don't appear to be major drivers of forecast error in this business. Most dominant is the SOH variable: A change of one standard deviation in the SOH variable is predicted to bring about almost a 0.9 standard deviation change in the forecast error metric, which is more than three times the effect of the Naïve Error variable and more than six times the effect of the CoV.

Table 1.2 The DNA Factors and Their Impact on Forecast Error

Global Regression Results	
DNA Factor	**Regression Coefficient**
Log(SOH)	0.8869
Log(Naïve error)	0.2908
CoV	0.1328
Log(#Customers)	0.0094
Length of SOH	0.0080
R-Square	91.5%

Notes:
All factors displayed were statistically significant.
All predictors have been centered and standardized (subtract the overall mean and divide by the standard deviation). This simplifies the determination of relative factor importance.
Only selected factors from the full model have been disclosed, since the detailed forecastability model is not transportable from one business to the next. Building a forecastability model for your particular business will provide more insight than reproducing the model shown.

Interpreting the SOH Coefficient

Previously, we showed a graph for one particular business, supporting the idea that as the yearly SOH volume increases, forecast error tends to decrease as a percentage of volume. At first glance, that negative relationship appears to be contradicted by the positive coefficient of 0.8867 for the SOH variable. The apparent contradiction is explained by the difference between the use of absolute error metric in the model and the percentage error (MAPE) metric in Figure 1.5. While a larger SOH volume leads to a larger absolute error, errors as a percentage of SOH volume decline. The calculation is shown in Table 1.3. Note the last two columns showing that as the SOH variable increases, the absolute error increases but the MAPE declines.

So long as the coefficient on the log-transformed SOH factor is less than one, higher SOH volumes lead to decreasing percentage errors and thus greater forecast-accuracy percentages.

The coefficient of variation (CoV) also appears as a significant factor (as shown in Table 1.2), but clearly not a dominant one. So while our results do affirm the pattern in Figure 1.4 that higher CoV items are associated with higher forecast errors and hence diminished forecast accuracy, the CoV cannot stand on its own as an indicator of forecastability.

Using the Model for Benchmarking

Figure 1.6 compares the (log of the) actual absolute forecast errors with those predicted by the forecastability model, for all SKUs and all businesses across all regions. The actuals on the *y*-axis are from current forecasting methods in use. These forecasting methods spanned the gamut, from advanced ERP planning modules to standalone forecasting software, Excel-based forecasting techniques to manual judgment forecasts. As an aside, we could also have included forecasting software as a DNA factor in the model to learn about how our various tools (or lack thereof) improve forecast accuracy (error), but we will leave that as a potential topic for future discussion.

Table 1.3 Building Intuition about MAPE and the SOH Coefficient

SOH	log(SOH)	log(AbsErr) = 0.8867*log SOH	AbsErr = 10^(logAbsErr)	Forecast Error (MAPE%)
10	1	0.8867	7.7	77.0%
100	2	1.7734	59.3	59.3%
1,000	3	2.6601	457.2	45.7%
10,000	4	3.5468	3,522.1	35.2%
100,000	5	4.4335	27,133.1	27.1%
1,000,000	6	5.3202	209,025.9	20.9%
10,000,000	7	6.2069	1,610,274.8	16.1%

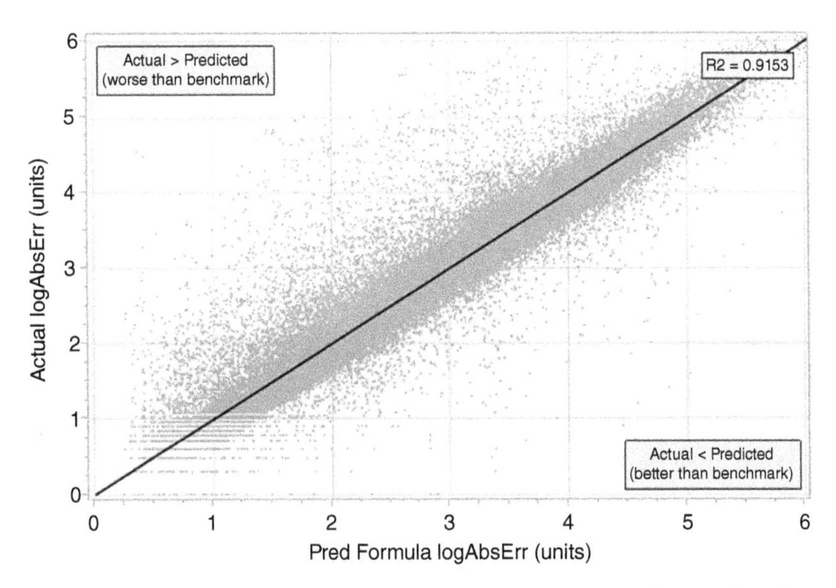

Figure 1.6 Actual vs. Predicted Benchmark Forecasting Errors (log units); All SKUs, All Businesses, All Regions

Note: The actual and predicted absolute forecast error (log units) are both measured over a 12-month period and reflect in-sample regression results.

The x-axis represents the predicted forecast error based on the item's forecastability DNA, that is, how difficult the item is to forecast. Higher predicted forecast error means "harder to forecast." Hence the x-axis represents the benchmark forecast error. Points in the area above the 45-degree line represent items for which the actual forecast error is larger than what would be predicted based on the benchmark. Points in this region suggest there may be an opportunity for improvement. We would still need to dig into the details to see if these worse-than-benchmark results are due to improper use of statistical models, non-value-added adjustments to the forecast, timing issues in the metric, inability to forecast promotions or new products, or something else awry with the nuts and bolts of our forecasting process.

Points in the area below the 45-degree line identify items for which the actual forecast error is less than the benchmark forecast error. Such results indicate that our forecast errors are lower than should be expected based on the model of forecastability DNA. While comforting, this does not necessarily imply that there is no further room for improvement. In these cases (actual less than predicted), we could raise the target by using the benchmark accuracy from one of the better-performing businesses as a goal. The mechanics of this process will be left as a potential topic for a future article.

Single-Item Benchmarking

Let's apply the forecastability model to one specific item. This item, used in the construction industry, was introduced 18 months ago: Recent forecasting errors totaled 18,554 units (absolute errors at a 60-day lead time summed over the last 12 months). Converted into percentages, the MAPE is 91.7%, implying a forecast accuracy of only 8.3%.

For this item, the DNA inputs were:

- Length of Sales Order History = 18 months
- Yearly Volume of SOH (units: last 12 months) = 20,224
- CoV (over last 12 months) = 0.58
- Naïve Forecast Error (units: last 12 months) = 11,384
- Number of Customers = 8
- Top 2 Customers = 58.4% of Sales
- And other DNA factors . . .

Loading these DNA factors into the forecastability model will give us a benchmark forecast accuracy for this SKU. We can then compare the current results (MAPE of 91.7%) to the benchmark MAPE to see if there is potential opportunity for improvement.

The forecastability model yields:

- Forecast error (units) = 9,763 (MAPE = 48.3%)
- Forecast accuracy benchmark = 100 − 48.3 = 51.7%

So our forecasts for this SKU are performing markedly worse than the benchmark. Indeed, they are less accurate than the naïve-model forecasts. The next step is to dig into the history of this SKU (Figure 1.7) to diagnose what we may have missed.

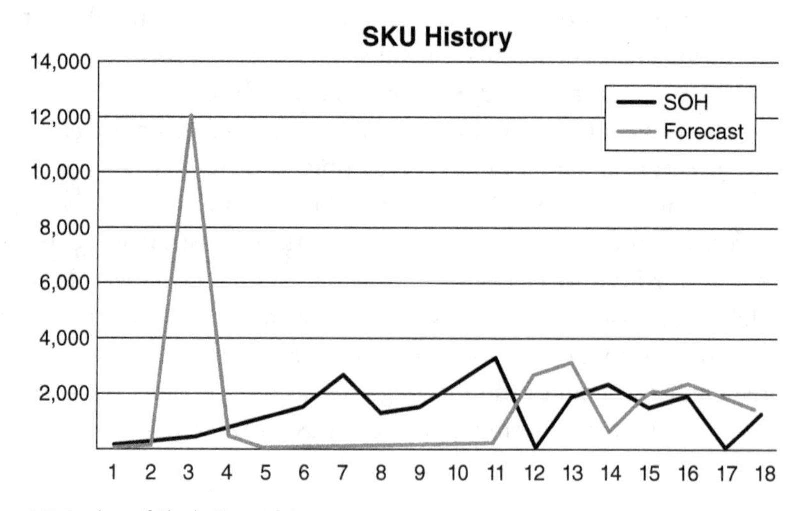

Figure 1.7 Review of Single-Item History

Note: The forecastability model uses the most recent 12 months of forecasts and actuals for modeling purposes. The full history is shown give an overview and context for discussion of forecasting over the SKU's life cycle.

We can see that the SOH has had a relatively low amount of month-to-month variation over the last 12 months. With a CoV of 0.58, it certainly should be much more forecastable than its recent forecast MAPE of 91.7%. The difficulty in forecasting appears to have been primarily driven by a lack of updating the forecast during months 5–11. Eventually the SKU sold through its initial inventory and ran out of stock during the 11th month, which affected sales and forecast error in the 12th month. The lack of sales in the 17th month requires a deeper investigation into causes; was it a brief change in the market or some type of data error in the ERP system? These are just a few of the ideas inspired by digging into the details, which in turn suggests a few areas for potential process improvement:

1. Implement tracking signals to ensure that any sustained differences between forecast and actuals are highlighted and quickly corrected.
2. Deploy a new-product-launch dashboard to ensure closer tracking of new products during initial 12 months of sales.
3. Create a system alert that highlights any SKUs where current forecast is greater than 0, recent SOH is greater than 0, but last month's SOH equals 0.

It is possible that current methods of continuous improvement for forecasting would have identified this particular SKU by its very high forecast MAPE—but an advantage to benchmarking using the forecastability-DNA approach is that it will also identify SKUs that are currently performing well using conventional metrics (e.g., ~40% forecast error), but could be performing even better (30% or less).

The power of the multivariate forecastability model also extends to understanding differences in forecastability between businesses while allowing us to generate customized forecast-accuracy targets for each business. We'll walk through an example now.

My Business Is Harder to Forecast

Knowing the key factors from the forecastability DNA for our overall business (Yearly Total SOH, Naïve Forecast Error, CoV, etc.) allows us to compare businesses objectively and quantitatively. We can start by looking at the average values of these factors for specific businesses at the SKU level, shown in Table 1.4.

Comparing Business 4 to Business 10 in the two listed regions, we see that an average SKU in Business 4 has higher volume, sells to fewer customers (Customer Count), and has similar length of history and variability (measured by CoV) as the typical SKU in Business 10. We would also note that Business 4 has half as many SKUs that need to be forecasted.

Table 1.4 Average Levels of the DNA Factors at the Business Region Level

Forecastability DNA Factor	Business 4, Region 3	Business 10, Region 2
SOH	68,689.25	13,638.65
NaiveFcstErr	30,395.17	7,893.98
CustomerCount	1.49	2.71
Length of History	10.43	10.53
CoV	0.96	0.94
SKU Count	349	861

Over the last 12 months, the accuracy achieved by these businesses (measured at the region level) is:

Business Unit	Forecast Accuracy (100%-MAPE)
Business 4, Region 3	34.5%
Business 10, Region 2	65.3%

Note that the forecastability model outputs the benchmark forecast error in units that we convert to forecast accuracy to allow easier comparisons between businesses.

The forecastability model crunches the DNA and gives the following as the benchmark forecast accuracy for each business:

Business Unit	Forecast Accuracy Benchmark
Business 4, Region 3	65.0%
Business 10, Region 2	60.5%

The forecastability DNA model also helps us understand objectively and in detail why we think Business 4 could markedly improve its forecast accuracy from its current level of 34.5%. The reasoning is:

- Business 4 has higher-volume items on average, which suggests it may be more forecastable overall than Business 10.
- Converting the average naïve forecast error per SKU of 30,395.17 for Business 4 into a naïve forecast accuracy of 55.7% also suggests the potential for improved accuracy in Business 4.
- By crunching all the forecastability DNA data, we see that the benchmark for Business 4 is calculated to be 65.0%, considerably better than recent forecast-accuracy results, which suggests that improvement is indicated for that business.

Compare how we objectively determined this target to the "standard" approach to target-setting. Following the traditional method, you'd likely hear, "Our current metric is 34.6%; our forecast accuracy goal next year will be 40.0%."

If we told them that a more appropriate goal is 65.0%, they might say, "My business is harder to forecast because of a, b, and c." Normally there isn't much we could offer in response, but with the forecastability DNA data in hand we can say, "Your CoV is similar to Business 10, your naïve accuracy is already 55%, and factoring in your number of customers, yearly sales volume (SOH), length of history, and the other genes in the forecastability DNA, a forecast accuracy better than 60% should be achievable." If the business is still skeptical, we could do further analysis to show how the items in their business are similar to many other items in other businesses that are already achieving higher forecast accuracies.

Conclusions

Forecastability and forecast-accuracy benchmarks are perennial topics of discussion in the forecasting world. Benchmarking across companies is a popular approach, but can be challenging because we don't usually know the details of how others calculate their metrics (lead time, level of aggregation, and what they scrub out, to name only a few of the unknowns), not to mention how difficult their business is to forecast. After all, even if we used the exact same metrics, few would argue that all businesses are exactly equal when it comes to forecasting difficulty.

The factors that vary both between and within businesses that can make forecasting more or less difficult can be considered part of the "forecastability DNA," which can be quantified and modeled in relation to forecastability and forecast accuracy (or error). Bearing in mind the dictum that "All models are wrong, but some are useful" from forecasting and statistics guru George Box, we can use the forecastability model to help us understand what makes our forecasting process tick, which can help us set realistic forecast-accuracy (or error) targets customized for the specifics of each item and area in the business, while pointing us in the direction of areas for potential improvement. Of course, the approach will not unequivocally state what the cause of the poor forecasting performance is, but it does support a management-by-exception approach to focusing where the opportunity for improvement is the greatest.

REFERENCES

Boylan, J. (2009). Toward a more precise definition of forecastability. *Foresight: International Journal of Applied Forecasting* 13 (Spring), 34–40.

Catt, P. (2009). Forecastability: Insights from physics, graphical decomposition, and information theory. *Foresight: International Journal of Applied Forecasting* 13 (Spring), 24–33.

Gelman, A., and Hill, J. (2007). *Data Analysis Using Regression and Multilevel/Hierarchical Models*. New York: Cambridge University Press.

Hawitt, D. (2010). Should you report forecast error or forecast accuracy? *Foresight: International Journal of Applied Forecasting* 18 (Summer), 46.

Kahn, K. (2006). In search of forecastability. Presentation at the Forecasting Summit. Orlando, FL, February.

Kolassa, S. (2008). Can we obtain valid benchmarks from published surveys of forecast accuracy? *Foresight: International Journal of Applied Forecasting* 11 (Fall), 6–14.

1.5 FORECAST ERRORS AND THEIR AVOIDABILITY*

Steve Morlidge

Several other recent articles have broken new ground in search of useful benchmarks of forecastability. New metrics have been proposed (and old ones criticized), new analytical approaches have been offered, and many new perspectives have emerged. Still, the search continues for what we might call an *industry standard*: a protocol for assessing forecastability.

Key concepts emerged from the earlier articles that helped clarify the meaning of forecastability and the challenges underlying its analysis:

- The lower and upper bounds of forecast accuracy—the worst and best accuracy to be expected.
- The relationship between the volatility of our sales histories (stability) over time and their forecastability.
- Limitations of the coefficient of variation in measuring forecastability and an alternative in a metric of entropy.

In continuing pursuit of this industry standard for assessing forecastability, Steve Morlidge addresses the question, "How good is a 'good' forecast?" Morlidge summarizes the innovations from earlier articles and the goes on to propose a simple, logical, and supportable metric to serve as the forecastability benchmark. This is a new perspective on forecastability and is a promising basis for further work on the subject.

The simplicity of the metric he creates should be very appealing to business forecasters, given that it offers a convenient way to compare forecast accuracy results across products. While it may never be possible to determine the best accuracy one can hope to achieve in forecasting any particular item, we can demonstrate what level of forecast error is unavoidable (because there will always be an element of randomness in our data)—a significant step toward being able to make objective statements about the lowest errors that are achievable.

---

* This article originally appeared in *Foresight: The International Journal of Applied Forecasting* (Summer 2013), and appears courtesy of the International Institute of Forecasters.

His approach is based on the ratio of forecast errors to the errors from a naïve model, where one forecasts no change from the present to the future. While not a new idea, he shows that, under common circumstances, ratios of the forecast errors from your model to those of a naïve model have natural lower bounds, which provide benchmarks for seeing if you have eliminated all but unavoidable error.

(For additional forecastability-related literature, see the Boylan, Schubert, and Morlidge reference sections.)

Beginnings

It all started in 2004.

I was working in a large multinational company, responsible for developing and promoting a performance-management initiative in the finance function. The books on managing change that I had been reading made it clear that bringing about change depends on having a "mission critical" problem—a burning platform—and identifying what you were doing as the solution. It was clear to me that our financial forecasting was a broken process. I needed to spur people into action, and I had spent over a year working up and promoting a solution to the problem. And then—to my good fortune, if not that of the shareholders—my company was forced to deliver the first profit warning in its proud history.

In a matter of weeks, I found myself at the heart of efforts to fight the fires that broke out across the business as a result of this public admission of failure. My first step was to draft a forecast policy, the reason for which was simple: Like most other companies, my employer had never formally defined what a good forecast should look like. Without a definition of success, it was little wonder that our forecast processes had failed so catastrophically. Fortunately, I had prepared myself well for this task.

Defining Success in Forecasting

In my research of the previous year, I had discovered that the science of forecasting in finance was primitive in the extreme. No one in the field seemed to have a clear idea about what constituted a good forecast. As fortune would have it, I had attached myself to a group that had been working for a number of years to improve planning and forecasting practice in the supply chain, and I learned a great deal—not all of it for the first time—that I was able to use in my developing ideas about how finance should go about things. The definition of success that our group used was this:

> *"A good forecast exhibits no bias and minimal variation."*

This definition correctly recognizes that systematic error (bias) and unsystematic error (variability or volatility) have different characteristics and consequences for the business. With a rapidity that was all but unprecedented, our definition of success (with a few tweaks to accommodate the peculiarities of financial forecasting) was adopted as a corporate policy.

Afterward, the company finance team with which I'd developed the new forecast policy invited me in for celebratory tea and biscuits. As we chatted, one team member asked me casually enough, "This is great, Steve, but how do we know if we have actually got a good forecast?"

Try as I might, I had no answer. The best I could do was, "Good question. Leave it with me." Like many simple questions, it was not as easy to answer as it perhaps first appeared.

Creating a Metric

Over the next few months, I was forced to come to terms with the subtlety of the problem and the depth of my ignorance on the subject. I formed a clear view of what kind of measurement system we needed to operationalize the policy that I had helped draft:

- It should be able to distinguish forecast error bias from forecast error magnitude (i.e., unsystematic variation).
- It should be actionable; being "accurate enough and quick" was better than "perfect and slow," since we needed to correct problems before they had a chance to overwhelm us.
- It had to recognize the difference between signal and noise; that is, it should alert us to real problems and deter us from intervening when there was no evidence of an issue problem.
- It should be simple to calculate and easy to communicate to nonexperts.
- It would quantify what constitutes an acceptable level of forecast accuracy.

I slowly came to understand that this final criterion presented the most formidable obstacle because it had three distinct facets:

1. How forecastable is the data set? Clearly, we cannot expect the same degree of error for a low-level forecast in a volatile market as for a high-level forecast in a stable market.
2. What proportion of the error is avoidable? Bias, the tendency of a forecast to systematically miss the actual demand (consistently either high or low), is avoidable in principle—but some portion of the forecast error is unavoidable because there is always going to be an element of randomness in our data. It is true that biases can arise after a major

structural change, but a good forecasting algorithm should be able to detect systematic error and correct for it before it builds up.

3. What is the business impact of the forecast error? For example, we might be happy to tolerate a high level of errors where the impact (in terms of cost of inventory, for example) is relatively low.

Unsurprisingly, these same questions have exercised the best minds in our field, as a review of past issues of *Foresight* makes abundantly apparent.

What the Experts Say

There is arguably no topic in forecasting more passionately debated than that of forecastability.

The most widely promoted approach is based on the intuitive insight that, generally, the more volatile the variable, the more difficult it is to forecast. There is a large body of empirical support for this concept. The coefficient of variation (CoV)—the ratio of the variation from the average in the data to the average value—is a standard measure of variability. Thus researchers have sought to correlate forecast accuracy with the CoV (Gilliland, 2010; Schubert, 2012).

One shortcoming with the CoV is that it does not always correlate well with forecast accuracy (Schubert, 2012); and even if it did measure actual forecast accuracy, it would not necessarily reflect forecastability (potential forecast accuracy).

Popular alternative approaches are based on comparisons of forecast accuracy with a benchmark such as the accuracy of a naïve forecast, where the actual for a period is used as the forecast for the subsequent period. Metrics employed in this approach are ratios of forecast errors from a designated model to the naïve forecast errors, and include Theil's U statistic (1966), the relative absolute error or RAE (Armstrong and Collopy, 1992), the mean absolute scaled error or MASE (Hyndman, 2006), as well as the concept of Forecast Value Added (Gilliland, 2013).

An advantage of using the naïve forecast as a benchmark is that it implicitly incorporates the notion of volatility, since the naïve forecast has the same level of variation as the variable itself. Errors associated with the naïve forecast are also probably a better predictor of forecastability for time-series purposes than the coefficient of variation because they measure period-to-period variation in the data. For example, a series where successive observations are highly positively correlated (so the series is forecastable) may drift away from the series' mean for several periods, thereby contributing to a high CoV. In contrast, the naïve forecast errors will be relatively small because the successive observations are similar.

A number of authors have expressed discomfort with using any forecast accuracy metric as a proxy for forecastability (Boylan, 2009). Peter Catt demonstrated (2009) how completely deterministic processes—and thus totally forecastable if you know the data generating process—can create very volatile data series. Attempts to find ways to measure forecastability directly have foundered on the self-referential nature of the problem: We can only assess the performance of a forecasting methodology by comparison with an unspecifiable set of all possible methodologies.

These authors have proposed alternative ways of assessing forecastability, such as through a profile of a "product DNA" (Schubert, 2012). It comes as no surprise that these methods are relatively complex and consequently more difficult to implement and interpret. A more straightforward approach emerges from the concept of avoidability.

Avoidability

Avoidability is closely related to forecastability. John Boylan (2009) defines forecastability as "the range of forecast errors that are achievable on average, in the long run." He argued that the upper bound of forecast error should be the naïve forecast error. This is an uncontroversial position since the naïve is the crudest forecast process imaginable—albeit one that professional forecasters often fail to beat in practice (Pearson, 2010). The lower bound or lowest achievable forecast error, Boylan indicates, could be impossible to determine because there are "endless forecasting methods that may be used. It is possible that a series is difficult to forecast and will yield high forecast errors unless a particular method is identified."

Avoidability sets a theoretical lower bound to the forecast error that is independent of the forecaster and the available tool set, and it can be quantified using a common error metric such as mean squared error (MSE) or mean absolute error (MAE). The theoretical lower bound may be achievable only with tools beyond the reach of the forecaster. What is achievable using existing technology defines forecastability.

What I was attempting to do all those years ago—without realizing it—was to build a forecasting control system. I have learned since I embarked on this quest that, without good feedback, no process can be relied on to consistently deliver a desired output. This fact surrounds us in nature, and it is at the heart of all of mankind's technological advances. Our bodies regulate the levels of many thousands of chemicals in a way that is very similar to how modern engine-management systems optimize the performance of our motor vehicles. In the same way, no forecast methodology, no matter how sophisticated, can consistently deliver a good performance unless we can find a way to measure and compare its performance to the desired result. Doing so enables us to make the timely corrections necessary to eliminate unnecessary and unwanted error (see Hoover, 2006).

It appears, then, that being able to determine what level of performance is achievable is not the icing on the forecasting cake after all; it is the difference between interesting mathematical theory and useful technology. Finding a way to break though the complexity surrounding these issues is imperative. Fortunately, recent work has suggested an approach.

The Way Forward: A Conjecture

In attempting to understand what constitutes an acceptable level of forecast performance, we start with these standard assertions:

1. First, there are no conceivable circumstances where forecasting performance should be consistently worse than that of the naïve forecast.
2. Second, the performance of any system that we might want to forecast will always contain noise.

With regard to number 2, we know that all extrapolation-based forecasting (i.e., time-series forecasting) rests on the assumption that there is a pattern (or signal) in the past data that will influence future outcomes, and that this signal is obscured by randomness. In addition, we should always expect that the signal will change at least a little bit as we move into the future—just how and how much are unknowable at present. So the job of a forecasting algorithm is to detect and mathematically describe the past pattern—having excluded the noise—and then apply it to extrapolate into the future.

A "perfect" forecasting algorithm would describe the past signal, leaving only errors that represent pure noise, and hence unavoidable. Since the errors from a naïve forecast are one way of measuring the observed amount of noise in data, my conjecture is that there is a mathematical relationship between these naïve forecast errors and the lowest possible errors from a forecast.

The Unavoidability Ratio

Prompted by this conjecture, Paul Goodwin (2013) provides a mathematical derivation of what this relationship might be. We summarize the results here:

> *When the pattern in the data is purely random, the ratio of the variance (mean squared error, MSE) from a perfect algorithm to the MSE of a naive forecast will be 0.5; that is, the perfect algorithm will cut observed noise (using the MSE measure) in half. Using the more practical measure of the ratio of the mean absolute error (MAE), a "perfect" algorithm would never achieve a ratio lower than 0.7 ($\sqrt{0.5}$).*

EXAMPLE

THE ASSUMPTIONS

- We have the perfect forecasting algorithm.
- The remaining errors are pure noise in the statistical sense that they are "stationary and independently and identically distributed with a mean of zero."
- The change in the signal from period to period is unaffected by the previous period's noise.

The Unavoidability Ratio

Under these assumptions, the ratio of the variance of pure error (that is, error from a perfect forecasting algorithm) to that of the errors from a naïve forecast model will be:

$$\frac{(\text{Variance of pure error})}{2 * (\text{Variance of pure error}) + (\text{Variance of period to period changes in signal}) + (\text{Mean change in signal})^2}$$

If there are no systematic changes in the signal (e.g., no trend or cyclical pattern), the second and third terms in the denominator become zero, leaving us with

$$\frac{(\text{Variance of noise})}{2 * (\text{Variance of noise})} = 0.5$$

for the best possible performance, and thus the definition of what constitutes unavoidable error.

This surprisingly simple result emerges from a particular set of assumptions about the data, which we enumerate in the accompanying boxed inset. The key assumption is that there is no trend, cyclical pattern to the historical data, or impact from causal variables.

Some might argue that this approach has limited value since it is not safe to assume that there will be no systematic changes in the signal; the existence of anything other than a flat trend, particularly if nonlinear, could lead to much lower theoretical minimum. However, there are many real-life situations where our assumptions can apply. For example, supply-chain forecasts are typically made at a very granular level using very short time intervals (typically buckets of one week). In these circumstances, both the mean and the variance of changes in the signal (per period) will probably be low relative to the level of noise, thus the theoretical limit of forecast performance is likely to stay close to the ratio of 0.5. Lower ratios are possible for series with complex signal patterns, but these are liable to be more difficult to forecast than those with a simple signal. So we would not expect to see performance much better than this limit because the theoretical possibility of improving performance would be offset by the practical difficulty of achieving it. From a practical point of view, the proposed standards could be the best we can hope to achieve.

In summary, an unavoidability ratio of 0.5 in terms of MSE or 0.7 with respect to the MAE represents a useful estimate of the lower bound for forecast error in a range of circumstances. The upper bound is defined by the naïve forecast itself, so that a rational forecast process will normally produce a ratio between 0.5 and 1.0. The better the forecasting methodology, the closer the statistic will be to 0.5; in some circumstances it may be possible to better this. Potentially, then, this insight might provide a useful way of measuring forecast quality; the only way to assess quite how useful is through empirical work.

So much for the theory. What about the practice?

The Empirical Evidence

We carried out two tests comparing the performance of a set of forecasts against the respective naïve forecasts. For reasons of simplicity, absolute errors were used and compared to a theoretical lower bound of 0.7.

The first test (Unit A) used 124 product SKUs over 52 consecutive weekly buckets. The sample is from a fast-moving consumer-goods manufacturer whose business is characterized by a high level of promotional activity, and thus incorporates extensive manual intervention of statistical forecasts based on market intelligence. These are circumstances where it might be possible to significantly better the theoretical minimum. The distribution of errors relative to those from the naïve forecast is shown in Figure 1.8.

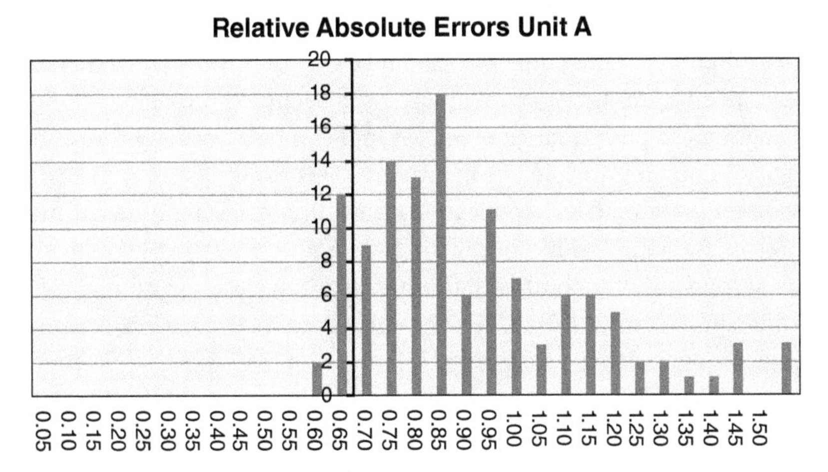

Figure 1.8 The Unavoidability Ratio (Absolute Errors Relative to Those of a Naïve Forecast) for Unit A

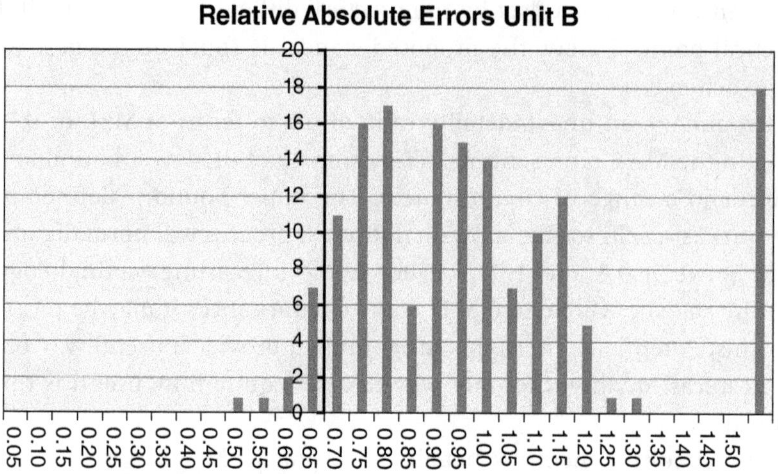

Relative Absolute Errors Unit B

Figure 1.9 The Unavoidability Ratio (Absolute Errors Relative to Those of a Naïve Forecast) for Unit B

The second example (Unit B, Figure 1.9) comes from a consumer-durables business with a very fragmented product portfolio. There is a lesser degree of manual intervention in the (statistical) forecast process, but items with intermittent and lumpy demand are common. In this case, the sample comprised 880 SKUs across 28 consecutive monthly buckets. With monthly buckets, we might expect to see less noise and more change in the signal, thus making ratios below 0.7 more likely.

There are two striking things about these examples.

First, relatively few items have a ratio that falls below 0.7 (2% in the case of Unit A, 9% for Unit B), and almost none fall below 0.5. This suggests that a ratio of somewhere around 0.5 (even using the MAE, lower using the MSE) may well represent a useful "lower bound" benchmark in practice.

Note that products like Units A and B (high levels of manual intervention and intermittent demand patterns) challenge the robustness of the avoidability principle. Even here, the unavoidability ratio seems to provide a sound basis for estimating the performance potential that can be achieved by any forecast process, not only in principle but in practice. This result opens up the prospect of a wide range of practical applications including meaningful benchmarking and forecast-tracking techniques.

The second striking point is that both cases have a large number of SKUs with ratios in excess of 1.0 (27% for Unit A and 26% for Unit B), meaning that forecast performance was worse than the naïve, most likely the result of inappropriate manual interventions in the forecast process. Mike Gilliland (2013) considers this situation to be a case of negative Forecast Value Added (FVA). It certainly exposes significant potential for improvement in forecast quality; it also shows that while we may theoretically benefit from making intelligence-driven interventions in the forecasting process, these benefits are often not realized in practice, as pointed out by Goodwin and Fildes (2007).

Of course, more work is needed to validate and then build on the theoretical foundations established here. Crucially, more empirical work is needed to determine how robust the approach is in a wider range of less amenable forecasting situations, such as products with pronounced seasonal patterns (for example, daily sales data in a retail environment). There may also be ways in which any shortcomings in the approach can be mitigated in practice.

The Next Step

While absolute precision in benchmarking forecasting performance is some distance off—and may prove impossible—our evidence suggests that it is possible to set rational quality criteria with more confidence than hitherto thought possible. In turn, this could open the way to developing approaches to measuring and managing forecast performance that are more useful in practice than existing methodologies.

To operationalize these insights and assess their usefulness in practice, I would welcome participation from companies in a collaborative effort to further test the methodology and help develop and refine practical applications of this approach.

REFERENCES

Armstrong, S., and F. Collopy (1992). Error measures for generalizing about forecasting methods: Empirical comparisons. *International Journal of Forecasting* 8, 69–80.

Boylan J. (2009). Towards a more precise definition of forecastability. *Foresight: International Journal of Applied Forecasting* 13 (Spring).

Catt, P. (2009). Forecastability: Insights from physics, graphical decomposition, and information theory. *Foresight: International Journal of Applied Forecasting* 13 (Spring).

Fildes, R., and Goodwin, P. (2007). Good and bad judgement in forecasting: Lessons from four companies. *Foresight: International Journal of Applied Forecasting* 8 (Fall).

Gilliland, M. (2010). *The Business Forecasting Deal.* Hoboken, NJ: John Wiley & Sons.

Gilliland, M. (2013). FVA: A reality check on forecasting practices. *Foresight: International Journal of Applied Forecasting* 29 (Spring), 14–18.

Goodwin, P. (2013). Theoretical gains in forecasting accuracy relative to naïve forecasts. Working paper, University of Bath.

Goodwin, P. (2009). Taking stock: Assessing the true cost of forecast errors. *Foresight: International Journal of Applied Forecasting* 15 (Fall).

Hoover, J. (2009). How to track forecast accuracy to guide forecast improvement. *Foresight: International Journal of Applied Forecasting* 14 (Summer).

Hoover, J. (2006). Measuring forecast accuracy: Omissions in today's forecasting engines and demand planning software. *Foresight: International Journal of Applied Forecasting* 4 (June).

Hyndman, R. (2006). Another look at forecast accuracy metrics for intermittent demand. *Foresight: International Journal of Applied Forecasting* 4 (Summer).

Pearson, R. (2010). An expanded prediction realization diagram for assessing errors. *Foresight: International Journal of Applied Forecasting*, Special Issue: Forecast Accuracy Measurement: Pitfalls to Avoid and Practices to Adopt.

Schubert, S. (2010). Forecastability: A new method for benchmarking and driving improvement. *Foresight: International Journal of Applied Forecasting* 26 (Summer 2012).

Theil, H. (1966). *Applied Economic Forecasting*. Amsterdam: North-Holland.

1.6 THE PERILS OF BENCHMARKING*

Michael Gilliland

Organizations often seek benchmarks to judge the success of their forecasts. Reliable benchmarks allow a company or agency to see if it has improved on industry standards and to assess whether investment of additional resources in forecasting is money well spent. But can existing benchmark surveys be trusted? Do they provide useful performance standards? The next two articles consider these issues.

For benchmarking, comparability is the key to usefulness. But Michael Gilliland shows that problems can occur when the data are inconsistent, inaccurate, and unreliable—or simply inappropriate. He offers three questions for evaluating a benchmark:

1. What is the source of the benchmark data, and is it trustworthy?
2. Is the measurement consistent across all respondents?
3. Is the measure appropriate?

Appropriateness is perhaps the most important consideration, as forecasting benchmarks fail to take into consideration the underlying forecastability of each respondent's data. Gilliland also warns of the danger of blindly copying the practices of "best-in-class" companies. Their exceptional forecast accuracy may be due less to admirable practices and more to having the easiest setting for forecasting demand.

Danger, Danger

Operational performance benchmarks are available from many sources, including professional organizations, journals, and consulting and benchmarking services. Appropriately constructed benchmarks provide insight into comparative performance and can be used to guide study of the practices of companies that head the benchmark lists. But published benchmarks should not be accepted blindly because there are a number of potential perils in the interpretation of benchmark data. Problems can occur when the data are

* This article originally appeared in *APICS e-NEWS* (Vol. 5, No. 23, December 6, 2005), and appears here courtesy of Jennifer Proctor, editor in chief of *APICS* magazine.

inaccurate, inconsistent, and unreliable—or simply inappropriate. Here are key questions to consider.

1. What is the source of the benchmark data, and is it trustworthy?

Is the benchmark based on rigorous audits of company data or based on unaudited responses to survey questionnaires? In an audit, the competence and integrity of the auditor must be trusted. But in a survey, the trust is placed in the knowledge and motivation of all the respondents. How many people really know the answers to the questions when they are filling out the survey?

2. Is the measurement consistent across respondents?

Survey-based benchmarks are particularly troublesome when the metric is complex or ambiguous. In the forecasting realm, a simple question such as, "What is your forecast error?" requires much further specification: What is the exact error formula to use; the organizational level at which the error is measured (stock keeping unit, warehouse, customer, region, total company); the time bucket (week, month, quarter); and the lag time? Respondents may be using entirely different methods to track their errors. Even formulas as similar sounding as mean absolute percent error (MAPE), symmetric MAPE, and weighted MAPE can give dramatically different results when applied to the same data.

3. Is the measure appropriate?

One of the purposes of benchmarking is to identify top performing companies so their practices can be emulated by others. But when it comes to forecasting performance, is it really fair to compare forecast error across companies when their demand patterns may not be equally forecastable? Even within an industry, such as apparel, one company may sell long lifecycle basic items with stable demand, while another sells only "fashion" items that change every season. It would be unrealistic to expect the fashion-item forecasters to perform as well as the basic-item forecasters.

Consider this worst-case scenario:

Company ABC appears at the top of a forecasting performance benchmark list for its industry. Consultants and academics swoop down on ABC to interview management, study the forecasting process, and publish guidelines for others wishing to follow ABC's "best practices." But just because ABC has the most accurate forecasts, does it mean its forecasting process is the best or even admirable?

What if ABC had it very easy to forecast demand? Further, what if ABC's elaborate forecasting process actually made the forecast accuracy *worse* than it would have been by using a simple method such as a random walk or moving average? These are certainly not the kinds of practices that other organizations should be emulating!

In this case, the benchmark metric (forecast accuracy) was not *by itself* appropriate. Just looking at forecast accuracy did not take into consideration the underlying difficulty (or ease) of ABC's forecasting problem. It did not compare ABC's results to the results it *would have achieved* by doing nothing and just using a simple method.

An alternative metric to benchmarking is comparing the results a company achieves to the results it would have achieved by using a different method or even by doing nothing. A generalization of this forecasting approach is to conduct forecast value added (FVA) analysis. FVA is defined as the change in a forecasting performance metric (such as MAPE or bias) that can be attributed to a particular step or participant in the forecasting process. FVA helps identify process activities that are adding value by making the forecast better and also helps identify those activities that are making the forecast worse. FVA analysis is consistent with lean—helping to streamline and improve a process by identifying (and eliminating) process waste. The benefit of the FVA approach is that it can help a company get better results with less effort.

Conclusion: Beware of judging operational performance based purely on industry benchmarks. Ask the questions outlined above to assess the validity of benchmark metrics. Do not copy the so-called best practices of others without verifying that these practices are indeed adding value and the reason for improved operational performance.

1.7 CAN WE OBTAIN VALID BENCHMARKS FROM PUBLISHED SURVEYS OF FORECAST ACCURACY?*

Stephan Kolassa

Stephan Kolassa dives deeper into benchmarking surveys and argues that it is difficult if not impossible to achieve comparability through external benchmarks.

Kolassa describes the many problems that plague benchmark surveys and advises companies to redirect their search from external to internal benchmarks. Internal benchmarks provide a better representation of the processes and targets the company has in place.

Benchmarks can be trusted only if the underlying process to be benchmarked is assessed in similar circumstances. But published surveys of forecast accuracy are not suitable as benchmarks because of incomparability in product, process, time frame, granularity, and key performance indicators. A better alternative for forecast improvement is a qualitative, process-oriented target. By focusing on process improvement, forecast accuracy and the use an organization makes of the forecasts will eventually be improved.

---

* This article originally appeared in *Foresight: The International Journal of Applied Forecasting* (Fall 2008), and appears here courtesy of the International Institute of Forecasters.

Introduction

Sales forecasters are frequently asked what a "good" forecast is; that is, what accuracy should be expected from the forecasting method or process?

This question is important for deciding how to allocate resources to the firm's forecasting function or forecast-improvement projects. If forecast accuracy is already as good as it can reasonably be expected to be, spending additional resources would be wasteful. Thus, the company can benefit from true benchmarks of forecasting accuracy.

By true benchmarks, I mean reliable data on the forecast accuracy that can be achieved by applying best practices in forecasting algorithms and processes. Unfortunately, published reports on forecasting accuracy are rare, and those that exist suffer from shortcomings that sharply limit their validity in providing forecast-accuracy benchmarks. Consequently, I believe it is a mistake to use benchmark surveys.

Published Surveys of Forecast Accuracy

The McCarthy Survey

(McCarthy et al., 2006) studied the evolution of sales forecasting practices by conducting surveys of forecasting professionals in 1984, 1995, and 2006. Their results (see Table 1.5) provide some evidence on forecast accuracy both longitudinally and at various levels of granularity, from SKU-by-location to industry level. The forecast horizons shown are (a) up to 3 months, (b) 4–24 months, and (c) greater than 24 months. The number of survey responses is denoted by n. All percentage figures are mean absolute percentage errors (MAPEs).

One of the study's general conclusions is that the accuracy of short-term forecasts generally deteriorated over time, as shown by the weighted-average MAPEs in the bottom row. Considering the ongoing and vigorous research on forecasting, as well as vastly improved computing power since 1984, this finding is surprising. The McCarthy team conjectured that the deterioration could be due to decreasing familiarity with complex forecasting methods (as they found via interviews), product proliferation, and changes in the metrics used to measure forecast accuracy over the past 20 years.

Indeed, the survey results do suffer from problems of noncomparability. For one, the numbers of respondents in 1995 and especially in 2006 were much lower than those in 1984. In addition, I presume that the participants in 2006 differed from those in 1984 and 1995, so that lower forecast quality could simply reflect differences in respondents' companies or industries. For example, the meaning of "SKU-by-location" may have been interpreted differently by respondents in different companies and industries. Similarly, "Product Line" and "Corporate" forecasts may mean different things to different respondents.

Table 1.5 MAPEs for Monthly Sales Forecast in 1984, 1995, and 2006 Surveys

Forecast Level	Horizon								
	≤ 3 Months			4 to 24 Months			> 24 Months		
	1984	1995	2006	1984	1995	2006	1984	1995	2006
Industry	8%	10%	15%	11%	12%	16%	15%	13%	7%
	n = 61	n = 1	n = 1	n = 61	n = 16	n = 10	n = 50	n = 36	n = 3
Corporate	7%	28%	29%	11%	14%	16%	18%	12%	11%
	n = 81	n = 2	n = 5	n = 89	n = 64	n = 31	n = 61	n = 42	n = 8
Product Line	11%	10%	12%	16%	14%	21%	20%	12%	21%
	n = 92	n = 4	n = 6	n = 95	n = 83	n = 34	n = 60	n = 25	n = 5
SKU	16%	18%	21%	21%	21%	36%	26%	14%	21%
	n = 96	n = 14	n = 5	n = 88	n = 89	n = 36	n = 54	n = 10	n = 3
SKU by Location		24%	34%		25%	40%		13%	
		n = 17	n = 7		n = 58	n =22		n = 5	
Weighted Average	15%	16%	24%						

So while the McCarthy survey provides some perspective on forecast accuracy at different times and levels, the usefulness of the figures as benchmarks is limited.

The IBF Surveys

The Institute of Business Forecasting regularly surveys participants at its conferences. The most recent survey results are reported in Jain and Malehorn (2006) and summarized in Table 1.6. Shown are MAPEs for forecast horizons of 1, 2, 3, and 12 months in different industries, together with the numbers of respondents. Jain (2007) reports on a similar survey taken at a 2007 IBF conference. The results are given in Table 1.7.

Tables 1.6 and 1.7 show large differences in forecasting accuracy among industries. For instance, the retail sector shows much lower errors than the more volatile computer/technology sector, especially for longer horizons. In general, the results show that forecast accuracy improves as sales are aggregated: Forecasts are better on an aggregate level than on a category level and better on a category level than for SKUs. And, while we should expect forecast accuracy to worsen as the horizon lengthens, the findings here are not always supportive. For example, at the Category and Aggregate levels in Consumer Products (Table 1.6), the 1-year-ahead MAPEs are lower than those at shorter horizons.

Table 1.6 MAPEs for Monthly Sales Forecast

Level	Horizon											
	1 Month			2 Months			1 Quarter			1 Year		
	SKU	Category	Aggregate	SKU	Category	Aggregate	SKU	Category	Aggregate	SKU	Category	Aggregate
Automotive	25% n = 3	5% n = 1	36% n = 1	31% n = 3	33% n = 2	25% n = 2	42% n = 1			46% n = 1		10% n = 1
Computer/ Technology	19% n = 4	14% n = 4	12% n = 7	33% n = 2	11% n = 2	18% n = 4	30% n = 3	16% n = 4	25% n = 6	17% n = 2	30% n = 1	31% n = 4
Consumer Products	27% n = 35	20% n = 23	15% n = 21	29% n = 20	22% n = 14	15% n = 10	33% n = 11	23% n = 7	14% n = 6	48% n = 4	19% n = 4	8% n = 3
Food/ Beverages	26% n = 16	15% n = 10	18% n = 11	28% n = 10	22% n = 4	36% n = 5	26% n = 8	21% n = 3	40% n = 4	19% n = 4	14% n = 2	48% n = 3
Healthcare	25% n = 7	15% n = 6	9% n = 6	27% n = 5	19% n = 5	17% n = 5	41% n = 5	24% n = 5	25% n = 5	30% n = 2	20% n = 2	15% n = 2
Industrial Products	22% n = 4	15% n = 7	7% n = 8	16% n = 2	14% n = 5	8% n = 6	17% n = 3	15% n = 6	10% n = 7	40% n = 2	21% n = 5	15% n = 6
Pharma	26% n = 5	20% n = 4	23% n = 4	30% n = 3	35% n = 2	33% n = 2	31% n = 4	25% n = 4	25% n = 3	34% n = 4	35% n = 4	28% n = 3
Retail	24% n = 7	18% n = 4	7% n = 4	17% n = 5	17% n = 6	8% n = 4	24% n = 4	10% n = 3	9% n = 4	23% n = 4	6% n = 2	6% n = 3
Telco				30% n = 1	10% n = 1	30§ n = 1	40% n = 1	15% n = 1	35% n = 1			
Others	28% n = 13	21% n = 9	17% n = 16	23% n = 7	20% n = 5	11% n = 10	25% n = 6	15% n = 5	14% n = 9	15% n = 4	18% n = 4	12% n = 8
Overall	26% n = 94	18% n = 68	13% n = 80	27% n = 58	20% n = 46	15% n = 51	30% n = 46	19% n = 37	17% n = 45	29% n = 27	21% n = 24	16% n = 33

Table 1.7 MAPEs for Monthly Sales Forecast

Level	Horizon											
	1 Month			2 Months			1 Quarter			1 Year		
	SKU	Category	Aggregate	SKU	Category	Aggregate	SKU	Category	Aggregate	SKU	Category	Aggregate
Consumer Products	29%	19%	16%	31%	20%	16%	35%	23%	22%	35%	28%	21%
Food and Beverages	27%	24%	24%	22%	12%	11%	23%	14%	15%	29%	18%	18%
Industrial Products	19%	17%	16%	28%	24%	18%	29%	22%	18%	36%	30%	17%

Unfortunately, the validity of these results is again problematic. The sample sizes were very small in many categories (Table 1.6), reflecting a low response rate by the attendees. Jain (2007) does not even indicate the number of responses behind the results in Table 1.7. In addition, these tables are based on surveys done at IBF conferences—which, after all, are attended by companies that are sensitive enough to the strategic value of forecasting to attend conferences on forecasting! Thus the MAPEs may not reflect average performance, but instead may represent lower errors at better-performing companies. Finally, while the forecast errors are shown separately for different industries—and one clearly sees large differences across industries—the industry categories are broadly defined and encompass a range of types of companies and products.

The M-Competitions

Since 1979, Spyros Makridakis and Michèle Hibon have been coordinating periodic forecasting competitions, the so-called M-Competitions. Three major competitions have been organized so far, with forecasting experts analyzing 1001 time series in the M1-Competition, 29 in the M2-Competition, and 3003 in the M3-Competition.

I will restrict the analysis here to the M2-Competition (Makridakis et al., 1993), which featured 23 series of company sales data. It attempted to model closely the actual forecasting process used in firms: Forecasters could include causal factors and judgmentally adjust statistical forecasts, and they were encouraged to contact the participating companies and obtain additional information that might influence sales. Table 1.8 shows the resulting MAPEs for monthly forecasts across different horizons, both for the average of 17 forecasting methods and for the "best" method (which I define here as the method that gave the best results, on average, across horizons up to 15 months ahead).

Table 1.8 MAPEs for Monthly Sales Forecast

Company	Industry	Number of Series	Forecast	1 Month	2 Months	1 Quarter	1 Year
Honeywell	Residential construction	6	Average Best (Naive method including seasonality)	N/A N/A	16.6% 5.1%	15.9% 6.7%	19.3% 13.5%
Squibb	Pharma	7	Average Best (Smoothing with dampened trend)	N/A N/A	9.1% 7.3%	10.6% 7.2%	28.1% 23.0%
Car company	Automotive	6	Average Best (Smoothing with dampened trend)	10.1% 8.0%	10.7% 9.5%	14.6% 14.6%	13.9% 14.2%
Aussedat-Rey	Paper	4	Average Best (Combination of smoothing methods)	3.7% 2.8%	5.6% 5.9%	6.8% 6.7%	5.2% 3.8%

The table reveals that forecast accuracy varied considerably across the four companies on a 1-year horizon, the best method yielding a MAPE of 23% for the pharma data and 3.8% for the paper data. The authors attributed the variations to different seasonalities and noise levels in the data, with pharma sales fluctuating much more strongly than paper sales. Unsurprisingly, forecast accuracy generally deteriorated as forecast horizons increased. Finally, quite simple methods—a naïve forecast, exponential smoothing with a dampened trend, or a combination of smoothing methods—beat more complex methods, including human forecasters using market information and judgmental adjustments. In particular, the Honeywell dataset showed that a simple, seasonally adjusted naïve method could be more accurate than other methods that were more complex.

However, even the results of the M2-Competition are problematic candidates for forecasting benchmarks. These companies represent a very small sample of industries, and the sample contains only one company per industry. In addition, very few time series per company were considered; for example, the only Honeywell series included were channel sales of a safety device and fan control. The latter makes it problematic even to extrapolate, from the MAPEs on the series chosen, the accuracy achievable for other Honeywell products.

Another problem is that very different series are being averaged. For instance, the six series for the car manufacturer include not only sales of three individual models (without specification of whether sales were national or international), but also total company sales and the total of the entire car industry. Conceivably, a method may forecast well for the entire automobile industry but break down when forecasting sales of a single model—a situation where life cycles need to be taken into account, although they may be less important on the aggregate level.

Finally, even though forecasting experts were encouraged to contact the companies for additional explanation and data, some experts consciously decided not to. They doubted that a sufficient understanding of the companies' markets could be formed within a short period (". . . it was hard to know what questions we should ask. . . ."). Subsequently, they acknowledged that their forecast was "not comparable with the likely accuracy of a judgmental forecast prepared within a business organization" (Chatfield et al., 1993).

Makridakis and colleagues never intended the results of the M-Competitions to be used as benchmarks against which forecasting performance of companies should be measured. Instead, the M-Competitions aimed at comparing different forecasting algorithms on standardized datasets. Their failure to provide benchmarks does not mean the results are uninformative to practicing forecasters. On the contrary, they guide practitioners to consider relatively simple methods when seeking to improve their methodologies.

What Is a Benchmark?

The concept of benchmarking is widely applied in business fields, from process benchmarking and financial benchmarking to IT performance benchmarking of new hardware. Common to any such endeavor is that measures of performance in similar and comparable fields are collected and analyzed in order to gain an understanding of what the best possible performance is.

In benchmarking, comparability is the key! Benchmarks can only be trusted if the underlying process to be benchmarked is assessed in similar circumstances. For instance, benchmarking profitability across "firms in general" fails the criterion of comparability; biotech and utility companies have widely different "normal" profitabilities, and using the best-in-class profitability of a biotech firm as a target for a utility is unrealistic.

Benchmarking is closely related to the search for best practices. Ideally, one would identify a performance benchmark and then investigate what factors enable achievement of the benchmark (Camp, 1989). For instance, an optimal sales forecast may be a result of very different factors: a good process for data collection, a sophisticated forecasting algorithm, or simply a clever choice of aggregating SKUs across stores and/or warehouses.

Any approach that leads to consistently superior forecasting performance would be a candidate for best practices. As forecasters, our search for benchmarks is really only part of our search for best practices. We try to optimize our forecasts and need to understand which part of our processes must be improved to reach this goal.

Problems with Forecast Accuracy Surveys

Can published figures on sales forecasting accuracy serve as benchmarks? My analysis indicates that the survey results suffer from multiple sources of incomparability in the data on which they are based. These include differences in industry and product, in spatial and temporal granularity, in forecast horizon, in metric, in the forecast process, and in the business model.

Product Differences. Going across industries or even across companies, we have to forecast sales of wildly dissimilar products. Sales of canned soup and lawn mowers behave very differently; their forecasting challenges will be different, too. A manufacturer of canned soup may be faced with minor seasonality as well as sales that are driven by promotional activities whose timing is under the manufacturer's control. Lawn mower sales, however, will be highly seasonal, depending crucially on the weather in early summer. Thus, it's reasonable to expect lawn mower sales to be more difficult to forecast than canned soup sales and to expect that even "good" forecasts for lawn mowers will have higher errors than "good" forecasts for canned soup.

The comparability problem arises when both canned soup and lawn mowers are grouped together as consumer products or products sold by the retail industry. This is nicely illustrated by the differences between the company datasets in the M2-Competition (Table 1.8). In addition, as I noted above, separate products of a single company may vary in forecastability. A fast-moving staple may be easily forecastable, while a slow-moving, premium article may exhibit intermittency—and consequently be harder to forecast.

Forecasts, moreover, are not only calculated for products, but also for services and/or prices. For manpower planning, a business needs accurate forecasts for various kinds of services, from selecting products for a retailer's distribution center to producing software. And in industries where price fluctuation is strong, forecasting prices can be as important as forecasting quantities. Problems of comparability may apply to price forecasts as well as to quantity forecasts. Although most published surveys have focused on quantities of non-service products, we can clearly see that benchmarking forecasts of services and prices face similar challenges.

Spatial Granularity. Published accuracy figures do not precisely specify the level of "spatial" granularity. When it comes to SKU-by-location forecasts, are we talking about a forecast for a single retail store, a regional distribution center (DC), or a national DC? Forecasting at all three locations may be important to the retailer. Forecasts at the national DC level will usually be of most interest to the manufacturer, as this is the demand from the retailer he normally faces—unless, of course, the manufacturer engages in direct store delivery (DSD), in which case he will certainly be interested in store-level sales and, it logically follows, store-level forecasts.

Aggregating sales from the retail stores serviced by a regional or national DC will usually result in more stable sales patterns. Consequently, forecasting at the retail store will usually be much harder than for the national DC. A given forecast error may be fine for a store forecast but unacceptably large for a DC forecast. Similarly, it will be easier to forecast car sales of General Motors in a mature and stable market, compared to car sales by a smaller company like Rolls-Royce, which builds limited runs of luxury cars for sale to aficionados.

Temporal Granularity. The time dimension of the forecasts reported in the surveys is often vague. Are the forecasts calculated for monthly, weekly, daily, or even intradaily sales? Forecasts for single days are important for retailers who need to replenish shelves on a daily basis, while weekly forecasts may be enough for supplying regional DCs. Manufacturers may only need to consider monthly orders from retailers' national DCs, but once again, in the case of DSD, they will need to forecast on a weekly or even daily level.

Just as aggregation of store sales to DC sales makes forecasting easier at the DC than in the store, it is usually easier to forecast monthly than weekly sales, easier to forecast weekly sales than daily sales, easier to forecast daily sales than intradaily sales. A given accuracy figure may be very good for a daily forecast but very bad for a monthly one.

Longer-term forecasting is harder than shorter-term, simply because the target time period is farther into the future. And long-range forecasts may differ in temporal granularity from short-range forecasts: Often, a retailer forecasts in daily (or even intradaily) buckets for the immediate next few weeks, on a monthly basis for forecasts 2–12 months ahead, and in quarterly buckets for the long term. These forecasts correspond, respectively, to operational forecasts for store ordering and shelf replenishment, to tactical forecasts for distribution center orders, and to strategic forecasts for contract negotiations with the supplier.

This example clearly illustrates that forecasts with different horizons may have different purposes and different users and be calculated based on different processes and algorithms. It's important to note that errors on different time horizons may have different costs: An underforecast for store replenishment will lead to an out-of-stock of limited duration, but an underforecast in long-range planning may lead a retailer to delist an item that might have brought in an attractive margin.

Key Performance Indicators (KPIs). The published surveys employ the MAPE—or a close variation thereof—as the "standard" metric for forecast accuracy. In fact, there is little consensus on the "best" metric for sales forecast accuracy. While the MAPE is certainly the most common measure used in sales forecasting, it does have serious shortcomings: asymmetry, for one, and error inflation if sales are low. These shortcomings have been documented in earlier *Foresight* articles by Kolassa and Schütz (2007), Valentin (2007), and Pearson (2007), who proposed alternative forecast-accuracy metrics. Catt (2007) and Boylan (2007) go further, encouraging the use of cost-of-forecast-error (CFE) metrics in place of forecast-accuracy metrics.

Because of the proliferation of forecast-accuracy metrics, you can't be certain if survey respondents have actually correctly calculated the metric reported.

Then there's the asymmetry problem. Overforecasts (leading to excess inventory) and underforecasts (lost sales) of the same degree may have very different cost implications, depending on the industry and the product. Excess inventory may cost more than lost sales (as with short-life products like fresh produce, or high-tech items that quickly become obsolete), or it can be the other way around (e.g., for canned goods or raw materials). The MAPE and its variants, which treat an overforecast of 10% the same as an underforecast of 10%, may not adequately address the real business problem. KPIs that explicitly address over- and underforecasts may be more meaningful to forecast users.

Forecast Horizon. Most studies report the forecast horizon considered; I wish all of them did. Many different forecast horizons may be of interest for the user, from 1-day-ahead forecasts for the retailer to restock his shelves, to 18-months-ahead (and more) forecasts for the consumer-product manufacturer who needs to plan his future capacity and may need to enter into long-term contractual obligations.

Forecast Processes. Forecasting accuracy is intimately related to the processes used to generate forecasts, not only to the algorithmic methods. In the past 25 years, forecasters have tried a number of ways to improve accuracy within a company's forecasting process, from structured judgmental adjustments and statistical forecasts (Armstrong, 2001) to collaborative planning, forecasting, and replenishment (CPFR) along the supply chain (Seifert, 2002). Yet the published surveys on forecast accuracy do not differentiate between respondents based on the maturity of their processes, whether a full-fledged CPFR effort or a part-time employee with a spreadsheet.

Benchmarking is deeply connected to process improvement (Camp, 1989). The two are, in a sense, inseparable. It follows that, as long as information on forecasting processes is not available, we really do not know whether reported MAPEs are "good" or "bad." Forecasting is an art that depends on good methods/algorithms and on sophisticated processes. Using results from purely scientific (what could be called in vitro or lab-based) forecasting competitions such as the M-Competitions or the recent competitions on Neural Network forecasting as benchmarks (Bunn and Taylor, 2001) will be difficult, as these competitions are often dissociated from the processes of the company that provided the data.

Business Model. The published surveys of forecast accuracy have examined business-to-consumer (B2C) sales in retail. In retail, we can only observe sales, not demand—if customers do not find the desired product on the shelf, they will simply shop elsewhere, and the store manager will usually be unaware of the lost sale. The information basis on which a forecast can be calculated is therefore reduced. We may want to forecast demand but only be able to observe historical sales.

This so-called censoring problem is especially serious for products where the supply cannot be altered in the short run, such as fresh strawberries. We may have a wonderful forecast for customer demand but miss sales by a large margin, simply because the stock was not high enough. Thus, comparing the accuracy of a strawberry sales forecast with a napkin sales forecast will be inappropriate: The censoring problems are more serious for strawberries than for napkins.

By contrast, in a business-to-business (B2B) environment, we often know the historical orders of our business clients, so even if the demand cannot be satisfied, we at least know how high it was. Therefore, B2B forecasts profit from much better historical data and should be more accurate than B2C forecasts.

Any published benchmarks on forecasts for products that could be sold either B2B or B2C are consequently harder to interpret than forecasts for "pure" B2B or B2C products.

Moreover, in a build-to-order situation, one may not even know the specific end-products that will be sold in the future. Here it makes sense to either forecast on a component level or to forecast sales volume in dollars rather than in units.

To summarize, none of the published sales forecasting studies can be used as a benchmark. All published indicators suffer from serious shortcomings regarding comparability of data and processes in which forecasts are embedded, as each industry and each company faces its own forecasting problems with its distinctive time granularity, product mix, and forecasting processes. The issues of incomparability have been recognized for many years (Bunn and Taylor, 2001) but have not been solved.

All studies published to date have averaged sales forecasts calculated on widely varying bases, used poorly defined market categories, and ignored the underlying forecast processes at work. These shortcomings are so severe that, in my opinion, published indicators of forecast accuracy can only serve as a very rudimentary first approximation to real benchmarks. One cannot simply take industry-specific forecasting errors as benchmarks and targets.

External vs. Internal Benchmarks

Are the survey problems of comparability resolvable? Could we, in principle, collect more or better data and create "real" benchmarks in forecasting?

The differences between companies and products are so large that useful comparisons among companies within the same market may be difficult to impossible. For instance, even in the relatively homogeneous field of grocery-store sales forecasting, I have seen "normal" errors for different companies varying between 20% and 60% (MAPE for 1-week-ahead weekly sales forecasts), depending on the number of fast sellers, the presence of promotional activities or price changes, the amount of fresh produce (always hard to forecast), data quality, etc. Thus, comparability between different categories and different companies is a major stumbling block.

In addition, industries differ sharply on how much information they are willing to provide to outsiders. I have worked with retailers who threatened legal action if my company disclosed that they were considering implementing an automated replenishment system. These retailers considered their forecasting and replenishment processes as so much a part of their competitive edge that there was no possibility of publishing and comparing their processes, even anonymously. It simply was not to be done. This problem is endemic in the retail market and makes benchmarking very difficult. It may be less prevalent in other markets, but it is still a problem.

My conclusion is that the quest for external forecasting benchmarks is futile.

So what should a forecaster look at to assess forecasting performance and whether it can be improved? I believe that benchmarking should be driven not by external accuracy targets but by knowledge about what constitutes good forecasting practices, independent of the specific product to be forecast.

The article by Moon, Mentzer, and Smith (2003) on conducting a sales forecasting audit and the commentaries that follow it serve as a good starting point to critically assess a company's forecasting practices and managerial environment. It's important to note that no one—not the authors of the paper, not the commentators, and none of the other works made reference to—recommended that you rely on or even utilize external forecast accuracy benchmarks. When discussing the "should-be" target state of an optimized forecasting process, they express the target in qualitative, process-oriented terms, not in terms of a MAPE to be achieved. Such a process-driven forecast improvement methodology also helps us focus our attention on the processes to be changed, instead of the possibly elusive goal of achieving a particular MAPE.

Forecast accuracy improvements due to process and organizational changes should be monitored over time. To support the monitoring task, one should carefully select KPIs that mirror the actual challenges faced by the organization. And historical forecasts as well as sales must be stored, so that you can answer the question, "How good were our forecasts for 2008 that were made in January of that year?" We can then evaluate whether, and by how much, forecasts improved as a result of an audit, a change in algorithms, the introduction of a dedicated forecasting team, or some other improvement project.

In summation, published reports of forecast accuracy are too unreliable to be used as benchmarks, and this situation is unlikely to change. Rather than look to external benchmarks, we should critically examine our internal forecast processes and organizational environment. If we focus on process improvement, forecast accuracy and the use an organization makes of the forecasts will eventually be improved.

REFERENCES

Armstrong, J. S. (2001). *Principles of Forecasting: A Handbook for Researchers and Practitioners*. New York: Springer.

Boylan, J. (2007). Key assumptions in calculating the cost of forecast error. *Foresight: International Journal of Applied Forecasting* 8, 22–24.

Bunn, D. W., and J. W. Taylor (2001). Setting accuracy targets for short-term judgemental sales forecasting. *International Journal of Forecasting* 17, 159–169.

Camp, R. C. (1989). *Benchmarking: The Search for Industry Best Practices That Lead to Superior Performance.* Milwaukee, WI: ASQC Quality Press.

Catt, P. (2007). Assessing the cost of forecast error: A practical example. *Foresight: International Journal of Applied Forecasting* 7, 5–10.

Chatfield, C., M. Hibon, M. Lawrence, T. C. Mills, J. K. Ord, P. A. Geriner, D. Reilly, R. Winkel, and S. Makridakis (1993). A commentary on the M2-Competition. *International Journal of Forecasting* 9, 23–29.

Jain, C. L. (2007). Benchmarking forecast errors. *Journal of Business Forecasting* 26(4), 19–23.

Jain, C. L., and J. Malehorn. (2006). *Benchmarking Forecasting Practices: A Guide to Improving Forecasting Performance,* 3rd ed. Flushing, NY: Graceway.

Kolassa, S., and W. Schütz (2007). Advantages of the MAD/MEAN ratio over the MAPE. *Foresight: International Journal of Applied Forecasting* 6, 40–43.

Makridakis, S., C. Chatfield, M. Hibon, M. Lawrence, T. Mills, K. Ord, and L. F. Simmons (1993). The M2-Competition: A real-time judgmentally based forecasting study. *International Journal of Forecasting* 9, 5–22.

McCarthy, T. M., D. F. Davis, S. L. Golicic, and J. T. Mentzer (2006). The evolution of sales forecasting management: A 20-year longitudinal study of forecasting practice. *Journal of Forecasting* 25, 303–324.

Moon, M. A., J. T. Mentzer, and C. D. Smith (2003). Conducting a sales forecasting audit (with commentaries). *International Journal of Forecasting* 19, 5–42.

Pearson, R. (2007). An expanded prediction-realization diagram for assessing forecast errors. *Foresight: International Journal of Applied Forecasting* 7, 11–16.

Seifert, D. (2002). *Collaborative Planning, Forecasting and Replenishment.* Bonn, Germany: Galileo.

Valentin, L. (2007). Use scaled errors instead of percentage errors in forecast evaluations. *Foresight: International Journal of Applied Forecasting* 7, 17–22.

1.8 DEFINING "DEMAND" FOR DEMAND FORECASTING*

Michael Gilliland

Demand forecasting is often uncritically based on histories of orders received, shipments/sales, or some combination of the two. But as Michael Gilliland explains in this article, the ultimate goal—a measurement of unconstrained true demand—is elusive and not always amenable to simple formulae based on orders and shipments.

Since true demand is not directly measurable, it must be forecast using an approximation constructed from the data we do have available (orders, shipments, backorders, etc.). There is a general belief that orders provide an upper bound to true demand, while shipments (or sales) provide a lower bound, but this is far too simplistic. The relationship depends on reactions to a failure to fill demand in the desired time frame.

So what to do? Recognizing the measurement difficulties, Gilliland suggests we can often derive a proxy for true demand that is "close enough" to be useful in generating an unconstrained forecast. Then, through sales and operations planning or other internal processes, the unconstrained forecast is merged with production/procurement capabilities and inventory availability to generate the "constrained forecast."

* This article originally appeared in *Foresight: The International Journal of Applied Forecasting* (Summer 2010), and appears here courtesy of the International Institute of Forecasters.

An important point is that forecasting performance evaluations should be based on the constrained forecasts, those that represent the organization's best guess at what is really going to happen after taking supply limitations into consideration. We can reliably measure the accuracy of the constrained forecast by comparing it to what really does happen (shipments, sales, or services provided).

Introduction: Unconstrained vs. Constrained Demand

Companies commonly characterize demand as "what the customers want, and when they want it," sometimes with the added proviso, "at a price they are willing to pay, along with any other products they want at that time." When businesses refer to demand, they mean unconstrained or true demand, which does not take into account their ability to fulfill demand. True demand is largely unobservable; so, as a practical matter, we can only approximate it with measurable quantities.

In contrast, the term constrained demand refers to how much demand can be fulfilled in light of limitations on the provision of the product or service demanded. Thus, constrained demand ≤ true demand.

A good forecast of demand, far enough into the future, allows an organization to invest in the facilities, equipment, materials, and staffing required to most profitably fulfill that demand. The planning process begins by loading demand histories into our forecasting software, with the purpose of creating an unconstrained demand forecast. Here, we encounter a problem: What is our operational definition of *demand?* What is the specific, systematic way we measure it?

A company needs to know how to measure true demand in order to provide the proper history for its forecasting models. Typically, you know your orders, shipments, and sales. You know calls handled at call centers, transactions processed at retail stores, and hours billed by consultants. You can track inventory, out-of-stocks, fill rates, back-orders, and cancellations. Still, while you have all these data, none yields the exact true demand.

Orders vs. True Demand

If customers place orders to express their "demand," and if the manufacturer services its customers perfectly by filling all orders in full and on time, then we have our operational definition. In this case, Demand = Orders = Shipments. If both order and shipment data are readily available in the company's system, then we have the historical demand data that we can use to feed our statistical forecasting models.

Unfortunately, few organizations service their customers perfectly—in other words, have an order-fill rate of 100%—so orders are not a perfect indicator of true demand. When some orders received cannot be filled in the customer's desired time frame, several different outcomes are possible:

1. An order that cannot be filled may be rejected by the company or canceled by the customer.
2. An unfilled order may be rolled ahead into a future time bucket.
3. If customers anticipate a shortage, they may inflate their orders to capture a larger share of an allocation.
4. If customers anticipate a shortage, they may withhold their orders, change the orders to a different product, or redirect their orders to an alternative supplier.

In the first case, the cancelled or rejected order may not appear in the demand history file. The omission means that current-period orders will understate true demand.

In the second case, the rolled-ahead order appears in a time bucket later than when it was placed by the customer, so true demand is overstated in future time buckets. That is, the order appears both in the original time bucket and again in future time buckets until the demand is filled or the order is cancelled.

In the third case, a savvy customer (or sales rep), anticipating that product scarcity will lead the supplier to impose an allocation formula (such as "fill all orders at 50%"), will now inflate the order—to twice the true demand, for example.

The fourth case, of withheld or redirected orders, is particularly harmful. Now the historical orders for the desired product do not include the withheld orders, once again understating true demand. Customers may truly want your product, but demand won't be reflected in your historical data because no order was placed. Worse, if customers order a product other than the one they really wanted because of a shortage of the original product, orders for this "second-best" or substitute product overestimate the true demand for the substitute product.

Finally, in a period of chronic supply shortages (due either to supply problems or demand much higher than anticipated), customers may go elsewhere, and all information on their demand is lost.

The assumption is often made that orders provide an upper bound (i.e., will be equal to or greater than true demand), but the four cases noted here reveal that there is no simple arithmetical connection between orders and true demand. In cases 1 and 4, orders will understate demand; in cases 2 and 3 (and sometimes 4, too), orders will overstate demand.

Shipments and Sales vs. True Demand

As with orders, there are also problems in using shipments to represent demand. Shipments are often perceived as a lower limit to true demand; that is, less than or equal to true demand. Thus, shipments and orders are thought to represent true demand's lower and upper bounds, respectively (e.g., Chockalingam, 2009).

We have noted above that cases 1 and 4 show that orders can understate true demand. Furthermore, in case 2, shipments can exceed true demand. This occurs when an unfilled order is rolled ahead into a future time bucket and then filled; the shipment then exceeds true demand in the time bucket in which it is finally shipped. Similarly, in case 4, shipments of a "second-best" product overstate the true demand for the substitute.

Seeking an Operational Definition of True Demand

More complex—but not necessarily better—operational definitions of true demand can be constructed by some hybrid of orders and shipments. Examples include:

1. Demand = (Shipments + Orders) / 2
2. Demand = Shipments + Incremental shortages
3. Demand = Shipments + Latest shortages

The first formula defines demand as halfway between orders and shipments. If order is 120 and shipment is 100, then demand = 110. It simply "splits the difference" by assuming half of the shortages represent legitimate demand, while the rest are due to order manipulation or other gamesmanship.

The second formula avoids overcounting repeat shortage rollovers by only adding increases in shortages to shipments. Therefore, if the shortage in time period t is 20, and the shortage in period $t + 1$ is again 20, then demand = shipments for period $t + 1$ (the shortage amount, 20, did not increase from the prior time period). If the shortage in period $t + 2$ is 25, the demand in period $t + 2$ is shipment + 5 (because there was an incremental 5 units of shortages from 20 to 25).

The third formula also avoids overcounting repeat shortages, in this case by including in demand only those shortages still showing at the end of the time bucket. The demand for a month will include all shipments of that month + unfilled orders of the last week only. If, for example, shortages in a four-week month were 10, 20, 40, and 30, the total demand for the month would be shipments + 30 (the last week's shortages). Table 1.9 illustrates various demand definitions over a one-month period (Gilliland, 2003).

As if this weren't complicated enough, most ERP systems save multiple dates for each order. These may include Order Entry Date, Order Promise Date, Revised Promise Date, Actual Shipment Date, and Customer Receipt Date. Even if companies reach a consensus on how to use order and shipment data, choosing among these dates adds another degree of difficulty in defining demand.

Table 1.9

Week	1	2	3	4	Month Total
Orders	50	50	60	60	220
Shipments	50	40	55	40	185
Shortages		10	5	20	35
Incremental shortage		10		15	25
Latest shortage				20	20

1. Demand = (Shipments + Orders) / 2 = (185 + 220) / 2 = 202.5
2. Demand = Shipments + Incremental shortages = (185 + 25) = 210
3. Demand = Shipments + Latest shortages = (185 + 20) = 205

Chockalingam (2009) illustrates two ways of calculating true demand, starting from either observed bookings (orders) or from observed (gross) shipments:

Observed Bookings

– Requested deliveries in the future

– Exaggerated customer orders

= True Demand

Observed (Gross) Shipments

+ Cuts (unfilled orders that are cancelled)

+ Backorders

– Carryovers

= True Demand

However, because of the vagaries of customer orders, these do not yield operational definitions of true demand. For one, we are unlikely to know the extent of "exaggerated customer orders." And the amount of "cuts" is a function of quantity ordered—yet we saw above that orders are not a reliable indicator of true demand.

To summarize, a suitable operational definition of demand may be unique to each organization and may be difficult to construct, given the available data. For a manufacturer, what a customer orders may not be the same as true demand, nor is true demand what the manufacturer actually ships. For a retailer, what is actually sold off the shelves may not be the same as true demand, either. For example, customers may not be able to find what they want in the store (due to out-of-stocks, or poor merchandise presentation and layout), so there is true demand but no recorded sale. In this case, they may buy a substitute product instead, for which we will record a sale, although there was no original demand.

Determining true demand for a service can be equally vexing. I may wish to stay at a bargain-rate hotel, but have to upgrade when my preferred choice is sold out. Or, I may call the cable company to complain about my television reception, only to hang up in frustration while trying to wade through their voice-menu system.

As a practical matter, while we can't know exactly what true demand really is, we can often come close enough to make the concept useful in forecasting and organizational planning. For manufacturers that do a good job at filling orders (say, 98%+), then shipments, orders, and true demand are virtually the same. Likewise, if a retailer's shelves are fully stocked (or nearly so), then point-of-sale data (cash-register receipts) may be an adequate representation of true demand.

Whether we can provide an accurate proxy for true demand or not, the errors made in approximating true demand can pale in comparison with forecast-model errors.

Making heroic efforts to capture a perfect history of true demand is unlikely to result in significantly improved forecasts and is probably not worth the effort.

True vs. Constrained Forecasts

Forecasts of true (unconstrained) demand provide the right starting point for the planning process (for example, see the *S&OP How-To Handbook* by Wallace and Stahl, 2008). The unconstrained forecast gives the supply chain an unfettered prediction of what customers are going to want in the future, allowing the organization to take action to meet this demand. If future demand is predicted to exceed the current available supply, the organization can hire workers or add shifts, build new facilities, or outsource production. Alternatively, the organization can take steps to reduce demand to levels it can fulfill, such as by increasing prices, dropping customers, or eliminating sales channels.

An output of the planning process is the constrained forecast, which accounts for anticipated supply limitations. The constrained forecast typically is not generated with a statistical model within the forecasting software, but is instead determined through the organization's planning process. It indicates the expected shipments, or expected sales, or expected services that will be provided. It represents the organization's best guess at what is really going to happen—what the shipments, sales, or services provided are really going to be.

Any gap between the true and the constrained forecasts is useful information for managing customer service. For example, when a manufacturer anticipates a shortage, customers can be contacted and their demand redirected to a future date (when their demand can be fulfilled) or to alternative products. It is a failure of management to continue the solicitation of orders when it is known in advance that those orders cannot be filled.

Assessing Forecast Accuracy and Making Financial Projections

Since we are unable to measure true demand reliably, we shouldn't base evaluations of forecast accuracy on our attempts to do so. The "true demand" forecast still serves a valuable purpose—as the starting point in the planning process—but any reports of its accuracy are immediately suspect.

Instead, it is appropriate to assess the accuracy of the forecast for constrained demand. This forecast—what we really expect to ship, sell, or service—is evaluated against what really does happen. Unlike the murky measurement of true demand, an organization should be able to measure unambiguously what really does ship or sell, or the amount of services it provides.

It's important that planners recognize the difference between the unconstrained and the constrained forecast. The planning process should always begin with the unconstrained forecast, nebulous though it may be, as this represents the potential opportunity. When future demand appears to exceed future supply, the organization can take steps to increase supply and meet that demand (or decide not to pursue it, or purposely reduce demand). In contrast, the constrained forecast is an outcome of the planning process and records what the organization ultimately expects to ship, sell, or service.

As a final note, financial projections should always be made from the constrained forecast. It makes no sense to project revenues for any unconstrained demand you know in advance you can't fulfill.

REFERENCES

Chockalingam, M. (2009). What is true demand? *Demand Planning Newsletter* (April). http://www.dem&Planning.net/Newsletters/DPnewsletter_april2009.html.

Gilliland, M. (2003). Fundamental issues in business forecasting. *Journal of Business Forecasting* 22 (2) (Summer), 7–13.

Wallace, T., and R. Stahl (2008). *Sales and Operations Planning: The How-To Handbook*, 3rd ed. T. F. Wallace & Co.

Portions of this material originally appeared in Gilliland, M. (2010), *The Business Forecasting Deal: Exposing Myths, Eliminating Bad Practices, Providing Practical Solutions*. Hoboken, NJ: John Wiley & Sons.

1.9 USING FORECASTING TO STEER THE BUSINESS: SIX PRINCIPLES*

Steve Morlidge

Based on his book, *Future Ready: How to Master the Art of Business Forecasting*, Steve Morlidge argues that business forecasting focuses too narrowly on the short-run forecast of a single variable. While helpful to synchronize demand and supply, this focus makes little contribution to the process of steering business performance. Instead, forecasters need to adopt a broader perspective on the role of strategic forecasting, and take a longer-range view on forecasts themselves.

Morlidge's remedy requires that professional forecasters face the challenges of forecasting the complex behavior of economic systems and address the reality that forecasting is not a stand-alone process. Rather, it exists as part of an organizational control system. Actions taken in response to a forecast (such as increased advertising) often invalidate the assumptions on which the forecast was originally based, making accuracy measurement problematical. Forecast errors might be the result of decisions made and actions taken, not a reflection of the quality of the forecasting process.

While appealing to forecasters to look beyond the short term, Morlidge provides six principles as a roadmap to process improvement. Like Charles Re Corr's article earlier in this chapter, these principles characterize what is needed to create a reliable business forecast to guide decision making.

Economic Forecasting Is Broken

"It's awful! How come no one saw it coming?" Queen Elizabeth spoke these words, in November, 2008, after a briefing on the credit crunch at the London School of Economics. The queen's question echoes that of people at all societal levels; economists and economic forecasters in particular do not currently enjoy a high reputation.

It is not just macroeconomic forecasting that is broken. The financial forecasts used by business executives have also proved highly fallible. "The financial crisis has obliterated corporate forecasts," reports *CFO Magazine* (Ryan, 2009); 70% of respondents to their recent survey said that they were unable to see more than one quarter ahead.

The problem is not restricted to bad economic times. According to the Hackett Group, only 18% of senior finance professionals are "highly satisfied" with their forecast process, and no wonder. On average, earnings forecasts are 13% out, knocking about 6% off their share price (EIU, 2007). Since 2005,

* This article originally appeared in *Foresight: The International Journal of Applied Forecasting* (Winter 2010), and appears here courtesy of the International Institute of Forecasters.

the 1,300 companies quoted on the London Stock Exchange have issued an annual average of 400 profit warnings, each resulting in a loss of value of 10% to 20% of market capitalization (Bloom and colleagues, 2009).

A survey recently conducted for KPMG of 540 senior executives (EIU, 2007) found that improved forecasting topped their priority ranking for the next three years. Ability to forecast results also leads the list of internal concerns for CFOs across the globe (Karaian, 2009).

The problems present a massive opportunity. From nearly 30 years' experience in finance, I can confirm that professional forecasting input is rare in the kinds of forecasts that interest CFOs: medium-term estimates of future revenues, earnings, cash flow, etc. At best, sales forecasts are used to inform short-term forecasts; even then, they are frequently adjusted. Industry surveys suggest forecasts are judgmentally adjusted 72% of the time, and a previous *Foresight* article suggests it could be as high as 91% (Goodwin and Fildes, 2007).

The Narrow Focus of the Forecasting Profession

Another take on this situation is that it represents an indictment of the forecasting profession. In writing this article, I was encouraged by *Foresight*'s editor to read the journal's previous issues. I found much to admire, including many things that I would have included in my book had I known about them before. Most of the contributions are engaging, practical, and intellectually rigorous—a very rare combination in business writing. However, I found very few addressing beyond the very short term. This is no fluke; I have seen little evidence elsewhere that the profession routinely contributes to business forecasting much beyond sales in the near term.

Why should the focus of forecasters be so narrow? Costs and profits are important business variables. Their behavior patterns are neither so obvious as to make the task of forecasting trivial, nor so chaotic as to make it futile. No one would argue that applying forecasting expertise to such problems is not worthwhile. Failure to forecast business performance can be catastrophic, and there is a desperate need for a more rigorous, scientific approach to the task.

If forecasting professionals are to make a bigger contribution to the management process, they must face two challenges.

Challenge #1: The Nature of Economic Systems

Traditional forecasting techniques are usually based on the premise that the future can be predicted by understanding the past. There is increasing recognition of the limitations of this approach. David Orrell and Patrick McSharry noted in their recent *Foresight* article (Orrell and McSharry, 2009), that real-world phenomena such as biological systems, weather patterns, and economic activity are complex and prone to unpredictable behavior, and that is why we can produce reasonable weather forecasts only for a few days ahead, despite decades of huge investment in technology. The phenomena that business forecasters deal with create even greater challenges. There are no economic laws to rival those that we know constrain the behavior of physical objects, and business executives are interested in forecasting beyond the very short term.

Furthermore, little attention is given to forecasting whole systems, as opposed to single variables or multiple instances of a single variable (usually sales or revenue). Steering a business requires forecasts of multiple interdependent variables: volume, price, materials costs, advertising and promotion, infrastructure expense, etc. If professionals shirk this task, then amateurs (such as accountants) will take it on.

A cause for optimism, however, is the growing awareness that discontinuities in systems behavior are not simply inconvenient blemishes in the data record, but matters of vital importance to forecasters and managers. Top executives are more interested in the message "Something is about to change/has changed" than they are in "Everything is as expected." So forecasters should try to anticipate these changes (Batchelor, 2009); if we cannot, we need to get better at spotting them quickly.

Challenge #2: The Organizational System

More attention needs to be paid to the organizational context in which forecasting activities sit. There are excellent articles about the impact of corporate politics on the integrity of forecasts (Finney and Joseph, 2009; Wallace and Stahl, 2009). Many others refer to the purpose of forecasting as informing decision making, but I see no references to the logical corollary that forecasting exists as part of an organizational control system, not as a standalone process. This means that forecasters have to comprehend and contribute to the ways in which targets are set and decisions made, rather than treating these as givens to be managed.

Viewing forecasting as part of a control process has methodological implications too. Take, for example, a fashion retailer. To steer business performance over the course of a season, managers have a range of levers at their disposal: prices, product range, advertising and promotions, store layout, opening hours, staff numbers, and so on. In response to a forecast, management may start, stop, bring forward, put back, and change planned initiatives or create new ones, and this process will repeat monthly or even weekly.

These decisions are taken in pursuit of some clearly stated corporate objective, in response to the actions of competitors, or to exploit competitors' perceived weaknesses. In these circumstances, historical patterns of behavior, upon which so much forecasting technique relies, are of limited value in forecasting future outcomes. Indeed, the value of some variables may be entirely the result of management discretion (e.g., the levels of advertising). Additionally, since management's actions taken in response to forecasts often invalidate the assumptions on which the forecasts were based, measuring forecast accuracy can be problematical. Forecast errors are likely to be the result of decisions taken, rather than a reflection of the quality of the forecast process, and the complexity and dynamism of the situation make it almost impossible to disentangle the impact of one from the other.

How we currently forecast in business is not necessarily wrong or futile. But if they are to make the kind of contribution to businesses they could (and should), forecasters must be more sensitive to the context in which they work, making necessary adjustments to their approach and techniques.

Forecasting is widely used in business to anticipate demand and synchronize with the capacity to fulfill that demand. I see no need for major changes here. Because businesses are designed to be responsive to demand, operational forecasting is short-term in nature. In the short term, systems are unlikely to change trajectory, and decisions made by the business will have limited effect on behavior patterns. The purpose of the short-term forecast is to coordinate an appropriate response to a system that is uncontrollable, just as we use short-term weather forecasts to help us decide what to wear. Consequently, the forecasting methodologies developed over the last few decades—built on the premise that the future will be rather like the past—can work well in these circumstances.

The traditional approach works less well beyond the short term. In the medium-to-long term, managers use forecasts to steer the business and may adopt a different course to what can be anticipated by a forecast based on past data. Also, the longer the time horizon, the greater the chance that the economic system will unpredictably change its behavior because of the nature of the system itself or because of decisions made by other actors, such as competitors. Here, boat racing is a better analogy than weather forecasting. A sailor will continuously reforecast and change course in anticipation of weather conditions, tides, and the movements of competitors.

Much of the opprobrium heaped on forecasters results from failure to recognize the fundamentally different roles that forecasting plays in these two sets of circumstances. The failure is not just of perception. Changes in approach are required if professional forecasters are to make effective contributions to managing business beyond the short term.

Prescription for Change

At a practical level, making these changes means:

- Forecasters have to dispel the notion, in our own and our customers' minds, that forecasting is prophecy. A forecast can be no more than a projection of what might happen, given a set of reasonable assumptions, one of which may be that recent trends will continue. Being able to anticipate outcomes, even imperfectly, means businesses can buy some time to prepare for what might lie ahead. Since the future can adopt any one of a number of trajectories, each of which may demand different responses, this also will involve making not one forecast, but a series of forecasts.

- Forecasters should dispense with the idea that increasing forecast accuracy is their primary aim (Oliva and Watson, 2006). A good medium-term business forecast is one that is accurate enough for the purposes of decision making. In practice, it should be unbiased and with acceptable margin for error. In addition, because we cannot assume the future will be like the past, measures of historic forecast performance have limited value. The focus should be on whether the current forecast is reliable for decision making now, using tools such as Trigg's Tracking Signal (Trigg, 1964).
- Since steering complex, integrated businesses involves a wide range of information and possible responses, forecasters need to handle a large, complex set of interdependent variables and deploy a range of forecasting methodologies, including judgmental forecasting techniques. Having a good understanding of the decision-making processes involved and making pragmatic, well-informed choices about data gathering and modelling is critical if the exercise is not to become hopelessly complicated.
- Forecasting should be perceived not as a stand-alone technical discipline but as part of an organization's performance-management system. This implies requirements for forecasters to have a broader understanding of business process, much more than simply integrating S&OP with the financials.

Another consequence is that there is a much bigger constituency for forecasters to manage. They must ensure that a wider range of business professionals have an appreciation of the fundamentals of good forecasting.

It may sound daunting, but I believe that the job of integrating professional forecasting into the day-to-day business-steering processes can be condensed into six simple principles. I hope these will provide a framework to facilitate the marriage of the skills of professional forecasters with the needs of their customers. Forecasters can use these principles as a map to help them colonize territory beyond the limits of their technical expertise. They also help general managers understand, utilize, and cultivate good forecasting practice.

Forecasting to Steer the Business: Six Principles

Principle 1: Mastering Purpose

Business forecasting is like navigation at sea:

> *It makes sense to plan before a journey, but the original plan (or budget) is often soon outdated because of changes in the weather or tides. Then you need to forecast where you are headed, so that you can determine the necessary corrective action to get to your destination.*

The first thing this example shows is that it's important to distinguish between a forecast (where you think you will be) and a target (where you want to be). Often there is a gap between a forecast and a target, at least until appropriate corrective actions (decisions) are taken—even then, except in the most stable environment, gaps are likely to open up again quickly.

It also helps us to understand the set of qualities needed in a good forecast.

- A good forecast is timely. If you are heading into trouble, a rough-and-ready forecast delivered quickly is much more valuable than a perfect one arriving too late for corrective action.
- It should be actionable. Do we need to make lean on the tiller? Hoist different sails? In business, this means that you need detail only if it is relevant to decision making. You'll probably require different information for forecasting than that used for budgeting. Much more information may be needed about "projects" (e.g., the impact of a new product launch); much less detailed information for "business as usual" (e.g., overhead costs).
- It should also be reliable. As I noted above, a forecast needn't be precise to be reliable; it has to be accurate enough for the purposes of decision making. In practice, it should be free from bias and with acceptable variation.
- It should be aligned. It would be no fun in a storm if every crew member had a different view of where the ship was heading and what course to steer in order to avoid the rocks, yet many businesses have competing "versions of the truth" produced by different functions. In these circumstances, decisions can become driven by corporate politics, slow, and fraught with risk.
- Finally, a forecast should be cost-effective.

Principle 2: Mastering Time

Time is critical to designing and running a forecast process. If a business had perfect information and could react instantaneously, forecasting would be unnecessary. Since this is not the case, two questions must be asked.

First, how far ahead do you need to forecast? The answer depends on how long it takes to enact a decision.

In this example, a supertanker needs to be able to see three miles ahead at all times, since it takes that long to stop. A speedboat, in contrast, requires much less forward visibility. In practice, this means that businesses need a rolling forecast horizon, based on the lead times associated with "steering actions." If an important steering decision—say, launching a new product—takes 12 months, then the business always needs 12 months' forward view. A traditional year-end financial forecast—where the forecast horizon declines the closer you get to year's end—is like overtaking on a blind bend. You have no idea of the possible outcome of your decision.

How frequently should you forecast? That depends on how quickly things change. A ship's captain needs to forecast more frequently in the busy Singapore Strait than she does in the wide-open spaces of the South Pacific. Accounting-period ends should not determine the timing of forecasts. Southwest Airlines, for instance, updates revenue forecasts daily, but aircraft-ownership costs (leases, depreciation, etc.) only once quarterly.

Principle 3: Mastering Models

Any forecast requires a model, a set of assumptions about the way the world works. This could be a statistical model, one extrapolating into the future from the past. Alternatively, it may be a causal factor model, based on the identification of key drivers. If the future is like the past, these kinds of models can be very effective.

However, often the world is too complex or the business is changing too fast to make such well-structured approaches workable. That is why business forecasting frequently relies on judgment: where the model is in the head of an expert or a larger number of people who "understand the business" or "know what is going on in the market." But human judgment has flaws, and managers can feel pressure to adjust forecasts to avoid "nasty surprises" or "sounding defeatist." Consequently, judgmental forecasts are prone to bias.

With forecast models, the trick is to understand the range of methodologies available, choose appropriately, then take steps to mitigate weaknesses. For example, it might be appropriate to use a statistical model to produce a baseline or "business as usual" volume forecast, and judgment to estimate the impact of decisions that alter the course of affairs (e.g., price changes).

Principle 4: Mastering Measurement

If you rely on a forecast to make decisions, the way that forecast is generated should have been reliable in the past. Yet, few businesses take the simple steps required to monitor their processes for evidence of bias so they can take action to eliminate it, if detected. As Jim Hoover notes in his article on the tracking of forecast accuracy (Hoover, 2009), most businesses fail to track forecast quality over time.

Those businesses that do attempt to monitor it often measure the wrong things at the wrong time. Forecast error needs to be measured over the short term—before decisions informed by the forecast have taken effect. To do otherwise is like blaming the navigator for having forecast a calamity that never occurred, precisely because the captain acted upon the forecast and changed course.

Also, forecasts need to be made frequently because it is important to distinguish between inevitable unsystematic error (variation) and systematic error (bias). A sequence of four errors with the same sign (positive or negative) is needed to be able to distinguish bias from the effects of chance. The common business practice of using quarterly forecasts to steer toward an annual target makes it impossible for managers to identify and correct a biased forecast in time.

Principle 5: Mastering Risk

Our only absolute certainty about the future is that any forecasts are likely to be wrong. Debate about the forecast should not focus on whether you have the right "single-point forecast," but how it might be wrong, why, and what to do about it. In particular, it is important to distinguish between *risk*—random variation around a realistic single-point forecast—and *uncertainty* resulting from a shift in the behavior of a system that invalidates the forecast.

A major contributor to the economic collapse earning the queen's comment was the overreliance of banks on risk models that failed to take account of some important sources of uncertainty. Whatever form your ignorance of the future takes, it is important to develop the capability to spot and diagnose deviations from forecast quickly and to create a playbook of potential actions enabling swift, effective response.

Principle 6: Mastering Process

Forecasting is neither art nor complex science. It is mainly a matter of applying modest amounts of knowledge, in a disciplined and organized fashion, as a process. A good process—like a good golf swing—produces good results.

Building a good process involves doing the right things in the right order (cultivating a good technique), over and over (grooving the swing). Those things that are responsible for bias (hooks and slices) should be designed out of the process (remodeling the swing), the results of the process continuously monitored (the score), and minor flaws corrected as they become evident. Again, as in golf, temperament is as important as technique. Blaming people for failures when the process is at fault is a sure way to encourage dishonest forecasting.

Efforts to improve forecasting processes can be undermined by behaviors associated with adjacent business processes such as traditional budgeting.

1. Budgeting does not recognize the distinction between a target and a forecast. Bias in forecasting is often associated with the desire not to show gaps between the two, either because a shortfall is interpreted as poor performance or a "lack of commitment" or because submitting an over-target forecast triggers a target increase.
2. Budgeting is incompatible with the need for rolling horizons built around decision-making lead times—everything is pegged to the financial year-end.
3. By fixing budgets on an arbitrary annual cycle, budgeting constrains an organization's ability to respond and therefore undermines the value of forecasting. Often appropriate, timely action cannot be taken because the department involved "hasn't got the budget."

Conclusions

There is an urgent need to improve the quality of the forecasts used to steer businesses, which hitherto have suffered from a lack of input from the professional forecasting community. To make the kind of contributions that businesses need, there must be a shift in understanding the role of forecasting and a complementary change in how forecasting methodologies are applied. Both require improved relationships between forecasting specialists and their business constituency.

The six principles of forecast mastery noted here help these two parties develop shared understanding of what it takes to create a reliable business forecast. Specifically, there must be the recognition:

1. That the PURPOSE of forecasting is to guide decision making, not to prophesy an outcome.
2. That TIMELINESS is important in managing the decision-making process.
3. That many different types of MODELS can be used to forecast, and that no one technique can be a "silver bullet."
4. That careful MEASUREMENT is needed to assess the reliability of forecasts.
5. That considerations of RISK should not be excluded from the forecast process.
6. That forecasting is part of a disciplined, collaborative, performance-management PROCESS.

REFERENCES

Batchelor, R. (2009). Forecasting sharp changes. *Foresight: International Journal of Applied Forecasting* 13 (Spring), 7–12.

Bloom, A., Wollaston, A. and McGregor, K. (2009). Analysis of profit warnings. Ernst and Young.

EIU (2007). *Forecasting with Confidence: Insights from Leading Finance Functions*. KPMG.

Finney, A., and M. Joseph (2009). The forecasting mantra: A holistic approach to forecasting and planning. *Foresight: International Journal of Applied Forecasting* 12 (Winter), 5–14.

Goodwin, P., and R. Fildes (2007). Good and bad judgment in forecasting: Lessons from four companies. *Foresight: International Journal of Applied Forecasting* 8 (Fall), 5–10.

Hoover, J. H. (2009). How to track forecast accuracy to guide forecast process improvement. *Foresight: The International Journal of Applied Forecasting* 14 (Summer), 17–23.

Karaian, J. (2009). By the numbers: Top ten concerns of CFOs. CFO Europe, September 2009, 11–12.

Oliva, R., and N. Watson (2006). Managing functional biases in organizational forecasts. *Foresight: International Journal of Applied Forecasting* 5 (Fall), 27–32.

Orrell, D., and P. McSharry (2009). A systems approach to forecasting. *Foresight: The International Journal of Applied Forecasting* 14 (Summer), 25–31.

Ryan, V. (2009). Future tense. *CFO* http://www.cfo.com/printable/article.cfm/12668080.

Trigg, D. W. (1964). Monitoring a forecasting system. *Operational Research Quarterly* 15, 271–274.

Various (2008). Aligning forecasting practice with market dynamics. The Hackett Group, Volume 12, Number 1.

Wallace, T., and B. Stahl (2009). Sales forecasting: Improving cooperation between the demand people and the supply people. *Foresight: International Journal of Applied Forecasting* 12 (Winter), 14–20.

1.10 THE BEAUTY OF FORECASTING*

David Orrell

Nobel economist Paul Krugman wrote in 2009 that "[t]he economics profession went astray because economists, as a group, mistook beauty, clad in impressive-looking mathematics, for truth." David Orrell, author of *Truth or Beauty: Science and the Quest for Order* (2012), now asks whether this same hubris has applied to forecasters in general.

Newton's law of gravity is held as the archetype of a beautiful theory—and a predictive model. It possesses the three key aesthetic properties of elegance, unity, and symmetry, and can accurately predict a broad range of phenomena. Orrell compares this to the widely used technique for estimating the risk for any financial asset, known as value at risk (VaR). While

* This article originally appeared in *Foresight: The International Journal of Applied Forecasting* (Winter 2014), and appears here courtesy of the International Institute of Forecasters.

VaR is mathematically elegant, incorporates assumptions of symmetry and stability, and unifies the description of a broad range of phenomena, it has failed on a regular basis. As Orrell tersely puts it, Newton's laws got us to the moon, and VaR got us to the financial crisis.

Citing empirical tests such as the M3 competition, simple models are often better at making predictions than more complicated models. But there is a distinction between simple models that involve few parameters (such as a random walk, or single exponential smoothing), and models like VaR that incorporate assumptions that were overly influenced by theoretical criteria such as symmetry or equilibrium.

Orrell concludes that because "living systems . . . resist the tidiness of mathematical laws," it is a risky business indeed to assume that these systems we seek to analyze are either easily depicted or predictable through elegant equations. So when it comes to predictive models, maybe it's OK if they are a little ugly.

Introduction

Most business forecasters would not associate their field with a quest for beauty. Excel spreadsheets are not renowned for their attractiveness. No one—even, I daresay, its inventors—would claim that a useful tool such as exponential smoothing, or even the "autoregressive integrated moving average," is the most beautiful formula ever devised.

But a sense of aesthetics plays an important, if subtle, role in many branches of science. Bertrand Russell wrote, "Mathematics, rightly viewed, possesses not only truth, but supreme beauty—a beauty cold and austere, like that of sculpture." The same kind of beauty is sought and appreciated by researchers in more applied areas as well—not just for its own sake, but because it often seems to indicate that one is on the right path.

The British physicist Paul Dirac went even further, arguing that "It is more important to have beauty in one's equations than to have them fit experiment." He demonstrated this by using an elegant equation to infer the existence of antimatter before it had been physically detected. Modern "theories of everything" such as supersymmetry are explicitly based on aesthetic ideas (e.g., lots of symmetry), though thus far to much less success.

Forecasters might not go to such extremes—they would not predict a recession or boom just because it "looked good"—but the models they use often carry in their bones a trace of mathematical elegance, which can either help or hinder their accuracy.

Perfect Model

Three key aesthetic properties are elegance, unity, and symmetry. Perhaps the archetype of a beautiful theory—and a predictive model—is Newton's law of gravity. The equation is mathematically simple and elegant. It unifies a broad range of phenomena—everything from the motion of the moon around the earth, to an apple falling to the ground. And it is highly symmetric, both spatially (it is the same in every direction) and in the sense that it produces a symmetric force (the earth pulls on the moon, but the moon also pulls back, causing tides). Physicists seek out symmetries in a system because these allow simplified mathematical representations that can be used to predict the system's behavior.

The success of this reductionist approach set a standard for other fields of science, including economics. Neoclassical economics was founded in the 19th century by economists such as William Stanley Jevons and Leon Walras, who took their inspiration directly from Newton. One of the great appeals of their theory was the physics-like way in which it reduced a complex world to a set of elegant equations. As Jevons put it in his 1871 book, *Theory of Political Economy*, these laws were to be considered "as sure and demonstrative as that of kinematics or statics, nay, almost as self-evident as are the elements of Euclid, when the real meaning of the formulae is fully seized."

The theory's key planks include rationality, stability, and uniformity (a large number of consumers and producers with similar characteristics), which together impose a kind of symmetry on the system. Rationality is a symmetry, because rational people with identical preferences will make the same decision given the same information. Stability is symmetry-in-time—if markets are in equilibrium, then the future looks like the past. And if markets are uniform in the sense that market participants have similar power and other characteristics, then that means transactions are symmetric.

Of course, no one thinks that people are perfectly rational, or that markets are perfectly stable or uniform, and much work has been done exploring deviations from these assumptions. But when it comes to what Krugman called the "impressive-looking mathematics" used in mainstream economic models, the world is a very rational, stable, and uniform place. The same hubris applies to certain forecasting models.

Economy at Risk

For example, policy makers often rely on economic predictions made using general equilibrium models. As the name suggests, these explicitly assume the existence of an underlying market equilibrium, and attempt to simulate how it will rationally adapt to changing conditions. Risk models used by banks also usually assume rational behavior and an underlying equilibrium.

Consider the development of the widely used technique known as value at risk (VaR), which is supposed to estimate the worst-case loss that an institution could face on a given financial position. Risk is calculated by taking historical data over a time window ranging from a few months to several years, depending on the case, and applying standard statistical techniques to give the likelihood of a particular loss in the future.

The model is based on the idea that prices are drawn to a stable equilibrium, but are perturbed randomly by the actions of independent investors or by unexpected news. These assumptions justify the use of elegant statistical methods such as the normal distribution. The risk of an asset can be reduced to a single number based on its historical variation.

Despite its popularity, and its intellectual attractiveness, the model has failed on a regular basis. In 2007, for example, the CFO of Goldman Sachs complained that they "were seeing things that were 25-standard-deviation moves, several days in a row." A 25-standard-deviation event is something that is not expected to happen even once in the duration of the universe—so if it happens several days in a row, you begin to realize there is a problem. In fact, market fluctuations do not follow a normal distribution. Like earthquakes, they are better described by a power-law distribution, which has "long tails" and therefore greater likelihood of extreme events.

Value at risk is certainly mathematically elegant. Just as Newton's equation can describe a broad range of phenomena, so VaR can give an estimate of risk for any financial asset. It incorporates assumptions of symmetry and stability. And like a financial law of gravity, it appears to make the trajectory of markets reassuringly rational and predictable. Unfortunately, it lacks empirical validity. Newton's laws of motion got us to the moon; VaR got us to the financial crisis.

Lessons from Business Forecasting

Empirical tests such as the M3 competition, described in Morlidge (2014), have often shown that simple models are better at making predictions than more complicated models. However, there is a distinction between empirical models that involve few parameters, and models that, like VaR, incorporate assumptions that were themselves overly influenced by theoretical criteria such as symmetry or equilibrium.

As I argue in *Truth or Beauty: Science and the Quest for Order* (Orrell, 2012), a concern with aesthetics has affected our choice of models in many areas of science, from string theory to weather prediction. Of course, not all forecasting or risk assessment tools suffer from the same drawbacks. In fact, I believe the business forecasting community has much to teach other fields about adopting an approach that is pragmatic and realistic.

Consider for example the traditional approach to climate forecasting. This involves producing a mechanistic model of the climate system, based on quasi-Newtonian equations of fluid flow, supplemented by empirical laws for things such as turbulent flow. As anyone who has worked with weather or climate models knows, they are not the most elegant of mathematical constructions;

however, they are still based on a reductionist approach which assumes that, in principle, the behavior of a system's components—and therefore the system itself—can be predicted using simple equations.

An alternative to the mechanistic method is to take a time-series modeling approach. For example, neural network models set up a network of artificial "neurons" that learn to detect patterns in past data. A recent study (Fildes and Kourentzes, 2011) showed that, for a limited set of historical data, a neural-network model outperformed a conventional climate model, while a combination of a time-series model with a conventional model led to an improvement of 18 percent in forecast accuracy over a 10-year period. Such time-series models are particularly good at spotting local variations, which tend to elude traditional models but are very relevant for policy makers.

So why have these statistical time-series techniques not been incorporated for use in official climate forecasts? I would venture that part of the reason is related to aesthetics—a topic that I doubt comes up much at meetings of the Intergovernmental Panel on Climate Change. Methods such as neural networks are based on a set of equations, but if you write them out they seem haphazard and strange. Instead of looking like good, mechanistic science, they look like a hack job.

But perhaps that awkwardness is just an expression of the fact that the system under analysis is not easily reconciled with simple equations. Living systems—such as a cell, a person, an economy, or even the climate (which is produced by life)—resist the tidiness of mathematical laws.

When it comes to predictive models, maybe it's OK if they are a little ugly. After all, as in life, looks don't count for everything.

REFERENCES

Fildes, R., and N. Kourentzes (2011). Validation and forecasting accuracy in models of climate change. *International Journal of Forecasting* 27 (4) (Oct–Dec), 968–995.

Morlidge, S. (2014). Do forecasting methods reduce avoidable error? Evidence from forecasting competitions. *Foresight: International Journal of Applied Forecasting* 32 (Winter), 34–39.

Orrell, D. (2012). *Truth or Beauty: Science and the Quest for Order*. New Haven, CT: Yale University Press.

CHAPTER 2

Methods of Statistical Forecasting

Instead of covering the basics of statistical modeling, this chapter aims to provide practical extensions of forecasting methods, including:

- Combining forecasts
- Handling outliers
- Forecasting in hierarchies
- Modeling extreme seasonality (items sell only during certain times of the year)

We also include a pair of articles on the growing application of data-mining techniques in forecasting, techniques that help identify variables potentially beneficial to forecasting models. Better models support management decision making, and can enhance organizational performance.

This chapter concludes with discussions of worst-case scenarios, downside risk assessment, and disruptive events, all issues given new attention after the 2008 global financial meltdown. Forecasting delivers its value by improving management decision making. A critical component of an informed decision is the proper assessment of uncertainty.

This compilation does not substitute for the many excellent books and articles about statistical modeling and other methodological aspects of business forecasting. While a "standard" text has been *Forecasting: Methods and Applications* (3rd Edition, 1998) by Makridakis, Wheelwright, and Hyndman, there are a number of recent offerings including the online, open-access textbook, *Forecasting: Principles and Practice* by Hyndman and Athanasopoulos, and *Principles of Business Forecasting* by Ord and Fildes. In 2014, *Foresight* published a compilation of *Forecasting Methods Tutorials*, providing useful nontechnical overviews of statistical forecasting methods.

2.1 CONFESSIONS OF A PRAGMATIC FORECASTER*

Chris Chatfield

Chris Chatfield draws on over 40 years of forecasting experience to make some practical recommendations about the choice and implementation of forecasting methods, and to offer advice to forecasting practitioners and consultants. Among Chatfield's key points:

- Overenthusiastic claims are often made by the inventor of a new method. While new methods may be a valuable addition to the forecaster's toolkit, they will not be a panacea for all forecasting problems.

* This article originally appeared in *Foresight: International Journal of Applied Forecasting* (Spring 2007), and appears here courtesy of the International Institute of Forecasters.

- When comparisons are fair, average differences between sensible methods applied to a sample of series are quite small, as in the M, M2, and M3 competitions. Large differences should be treated with suspicion.
- The Holt-Winters method remains a good, robust way of forecasting data showing trend and seasonality. ARIMA modeling is recommended only for a series showing short-term correlation where the variation is not dominated by trend and seasonality.
- Prediction intervals ignore model uncertainty. So rather than forecast with a single model or a single set of assumptions, we could use a model-averaging approach to incorporate the effect of model uncertainty.
- Publication bias, whereby forecasters do not report their failures, gives an unfair reflection of the accuracy of more complicated methods. Editors should be encouraged to publish negative results as well as positive ones.
- It remains as important as ever to understand the context of the forecasting problem, to clarify the objectives, and to plot the data.

Introduction

This paper presents some instructive highlights (and lowlights!) from a career in time-series forecasting that began in 1964. We can expect to learn from both our successes and failures, and I encourage forecasters to report both as we learn from both. I use the word *pragmatic* in the title to mean being sensible and practical and hope this applies to my work.

My reflections will touch on longstanding time-series methods, such as Holt-Winters exponential smoothing and Box-Jenkins, and on some newer methods based on neural networks, state-space formulations, and GARCH models. I will also discuss what is meant by a "best" forecast.

Turning to implementation issues, I will discuss the construction of prediction intervals, the handling of model uncertainty, the combining of forecasts, and the effect of differing numbers of items to be forecasted. Publication bias is of concern to me and I will also address that problem.

For the forecasting consultant, I will make a number of practical recommendations, including the importance of looking at the data, understanding the context, using common sense, ensuring that forecast comparisons are fair, and preferring simple (but not simplistic) forecasting methods. Finally I will comment more generally on forecasting today and in the future.

Some History

Forecasting has been described as "the art of saying what will happen and then explaining why it didn't." The converse is also true, namely saying what won't happen and then explaining why it did. Looking through history, one cannot help being struck by the way that forecasts have gone wrong, my own included.

Apocryphal stories include one about the founder of IBM, who, in 1947, is alleged to have said, "I think there is a world market for about five computers." Clearly, basing predictions on past events can be a recipe for disaster, and yet that is exactly how forecasts are typically made. So, are there ways in which uncertainty can be reduced and accuracy improved? Fortunately, there are, though the perceptive forecaster will still realize that the future may not be like the past and that the longer the forecasting horizon, the greater the uncertainty.

Time-series forecasting is a fairly recent phenomenon. Before 1960, the only statistical techniques employed for trend and seasonality were a linear regression on time and a constant seasonal pattern. A big step forward came with the development of exponential smoothing (ES) around 1960 by Robert Brown and Charles Holt. Their forecasting method for data showing both trend and seasonality is customarily called the Holt-Winters method.

As early as 1960, John Muth showed that simple exponential smoothing (no trend or seasonality) was optimal for a model called random walk plus noise, and various other versions of ES have been found to be optimal for a variety of other models, including state-space models with non-constant variance (Chatfield et al., 2001). By *optimal,* we mean that the forecasting formula minimizes the mean square deviation between observed and predicted values for the given model. ES methods are easy to use and employ a natural updating procedure, whereby revisions to forecasts only depend on the latest observed value.

In the mid-1960s, George Box and Gwilym Jenkins began work on a class of models called autoregressive integrated moving average (ARIMA) models and the forecasting approach that was optimal for it. Their 1970 book, now in its 3rd edition (Box et al., 1994), continues to be hugely influential, not only for its coverage of ARIMA modeling, but also for some more general statistical ideas, such as how to carry out model building in an iterative way, with an initial "guessed" model being modified as the analysis progresses and more data become available.

I was fortunate to become a graduate student of Gwilym Jenkins in 1964, though it should be said that the emphasis of our research at that time was on controlling the value of a random process rather than on forecasting (although the two problems are clearly related). It is also salutary to remember that I began my research using paper tape and then punched cards and had to write all my own programs. (Those were the bad old days.) Forecasters today have a range of computers, laptops, and software that early researchers could not possibly have imagined.

Over the years there has been an explosion of alternative methods, such as structural modeling (based on state-space models) and Bayesian forecasting, not to mention more esoteric methods such as those based on nonlinear models. The latter include neural networks as well as GARCH models for changes in variance. When a new method has been proposed, overenthusiastic claims have often been made by the inventor. It is now generally recognized that while new models may be a valuable addition to the forecaster's toolkit, they will not be a panacea for all forecasting problems. This has certainly been my experience, and the fair comparison of forecasting methods has been an important area of research.

When I took my first time-series course in 1964 and taught my first course in 1968, there were no suitable texts available at all. Now there are numerous good books at a variety of mathematical levels covering the basics of time-series analysis as well as forecasting. This makes life much easier for the forecaster. Apart from my own books (Chatfield, 2001, 2004), my favorites include Granger and Newbold (1986, but still useful), Diebold (2004), and (slightly more mathematical) Brockwell and Davis (2002).

Forecasting Methods

ARIMA

ARIMA models were the subject of my first controversial forecasting research study back in the early 1970s and continue to be of wide interest. With no software available to implement ARIMA forecasting at that time, my then-research-student, David Prothero, wrote a suite of programs to carry out the steps outlined in the Box-Jenkins book. Our first attempt at modeling led to forecasts that were intuitively implausible when plotted. We reported this work in a paper read to the Royal Statistical Society (Chatfield and Prothero, 1973), probably the first published case study, and also described our attempts to get around the problems.

In the tradition of the Society, a lively discussion ensued, during which we were told that we should have used a cube-root transformation rather than logarithms. This seemed to us, then, and still does today, to be a rather ill-advised suggestion. The discussion showed us how fiercely people will defend their corner when comparing different methods, but also convinced us that ARIMA models would not always work well. The importance of plotting data and forecasts was paramount. Nowadays, I would only recommend ARIMA modeling for a series showing short-term correlation where the variation is not dominated by trend and seasonality, provided the forecaster has the technical expertise to understand how to carry out the method. This is based on my experience with real data and on the results of forecasting competitions, which show that ARIMA modeling does no better than simpler methods for series showing substantial trend and seasonality.

Exponential Smoothing (Holt-Winters)

Different forms of exponential smoothing continue to be widely used, especially when large numbers of series need to be forecasted. Over the years,

I have made a number of comparative studies using Holt-Winters for data showing trend and seasonality. Generally speaking, I have found this to be a good, straightforward method whose forecasting accuracy compares well with more complicated methods (e.g., Chatfield, 2001, Chapter 6). Note that trend (which can be global or local) and seasonality (which can either be estimated or removed) are often key sources of variation but remain difficult to assess. There is no unique way of disentangling the effects of trend and seasonality, and these effects may change through time.

I recommend exponential smoothing for many problems, especially when there are large numbers of series to predict, and appropriate software is now widely available. The forecaster should make sure that the software optimizes the smoothing weights and is good enough to choose an appropriate form of ES. An important update of research in this area is given by Gardner (2006).

Neural Nets

Neural nets (NNs) have been used for forecasting since about 1990. They are a nonlinear class of models with a potentially large number of parameters. In an IJF Editorial in 1993, I asked whether neural nets were a forecasting breakthrough or a passing fad, a question that can be asked of many new methods. In my experience, it is possible to get reasonable results with NNs, but I have also found many practical difficulties. The analyst still needs to carry out careful model identification to get good results and a black-box approach should be avoided. NNs work best for long series (several thousand observations) showing nonlinear properties but struggle to beat simpler alternative methods for shorter series, especially when the variation is dominated by trend and seasonality. This may not be the impression gained from the literature, but this is partially explained by publication bias, which I comment on below.

State-Space Models

There are several classes of models that can be regarded as state-space models. They include structural models (Harvey, 1989), the Bayesian dynamic linear models of West and Harrison (1997), and the unobserved components models used by economists. These classes can all be expressed in state-space form and are essentially trying to do the same thing, despite the different nomenclature. All are updated by something very close to the Kalman filter, which is a general way of updating estimates of the system parameters when a new observation becomes available. Note that exponential smoothing is a simple example of such a filter. In some ways state-space models are more versatile than ARIMA models and can have the advantage of providing explicit estimates of trend and seasonality. More widely available software is needed, and I am puzzled as to why software vendors have not provided it.

Multivariate Forecasting

Models with Explanatory Variables

In principle, one expects multivariate models to give better forecasts than univariate models. However, this is not always the case. In many models with explanatory variables, genuine out-of-sample forecasts of the dependent variable require forecasts of future values of explanatory variables, and this increases forecast uncertainty. My limited experience with vector ARIMA models has found them theoretically challenging and difficult to fit in practice. Perhaps we should confine attention to simple vector AR models. Box-Jenkins transfer-function models are somewhat easier to fit but require that the dependent variable does not affect the explanatory variables. Econometric models are outside my area of expertise but seem to require skilled judgment.

Nonlinear Models

There has been much recent interest in a variety of nonlinear models, over and above neural networks mentioned earlier. While nonlinear models are very interesting from a theoretical point of view, I have yet to see much evidence that they can provide better empirical forecasts than appropriate linear models. Tests for detecting nonlinearity have been developed, as have methods for model-fitting, but they can be very difficult to perform. Clearly there is much to do to make them worthwhile in practice.

One special, and rather different, class of nonlinear models is that called GARCH (generalized autoregressive conditional heteroscedastic) models. They are used to model changes in the local variance, rather than the actual observed variable. I remain suspicious of GARCH models, as I think they have a number of potential problems (although I admit that I haven't tried them in practice). For example, I do not like the deterministic nature of the equation used to update the local variance, and I have seen little empirical evidence that GARCH models actually fit real data. Indeed, it is difficult to evaluate GARCH models because one does not directly observe the local variance. Moreover, many series show periods when the local variance is more or less constant, and times when there is a sudden increase in variance for a short time or perhaps for a longer period. This sort of behavior, often driven by known external events, is usually evident when looking at a simple time plot of the observed data and cannot adequately be captured by a GARCH model. There are several alternative types of volatility models that I prefer to GARCH.

Computationally Intensive Methods

There is much current research on the use of computationally intensive methods, such as the Markov Chain Monte Carlo (MCMC) method, to solve a variety of statistical problems, including forecasting. They can be useful when no analytic solution exists. However, there is a major difficulty in that there is no obvious way to check the results. Thus the methods worry me. In particular, what does one do if the results do not look "right"? I do not know the answer.

Which Method Is Best?

Although this question is crucial for forecasters, we now know that there is no simple answer. The choice of method depends on the type of problem, the length of the series, the forecasting horizon, the number of series to forecasts, the level of expertise available, and other factors.

We also need to be clear as to what we mean by "best." The choice of metric to measure forecasting accuracy is crucial. To compare accuracy over multiple series, the metric must be scale-independent to ensure that we are comparing like with like. We also need to carefully consider other questions relating to forecast evaluation and model comparison, such as when is it a good idea to split a time series into a training set (to fit the model) and a test set (to evaluate model forecasts), and how this should be done. It is also essential that all forecasts are genuine out-of-sample (ex ante) forecasts, applied with the same degree of expertise. Having taken part in several comparative studies, I can say that it is surprising how often one method is found to have an unfair advantage over others. We need transparency, full disclosure of all relevant information, so that replication can take place. We also need to ensure that different methods use exactly the same information.

When comparisons are fair, we find that average differences between sensible methods, applied to a sample of series, are quite small, as in the M, M2, and M3 competitions. Indeed I would go further and say that large differences should be treated with suspicion. It may be, for example, that forecasters are using future information, perhaps inadvertently, so that forecasts are not ex ante, and I have known several cases where further study showed that a method was not as good as first suggested. One recent example that caught my eye is the use of what are called Dynamic Artificial Neural Networks (DANNs). I had not heard of these models, but the results of Ghiassi et al. (2005) appeared to show that DANNs gave considerably better forecasts for six well-known series than alternative methods. Can we believe these results? Is the approach a real breakthrough or is there something wrong? I find it hard to believe such an implausible improvement. Moreover, I cannot understand the theory or the practical details of the method and so cannot replicate the results. Thus, until I see an independent researcher get similar results with DANNs, I have to regard the case as not proven.

Even when differences between methods are substantial enough to be interesting, but not so large as to raise disquiet, there still remains the question as to how we can tell if differences are in fact large. One might expect to carry out tests of significance to assess differences between methods. Indeed Koning et al. (2005) say that "rigorous statistical testing" is needed in "any evaluation of forecast accuracy." However, samples of time series are not a random sample, and different methods are applied by different people in different ways. Thus, in my view significance tests are not valid to tackle this question. Rather, I think it more important to assess whether differences are of practical importance. At the same time, we should check whether forecasts have been calculated in comparable ways. Indeed, how the results of forecasting competitions, and significance tests thereon, are relevant to ordinary forecasting is still unclear.

Implementation of Forecasting Methods

Interval Forecasts

The forecasting literature has tended to concentrate on point forecasts, even though interval forecasts are often more informative. This latter type usually involves finding an upper and lower limit within which the future value is expected to lie with a given probability. I also like the related approach using density forecasts, perhaps presented as fan charts. I reviewed this whole area in Chatfield (2001, Chapter 7).

Model Uncertainty

Interval forecasts are usually calculated conditional on a fitted model, often a best-fit model. This leads to a related topic that has interested me, namely the study of *model uncertainty*. Forecasters often forget that their fitted model is unlikely to be the "true" model and that model uncertainty generally increases the forecast error variance. Sadly, this effect is usually ignored, which partly explains why out-of-sample forecasting accuracy is often disappointing compared with within-sample fit. Analysts may think a narrow interval forecast is a good idea, but experience suggests that a wider interval may be more realistic. A nice example is given by Draper (1995). Forecasts of oil prices in 1986 were made in 1980 using 12 different scenarios, and ranged from \$29 to \$121 per barrel. A typical 90% prediction interval was \$27 to \$51. The actual mid-1986 price was \$11 per barrel, which lay outside every prediction interval calculated. Rather than forecast with a single model or a single set of assumptions, Draper used a model-averaging approach to incorporate the effect of model uncertainty. This gave the interval \$20 to \$92, which was wider (and therefore better), but was still not wide enough. Of course the price at the time of writing appears to be heading outside the upper limit of these intervals, thus illustrating the difficulty of forecasting the future of a volatile variable. This topic is reviewed in Chatfield (2001, Chapter 8).

Combining Forecasts

The use of a single, perhaps best-fit model is often inappropriate and stems from the idea that there must be a true model, if only one could find it. The forecaster should consider combining forecasts or getting a range of forecasts under different conditions—often called *scenario forecasting*.

Different approaches to forecasting are appropriate for different situations. This obvious truth is often overlooked when people argue about the best forecasting procedure. The many different approaches are complementary, rather than competitive. For example, some approaches are primarily empirical, while others are more theoretical. Both have their place, and often a combination is better.

The Number of Items to Be Forecast

The problems involved in forecasting a few series are quite different from those involved with forecasting many series, perhaps hundreds or even thousands. Univariate methods are useful when forecasting lots of series as well as giving a yardstick in stable situations. Multivariate methods should be used only for small numbers of series, especially when there are known causal variables.

Publication Bias

In medical research, it is well known that researchers tend to publish encouraging results but suppress poor or disappointing results. In my experience, the same is true of forecasting. This can give an important source of bias when assessing forecasting results. For example, I know of two instances where people suppressed the poor results obtained using NNs for commercial reasons. How can this be prevented, at least partially? I think editors should be encouraged to publish negative results as well as positive ones, just as nonsignificant effects can be as important as significant ones in medical research. We should not be using forecasting methods (or medical drugs) that are not efficacious.

Experience in Consulting

Like most subjects, forecasting is best learned by actually doing it. This section gives some practical advice based on many years' experience. The first point is that forecasters sometimes find that forecasts can go horribly wrong. This means that avoiding trouble is more important than achieving optimality. It can certainly be dangerous to rely on thinking that there is a true (albeit unknown) model from which optimal forecasts can be found.

The really important advice is as follows:

- Before you start, it is essential to understand the context. Ask questions, if necessary, so that the problem can be formulated carefully. Do the objectives need to be clarified? How will the forecast actually be used? Do you have all the relevant information?

- Check data quality. Do you have good data, whatever that means? How were they collected? Do they need to be cleaned or transformed?
- Draw a clear time-plot and look at it. Can you see trend or seasonality? Are there discontinuities or any other interesting effects?
- Spend time trying to understand, measure, and, if necessary, remove the trend and seasonality.
- Use common sense at all times.
- Be prepared to improvise and try more than one method.
- Keep it simple.
- Consult the 139 principles in Armstrong (2001, page 680), of which the above are an important subset. They come from theory, empirical evidence, and bitter experience.

REFERENCES

Armstrong, J. S. (Ed.) (2001). *Principles of Forecasting: A Handbook for Researchers and Practitioners*. Norwell, MA: Kluwer.

Box, G. E. P., G. M. Jenkins, and G. C. Reinsel (1994). *Time-Series Analysis, Forecasting and Control*, 3rd ed. Englewood Cliffs, NJ: Prentice-Hall.

Brockwell, P. J., and R. A. Davis (2002). *Introduction to Time Series and Forecasting*, 2nd ed. New York: Springer.

Chatfield, C. (2004). *The Analysis of Time Series*, 6th ed. Boca Raton: Chapman & Hall/CRC Press.

Chatfield, C. (2002). Confessions of a pragmatic statistician. *The Statistician* 51, 1–20.

Chatfield, C. (2001). *Time-Series Forecasting*. Boca Raton: Chapman & Hall/CRC Press.

Chatfield, C., A. B. Koehler, J. K. Ord, and R. L. Snyder (2001). Models for exponential smoothing: A review of recent developments. *The Statistician* 50, 147–159.

Chatfield, C., and D. L. Prothero (1973). Box-Jenkins seasonal forecasting: Problems in a case study. *Journal of the Royal Statistical Society*, Series A, 136, 295–352.

Diebold, F. X. (2004). *Elements of Forecasting*, 3rd ed. Cincinnati: South-Western.

Draper, D. (1995). Assessment and propagation of model uncertainty. *Journal of the Royal Statistical Society* Series B, 57, 45–97.

Gardner, E. S. Jr. (2006). Exponential smoothing: The state of the art—part II. *International Journal of Forecasting* 22, 637–666.

Ghiassi, M., H. Saidane, and D. K. Zimbra (2005). A dynamic artificial neural network model for forecasting time series events. *International Journal of Forecasting* 21, 341–362.

Granger, C. W. J., and P. Newbold (1986). *Forecasting Economic Time Series*, 2nd ed. Orlando: Academic Press.

Harvey, A. C. (1989). *Forecasting, Structural Time Series Models and the Kalman Filter.* Cambridge: Cambridge University Press.

Koning, A. J., P. H. Franses, M. Hibon, and H. O. Stekler (2005). The M3 competition: Statistical tests of the results. *International Journal of Forecasting* 21, 397–409.
West, M., and J. Harrison (1997). *Bayesian Forecasting and Dynamic Models*, 2nd ed. New York: Springer-Verlag.

2.2 NEW EVIDENCE ON THE VALUE OF COMBINING FORECASTS*

Paul Goodwin

Combining forecasts from multiple, independent sources has long been recognized as a way to improve forecast accuracy. Andreas Graefe and colleagues provide an excellent summary of the literature in "Combining Forecasts: An Application to Elections," appearing in the *International Journal of Forecasting* in 2014. They conclude that "the simple method of combining is one of the most useful procedures in a forecaster's toolkit," and note that the costs of combining are likely to be trivial compared to the potential gains.

In this brief article, Paul Goodwin looks at reasons why combining forecasts seems to work. Among these are (1) different models use different information, so that combined models draw from a wider set of information, and (2) the biases of individual models may cancel out, leading to a truer combined forecast.

Goodwin also discusses alternative weighting schemes for combining forecasts. While there often is no need to take other than a simple average of individual forecasts, he reports on studies advocating the Akaike Information Criterion (AIC) for weights, and on "trimmed means" (removing the high and low forecasts before averaging).

One of the major findings of forecasting research over the last quarter century has been that greater predictive accuracy can often be achieved by combining forecasts from different methods or sources. Combination can be a process as straightforward as taking a simple average of the different forecasts, in which case the constituent forecasts are all weighted equally. Other, more sophisticated techniques are available, too, such as trying to estimate the optimal weights that should be attached to the individual forecasts, so that those that are likely to be the most accurate receive a greater weight in the averaging process. Researchers continue to investigate circumstances where combining may well be useful to forecasters and to compare the accuracy of different approaches to combining forecasts.

Forecast Combination and the Bank of England's Suite of Statistical Forecasting Models

George Kapetanios and his colleagues (Kapetanios et al., 2008) have recently evaluated the potential advantages of combining forecasting data at the Bank

* This article originally appeared in *Foresight: International Journal of Applied Forecasting* (Winter 2009), and appears here courtesy of the International Institute of Forecasters.

of England, where quarterly forecasts of inflation and GDP growth are made. The bank has a suite of different statistical forecasting methods available. They include extremely simple approaches, such as the naïve (or random walk) method where the forecasts are equal to the most recent observation. More sophisticated and complex methods in the suite include autoregression, vector-autoregressions (VARs), Markov switching models, factor models, and time-varying coefficient models.

The researchers assessed the value of combining forecasts from the methods available using two different approaches. The first involved taking a simple mean of the forecasts generated by the methods in the suite. The second involved weighting the individual forecasts based upon the Akaike information criterion (AIC). Many commercial forecasting packages report the AIC, which is a measure that takes into account how well a model fits past data but also penalizes the model for complexity, based on the number of parameters it contains. Thus, forecasts from relatively simple models that provided a good fit to past observations received a greater weight in the averaging process than more complex or poorer fitting models.

The accuracy of the two types of combined forecasts was assessed over a range of forecast horizons using the relative root mean squared error (RRMSE) statistic. This compares the square root of the sum of squared forecast errors to those of a benchmark forecasting method (in this case, the benchmark was the autoregressive forecast). The researchers reported that "it is striking that forecast performance . . . is improved when forecasts are combined and the best forecast combinations for both growth and inflation are those based on the [Akaike] information criterion." The Kapetanios group concluded that "combinations of statistical forecasts generate good forecasts of the key macroeconomic variables we are interested in."

Similar benefits of combining have also recently been reported in studies by David Rapach and Jack Strauss (Rapach and Strauss, 2008), who forecast U.S. employment growth, and Jeong-Ryeol Kurz-Kim (Kurz-Kim, 2008), who forecasts U.S. GDP growth. The latter study combined forecasts from the same method (autoregression) that was implemented in different ways.

Why Did Combining Work?

The researchers suggest a number of reasons. Different models use different sets of information, and each model is likely to represent an incomplete view of the process that is driving the variable of interest. Combined forecasts are therefore able to draw on a wider set of information. In addition, some of the constituent forecasting methods may be biased, in that they consistently forecast too high or too low. When several methods are combined, there is a likelihood that biases in different directions will counteract each other, thereby improving accuracy.

Trimmed Means

While the more sophisticated AIC-based weights performed best in the Kapetanios et al. study, the simple mean also did well in both this and the Rapach and Strauss study. The simple mean does have advantages. For one thing, it is easy to implement and explain. It also avoids the need to estimate the optimum set of weights to attach to the forecasts—in many practical circumstances, there may be insufficient data to reliably make these estimates.

However, the simple mean also has the disadvantage of being sensitive to extreme forecasts: If there is an outlying forecast in the set that is being averaged, it will have undue influence on the combined forecast. This has led some researchers (e.g., Armstrong, 2001) to argue that the highest and lowest forecasts should be removed from the set before the mean is calculated. The resulting average is called a trimmed mean.

Victor Jose and Robert Winkler (Jose and Winkler, 2008) recently investigated whether trimmed means lead to more accurate combined forecasts. They explored the effects of applying different degrees of trimming (e.g., removing the two highest and two lowest forecasts from the set before averaging, or the three highest and three lowest, and so on). In addition, they evaluated whether an alternative form of averaging, the Winsorized mean, was more effective. Rather than removing the highest and lowest forecasts, the Winsorized mean alters their values, making them equal to the highest and lowest forecast values that remain. For example, consider these sales forecasts from five different methods: 23, 34, 47, 53, 86. If we decide to leave off the two "outside" forecasts, our trimmed mean will be the mean of 34, 47, and 53 (i.e., 44.7). In contrast, the Winsorized mean will be the mean of 34, 34, 47, 53, and 53 (i.e., 44.2). It is quickly apparent that these two types of modification only make sense when you have at least three forecasts to work with. Also, the two methods yield differing results only when there are a minimum of five forecasts to combine.

The researchers tested these approaches by combining the forecasts of 22 methods for the 3003 time series from the M3 competition (Makridakis and Hibon, 2000). Additionally, they carried out similar tests on the quarterly nominal GDP forecasts from the Federal Reserve Bank of Philadelphia's Survey of Professional Forecasters. They found that both trimming and Winsorization yielded slightly more accurate forecasts than the simple mean; they also outperformed all of the individual forecasting methods. There was, however, little to choose between trimming and Winsorization. Moderate degrees of trimming, removing 10 to 30% of the forecasts, seemed to work best. For Winsorization, replacing 15 to 45% of the values appeared to be most effective. I would point out that greater amounts of trimming or replacement yielded greater accuracy when there was more variation in the individual forecasts. This is probably because highly variable sets of forecasts contained extreme values.

Conclusions

All of this suggests that when you have access to forecasts from different sources or methods (e.g., different statistical methods or judgmental forecasts from different experts), combining these forecasts is likely to be an effective way of improving accuracy. Even using relatively simple combination methods will be enough to yield improvements in many cases. Whatever your area of forecasting, combining forecasts is certainly worth a long, close look.

REFERENCES

Armstrong, J. S. (2001). Combining forecasts. In J. S.Armstrong (Ed.), *Principles of Forecasting: A Handbook for Researchers and Practitioners*. Norwell, MA: Kluwer Academic Publishers, 417–439.

Jose, V. R., and R. L. Winkler (2008). Simple robust averages of forecasts: Some empirical results. *International Journal of Forecasting* 24, 163–169.

Kapetanios, G., V. Labhard, and S. Price (2008). Forecast combination and the Bank of England's suite of statistical forecasting models. *Economic Modeling* 24, 772–792.

Kurz-Kim, J-R (2008). Combining forecasts using optimal combination weight and generalized autoregression. *Journal of Forecasting* 27, 419–432.

Makridakis, S., and M. Hibon (2000). The M-3 competition: Results, conclusions and implications. *International Journal of Forecasting* 16, 451–476.

Rapach, D. E., and J. K. Strauss (2008). Forecasting U.S. employment growth using forecast combining methods. *Journal of Forecasting* 27, 75–93.

2.3 HOW TO FORECAST DATA CONTAINING OUTLIERS*

Eric Stellwagen

In the practice of business forecasting, we often encounter historical data that contain outliers—data values that are unusually large or small, that fall well above or below what we would expect for a given time period. The easiest (and most common) thing to do is to "mask" the outliers (i.e., remove them from the data) and ignore them. Aren't they just annoyances that make it harder to construct a good model of the history?

Removing or adjusting the outliers lets you fit a simpler and more aesthetically pleasing model to the time-series data. This is the "principle of parsimony" at work. The model, based on better behaving data, won't propagate the erratic spikes and troughs of true history, and you end up with a nicer, more stable view of the future. The future, in fact, starts to look pretty well-behaved and predictable, which is the way forecasters (and business managers) like it! However, the gratuitous masking of outliers can have an ugly downside.

* This article was adapted from *Forecasting 101: How to Forecast Data Containing Outliers* by Eric Stellwagen originally published in the September 2007 issue of the *Forecast Pro Trends Newsletter* and is reprinted with permission.

Eric Stellwagen notes that outliers "scream out" to us about additional risk and uncertainty in the historical data. Simply ignoring them can be dangerous, leading to excessive (and unjustified) confidence in our forecasts. He then describes three better approaches to outlier handling:

- Outlier correction
- Separation of demand streams
- Event modeling

What's important to remember is that unusual and annoying things have happened in the past and will probably recur in the future. When we blindly remove the outliers from our historical data, we are ignoring an important source of information on how ill-behaved the world can really be.

An outlier is a data point that falls outside of the expected range of the data (i.e., it is an unusually large or small data point). If you ignore outliers in your data, there is a danger that they can have a significant adverse impact on your forecasts. This article surveys three different approaches to forecasting data containing outliers, discusses the pros and cons of each, and makes recommendations about when it is best to use each approach.

Option #1: Outlier Correction

A simple solution to lessen the impact of an outlier is to replace the outlier with a more typical value prior to generating the forecasts. This process is often referred to as Outlier Correction. Many forecasting solutions offer automated procedures for detecting outliers and "correcting" the history prior to forecasting.

Correcting the history for a severe outlier will often improve the forecast. However, if the outlier is not truly severe, correcting for it may do more harm than good. When you correct an outlier, you are rewriting the history to be smoother than it actually was and this will change the forecasts and narrow the confidence limits. This will result in poor forecasts and unrealistic confidence limits when the correction was not necessary.

Recommendations:

1. If the cause of an outlier is known, alternative approaches (such as option #2 and #3 below) should be considered prior to resorting to outlier correction.
2. Outlier correction should be performed sparingly. Using an automated detection algorithm to identify potential candidates for correction is very useful; however, the detected outliers should ideally be individually reviewed by the forecaster to determine whether a correction is appropriate.

3. In cases where an automated outlier detection and correction procedure must be used (for example, if the sheer number of forecasts to be generated precludes human review), then the thresholds for identifying and correcting an outlier should be set very high. Ideally, the thresholds would be calibrated empirically by experimenting with a subset of the data.

Option #2: Separate the Demand Streams

At times, when the cause of the outlier is known, it may be useful to separate a time series into two different demand streams and forecast them separately. Consider the following three examples.

Example A: A pharmaceutical company's demand for a given drug consists of both prescription fills (sales) and free goods (e.g., samples distributed free of charge to physicians). The timing of the distribution of free goods introduces outliers in the time series representing total demand. Separating the demand streams yields an outlier-free prescription fills series and allows different forecasting approaches to be used for each series—which is appropriate since the drivers generating the demand are different for the two series.

Example B: A manufacturing company's demand normally consists of orders from its distributors. In response to an unusual event, the government places a large one-time order that introduces a significant outlier into the demand series, but does not impact base demand from the distributors. Separating the demand streams yields an outlier-free distributor demand series and allows the forecast for the government's demand series to be simply set to zero.

Example C: A food and beverage company sells its products from both store shelves and promotional displays (e.g., end caps, point-of-sale displays, etc.). It has access to the two separate demand streams. Although it is tempting to forecast these two series separately, it may not be the best approach. Although the promotional displays will increase total demand, they will also cannibalize base demand. In this example it may be better to forecast total demand using a forecasting method that can accommodate the promotions (e.g., event models, regression, etc.).

Recommendations:

- Separating the demand streams should only be considered when you understand the different sources of demand that are introducing the outliers.
- If the demand streams can be separated in a "surgically clean" manner, you should consider separating the demand streams and forecasting them separately.
- In cases where the demand streams cannot be cleanly separated, you are often better off working with a single time series.

Option #3: Use a Forecasting Method that Models the Outliers

Outliers can be caused by events of which you have knowledge (e.g., promotions, one-time orders, strikes, catastrophes, etc.) or can be caused by events of which you have no knowledge (i.e., you know that the point is unusual, but you don't know why). If you have knowledge of the events that created the outliers, you should consider using a forecasting method that explicitly models these events.

Event models are an extension of exponential smoothing that are particularly well suited to this task. They are easy to build and lend themselves well to automation. Another option is dynamic regression.

Unlike time-series methods, which base the forecasts solely on an item's past history, event models and dynamic regression are causal models, which allow you to bring in additional information such as promotional schedules, the timing of business interruptions, and (in the case of dynamic regression) explanatory variables.

By capturing the response to the events as part of the overall forecasting model, these techniques often improve the accuracy of the forecasts as well as providing insights into the impact of the events.

Recommendation:

- In instances where the causes of the outliers are known, you should consider using a forecasting method that explicitly models the events.

Summary

Ignoring large outliers in your data often leads to poor forecasts. The best approach to forecasting data containing outliers depends on the nature of the outliers and the resources of the forecaster. In this article, we have discussed three approaches—outlier correction, separating the demand streams, and modeling the outliers—which can be used when creating forecasts based on data containing outliers.

2.4 SELECTING YOUR STATISTICAL FORECASTING LEVEL*

Eric Stellwagen

Many software packages support *hierarchical forecasting*, in which you define the hierarchical relationship of your products and locations, create forecasts at one or more levels, and then reconcile the forecasts across the full hierarchy.

In a *top-down* approach, you generate forecasts at the highest level and apportion them down to lower levels. In *bottom-up* forecasting, you generate forecasts at the bottom (most granular)

* This article was adapted from *Selecting Your Statistical Forecasting Level: How Low Should You Go?* by Eric Stellwagen, originally published in *The Forecast Pro Blog*, 12/04/2013, and is reprinted with permission.

level of the hierarchy, then aggregate to obtain forecasts at higher levels. In the commonly used *middle-out* approach, you generate forecasts at some intermediate level, sum them up to higher levels, and apportion them down to more granular levels.

By starting with the question, "Can it be simpler?" Eric Stellwagen notes that the hierarchy should include only the minimum number of levels needed for forecasting. Quite clearly, there are costs associated with overly lush hierarchies: much more data to store and process (slowing down system performance), and more work for the forecast analyst (with more levels of forecasts to monitor and maintain).

Once the hierarchy is defined, the next decision is the level at which to generate the statistical forecasts. Stellwagen illustrates how the most granular level can be ill-behaving, or lacking sufficient data to forecast using statistical methods. It is often best, therefore, to forecast at a higher level (where data are sufficiently well-behaved) and then use an allocation scheme to apportion the forecast to lower levels.

Although not covered in Stellwagen's article, one reason for the common "worst practice" of too many hierarchy levels is the confusion of forecasting needs with reporting needs. For example, an apparel manufacturer may need to know how many white, black, red, and yellow t-shirts are forecast, so the appropriate amount of dye can be procured. But this doesn't mean the *color* needs to be a level in the hierarchy.

Color is a product *attribute*. The proper way to forecast color demand is to export item-level forecasts to a reporting system, then aggregate the item forecasts according to their color attribute. In this way, additional levels desired for reporting can be handled outside the forecasting hierarchy.

Many organizations need to generate forecasts at very detailed levels. For example, a consumer products company may need an SKU-by-customer forecast, a shoe manufacturer may need a shoe-by-size forecast, or an automobile manufacturer may need a parts-level forecast. One approach to generating low-level forecasts is to apply statistical forecasting methods directly to the lowest-level demand histories. An alternative approach is to use statistical forecasting methods on more aggregated data and then to apply an allocation scheme to generate the lower-level forecasts.

Deciding on the lowest level at which to generate statistical forecasts and deciding how to allocate a statistical forecast to lower levels can have a major impact on forecast accuracy. This article examines some of the issues surrounding these decisions including how the "forecastibility" of data changes at different levels of aggregation.

Can It Be Simpler?

Prior to deciding what levels of your forecasting hierarchy should be forecasted using statistical models, it is useful to consider whether your forecasting hierarchy can be simplified. Just because you have access to very detailed information, does not mean it should be forecasted. If a forecasting level is not strictly required—it should not be included in your forecasting hierarchy. Your goal is to always keep your forecasting hierarchy as simple as possible, while still getting the job done.

If your management asks whether you can generate a forecast at a lower level than you are currently forecasting, you may need to educate them about why this may not be the best choice. You will need to explain that the forecasts are likely to be less accurate than your current forecasts, that forecasting at a lower level will complicate the forecasting process considerably, and question whether such forecasts are truly needed by the organization. As Einstein put it, "Everything should be made as simple as possible, but not simpler."

Do You Have Enough Structure?

Figure 2.1 shows monthly sales for a brand of cough syrup. Figure 2.2 shows monthly sales for a specific SKU. The company assigns a unique SKU number to each flavor-by-bottle size combination that it produces.

Consider the two graphs. Notice that at the brand level, there is more structure to the data. The seasonal pattern is readily apparent and there is less "noise" (random variation). More than three years of demand history is available at the brand level, while only 10 months of history exists for the recently introduced SKU. In general, when you disaggregate data, the result is lower volume, less structure, and a data set that is harder to forecast using statistical methods.

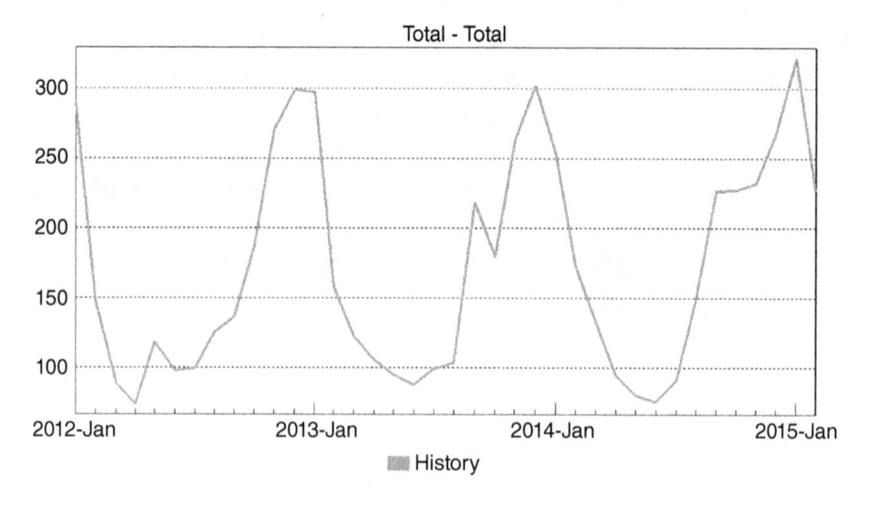

Figure 2.1 Monthly Sales for Cough Syrup Brand

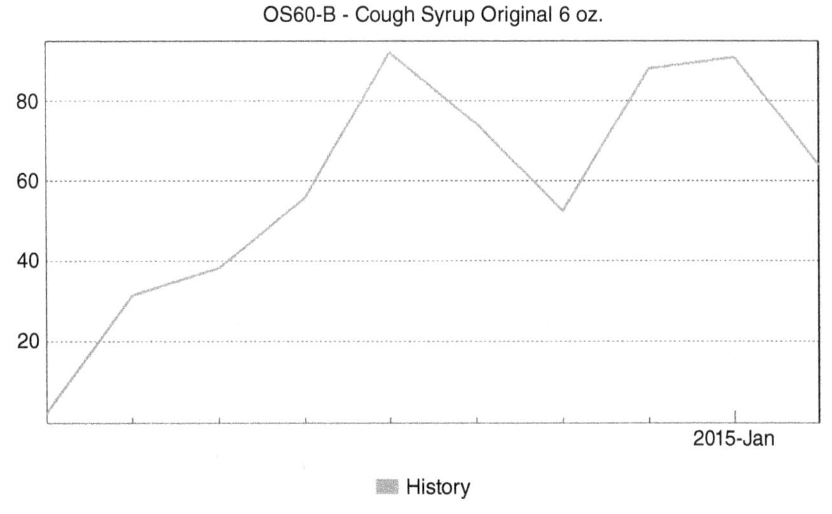

Figure 2.2 Monthly Sales for Cough Syrup SKU

Many organizations that need to generate low-level forecasts discover that at the lowest levels there is not enough structure to generate meaningful statistical forecasts directly from the low-level data. In these cases there is little choice but to generate the lowest-level forecasts not with statistical models, but rather by using some type of top-down allocation scheme.

Are the Relationships Between Levels Changing in Time?

A statistical model uses past demand history to forecast how things are changing in time. If there is a relationship between two levels of your hierarchy that is time independent, then you may be able to define an allocation scheme to forecast the lower level rather than trying to forecast it based on history.

For example, a shoe manufacturer needs a forecast for a men's running shoe for each size manufactured. The demand for the specific style of shoe is changing in time, so the shoe-level forecast should be generated using a statistical method to capture the change. On the other hand, the size of runners' feet is not changing rapidly in time, so the by-size forecasts can be generated by allocating the shoe-level forecast to the sizes using a size distribution chart.

Another example might be an automobile manufacturer who uses a statistical model to forecast vehicle sales and then allocates via a bill of materials to generate a parts-level forecast.

In both of these examples, because the relationship between the levels is known and not changing in time, the allocation approach will likely be more accurate than trying to statistically model the lower-level data.

Summary

Deciding how to organize your forecasting hierarchy and how to forecast each level can have deep ramifications on forecast accuracy. As you make these important decisions, you need to: (1) question whether you have simplified your hierarchy as much as possible; (2) determine what levels have enough structure for you to apply statistical methods directly to the data, and (3) understand the relationships between the levels—particularly those where a logical allocation scheme could be used to generate the lower-level forecasts.

2.5 WHEN IS A FLAT-LINE FORECAST APPROPRIATE?*

Eric Stellwagen

Flat-line forecasts occur when no trend or seasonality is detected in the time-series data, and all the ups and downs of history are treated as random noise.

While flat-line forecasts are often the most appropriate representation of what is going to happen in the future, Stellwagen recognizes that management may reject them or require an explanation. To make such forecasts acceptable to management and improve their usefulness for planning, confidence limits can be added to show the expected range of fluctuation.

Using an example from spare parts forecasting (with intermittent, very low volume demand), Stellwagen shows how the flat-line forecast shows the expected demand (and can be used to forecast revenue for spare part sales). The upper confidence limit can be used to determine how many spare parts to keep in inventory.

A forecasting technique that generates a forecast based solely on an item's past demand history is referred to as a time-series method. Typically, time-series methods will capture structure in the history—such as current sales levels, trends, and seasonal patterns—and extrapolate them forward.

When the data are not trended and are not seasonal, a time-series method will often generate a flat-line forecast reflecting the current sales level. Because

* This article was adapted from *Forecasting 101: When Is a Flat-line Appropriate and What Does It Tell You About Your Demand?* by Eric Stellwagen, originally published in *The Forecast Pro Blog*, 1/08/2014, and is reprinted with permission.

a flat line is often an implausible scenario for the future, delivering a flat-line forecast to management may require explaining the distinction between a scenario for the future and a statistical forecast of the future. This article explains this distinction and discusses when a flat-line forecast is and is not appropriate.

Consider the two data sets shown below. Figure 2.3 represents monthly demand for an expensive spare parts assembly needed to maintain commercial equipment. Notice that the historic demand consists of integers and has equaled either 0, 1, 2, 3, or 4 units in any given month.

Figure 2.4 represents annual rainfall in a city in Brazil for the period 1849–1920. Notice that historically it has rained anywhere from 50 to 250 centimeters per year and the amount of rainfall can vary quite widely from year to year.

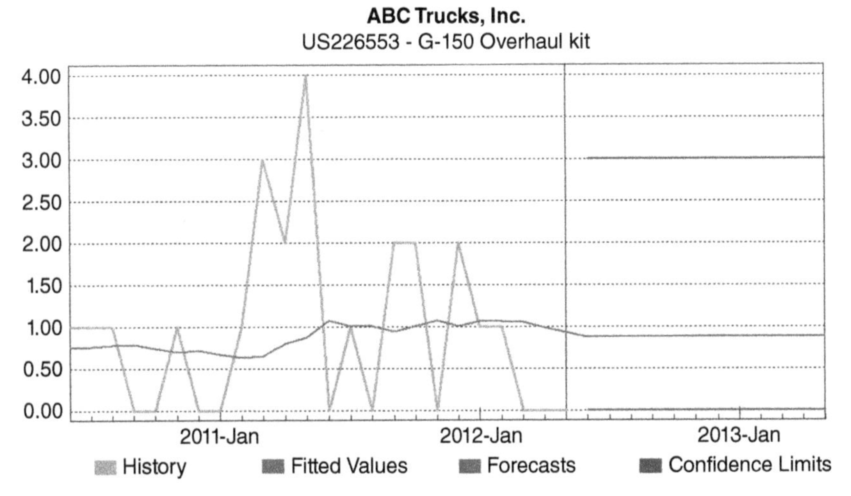

Figure 2.3 Monthly Demand

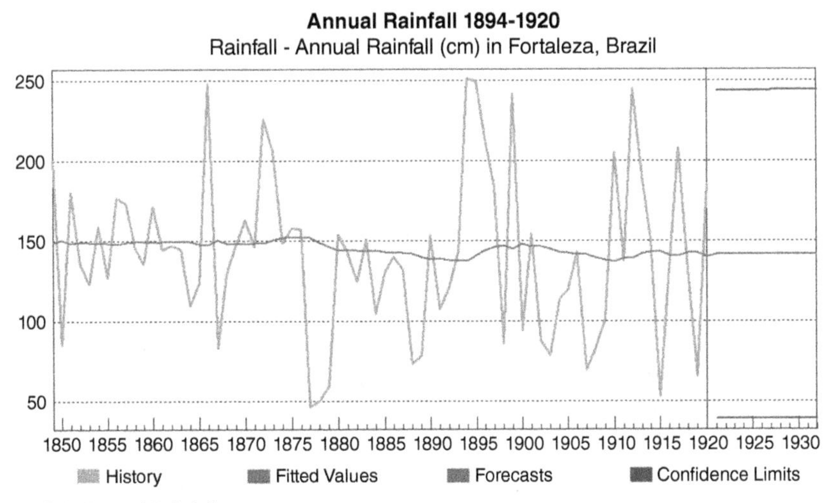

Figure 2.4 Annual Rainfall

Neither data set is trended. Neither data set is seasonal. Thus, their forecasts are not trended and are not seasonal—they are flat. This does not indicate that the future demand for the spare parts assembly or rainfall will be flat—these amounts will continue to fluctuate in the future—it just indicates that how these amounts will fluctuate is not predictable based solely on the historic data. The expected range of the fluctuations is shown by the confidence limits.

Let's take a closer look at our spare parts assembly. The forecast is 0.9 units per month and the upper confidence limit is set to 97.5%. Notice that the forecast is not a possible scenario for the future—we will not sell 0.9 units per month for the next 12 months—in all likelihood we will continue to sell either 0, 1, 2, 3, or 4 units in any given month. The problem is that the timing and size of the future orders is not knowable from the past history. So what does our forecast tell us, and how do we use it?

In the statistical sense, the forecast is the expected value for the future periods. It is the point at which (according to the model) it is equally likely that the actual value will fall above or below. If we are trying to estimate expected revenue for our spare parts assembly, this is exactly what we want. We can take our forecasts and multiply them by our average selling price to determine our expected revenues. If we want to know how many spare parts assemblies to keep in inventory, we use our upper confidence limit.

Notice that even though our data are highly variable and our forecast is flat, the accuracy of the forecast and confidence limits still has a major impact on our revenue planning and inventory policies. Thus, it is important to generate the most accurate forecast possible, even when the forecast is a flat line.

2.6 FORECASTING BY TIME COMPRESSION*

Udo Sglavo

Extreme seasonality occurs when an item sells only during a particular time of the year, with zero sales the rest of the time. This is a familiar situation for retailers, who only stock certain items "in season." Note that extreme seasonality is distinct from the normal patterns of *intermittent demand*, in which frequent periods of zero sales are interspersed with periods of non-zero sales.

Udo Sglavo describes a novel way to generate forecasts in situations of extreme seasonality. Traditional time-series forecasting methods, even when enhanced by the use of event flags to identify the selling period, can be heavily influenced by all of the zero values outside the selling period, and perform poorly as a result.

* This article was adapted from the SAS whitepaper "Forecasting by Time Compression: Forecasting Highly Seasonal Items in Retail."

Using the time-compression method, all observations outside the selling season are compressed into one observation having zero sales. For example, if an item is sold for 10 weeks of the year, the compressed series will be 12 observations for the year. At this point, regular time-series methods can be applied to the compressed weekly series, setting the "seasonality" parameter to 12 (instead of 52, as it would normally be with weekly data).

After a model is selected and forecasts are generated, the results are uncompressed, adding back in all the zero-sales weeks to return to a 52-week year. This approach may provide forecast accuracy that is superior to using traditional methods.

Introduction

Demand forecasting is a challenging activity. This is particularly true for the retail industry, where more rigorous forecasting and planning processes and statistical tools are beginning to augment the "art" of merchandising and replenishment.

Retailers want to know what will sell at which price points, what promotions will be most effective, and what will be the best clearance strategy when a product is out of season. These questions all have a basis in forecasting.

Forecasting is considered an important function, and it follows the same iterative process with each forecasting and planning cycle. The process usually involves generating updated forecasts based on the most recent data, reconciling forecasts in a hierarchical manner, identifying and remedying problematic forecasts, adding judgmental overrides to the forecasts based on business knowledge, and publishing the forecasts to other systems or as reports. However, many organizations still rely solely on readily available tools that their employees are comfortable with rather than using specialized forecasting software.

Given the relatively small number of forecasters in most organizations, a large degree of automation is often required to complete the forecasting process in the time available for each planning period. Retailers still may be faced with some types of forecasts that need special consideration—for example, forecasting the demand of products that are only sold during one season, or around a holiday.

This paper will suggest an approach for dealing with these kinds of highly seasonal forecasts. It provides an illustrative example based on real-life data.

The Challenge

Retailers are commonly faced with producing predictions for items that are only sold at a certain time of the year. A typical example would be special items that are available only during a short season—such as a holiday period. The

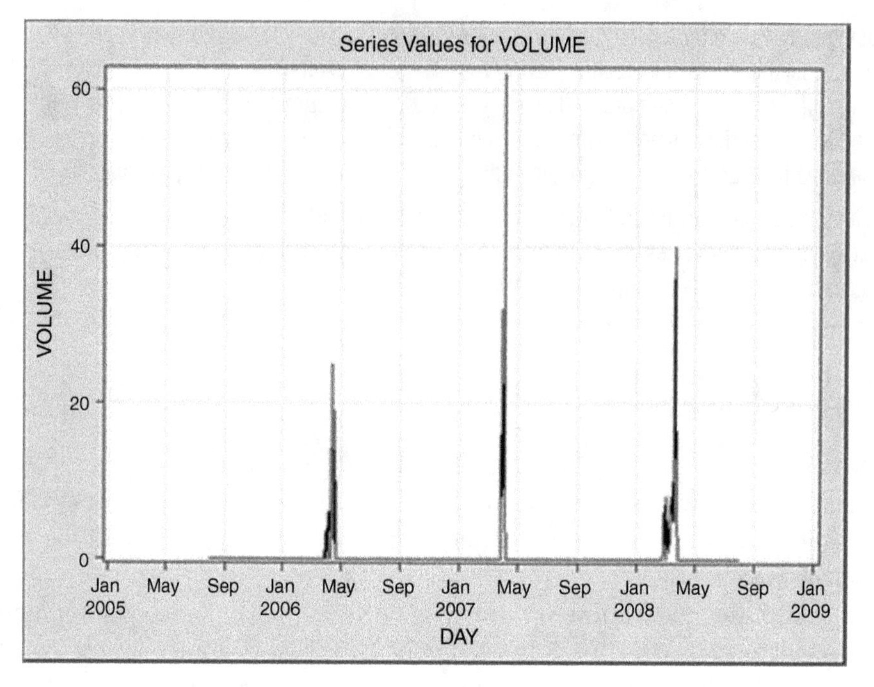

Figure 2.5 Daily Sales Volume

challenge for a typical retailer is to produce a forecast for these types of items, because they need to let their suppliers know in advance how many items they will need. Sometimes the lead time can be up to six months or more. Ordering too few items will result in stockouts, which lead to lost revenue and customer dissatisfaction. At the same time, ordering too many items will result in overstocks, leading to waste or costly markdowns.

From a statistical forecasting perspective, tackling this challenge is difficult. Most values of the underlying time series will be zero (when the product is out of season)—but there are huge sales spikes when the product is in season.

A typical graphical representation for such an item is provided in Figure 2.5. In this case, we are trying to model a special beverage, which is sold only during Easter. The data at hand is in a daily format—beginning on Monday, August 1, 2005, and ending on Thursday, July 31, 2008.

Our task is to come up with a forecast for the Easter period 2009 in weekly numbers.

Approach 1: Traditional Forecasting

As a first step, we will try to fit traditional statistical forecasting models. Because we need to provide weekly forecasts, we will first aggregate the daily data to weekly levels (see Figure 2.6). This will remove some of the random noise in the data. We also will add additional values to our time series to get complete

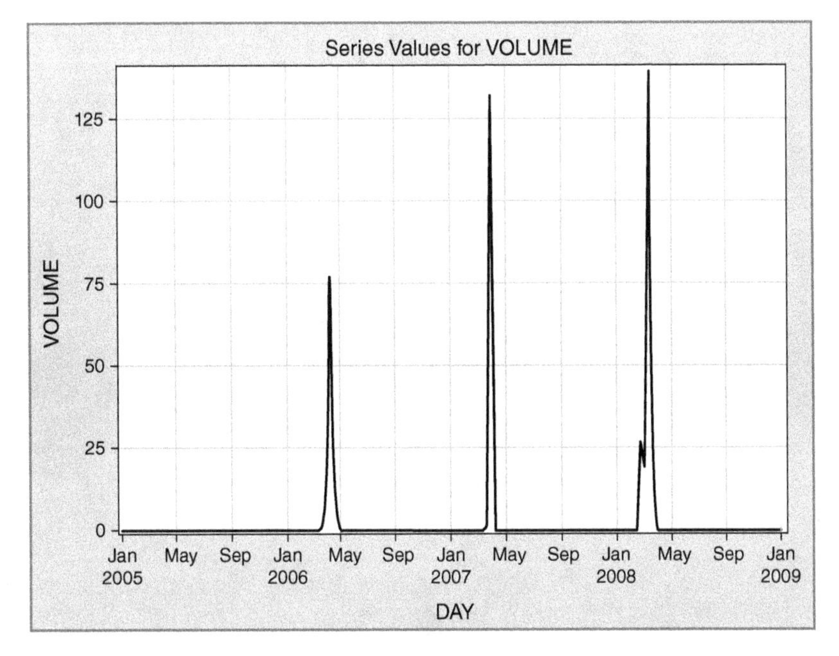

Figure 2.6 Weekly Sales Volume

yearly information. This can be done easily, as we know the sales before and after the Easter selling period are zero.

Because no sales information was provided for Easter 2005, we will drop the year 2005 from our analysis. After doing this we can use forecasting software to come up with a decent forecasting model. In addition, we will define some events that flag the Easter holiday—hoping that this information will improve the models. For this retailer, the sales pattern of the Easter beverage always starts three weeks before Easter and continues through one week after Easter.

After using these steps, it occurs to us that while the forecasting software is capable of identifying the Easter pattern (Figure 2.7), it does not identify the sales increase accurately enough (Figure 2.8). This behavior is caused by the particular structure of our data, which contains mostly zeros.

Approach 2: Forecasting by Time Compression

Rather than trying to come up with better statistical forecasting models by fine-tuning our initial model, we want to try an alternative approach. Our idea is to compress the data by putting all dates that are zero into one bucket. Then we want to create a forecasting model based on this new time series. After forecasting we will transform the data back to its original format.

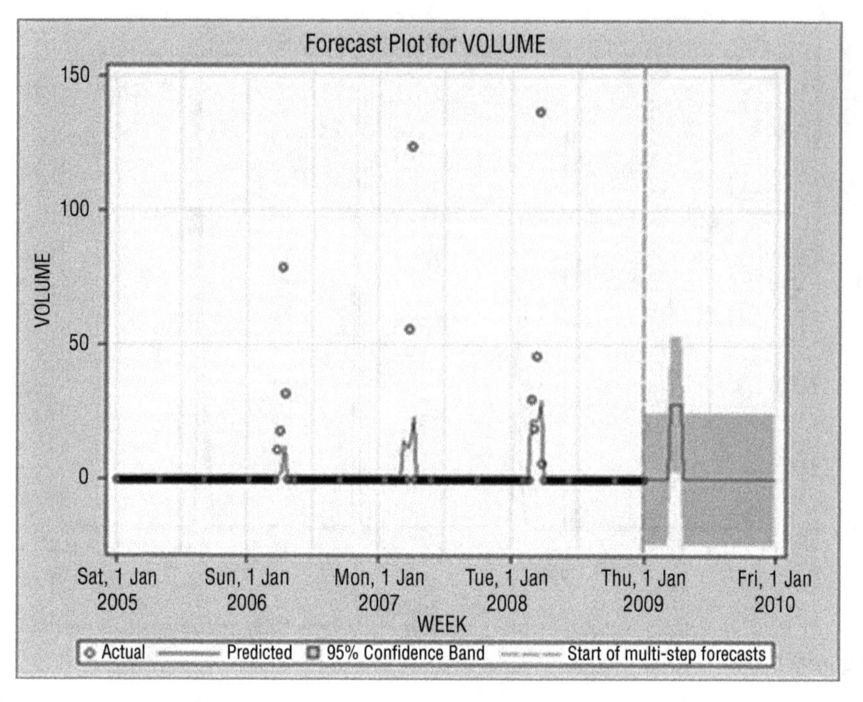

Figure 2.7 Forecast Model Generated by Forecasting Software

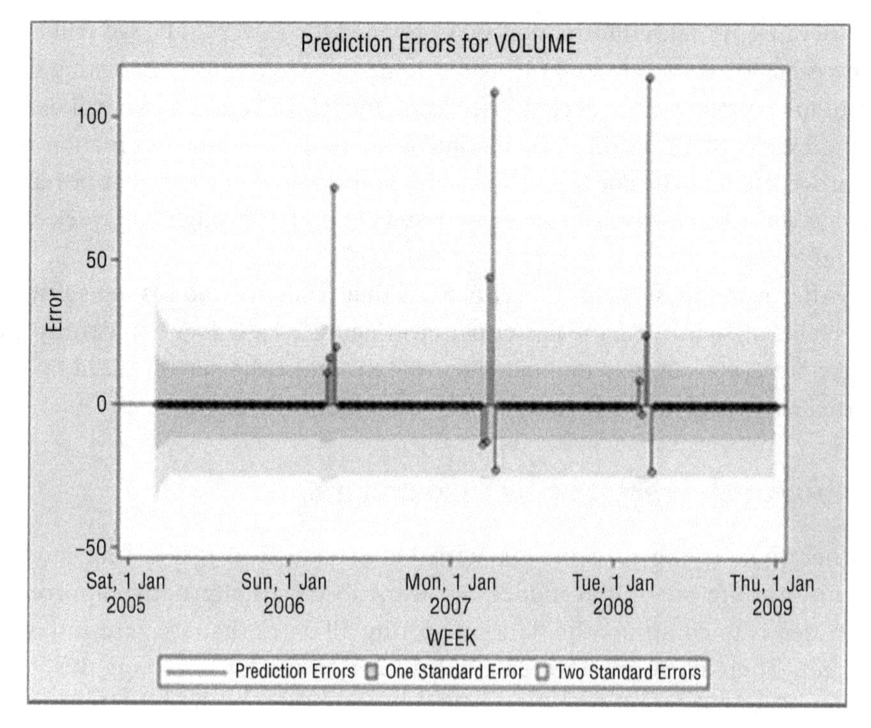

Figure 2.8 Model Fit Errors

Step 1: Compress Time Dimension of Original Series

To compress our original time series, we need to flag the Easter event first and then merge all observations that do not happen during the Easter event into another observation (with volume zero). Due to the structure of the sales pattern (sales occur beginning three weeks before Easter, during Easter week, and for one week after Easter), our "Easter event" bucket will consist of five points. We then compress all of the year's time periods before the Easter event into one point (with value zero), and all time periods after that for the year into one point (with value zero). This results in seven observations per year (Figure 2.9). Note that this also indicates our seasonality pattern (which is seven).

Step 2: Create Forecasting Model and Predictions

After creating the new series we can fit traditional statistical forecasting models using our forecasting software. In our case, an additive-winters exponential method gives the most appropriate fit (Figure 2.10).

Step 3: Transforming Forecasts Back to Original Time Format

Because we know about the future Easter period, it is fairly easy to back-transform the data into its original format. Again we will assume that no sales occur outside of the selling period, and we will set these values to zero in the forecasting horizon (Figure 2.11).

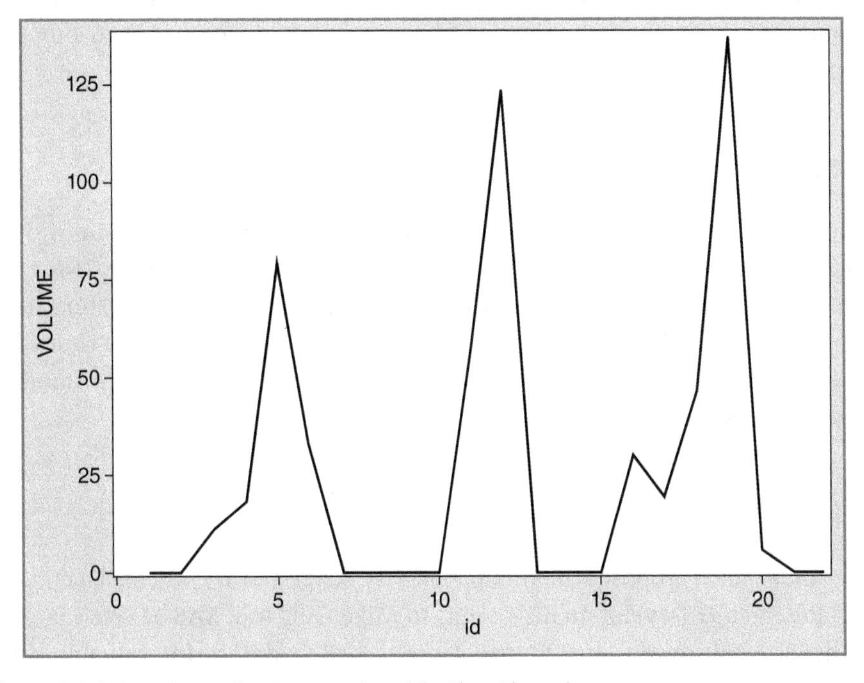

Figure 2.9 Sales Volume after Compression of the Time Dimension

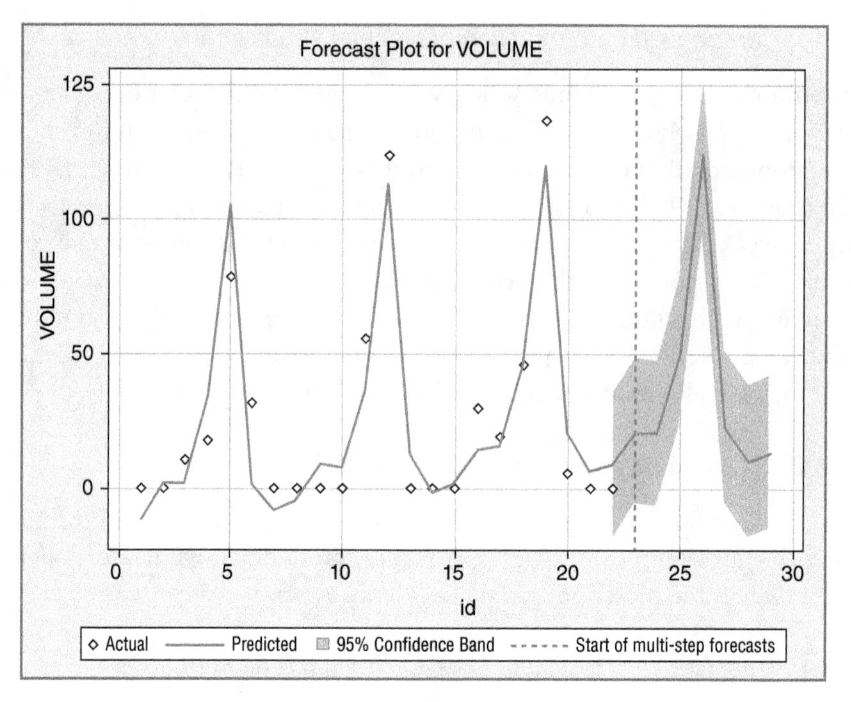

Figure 2.10 Forecast Model of the Compressed Volume

As we can see (Figure 2.12), our new forecasts not only identify our sales pattern accordingly; this time we get a better overall fit to history and, more important, we get better estimates of the sales spike compared to our first approach.

Conclusion

Forecasting data of highly seasonal items (items that are sold only for a short time during the year, but with large volumes) is a challenging task. Using the compression approach introduced in this paper, traditional forecasting techniques can be applied to transformed time series. Initial results seem to suggest that the accuracy of such an approach could be superior to a more standard way of time-series modeling.

Acknowledgments

The initial idea proposed in this paper was suggested by Michael Leonard, SAS Research & Development. Thanks to Mike Gilliland, SAS Marketing, Bob Lucas, SAS Education, and Snurre Jensen, SAS Denmark for valuable comments on the draft of this paper.

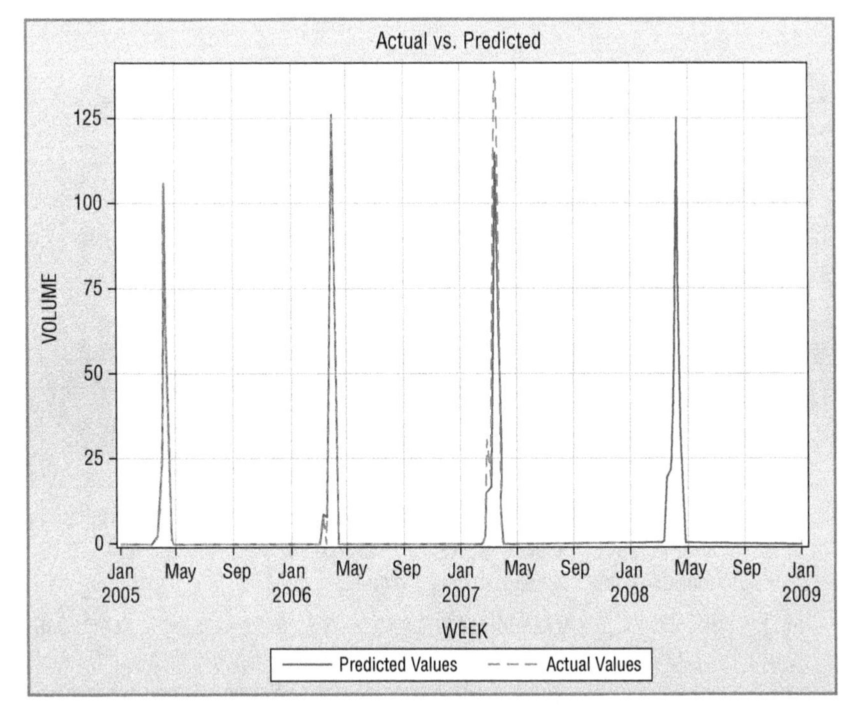

Figure 2.11 Sales and Forecast (after Transformation back to Weekly)

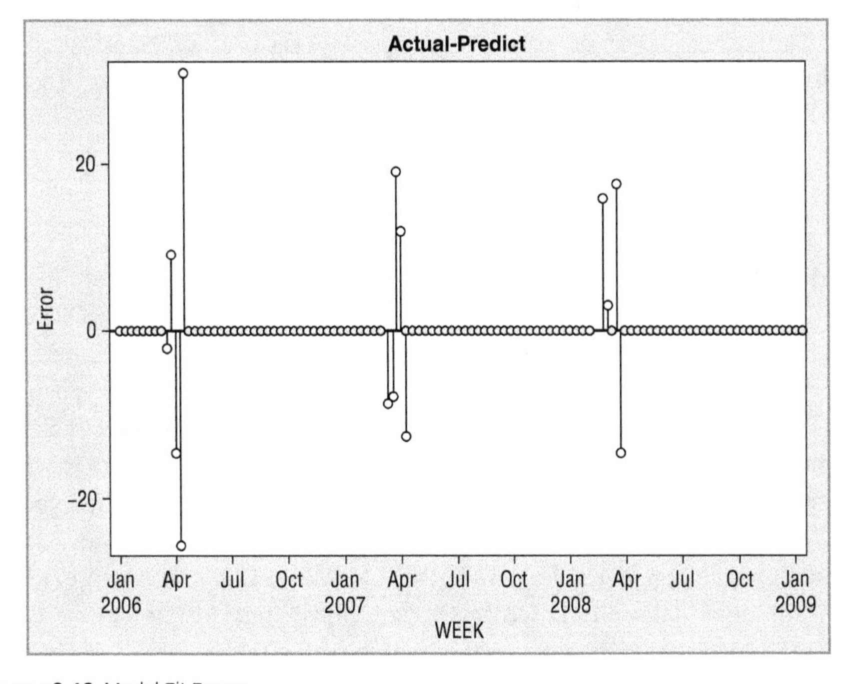

Figure 2.12 Model Fit Errors

REFERENCES

Brocklebank, John C., and David A. Dickey (2003). *SAS for Forecasting Time Series*, Second Edition. Cary, NC: SAS Institute and John Wiley & Sons.

Box, G. E. P, G. M., Jenkins, and G. C. Reinsel (1994). *Time Series Analysis: Forecasting and Control*. Englewood Cliffs, NJ: Prentice Hall, Inc.

Makridakis, S. G., S. C. Wheelwright, and R. J. Hyndman (1997). *Forecasting: Methods and Application*. New York: John Wiley & Sons.

2.7 DATA MINING FOR FORECASTING: AN INTRODUCTION

Chip Wells and Tim Rey

The next two articles are adapted from the book *Applied Data Mining for Forecasting Using SAS®* by Rey, Kordon, and Wells (2012). Chip Wells and Tim Rey show how to apply data-mining methods to large-scale forecasting, where there may be thousands of series to be forecast, and thousands of possible explanatory variables.

Data mining is not used for univariate forecasting methods such as exponential smoothing, where the values of the time series itself (e.g., weekly sales) are the only data used, which is to say there are no explanatory variables. However, for regression models and other methods that incorporate explanatory variables (e.g., price, advertising, economic conditions, weather, etc.), data mining can be used to identify the most relevant variables to include in the model.

This article includes a list of available time-series data sets, from both government and commercial sources. Many of the data services are free and there are systems available to automatically load external time series into an organization's internal databases.

There are also useful references on the data mining process known as *variable* or *feature selection*, which is how many candidate explanatory variables are reduced to a limited number for inclusion in the forecasting model.

Introduction, Value Proposition, and Prerequisites

Big data means different things to different people. In the context of forecasting, the savvy decision maker needs to find ways to derive value from big data. Data mining for forecasting offers the opportunity to leverage the numerous sources of time-series data, both internal and external, now readily available to the business decision maker, into actionable strategies that can directly impact profitability. Deciding what to make, when to make it, and for whom is a complex process. Understanding what factors drive demand, and how these factors (e.g., raw materials, logistics, labor, etc.) interact with production processes or demand and change over time, are keys to deriving value in this context.

Traditional data-mining processes, methods, and technology oriented to static type data (data not having a time-series framework) have grown immensely in the last quarter century (Fayyad et al. (1996), Cabena et al.

(1998), Berry (2000), Pyle (2003), Duling and Thompson (2005), Rey and Kalos (2005), Kurgan and Musilek (2006), Han et al. (2012)). These references speak to the process as well as myriad of methods aimed at building prediction models on data that does not have a time-series framework. The idea motivating this paper is that there is significant value in the interdisciplinary notion of data mining for forecasting. That is, the use of time-series based methods to mine data collected over time.

This value comes in many forms. Obviously being more accurate when it comes to deciding what to make when and for whom can help immensely from an inventory cost reduction as well as a revenue optimization view point, not to mention customer satisfaction and loyalty. But there is also value in capturing a subject matter expert's knowledge of the company's market dynamics. Doing so in terms of mathematical models helps to institutionalize corporate knowledge. When done properly, the ensuing equations become intellectual property that can be leveraged across the company. This is true even if the data sources are public, since it is how the data is used that creates intellectual property, and that is in fact proprietary.

There are three prerequisites to consider in the successful implementation of a data mining for time-series approach: understanding the usefulness of forecasts at different time horizons, differentiating planning and forecasting, and, finally, getting all stakeholders on the same page in forecast implementation.

One primary difference between traditional and time-series data mining is that, in the latter, the time horizon of the prediction plays a key role. For reference purposes, short-ranged forecasts are defined herein as 1 to 3 years, medium-range forecasts are defined as 3 to 5 years, and long-term forecasts are defined as greater than 5 years. The authors agree that anything greater than 10 years should be considered a scenario rather than a forecast.[1] Finance groups generally control the "planning" roll up process for corporations and deliver "the" number that the company plans against and reports to Wall Street. Strategy groups are always in need for medium (1–3 years) to long range (3+ years) forecasts for strategic planning. Executive sales and operations planning (ESOP) processes demand medium range forecasts for resource and asset planning. Marketing and Sales organizations always need short to medium range forecasts for planning purposes. New business development incorporates medium to long-range forecasts in the NPV process for evaluating new business opportunities. Business managers rely heavily on short- and medium-term forecasts for their own businesses data but also need to know the same about the market. Since every penny a purchasing organization can save a company goes straight to the bottom line, it behooves a company's purchasing organization to develop and support high-quality forecasts for raw materials, logistics costs, materials and supplies, as well as services.

However, regardless of the needs and aims of various stakeholder groups, differentiating a "planning" process from a "forecasting" process is critical. Companies do need to have a plan that is aspired to. Business leaders have to be responsible for the plan. But, to claim that this plan is a "forecast" can be disastrous. Plans are what we "feel we can do," while forecasts are mathematical estimates of what is most likely. These are not the same, and both should be maintained. The accuracy of both should be tracked over a long period of time. When reported to Wall Street, accuracy is more important than precision. Being closer to the wrong number does not help.

Given that so many groups within an organization have similar forecasting needs, a best practice is to move toward a "one number" framework for the whole company. If Finance, Strategy, Marketing/Sales, Business ESOP, NBD, Supply Chain, and Purchasing are not using the "same numbers," tremendous waste can result. This waste can take the form of rework and/or mismanagement given an organization is not totally lined up to the same numbers. This then calls for a more centralized approach to deliver forecasts for a corporation, which is balanced with input from the business planning function. Chase (2013) presents this corporate framework for centralized forecasting in his book *Demand-Driven Forecasting.*

Raw ingredients in a successful forecasting implementation are historical time-series data on the *Y* variables that drive business value and a selected group of explanatory (*X*) variables that influence them. Creating time-series data involves choosing a time interval and method for accumulation. Choosing the group of explanatory variables involves eliminating irrelevant and redundant candidates for each *Y*.[2] These tasks are interrelated. For example, if demand is impacted by own price and prices of related substitute and complementary goods, and if prices are commonly reset about once a month, then monthly accumulation should give the analyst the best look at candidate price correlation patterns with various demand series.

The remainder of this article presents an overview of techniques and tools that have proven to be effective and efficient in producing the raw materials for a successful forecasting analysis. The context of the presentation is a large scale forecasting implementation, and *Big Data*—that is, thousands of *Y* and candidate *X* series, is the starting point.

Big Data in Data Mining for Forecasting

Big Data Source Overview

Over the last 15 years or so, there has been an explosion in the amount of external time series based data available to businesses. Commercial sources include: Global Insights, Euromonitor, CMAI, Bloomberg, Nielsen, Moody's,

Economy.com, and Economagic. There are also government sources such as: www.census.gov, www.stastics.gov.uk/statbase, IQSS database, research .stlouisfed.org, imf.org, stat.wto.org, www2.lib.udel.edu, and sunsite.berkeley .edu. All provide some sort of time-series data—that is, data collected over time inclusive of a time stamp. Many of these services are for a fee; some are free. Global Insights (ihs.com) alone contains over 30,000,000 time series.

This wealth of additional information actually changes the way a company should approach the time-series forecasting problem in that new methods are necessary to determine which of the potentially thousands of useful time series variables should be considered in the exogenous variable forecasting problem. Business managers do not have the time to "scan" and plot all of these series for use in decision making.

Many of these external sources offer databases for historical time-series data but do not offer forecasts of these variables. Leading or forecasted values of model exogenous variables are necessary to create forecasts for the dependent or target variable. Other services, such as Global Insights, CMAI, and others, do offer lead forecasts.

Concerning internal data, IT Systems for collecting and managing data, such as SAP and others, have truly opened the door for businesses to get a handle on detailed historical static data for revenue, volume, price, costs, and could even include the whole product income statement. That is, the system architecture is actually designed to save historical data. Twenty-five years ago, IT managers worried about storage limitations and thus would "design out of the system" any useful historical detail for forecasting purposes. With the cost of storage being so cheap now, IT architectural designs have included "saving" various prorated levels of detail so that companies can take full advantage of this wealth of information.

Relevant Background on Time-Series Models

A couple of important features about time-series modeling are important at this point. First, the one thing that differentiates time-series data from simple static data is that the time-series data can be related to "itself" over time. This is called *serial correlation*. If simple regression or correlation techniques are used to try and relate one time series variable to another, and ignore possible serial correlation, the businessperson can be misled. So, rigorous statistical handling of this serial correlation is important.

The second feature is that there are two main classes of statistical forecasting approaches to consider. First there are *univariate* forecasting approaches. In this case, only the variable to be forecast (the Y or dependent variable) is considered in the modeling exercise. Historical trends, cycles, and seasonality of the Y itself are the only structures considered when building the forecasting model. There is no need for data mining in this context.

In the second approach—where the plethora of various time-series data sources comes in—various *X* or independent (exogenous) variables are used to help forecast the *Y* or dependent variable of interest. This approach is considered exogenous variable forecast model building. Businesses typically consider this value added; now we are trying to understand the *drivers* or *leading indicators*. The exogenous variable approach leads to the need for data mining for forecasting problems.

Though univariate or *Y*-only forecasts are often times very useful, and can be quite accurate in the short run, there are two things that they cannot do as well as the multivariate forecasts. First and foremost is providing an understanding of "the drivers" of the forecast. Business managers always want to know what "variables" (and in this case means what other time-series) "drive" the series they are trying to forecast. *Y*-only forecasts do not accommodate these drivers. Second, when using these drivers, the exogenous variable models can often forecast further and more accurately than the univariate forecasting models.

The recent 2008/2009 recession is evidence of a situation where the use of proper *X*s in an exogenous variable leading-indicator framework would have given some companies more warning of the dilemma ahead. Univariate forecasts were not able to capture this phenomenon as well as exogenous variable forecasts.

The external databases introduced above not only offer the *Y*s that businesses are trying to model (like that in NAICS or ISIC databases), but also provide potential *X*s (hypothesized drivers) for the multivariate (in *X*) forecasting problem. Ellis (2005) in "Ahead of the Curve" does a nice job of laying out the structure to use for determining what *X* variables to consider in a multivariate in *X* forecasting problem. Ellis provides a thought process that, when complemented with the data mining for forecasting process proposed herein, will help the business forecaster do a better job identifying key drivers as well as building useful forecasting models.

The use of exogenous variable forecasting not only manifests itself in potentially more accurate values for price, demand, costs, etc. in the future, but it also provides a basis for understanding the timing of changes in economic activity. Achuthan and Banerji (2004), in *Beating the Business Cycle,* along with Banerji (1999), present a compelling approach for determining potential *X*s to consider as leading indicators in forecasting models. Evans et al. (2002) as well (www.nber.org and www.conference-board.org) have developed frameworks for indicating large turns in economic activity for large regional economies as well as specific industries. A part of the process they outline identifies key drivers. In the end, much of this work speaks to the concept that, if studied over a long enough time frame, many of the structural relations between *Y* and *X* are fairly stable. This offers solace to the business decision maker and forecaster willing to learn how to use data mining techniques for forecasting in order to mine the time-series relationships in the data.

Many large companies have decided to include external data, such as that found in Global Insights as mentioned above, as part of their overall data architecture. Small internal computer systems are built to automatically move data from the external source to an internal database. This, accompanied with tools used to extract internal static data, allows bringing both the external *Y* and *X* data alongside the internal. Oftentimes the internal *Y* data are still in transactional form. Once properly processed, or aggregated, e.g., by simply summing over a consistent time interval like month and concatenated to a monthly time stamp, this time stamped data becomes time-series data. This database would now have the proper time stamp, include both internal and external *Y* and *X* data, and be all in one place. This time-series database is now the starting point for the data mining for forecasting multivariate modeling process.

Feature Selection: Origins and Necessary Refinements for Time Series

Various authors have defined the difference between *data mining* and classical statistical inference; Hand (1998), Glymour et al. (1997), and Kantardzic (2011) are notable examples. In a classical statistical framework, the scientific method (Cohen and Nagel, 1934) drives the approach. First, there is a particular research objective sought after. These objectives are often driven by first principles or the physics of the problem. This objective is then specified in the form of a hypothesis; from there a particular statistical "model" is proposed, which then is reflected in a particular experimental design. These experimental designs make the ensuing analysis much easier in that the *X*s are independent, or orthogonal to one another. This othogonality leads to perfect separation of the effects of the "drivers" therein. So, the data are then collected, the model is fit, and all previously specified hypotheses are tested using specific statistical approaches. Thus, very clean and specific cause and effect models can be built.

In contrast, in many business settings a set of "data" often times contains many *Y*s and *X*s, but has no particular modeling objective or hypothesis for being collected in the first place. This lack of an original objective often leads to the data having irrelevant and redundant candidate explanatory variables. Redundancy of explanatory variables is also known as *multicollinearity*—that is, the *X*s are actually related to one another. This makes building cause-and-effect models much more difficult. Data mining practitioners will "mine" this type of data in the sense that various statistical and machine learning methods are applied to the data looking for specific *X*s that might "predict" the *Y* with a certain level of accuracy. Data mining on static data is then the process of determining what set of *X*s best predicts the *Y*(s). This is a different approach than classical statistical inference using the scientific method. Building adequate *prediction* models does not necessarily mean an adequate *cause-and-effect* model was built.

Considering time-series data, a similar framework can be understood. The scientific method in time-series problems is driven by the "economics" or "physics" of the problem. Various "structural forms" may be hypothesized. Often times there is a small and limited set of *X*s, which are then used to build multivariate times-series forecasting models or small sets of linear models that are solved as a "set of simultaneous equations." Data mining for forecasting is a similar process to the "static" data-mining process. That is, given a set of *Y*s and *X*s in a time-series database, what *X*s do the best job of forecasting the *Y*s? In an industrial setting, unlike traditional data mining, a "data set" is not normally readily available for doing this data mining for forecasting exercise. There are particular approaches that in some sense follow the scientific method discussed earlier. The main difference herein will be that time-series data cannot be laid out in a *designed-experiment* fashion.

With regard to process, various authors have reported on data mining for static data. A paper by Azevedo and Santos (2008) compared the KDD process, SAS Institute's SEMMA process (Sample, Explore, Modify, Model, Assess), and the CRISP data-mining process. Rey and Kalos (2005) review the data-mining and modeling process used at the Dow Chemical Company. A common theme in all of these processes is that there are many candidate explanatory variables, and some methodology is necessary to reduce the number of *X*s provided as input to the particular modeling method of choice. This reduction is often referred to as Variable or Feature selection. Many researchers have studied and proposed numerous approaches for variable selection on static data (Koller and Sahami (1996), Guyon and Elisseeff (2003), etc.). One of the expositions of this article is an evolving area of research in variable selection for time-series type data.

NOTES

1. An important and related idea is that the range of the forecast horizon is a function of number of intervals in it. For example, a two-year horizon could be considered "short range" if the data has been accumulated to a year interval. Conversely, forecasting the level or rate of a variable at noon tomorrow may be considered long range if the data have a minute interval.
2. In a large-scale forecasting scenario, a useful first step in data mining for forecasting is to group *Y* variables based on product type, geographic distribution, or some other characteristic that drives common systematic variation. Candidate explanatory variables can then be selected for *Y* groups.

REFERENCES

Achuthan, L., and A. Banerji (2004). *Beating the Business Cycle*. New York: Doubleday.

Azevedo, A., and M. Santos (2008). KDD, SEMMA and CRISP-DM: A Parallel Overview. *Proceedings of the IADIS*.

Banerji, A. (1999). The lead profile and other nonparametrics to evaluate survey series as leading indicators. *24th CIRET Conference*.

Berry, M. (2000). *Data Mining Techniques and Algorithms*. Hoboken, NJ: John Wiley & Sons.

Cabena, P., P. Hadjinian, R. Stadler, J. Verhees, J., and A. Zanasi (1998). *Discovering Data Mining: From Concept to Implementation*. Englewood Cliffs, NJ: Prentice Hall.

Chase, C. (2013). *Demand-Driven Forecasting* (2nd ed.). Hoboken, NJ: John Wiley & Sons.

Cohen, M., and E. Nagel (1934). *An Introduction to Logic and Scientific Method*. Oxford, England: Harcourt, Brace.

CRISP-DM 1.0, SPSS, Inc., 2000.

Data Mining Using SAS Enterprise Miner: A Case Study Approach. Cary, NC: SAS Institute, 2003.

Duling, D., and W. Thompson (2005). What's New in SAS® Enterprise Miner™ 5.2. SUGI-31, Paper 082–31.

Ellis, J. (2005). *Ahead of the Curve: A Commonsense Guide to Forecasting Business and Market Cycles*. Boston, MA: Harvard Business School Press.

Evans, C., C. Liu, and G. Pham-Kanter (2002). The 2001 recession and the Chicago Fed National Activity Index: Identifying business cycle turning points. *Economic Perspectives* 26(3):26–43.

Fayyad, U., G. Piatesky-Shapiro, P. Smyth, and R. Uthurusamy (eds.). (1996). *Advances in Knowledge Discovery and Data Mining*. AAAI Press.

Glymour, C. et al. (1997). Statistical themes and lessons for data mining. *Data Mining and Knowledge Discovery* 1, 11–28. Netherlands: Kluwer Academic Publishers.

Guyon, I., and A. Elisseeff (2003). An introduction to variable and feature selection. *Journal of Machine Learning Research* 3 (3), 1157–1182.

Han, J., M. Kamber, and J. Pie (2012). *Data Mining: Concepts and techniques*. Amsterdam: Elsevier, Inc.

Hand, D. (1998). Data mining: Statistics and more? *The American Statistician* 52 (2), 112–118.

Kantardzic, M. (2011). *Data Mining: Concepts, Models, Methods, and Algorithms*. Piscataway, NJ: IEEE Press.

Koller, D., and M. Sahami (1996). Towards optimal feature selection. *International Conference on Machine Learning* 284–292.

Kurgan, L., and P. Musilek (2006). A survey of knowledge discover and data mining process models. *The Knowledge Engineering Review* 21 (1), 1–24.

Pyle, D. (2003). Business modeling and data mining. *Elsevier Science*.

Rey, T., and A. Kalos (2005). Data mining in the chemical industry. *Proceedings of the Eleventh ACM SIGKDD*.

2.8 PROCESS AND METHODS FOR DATA MINING FOR FORECASTING

Chip Wells and Tim Rey

Wells and Rey continue with presentation of a framework for implementing data mining directed to forecasting. It begins with understanding the strategic objectives of the business leadership.

Forecasting is a subset of *predictive modeling*. Its distinguishing feature is that the available data are in the form of time series (data in equally spaced time buckets such as weeks). When undertaking a data-mining project, transactional data (such as cash register receipts) may have to be accumulated into time series (daily sales revenue), and then further aggregated (e.g., weekly sales, quarterly sales) into a time-series hierarchy.

How granular these aggregations are is an important consideration—the intervals impact underlying patterns that determine forecastability. Consider a retailer who changes prices each week (some items going on sale, others coming off sale). If data are aggregated to monthly, detail of the price variation would be lost, diminishing their value for forecasting.

Other data preparation considerations are discussed, including the particular *roll-up method* utilized. Summing is appropriate for many things (units sold, revenue); averaging (for cost of goods) and minimum or maximum may be most suitable for inventory level. The key is to choose a method that best reveals the systemic patterns in the time series.

Wells and Rey emphasize that stakeholders with knowledge of the data can help the analyst understand the many available variables. The goal is to reduce possibly thousands of candidate variables to at most a few hundred (the *variable reduction* step) and, through *variable selection* via statistical and judgmental means, determine which of them to ultimately use in the forecasting models.

Integrating data mining and forecasting can provide the highest quality forecasts possible. It facilitates access to thousands of candidate variables and can do so in an expedient and cost effective manner.

This article provides a framework and overview of various methods for implementing a data mining for forecasting analysis (see Figure 2.13). Further details on process and methodologies as well as step-by-step applied examples are given in Rey et al. (2012), *Applied Data Mining for Forecasting Using SAS®*.

The process for developing time-series forecasting models with exogenous variables starts with understanding the strategic objectives of the business leadership sponsoring the project.

This is often secured via a written charter so as to document key objectives, scope, ownership, decisions, value, deliverables, timing, and costs. Understanding the system under study with the aid of the business subject-matter experts provides the proper environment for focusing on and solving the right problem. Determining from here what data help describe the system previously

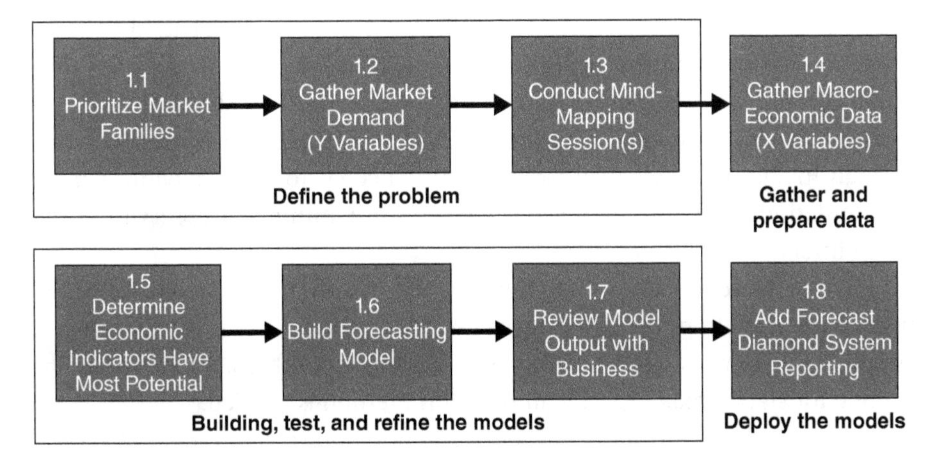

Figure 2.13 Model Development Process

defined can take some time. In the end, it has been shown that the most time consuming step in any data-mining prediction or forecasting problem is in the data processing step where data is created, extracted, cleaned, harmonized, and prepared for modeling. In the case of time-series data, there is often a need to harmonize the data to the same time frequency as the forecasting problem at hand.

Time-Series Data Creation

A key element in the process illustrated above is the selection of the time interval and accumulation method for analysis. Various stakeholder groups will have preferred intervals and summary methods that integrate well with their planning and reporting processes. However, the selection of the interval and method of implementation for time-series data mining and subsequent modeling should be based on the answer to the following question; What roll-up method yields the best "look" at systematic patterns of interest in the data? These include price effects, seasonality, technological cycles, and so on.

A fact that forecast stakeholder groups sometimes fail to fully appreciate is that the data are created in the process of a time-series analysis. Choices of an accumulation (transformation of time stamped into time-series data) and aggregation (creation of time-series hierarchies) intervals impact underlying patterns that determine the forecastability (or not) of data that flow into the models. For example, if prices are reset about once a week, but the selected interval is month or quarter, then variation in prices would likely be overly smoothed, and the forecastability of the data may be diminished.

Further, a roll-up method must be chosen. Total (sum) usually works well to construct an observation of units of demand per interval, and average is a reasonable choice for prices. However, the analyst must understand the data, and choose a method that will provide a conduit for systemic patterns to be emphasized in the time series. For example, inventories at levels around historical averages may have very little impact on demand. However, very low or high inventory levels may strongly influence customer behavior. A better accumulation method may be the maximum or minimum observation in a given interval in this case.

Given an interval and roll-up method, there is often a need to handle missing values. This may be in the form of forecasting forward, back casting, or simply filling in missing data points with various algorithms. So, just as in data mining for static data, a specific imputation method is needed.[1]

Three methods for input variable reduction and selection in a time-series setting are outlined below. In application, any one is usually implemented in an iterative way. That is, an accumulation interval and method are proposed, and a given method is run. Results are assessed for plausibility, correlation strength, and robustness by analysts and subject matter experts. Given the time available and the value of the series to be forecast, alternative intervals and methods are tried. The end goal is to find an interval and accumulation method that leads to the selection of unique explanatory variables whose variation is strongly correlated with and that leads variation in the *Y* variables.

Two Phases of Data Mining for Forecasting

The initial phase of the analysis is centered on the variable reduction step. In variable reduction, subject matter expertise is combined with various approaches (see below) to reduce the number of *X*s being considered while at the same time "explaining" or "characterizing" the key sources of variability in the *X*s regardless of the *Y*s. The goal is to reduce a large group of, possibly, thousands of candidate *X* variables down to a group size of a couple hundred. Stakeholders with knowledge of the data are instrumental here in helping analysts understand how variables are denominated and derived, what variables are truly redundant (e.g., different names for the same thing), and what *X*s are hypothesized to play key roles within various business lines and regions.

The later phase of a data mining for forecasting analysis is focused on variable selection. Variable selection relies more heavily on algorithms, and this step contains supervised methodologies since the *Y*s are now being considered. Various methods (some are outlined later) assess the candidate *X*s for correlation with the *Y*s. If a correlation exists, further steps are centered on identifying its dynamic structure (e.g., contemporaneous, lead, or delay). Subject-matter experts continue to play a role in variable selection. Their judgment in assessing the magnitude, robustness, and plausibility of automated feature selection algorithm results is a final sanity check that helps to ensure forecasts are as precise as possible.

Three Methods for Data Mining in Time Series

One of the key problems with using static variable reduction and variable selection approaches on time-series data are that, in order to overcome the method not being time-series based, the modeler has to include lags of the *X*s in the problem. This dramatically increases the size of the variable selection problem. For example, if there are 1,000 *X*s in the problem, and the data interval is quarter, the modeler would have to add a minimum of four lags for each *X* in the variable reduction or selection phase of the project. This is because the *Y* and *X* are potentially correlated at any or all positive lags of *Y* on *X*, 1 to 4, and thus now there are 4,000 "variables" to be processed.

In the traditional data-mining literature on static or "non" time-series data, many researchers have proposed numerous approaches for variable reduction and selection on static data (again Koller and Sahami (1996), Guyon and Elisseeff (2003), etc.). The serially correlated structure and the potential for correlation between candidate *X*s and *Y*s at various lags makes implementing traditional data mining techniques on time-series data problematic. New techniques are necessary for dimension reduction and model specification that accommodate the unique aspects of the problem. Below, we present three methods that have been found to be effective for mining time-series data.

1. A similarity analysis approach can be used for both variable reduction and variable selection. Leonard et al. (2008) introduce an approach for analyzing and measuring the similarity of multiple time-series variables. Unlike traditional time-series modeling for relating *Y* (target) to an *X* (input) similarity analysis leverages the fact that the data is ordered. A similarity measure can take various forms but essentially is a metric that measures the distance between the *X* and *Y* sequences keeping in mind ordering. Similarity can be used simply to get the similarity between the *Y*s and the *X*s but it can also be used as input to a variable clustering algorithm to then get clusters of *X*s to help reduce redundant information in the *X*s and thus reduce the number of *X*s.

2. A cointegration approach for variable selection is implemented. Engle and Granger (2001) discuss a cointegration test. Cointegration is a test of the economic theory that two variables move together in the long run. The traditional approach to measuring the relationship between *Y* and *X* would be to make each series stationary (generally by taking first differences) and

then see if they are related using a regression approach. This differencing may result in a loss of information about the long-run relationship. Differencing has been shown to be a harsh method for rendering a series stationary. Thus cointegration takes a different tack. First, the simple OLS regression model (called the cointegrating regression), where X is the independent variable, Y is the dependent variable, t is time, α and β are coefficients, and ε is the residual. The actual test statistic used to see if the residuals of the model are stationary is either the Dickey-Fuller test or the Durbin Watson test. In the implementation examples below the Dickey-Fuller test is used.

3. A cross-correlation approach for variable selection is described. A common approach used in time-series modeling for understanding the relationship between Y and X is called the cross-correlation function (CCF). A CCF is simply the bar chart of simple Pearson product moment correlations for each of the lags under study.

We have automated all of these methods and combine them into one table for review by the lead modeler and a panel of subject matter experts (see Table 2.14).

In these big data, time-series variable reduction and variable selection problems, we combine all three, along with the prioritized list of variables the business SMEs suggest, into one research database for studying (see Table 2.15).

Next, various forms of time-series models are developed; but, just as in the data mining case for statics data, there are some specific methods used to guard against overfitting that help provide a robust final model. This includes, but is not limited to, dividing the data into three parts: model, hold out, and out of sample. This is analogous to training, validating, and testing data sets in the static data-mining space. Various statistical measures are then used to choose the final model. Once the model is chosen, it is deployed using various technologies.

First and foremost, the reason for integrating data mining and forecasting is simply to provide the highest quality forecasts as possible. The unique advantage to this approach lies in having access to literally thousands of potential Xs and now a process and technology that enables doing the data mining on time-series type data in an efficient and effective manner. In the end, the business receives a solution with the best explanatory forecasting model as possible. With the tools now available through various technologies, this is something that can be done in an expedient and cost efficient manner.

Now that models of this nature are easier to build, they can then be used in other applications inclusive of scenario analysis, optimization problems, as well as Simulation problems (linear systems of equations as well as nonlinear system dynamics). So, all in all, the business decision maker will be prepared to make better decisions with these forecasting processes, methods, and technologies.

NAME OF FORMER VARIABLE	Cluster	RSQUARED	Overall_fit_metri	CCF_impact_factor	Coint	XYsimilarity
SA_XNET_NetExports_Q	2	0.75353	1.06783	0.41089	0.82275	1.2136
US_IndProdTextileCarpet_Q	3	0.88058	1.05689	0.96827	0.30134	1.41755
Ratio_NatGas_Crude_Q	10	0.76041	1.00322	0.35933	0.01225	1.13092
EMEA_D17_Purchases_USR_A	10	0.93457	0.95842	0.10296	0.03182	0.95809
EMEA_D341T2_CapEx_USR_A	2	0.90305	0.93874	0.12241	0.24041	1.2694
GB_UKIP3825_IP_Oequip_Q	14	0.76552	0.91922	0.91594	0.30694	1.29469
DE_RSH_RetailSales_M	23	0.92545	0.91316	1.04961	0.21038	1.35571
EMEA_D17_TotalSales_USR_A	10	0.93171	0.89764	0.03428	0.06698	0.98287
EMEA_D17_AppCons_USR_A	10	0.94363	0.8833	0.06878	0.00804	0.69742
GB_UKIPTOT_ProdIDX_Total_Q	14	0.92461	0.87273	1.0093	0.27083	1.38147
EMEA_D17_ValueAdded_USR_A	10	0.91154	0.85845	0	0.01527	1.02758
US_DemandPaintsCoatings_Q	3	0.64531	0.83516	0.81584	0.29373	1.34716
US_PPI_Semiconductors_Q	23	0.93715	0.83511	0.06393	0.0143	0.64068
ECRI_UKCSI_Growth_M	2	0.9333	0.72088	0.11517	0.13984	1.13519
GB_UKIP3831A_IP_Emach_Q	23	0.9621	0.68237	1.01475	0.33737	1.31429
ECRI_FRCMI_Level_M	10	0.93054	0.67723	0.96632	0.23854	1.42202
GB_UKIP3832_IP_Cequip_Q	14	0.42833	0.67295	1.16686	0.15831	1.31584
EMEA_D17_OpProfit_USR_A	10	0.86821	0.67029	0	0.10978	0.85769
DE_CRUDE_GAS_IP_Q	23	0.90158	0.6047	0.23504	0.24053	1.28992
EMEA_D341T2_OpProfit_USR_A	18	0.88417	0.6027	0.12454	0.23764	1.27323
EMEA_D36_ValueAdded_USR_A	10	0.96373	0.6014	0.1382	0.1756	1.36848
US_DemandElecWireCable_Q	10	0.80881	0.58226	0.83917	0.31734	1.29785
EMEA_A_Purchases_USR_A	1	0.97916	0.56493	0.81553	0.26345	1.31931
EMEA_D343_ValueAdded_USR_A	2	0.94043	0.56254	0.12296	0.27745	1.31606
EMEA_D34_OpProfit_USR_A	18	0.84732	0.55947	0.18405	0.41904	1.25575
EMEA_D34_CapEx_USR_A	2	0.97543	0.54202	0.12235	0.19853	1.24471
ECRI_UKCEI_Growth_M	2	0.92079	0.53747	0.13727	0.27509	1.01952
EMEA_A_TotalSales_USR_A	1	0.96984	0.53109	0.63316	0.2083	1.34253
EMEA_A_AppCons_USR_A	1	0.97568	0.52896	0.87562	0.2914	1.31233
WO_D17_OpProfit_USR_A	15	0.7888	0.5221	0.12699	0.07719	1.04882
US_DemandHydCement_Q	14	0.90516	0.503	0.99844	0.21543	1.31523
US_PPI_Coal_Q	8	0.9042	0.49311	1.05662	0.27391	1.46314
EMEA_Infrastr_USR_A	1	0.96235	0.48859	0.2685	0.73566	1.44824
EMEA_D34_ValueAdded_USR_A	2	0.95011	0.48524	0.11406	0.34027	1.2608
ECRI_FRLMI_Level_M	22	0.93451	0.47742	1.07022	0.15624	1.46193
SA_CR_Priv_Consumption_Q	4	0.96182	0.45843	0.33415	0.29073	1.1502
EMEA_GovtCons_USR_Q	21	0.92775	0.45494	0.1373	0.38077	1.40476
EMEA_D341T2_ValueAdded_USR_A	2	0.95336	0.44433	0.11341	0.28652	1.27862
EMEA_D343_OpProfit_USR_A	7	0.78424	0.44147	0.1242	0.25144	1.30967

Figure 2.14 Table Prepared for Review

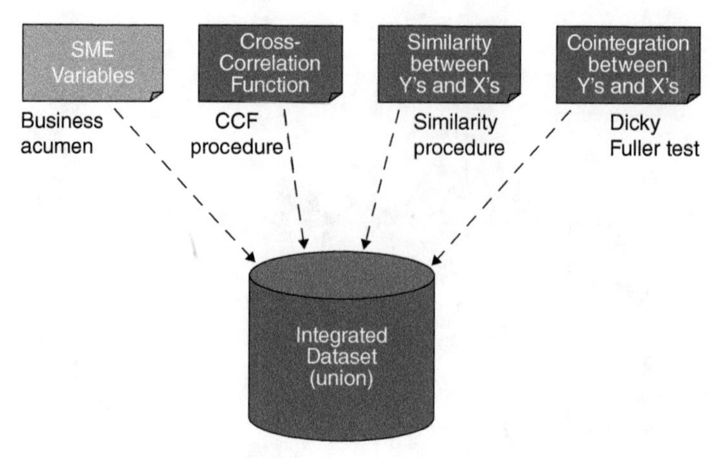

Figure 2.15 Research Database

NOTE

1. Traditional imputation methods for interval-valued variables, like average, usually perform poorly for time-series data. A straightforward and useful approach is to impute missing values using the one-step-ahead forecast from a simple time-series class of models like exponential smoothing.

REFERENCES

Engle, R., and W. Granger (2001). *Long-Run Economic Relationships: Readings in Cointegration*. New York: Oxford University Press.

Guyon, I., and A. Elisseeff (2003). An introduction to variable and feature selection. *Journal of Machine Learning Research* 3 (3), 1157–1182.

Koller, D., and M. Sahami (1996). Towards optimal feature selection. *International Conference on Machine Learning* 284–292.

Leonard, M., T. Lee, J. Sloan, and B. Elsheimer (2008). An introduction to similarity analysis using SAS®. SAS Institute White Paper.

Rey, T., A. Kordon, and C. Wells (2012). *Applied Data Mining for Forecasting Using SAS®*. Cary, NC: SAS Institute Inc.

2.9 WORST-CASE SCENARIOS IN FORECASTING: HOW BAD CAN THINGS GET?*

Roy Batchelor

Conventional business forecasting systems are not set up to tell us about extreme events. That is the conclusion drawn by Roy Batchelor in this discussion of *downside risk*.

* This article originally appeared in *Foresight: International Journal of Applied Forecasting* (Summer 2010), and appears here courtesy of the International Institute of Forecasters.

The problem is that standard statistical models provide misleading evidence for defining the "worst-case" possibilities when there is a serious shock to the business, as happened during the world's 2008 financial crisis. Typical worst-case forecasts are liable to be less severe than the worst that actually plays out. While recognition of this caveat is important in itself, there are ways to model the impacts of extreme events and thus derive a realistic indication of downside risk.

Batchelor illustrates what needs to be done to more accurately determine how bad things can get. Among his key points:

- Serious shocks normally increase the volatility of sales: This extra volatility has to be modeled appropriately.
- One modeling approach used in finance is called GARCH, a method that assumes that volatility and hence expected forecast errors increase after a large external shock.

Batchelor provides a case study of automobile sales to illustrate how a GARCH model provides a more realistic forecast of the downside risk facing this industry.

When forecasting extreme events, it is important to understand that the worst is yet to come. The worst thing that has already happened so far is just a *best-case* estimate of the worst that can possibly happen. Things can always get worse than they have ever been before.

Worst-Case Damage from a Blowout in the Gulf of Mexico

According to news reports, the main contingency plan foresaw a blowout with a worst-case spill of 40 million gallons in total. During the first three months, millions of gallons have been gushing per day. Regulatory agencies based their efforts on worst-case scenarios that weren't nearly worst case.

Introduction

Throughout the recent recession, companies have watched sales and production shrink by unprecedented amounts. Month after month, outturns have not merely fallen short of central forecasts but have crashed through the lower limits of prediction intervals churned out by statistical models. Conventional business-forecasting systems are just not set up to tell us about extreme events.

Downside risk has long been a central concern of financial forecasters. In the financial markets, high volatility in prices means large potential losses for investors, and risk-averse hedgers will pay more for insurance against adverse events. Option pricing theory ties the cost of insurance directly to the forecast of volatility of future price changes. A massive academic and practitioner literature has sprung up, focused on getting good predictions of whether share prices, currencies, and commodities are likely to become more or less volatile in the future.

Volatility changes can be forecast. Day-to-day price changes are close to random, but the volatility of these price changes is serially correlated: If there is a big price change (up or down) on one day, it is more likely than not that there will be a big price change the following day (down or up, we don't know which).

More recently, downside risk has become an important issue for business forecasters who are concerned with future sales, rather than prices on the financial markets. Most companies try to define *worst-case scenarios* for sales. Models of inventory control rely heavily on estimates of the future volatility of demand. Yet somehow, the well-developed technology of volatility forecasting has not been transferred into the business domain. To see what that would involve, I have set out below the procedure for defining a worst-case scenario that would follow from reading a basic business forecasting text. Then I illustrate how the transfer of a small piece of volatility forecasting technology—the GARCH variance model—from a financial to a business-forecasting environment can help quantify downside risk.

A Standard View of New Car Sales

Consider the point of view of a forecaster trying to predict new-car sales in the U.S. through the 2008–2009 recession. Imagine we are in early September 2008. We have a preliminary estimate of August sales of around 630 thousand vehicles. This was about 10% lower than August of a year earlier, but still well within the range of 500–800 thousand that had been the norm since 2000. Visual inspection of the monthly data on Figure 2.16 suggests that a worst-case scenario would be monthly sales below 500 thousand, an event that happened in only three of the previous 103 months.

To generate a forecast for September 2008 onwards, we need a model for car sales. I have used a conventional time-series representation using data back to 1980, a seasonal ARIMA model. The forecasts from this model are shown on Figure 2.17, in the form that is generated by most standard business-software packages. This shows expected sales (light gray line) and upper and lower bounds to the 95% prediction interval. The idea is that, in 95% of forecast months, sales should lie within these limits. Sales are forecast to be around 600 thousand cars per month, with some seasonal fluctuations. The bad case is for sales to fall below 494 thousand in September. The estimated reliability of the central forecast is reflected in its standard error, which we could loosely define as the size of a typical monthly error. Larger values of the standard deviation imply less reliability. This lower bound is around two standard errors below the expected level of sales, so the standard error of our one-month-ahead forecast is about $\frac{1}{2} \times (600 - 494) = 53$ thousand cars, or about 9% of the central forecast.

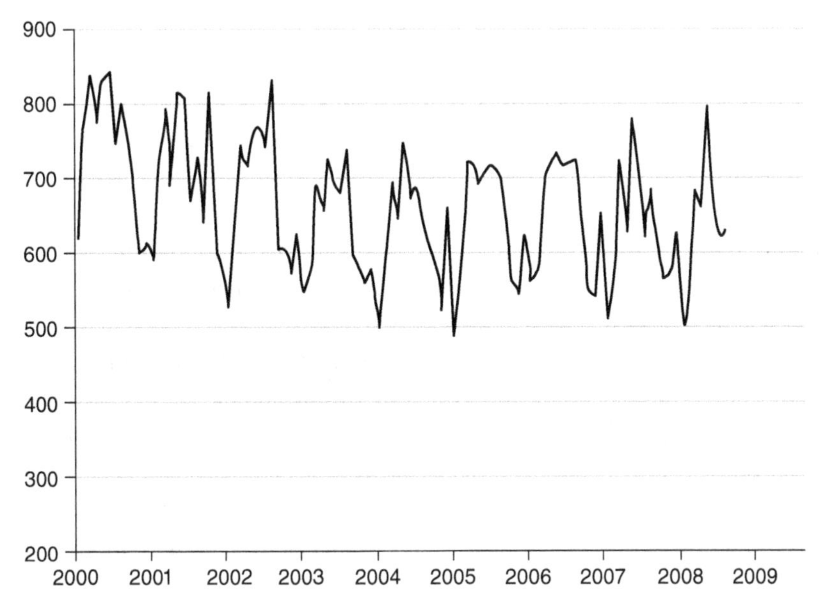

Figure 2.16 New Car Sales, January 2000–August 2008 (thousands)

What actually happened in September 2008, the month of the Lehman bankruptcy, was that consumer confidence plummeted, spending contracted across the economy, and car sales fell to an all-time low of 481 thousand, below the model's bad-case estimate. Of course, we expect there to be two to three months in every decade when sales fall below the lower prediction bound. This was an extreme adverse event, and leads to our key question: Given such a shock, how much worse can things get?

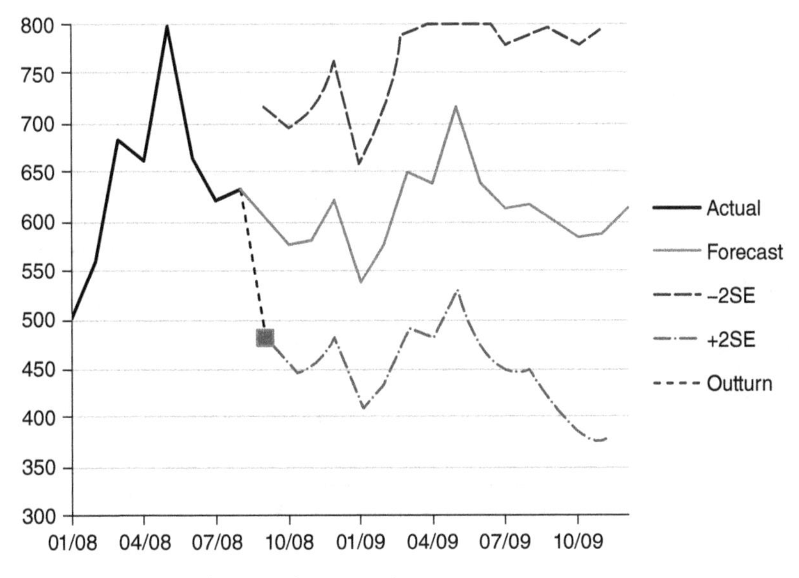

Figure 2.17 Forecasts and Outturn for September 2008

Let's stick with our conventional model and make a new set of forecasts for October 2008 and beyond, in light of information about the collapse in sales in September. The new path of expected sales and lower bound to the 95% prediction interval are shown in Figure 2.18. Sales are predicted to rebound to 505 thousand and then continue along a path somewhat lower than had been forecast a month earlier. Very sensibly, part of the fall in sales in September is treated as a temporary effect that will be offset in the following month, and part is treated as a signal that the underlying level of the series has permanently fallen.

Less sensible is what happens to the prediction interval. The bad case is now for sales to be 413 thousand. This is 92 thousand below the mean forecast, suggesting a standard error of 92/2 = 46 thousand. This is actually lower than a month earlier, and still only 9% of the new mean forecast. So, after the worst shock to car sales in living memory, the standard business-forecasting model suggests that our forecasts will be just as reliable as they were before the shock happened!

To underline how unrealistic this is, Figure 2.18 also shows that sales in October again fell below the model-generated lower prediction bound. Two successive outcomes below the lower bound is a very unusual occurrence and should make us reconsider how our bad-case forecast has been constructed. We could keep going—but, month after month, the standard error of the one-month-ahead forecast would stay stuck at about 9% of the forecast level, regardless of whether the economic conditions were calm or stormy.

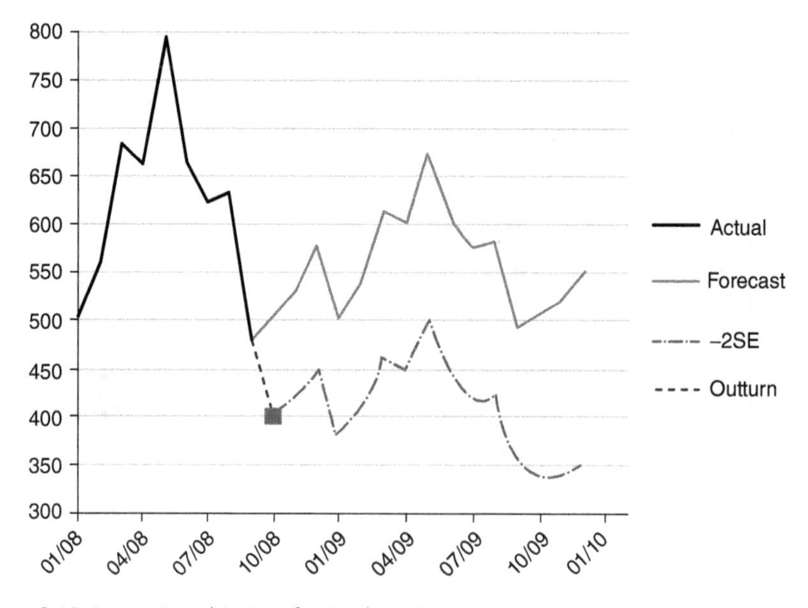

Figure 2.18 Forecasts and Outturn for October 2008

Time-Varying Volatility in Car Sales

The problem is that conventional time-series and regression models assume that the distribution of shocks to the system stays unchanged over time. Sometimes shocks are large and sometimes small, but these are treated as random draws from an underlying probability distribution that has a constant volatility. Prediction intervals from these models are based on an estimate of the average volatility of residuals over the whole sample used in model estimation. When a new observation appears, no matter how extreme it is, it has only a marginal effect on the estimated variance of residuals, and hence scarcely affects prediction intervals.

This assumption of constant volatility of shocks—called homoscedasticity—is not one that would be entertained in any model of financial markets, where it is plain that periods of steady growth in markets are punctuated by booms and crashes, during which volatility rises sharply. Since the Nobel Prize–winning economist Rob Engle developed the so-called ARCH (autoregressive conditional heteroscedasticity) model in the 1980s, it has become standard to characterize financial time series by some variant of this model. Financial economists are also reluctant to assume that shocks are normally distributed, preferring *fat-tailed* distributions such as the *t*-distribution, which allow extreme events to occur more frequently than suggested by the normal curve.

In the most popular "generalized ARCH" or GARCH model, there is some long-term underlying average variance, but in the short term the variance of potential shocks can rise above this underlying level if there is an unexpectedly large shock (= large forecast error) to the series being modeled. I describe the GARCH model in the article appendix.

Regression packages churn out tests for normality in residuals (Jarque Bera test) and for ARCH errors (Engle's Lagrange multiplier test). These are often ignored because they do not bias central forecasts. They are critical, however, for constructing prediction intervals. Therefore, we can easily test whether shocks to car sales can be described by a GARCH model and whether their distribution contains more extreme events than normal. The answer is yes, and yes. Volatility in car sales does rise after unusually large and unexpected increases and decreases in sales. When shocks occur, there are more large changes than the normal curve would lead us to expect.

Let's revisit the forecasts for September and October 2008, using the same ARIMA model for car sales but allowing the distribution of shocks to be fat-tailed and have time-varying volatility. Figure 2.19 shows the effect of the GARCH assumption on the mean forecast and the lower prediction interval bound. The mean forecast is unchanged. However, the large shock that occurred in September 2008 has caused the model to revise sharply upward its

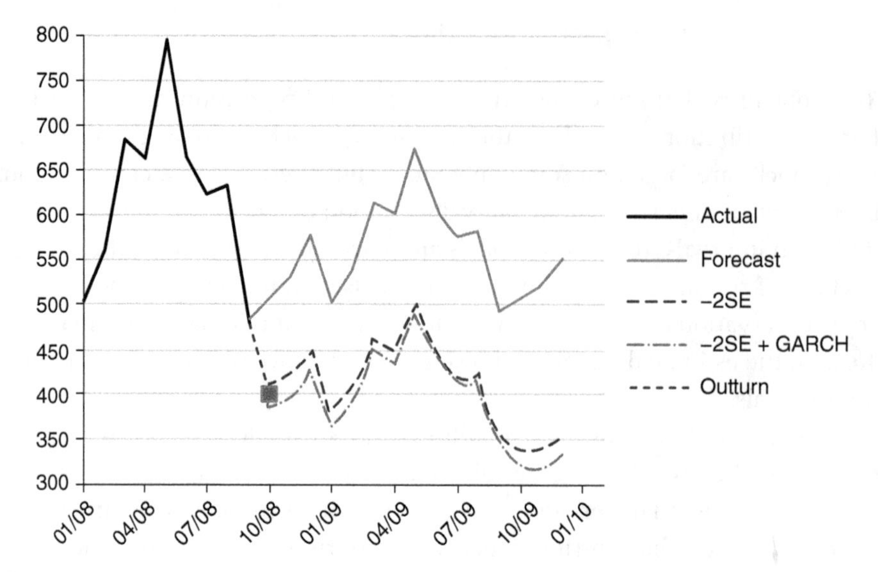

Figure 2.19 Lower 95% Prediction Bounds: Conventional vs. GARCH

estimate of the likely volatility of future shocks. The lower prediction bound for October is now 386 thousand, much lower than the 413 thousand estimated by the conventional model.

The outturn of 400 thousand is now inside rather than outside the prediction interval, and in that sense is less surprising. The fact that the October outturn is well below its expected value also means that, when we make our forecast for November, the GARCH model will again predict that volatility will be high, the prediction interval will be large, and the bad case will again be pretty bad.

Figure 2.20 shows the GARCH model estimates of how the standard deviation of shocks in the car market has changed from month to month since 2000. Although the average volatility is indeed around 9%, it can change drastically from year to year, and the very steep rise to over 15% in the recent recession shows that models of car sales that neglect changes in volatility provide us with a very poor guide to the risks faced by producers and dealers.

Note, by the way, that the most recent peak in volatility was due not to a collapse in sales, but to the splurge of buying in August 2009 in response to the "cash for clunkers" scheme that subsidized the replacement of old cars by new, more fuel-efficient vehicles.

Concluding Remarks

I have looked here at just one way of refining estimates of prediction intervals, using a simple model of time-varying volatility. There are many other ingenious devices for looking at downside risk in the financial-risk manager's

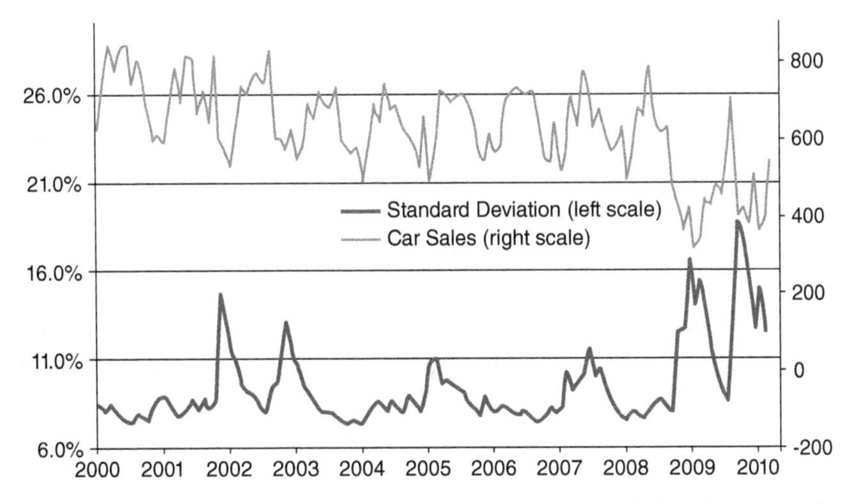

Figure 2.20 GARCH Estimates of a Time-Varying Volatility (Standard Deviation) of New-Car Sales

toolkit. For example, some analysts ignore all but the most extreme events and use special extreme value distributions to approximate the shape of the left tail of probability distributions. These methods are viable only if we have many observations on extreme events, and this in turn depends on the availability of high frequency, daily, or intraday data over a long time period—conditions that rule out most mainstream business-forecasting applications.

Business forecasters don't often take prediction intervals seriously and have some incentives to keep quiet about them. Most of the time, the intervals look very scary. With moderate sample sizes, the conventional 95% prediction interval for three to four steps ahead typically encompasses the whole range of historic data, and colleagues and clients might be tempted to conclude that you are saying, "Anything can happen."

Unfortunately, this is true. Indeed, results from forecasting competitions consistently tell us that, if anything, statistical prediction intervals are too narrow, since we can rarely identify the true model driving our data, and all series are subject to unforecastable structural change.

Frank Sinatra had the lyric "The best is yet to come" inscribed on his tombstone. When forecasting extreme events, it is important to understand, as well, that the worst is yet to come. The worst thing that has already happened in the sample is an upper estimate of the worst thing that can possibly happen. The honest answer to the question "How bad can things get?" is that they can always be worse than they have ever been before.

The value of models with time-varying volatility is that they help us quantify exactly how much worse things can get: whether right now we are confronted with a low or a normal degree of risk, or whether—as in September

2008—volatility is unusually high, and one of these unprecedentedly bad outcomes is most likely to occur.

Appendix: The GARCH Model

Suppose we are using time-series data to forecast a target variable y_t, based on a set of predictors x_t. Our standard regression model is $y_t = bx_t + u_t$ where b is a vector of coefficients, and the u_t are regression residuals ("shocks" that cannot be explained by the predictors x). The standard assumption is that the u_t are normally distributed and have a standard deviation σ that is constant over time.

The GARCH model allows σ to vary over time. Specifically, if at time $t - 1$ there was a big shock (so the squared residual u_{t-1}^2 is large), then volatility σ will rise. Conversely, if the last residual was small, then σ will fall. The exact formula used is $\sigma_t^2 = a_0 + a_1 u_{t-1}^2 + a_2 \sigma_{t-1}^2$. The larger the size of a_1 relative to a_2, then the greater the influence will be of the latest shock on our new estimate of volatility. The closer a_2 is to 1, the more long-lived will be the effect of a large shock on the volatility of Y in subsequent time periods.

The distribution of the shocks u_t need not be normal, and in the case of car sales follows a t-distribution with 8 degrees of freedom, showing that there are many more extreme events. In this case, the 95% prediction interval is not $\pm 2\sigma$, but $\pm 2.3\sigma$, making the margin of uncertainty wider and the worst-case scenario even worse.

For the U.S. car market, a_1 is 0.2 and highly significant, meaning that an unexpected 10% fall in sales leads to a rise of $\sqrt{(0.2 * 0.1^2)} = 4.5\%$ in the standard deviation of car sales in the following month. Therefore, if volatility had been around 8% of sales, an unexpected 10% fall in sales would cause volatility to rise to 12.5% of car sales—exactly what happened between September and October 2008.

The coefficient a_2 is 0.6, so the shock has a half-life of $1/(1 - 0.6) = 2.5$ months. That is, after the initial large impact of the shock, in the absence of further shocks volatility will die away toward a baseline level quite quickly over the following months.

There are many variants of the GARCH model. With car sales, reactions to good news and bad news are the same. This is why volatility rose after the unexpected surge in sales in August 2009. However, with stock prices, a large fall in the market increases volatility much more than a large rise, so when modeling the stock market the coefficient a_1 would be higher for negative shocks than for positive shocks.

A relatively nontechnical review of GARCH is given in Robert Engle (2001), "GARCH 101: The Use of ARCH/GARCH Models in Applied Econometrics," *Journal of Economic Perspectives* 15 (4), 157–168, downloadable at http://pages.stern.nyu.edu/~rengle/Garch101.doc.

2.10 GOOD PATTERNS, BAD PATTERNS*

Roy Batchelor

Forecasting by analogy is a common approach to new-product forecasting. Sales of previous products with attributes similar to the new product will, it is presumed, guide us to a more accurate sales forecast for the new product. But, as discussed in Michael Gilliland's "Worst Practices in New Product Forecasting" in Chapter 4, planners are apt to select inappropriate analogies—even "cherry picking" only the best performing previous products to justify a higher forecast for the new product. In this article, Roy Batchelor takes a broader look at the benefits and foibles of prediction from patterns.

When a disruptive event occurs (such as a new product introduction, a company takeover bid, or an economic crisis), our natural reaction is to try to predict its impact by looking for analogies whose outcomes are known. But while past occurrences of an event can serve as analogies for forecasting the impact of the new occurrence, Batchelor argues that the reliability of the analogy lies in the proper balance of data interpretation and good judgment.

Pattern-based forecasts can go horribly astray, as happened with a 2009 forecast of U.S. employment recovery based on analogy to several previous recessions. The problem lies in knowing which prior events are genuinely analogous to the current forecasting problem. In this case, the post-2008 recession was caused by a credit crisis, not by monetary policy or oil prices, as in the selected analogies. Based on the wrong analogies, the forecast drastically overestimated the speed of employment recovery.

Uncritical examination of the past data can lead to false analogies—the extrapolation of patterns that do not apply to the case at hand. Uncritical use of any and all apparently relevant data gives us statistically good-looking results, but at the expense of ignoring critical features of the event under scrutiny.

On the other hand, Batchelor notes, if we overtheorize about the current event without the capacity to build a credible statistical model, we may wind up looking at very few analogies, and placing too much weight on our fallible judgment.

Good judgment needs to be grounded in a coherent and data-congruent theory. Bad judgment is the result of belief, wishful thinking, and anecdote.

Introduction

When a disruptive event occurs, our natural reaction is to try to predict its impact by looking for analogies whose outcomes are known. In the financial markets, this is the basis for the event study methodology that analysts have used for over 40 years to predict the effects of corporate actions like takeovers and bond downgrades. In this article, we describe the method and look at whether and how it can be extended to mainstream business and economic

* This article originally appeared in *Foresight: International Journal of Applied Forecasting* (Spring 2012), and appears here courtesy of the International Institute of Forecasters.

forecasting problems. The key to success is finding the right analogies, which in turn requires a judicious blend of domain knowledge and data mining.

Good Patterns

Suppose we want to know what is likely to happen to the share price of a particular company before and after a takeover bid. There are unlikely to be similar events in the past history of the company, and share prices are in any case very volatile. In this situation, time-series analysis and causal model building are not of much use. However, many other companies have been subjected to takeover bids in the past, and we can learn by pooling data from these episodes and searching these data for patterns. This is the basis for the highly influential and intuitively appealing event study methodology introduced by Fama, Fisher, Jensen, and Roll (1969) and surveyed by John Binder (1998).

The idea is to collect share-price data on a sample of target companies for the days before and after the takeover announcement and line up these share-price windows to see if any patterns are apparent. Figure 2.21 illustrates the results of this process, for a small sample of five companies. The gray lines show the (excess = risk-adjusted) returns that an investor in each of these companies would have made by buying the shares 60 days ahead (day −60) of the takeover announcement (on day 0).

The experiences of the companies differ, but by averaging these returns we can see a pattern emerge, shown by the black line in the figure. Typically, there are no excess returns to be made until about 20 days before the

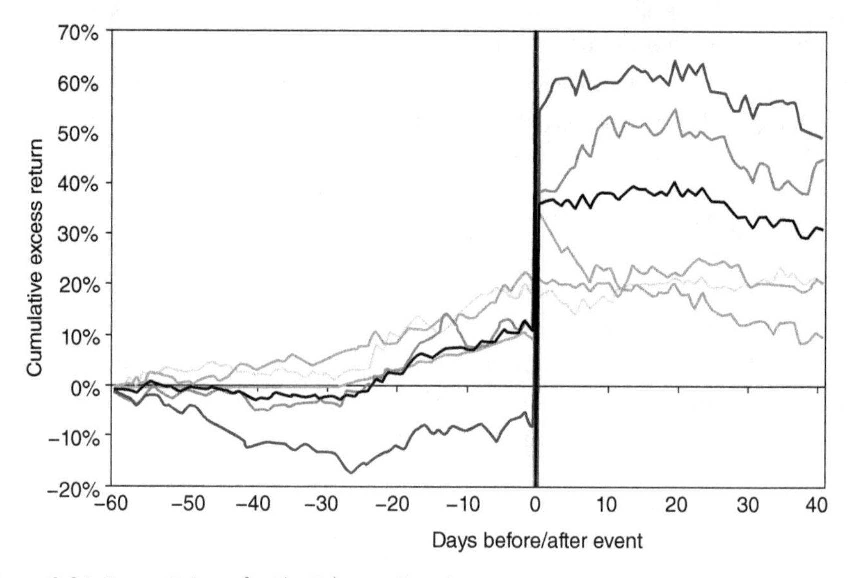

Figure 2.21 Excess Returns for Five Takeover Targets

takeover announcement, when returns gradually rise to around 10%. On the day of the announcement, share prices jump sharply by an additional 20%, and remain stable thereafter. This is why many hedge funds invest a lot of time and ingenuity in trying to identify potential takeover targets. It also explains why regulatory agencies try to identify and prosecute the insiders whose actions must be responsible for driving prices up before the public announcement of the takeover.

This is a straightforward and intuitive approach to forecasting, and we see examples in many other contexts, with varying degrees of sophistication. At the high-tech end of the forecasting business, statisticians trying to make sense of long but apparently erratic time series use nearest neighbor methods to look at the past history of the series to make forecasts based on patterns closest to those observed in the recent past. In organizations with sales and inventory data on many products, there are demonstrable benefits to pooling data for products that are related, especially if we weight these according to their similarity to the product we are trying to forecast (Duncan and colleagues, 2001). In the very practical business of figuring out the likely path for sales of new pharmaceutical or electronics products, planners often line up the sales paths following earlier launches of similar products and conjecture that the new product will follow a similar trajectory.

Bad Patterns

In the wrong hands, however, pattern-based forecasts can go horribly astray. The problem lies in knowing which prior events are genuinely analogous to the current forecasting problem. To illustrate, here are two examples of bad uses of a good methodology. In the first, data have been used uncritically, and not enough judgment has been applied. In the second, too much (biased) judgment has been applied, allowing forecasters to ignore relevant but unwelcome data.

Example 1: Not Enough Judgment

Since recession hit in 2008, newspapers and the blogosphere have been full of pictures trying to chart the likely progress of output and employment by looking at past recessions. Figure 2.22 provides a chart of U.S. nonfarm employment published on a website in February 2009. The lines show employment in the 60 months following the peak of each postwar U.S. business cycle. The path of employment in 2008 is shown by the firm black line, and the hope of the author was that previous patterns would give some guidance as to where it will go in 2009 and beyond.

On the basis of the observation that employment bounced back healthily in previous recessions, the author—no names will be mentioned—wrote:

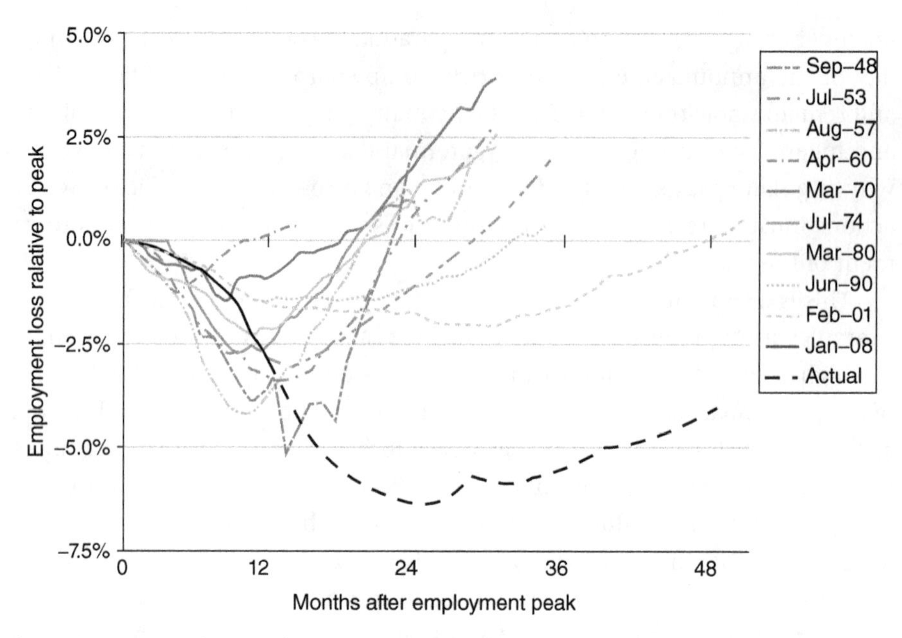

Figure 2.22 U.S. Nonfarm Employment and Forecast

> *. . . a forecast of job losses continuing for another 6 to 9 months would not be out of line. Furthermore, looking at past cycles, one would expect it will be at least a year (possibly more if the recovery looks more like that after the 2001 recession) before employment reaches the previous peak. Personally, my expectation is that it will take 18 to 24 months (from now) to get back to the previous peak.*

In other words, recovery was projected to follow the dashed line (two short dashes between a long dash) in the figure. What actually happened is shown by the black dashed line. Employment continued to fall, and at this time of writing—four years after the recession hit—is still almost 5% below its peak.

The problem here is that the current recession in the U.S. is not analogous to past U.S. recessions, most of which were driven by monetary policy or oil prices. How is this recession a different animal? In their fine book *This Time Is Different*, Reinhart and Rogoff (2009) look across financial crises in many countries in a longer sweep of history. They show that because the current crisis is driven by a failure of credit, better analogies can be found in the depressing experiences of Japan after its stock-market collapse, the Scandinavian economies after their banking crises in the 1990s, and the earlier travails of indebted emerging economies in Asia and South America. In short, the error in Figure 2.22 is that not enough judgment or theorizing has gone into choosing the sample of analogous events.

Sometimes we can get away with being sloppy about this. Consider a hedge fund that has identified some pattern predictive of a takeover. Each takeover has unique elements, and while analysts try to control for these, there will be instances where returns are lower than forecast, and others where returns are higher, and many cases where no takeover occurs. However, there will be many takeovers during the year, and the fund can act on the average patterns uncovered by its model, knowing that idiosyncratic behavior of individual shares will average out over a series of investments.

This kind of diversification of risk in forecast errors is not always possible, and definitely not in the case of costly one-off events like recessions. Similarly, the whole viability of a company may rest on the success of a single new product. When no diversification of risk is possible, the potential loss from an incorrect model is greater and possibly grievous. In these cases, a lot more attention needs to be paid to whether the events being pooled are truly analogous to the company's product launch.

Example 2: Not Enough Data

The more care we take in finding exact analogies to the event we are trying to predict, the less hard data remain to be used, and the more we must rely on judgment rather than statistical analysis. As reported frequently in *Foresight* articles, judgment is not always as reliable as judges assume, and experts are rarely as expert as we would like. Good judgment—as in the Reinhart and Rogoff study—needs to be grounded in a coherent and data-congruent theory. Bad judgment is the result of belief, wishful thinking, and anecdote.

In the field of pattern-based forecasting, there are plenty of examples of bad judgment. In particular, many "chart analysts" in financial markets make forecasts based on patterns that have little theoretical or empirical support.

Figure 2.23 illustrates the very popular head and shoulders pattern. The bars show daily ranges of share prices, green for rising, red for falling. The narrative here is that after prices have risen, sellers come in and the price falls back (left shoulder). Buyers then reenter the market and drive the price higher still (head). After the price falls back again, buyers reenter the market but fail to drive the price above its previous high (right shoulder). When the price falls below the neckline joining the most recent troughs, as in Figure 2.23, this is a sell signal as the price is forecast to fall further.

It would be nice to report that this pattern was developed from extensive event studies where the paths of prices after such patterns were tracked and averaged. However, refereed empirical studies in the area (Osler, 1998; Chang and Osler, 1999) do not find significant predictive power or profitability in the

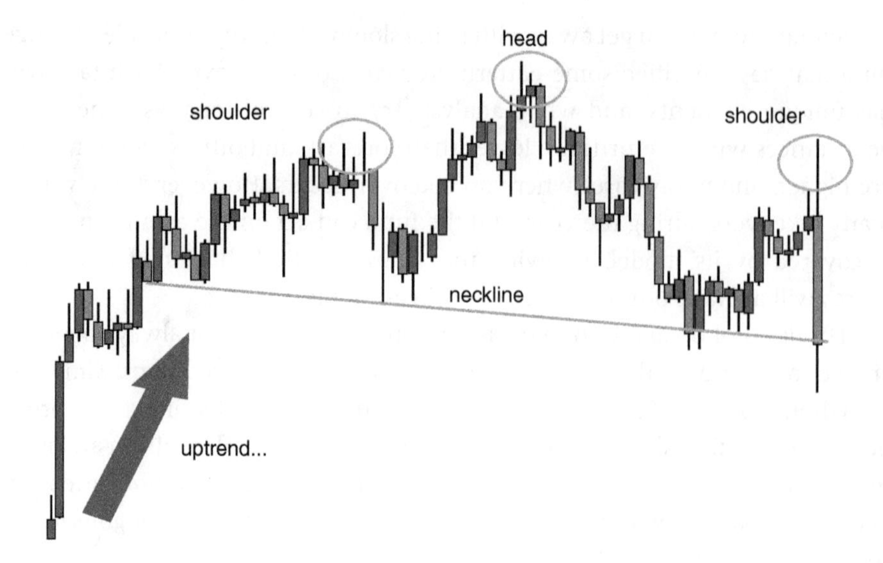

Figure 2.23 Head and Shoulders Stock Price Pattern

head-and-shoulders formation. The only support for this pattern comes from the anecdotes of traders.

It is human nature to look for patterns in the world around us. This is how we have made progress in science and social relationships. Unfortunately, this instinct sometimes finds inappropriate applications. In this case, it is likely that the head and shoulders pattern is a product of the illusion of control, the human tendency to construct patterns even from random data. Looking at a short run of share prices through half-closed eyes, it is pretty easy to start seeing waves, and flags, and double tops, and imagining that there is order in this very disordered environment, especially if there are financial rewards waiting for anyone who can make sense of it.

To be fair to chart analysts, best practice would require them to trade not only on the signal given in Figure 2.20, but to seek confirmation of its validity, either in the larger pattern of the time series or in the behavior of related variables. Specifically they should check that the pattern was preceded by a sustained uptrend and look carefully at the volume of trading around the turning points and breaks in the pattern (see stockcharts.com, 2012). Unfortunately, lengthening the time series and expanding the set of variables considered reduces the number of trading opportunities and delays their execution, both severe tests of traders' discipline.

Conclusion

The "event study/pattern overlay" methodology offers benefits to forecasters in situations where we do not have a long run of time-series data or where the process driving our data has been disrupted by some structural break. This covers pretty much all real-world forecasting problems.

This article has considered what is likely to determine the effectiveness of using the event-study methodology outside finance applications. Even from these simple considerations, it is clear that there is a tradeoff between the exercise of judgment and the use of data.

On the one hand, the uncritical use of any and all apparently relevant data—as in the recession forecasting example—may give us statistically good-looking results, but at the expense of ignoring critical features of the event under scrutiny.

On the other hand, if we overtheorize about the current event, look at longer runs of data, or try to weight many related variables but without the capacity to build a credible statistical model, we may wind up looking at very few analogies and placing too much weight on our fallible judgment.

REFERENCES

Binder, J. (1998). The event study methodology since 1969. *Review of Quantitative Finance and Accounting* 11, 111–137.

Chang, K. P. H., and C. Osler (1999). Methodical madness: Technical analysis and the irrationality of exchange-rate forecasts. *Economic Journal* 109 (458), 636–661.

Fama, E. F., L. Fisher, M. C. Jensen, and R. Roll (1969). The adjustment of stock prices to new information. *International Economic Review* 10 (1), 1–21.

Osler, C. L. (1998). Identifying noise traders: The head-and-shoulders pattern in U.S. equities. Staff Reports 42, Federal Reserve Bank of New York.

Reinhart, C. M., and K. S. Rogoff (2009). *This Time Is Different.* Princeton University Press.

stockcharts.com (2012). Head and shoulders top (reversal). Available: http://stock-charts.com/school/doku.php?id=chart_school:chart_analysis:chart_patterns:head_and_shoulders_t. Last accessed 29 February 2012.

CHAPTER 3

Forecasting Performance Evaluation and Reporting

Process improvement begins with process measurement. But it can be a challenge to find the right metrics to motivate the desired behavior. A simple example is provided by Steve Morlidge (in an article later in this chapter) for the case of intermittent demand:

> *When 50% or more of the periods are zero, a forecast of zero every period will generate the lowest average absolute error—irrespective of the size of the nonzero values. Yet forecasting zero every period is probably the wrong thing to do for inventory planning and demand fulfillment.*

There are dozens of available forecasting performance metrics. Some, like mean absolute percent error (MAPE), represent error as a percentage. Others, like mean absolute error (MAE), are *scale dependent*; that is, they report the error in the original units of the data. *Relative-error metrics* (such as Theil's U or forecast value added (FVA)) compare performance versus a benchmark (typically a naïve model). Each metric has its place—a situation where it is suitable to use and informative. But there are also countless examples (many provided in the articles below) where particular metrics are unsuitable and lead decision makers to inappropriate conclusions.

After Len Tashman's opening overview and tutorial on forecast accuracy measurement, this chapter provides a critical exploration of many specific metrics and methods for evaluating forecasting performance. It covers some innovative approaches to performance reporting—including the application of statistical process control methods to forecasting. And it concludes with the most fundamental—yet frequently unasked—question in any performance evaluation: Can you beat the naïve forecast?

3.1 DOS AND DON'TS OF FORECAST ACCURACY MEASUREMENT: A TUTORIAL*

Len Tashman

In this introductory tutorial, Len Tashman surveys the underlying concepts of forecast accuracy measurement. Many of these concepts will be explored further in the articles that follow.

---

* This article was adapted from the *Foresight* Guidebook entitled *Forecast Accuracy Measurement: Pitfalls to Avoid and Practices to Adopt,* and appears here courtesy of the International Institute of Forecasters.

Perhaps the most basic concept is to distinguish a model's fit to history from its ability to forecast the future. Failing to recognize this distinction, and reporting fit as an indicator of forecast accuracy, is the first of 16 taboos spread throughout the article. Tashman goes on to review the various approaches for assessing forecast accuracy, the particular metrics used to measure accuracy (and their flaws), and methods for benchmarking and determining forecastability.

The tutorial concludes with discussion of the costs of forecast error. Tashman notes that forecast accuracy metrics do not reveal the financial impact of forecast error—this requires a separate calculation—and improved accuracy does not automatically translate into cost savings or other operational benefits. Rather, such benefits arise from better decisions and planning that (we hope) are a consequence of more accurate forecasts. (Of course, as will be discussed in Chapter 4, forecasting is a politicized process. Organizations will not reap the benefits of more accurate forecasting if management fails to use the forecasts to drive better planning decisions.)

As a forecaster, you've acquired a good deal of knowledge about statistical measurements of accuracy, and you've applied accuracy metrics alongside a large dose of common sense. This tutorial is designed to confirm your use of appropriate practices in forecast accuracy measurement, and to suggest alternatives that may provide new and better insights.

Perhaps most important, we warn you of practices that can distort or even undermine your accuracy evaluations. You will see these listed below as *taboos*—errors and omissions that must be avoided.

The Most Basic Issue: Distinguish In-Sample Fit from Out-of-Sample Accuracy

Using a statistical model applied to your sales history of daily, weekly, monthly, or quarterly data, possibly modified by judgmental adjustments, you generate forecasts for a certain number of periods into the future. We'll use month as the general time interval. The question, "How accurate is your model?"—a question that contributes to decisions on whether the model is reliable as a forecasting tool—has two distinct components:

A. **In-Sample or Fitting Accuracy**: How closely does the model track (fit, reproduce) the historical data that were used to generate the forecasts? We call this component *in-sample accuracy.* If you used the most recent 36 months of history to fit your model, the metrics of in-sample fit reveal the proximity of the model's estimates to the actual values over each of the past 36 months.

B. **Out-of-Sample or Forecasting Accuracy**: How closely will the model predict activity for the months ahead? The essential distinction from fitting accuracy is that you are now predicting into an unknown future, as opposed to predicting historical activity whose measurements were known to you. This forecasting accuracy component is often called *out-of-sample accuracy,* since the future is necessarily outside the sample of historical data we have about the past.

The best practice is to calculate and report measurements of both fitting and forecasting accuracy. The differences in the figures can be dramatic, and the key is to avoid taboo #1.

Taboo #1: Measuring *fitting* accuracy, but reporting the results as indicators of *forecasting* accuracy.

Volumes of research tell us that you cannot judge forecasting accuracy by fitting accuracy. For example, if your average error in-sample is found to be 10%, it is very probable that forecast errors will average substantially more than 10%. More generally put, in-sample errors are liable to understate errors out of sample. The reason is that you have calibrated your model to the past but you cannot calibrate to a future that has yet to occur.

How serious can violation of Taboo #1 be? If in-sample errors average 10%, how much larger than 10% will forecast errors be? A bit, twice the 10% figure, five times this figure, or 100 times this figure? That depends upon how closely the near future tracks the recent past, but it would not be surprising to find that out-of-sample errors are more than double the magnitude of in-sample errors.

The point to remember is this: The use of in-sample figures as a guide to forecasting accuracy is a mistake (a) that is of a potentially major magnitude; (b) that occurs far too often in practice; and (c) that is perpetuated by omissions in some, and perhaps most, forecasting software programs (think Excel, for example). The lack of software support is one reason that this mistake persists.

So how do you keep the distinction between fitting and forecasting accuracy clearly delineated?

Assessing Forecast Accuracy

There are at least three approaches that can be used to measure forecasting accuracy. These are:

1. Wait and see in real time
2. Use holdout samples
3. Create retrospective evaluations

While there are variations on these themes, it is worthwhile understanding their basic similarities and differences.

Real-Time Evaluations

A company commits to a forecast for "next month" on or before the last day of the current month. This is a forecast with a one-month lead-time, or one-month horizon. We call it a one-month-ahead forecast.

Suppose the May forecast is presented by April 30. Soon after May has elapsed, the activity level for this month is a known fact. The difference between that level and what had been forecast on April 30 is the forecast error for the month of May, a one-month-ahead forecast error.

The company has developed worksheets that show the actuals, forecasts, and errors-by-month over the past few years. They use these figures to compare alternative forecasting procedures and to see if accuracy is improving or deteriorating over time.

The real-time evaluation is "pure" in that forecasts for the next month do not utilize any information that becomes known after the month (May) begins. One disadvantage here is that there is more than a month's lag before the next accuracy figure can be calculated.

The most critical lead-time for judging forecast accuracy is determined by the order/replenishment cycle. If it takes two months, on average, to obtain the resources to produce the product or service, then forecasting accuracy at two months ahead is the critical lead-time.

Taboo #2: Failing to specify the critical lead-time when assessing forecast accuracy.

There is also an inconvenience to real-time evaluations. These normally must be done outside the forecasting tool, requiring creation of worksheets to track results. If the company wishes to learn how accurately it can forecast more than one month ahead—for example, forecasting with lead-times of two months, three months, or longer—it will need to create a separate worksheet for each lead-time.

Holdout Samples

Many software tools support holdout samples. They allow you to divide the historical data on an item, product, or family into two segments. The earlier segment serves as the fit or in-sample period; the fit-period data are used to estimate statistical models and determine their fitting accuracy. The more recent past is held out of the fit period to serve as the test, validation, or out-of-sample period: Since the test-period data have not been used in choosing or fitting the statistical models, they represent the future that the models are trying to forecast. Hence, a comparison of the forecasts against the test-period data is essentially a test of forecasting accuracy.

Peeking

Holdout samples permit you to obtain impressions of forecast accuracy without waiting for the future to materialize (they have another important virtue as well, discussed in the next section). One danger, however, is peeking, which is what occurs when a forecaster inspects the holdout sample to help choose a model. You can't peek into the future, so peeking at the held-out data undermines the forecast-accuracy evaluation.

Another form of the peeking problem occurs when the forecaster experiments with different models and then chooses the one that best "forecasts" the holdout sample of data. This overfitting procedure is a no-no because it effectively converts the out-of-sample data into in-sample data. After all, how can you know how any particular model performed in the real future, without waiting for the future to arrive?

In short, if the holdout sample is to provide an untainted view of forecast accuracy, it must not be used for model selection.

Taboo #3: Basing model selection on the holdout sample.

Single Origin Evaluations

Let's say you have monthly data for the most recent 4 years, and have divided this series into a fit period of the first 3 years, holding out the most recent 12 months to serve as the test period. The forecast origin would be the final month of year 3. From this origin, you forecast each of the 12 months of year 4. The result is a set of 12 forecasts, one each for lead-times 1–12.

What can you learn from these forecasts? Very little, actually, since you have only one data point on forecast accuracy for each lead-time. For example, you have one figure telling you how accurately the model predicted one month ahead. Judging accuracy from samples of size 1 is not prudent. Moreover, this one figure may be "corrupted" by occurrences unique to that time period.

Further, you will be tempted (and your software may enable you) to average the forecast errors over lead-times 1–12. Doing so gives you a metric that is a mélange of near-term and longer-term errors that have ceased to be linked to your replenishment cycle.

Taboo #4: Calculating a forecast-error metric by averaging errors at different lead-times.

Rolling Origin Evaluations

The shortcomings of single-origin evaluations can be overcome in part by successively updating the forecast origin. This technique is also called a rolling-origin evaluation. In the previous example (4 years of monthly data, the first 3 serving as the fit period and year 4 as the test period), you begin the same way, by generating the 12 forecasts for the months of year 4 . . . but you don't stop there.

You then move the first month of year 4 from the test period into the fit period, and refit the same statistical model to the expanded in-sample data. The updated model generates 11 forecasts, one each for the remaining months of year 4.

The process continues by updating the fit period to include the second month of year 4, then the third month, and so forth, until your holdout sample is exhausted (down to a single month). Look at the results:

12 data points on forecast accuracy for forecasting one month ahead

11 data points on forecast accuracy for forecasting two months ahead

. . .

2 data points on forecast accuracy for forecasting 11 months ahead

1 data point on forecast accuracy for forecasting 12 months ahead.

If your critical lead-time is 2 months, you now have 11 data points for judging how accurately the statistical procedure will forecast two months ahead. An average of the 11 two-months-ahead forecast errors will be a valuable metric and one that does not succumb to Taboo #3.

Performing rolling-origin evaluations is feasible only if your software tool supports this technique. A software survey that Jim Hoover and I did in 2000 for the Principles of Forecasting project (Tashman and Hoover, 2001) found that few demand-planning tools, spreadsheet packages, and general statistical programs offered this support. However, dedicated business-forecasting software packages do tend to provide more adequate support for forecasting-accuracy evaluations.

> Taboo #5: Continuing to rely on software tools that do not support adequate out-of-sample evaluations.

How Much Data to Hold Out?

There are no hard and fast rules. Rather, it's a balancing act between too large and too small a holdout sample. Too large a holdout sample and there is not enough data left in-sample to fit your statistical model. Too small a holdout sample and you don't acquire enough data points to reliably judge forecasting accuracy.

If you are fortunate to have a long history—say, 48 months of data or more—you are free to make the decision on the holdout sample based on common sense. Normally, I hold out the final year (12 months), using the earlier years to fit the model. This gives a picture of how that model would have forecast each month of the past year.

If the items in question have a short replenishment cycle—2 months, let's say—you're interested mainly in the accuracy of 2-months-ahead forecasts. In this situation, I recommend holding out at least 4 months. In a rolling-origin evaluation, you'll receive 4 data points on accuracy for one month ahead and 3 for two months ahead. (Had you held out only 2 months, you'd receive only 1 data point on accuracy for your 2-months-ahead forecast.) I call this the H+2 rule, where H is the forecast horizon determined by your replenishment cycle.

When you have only a short history, it is not feasible to use a holdout sample. But then statistical accuracy metrics based on short histories are not reliable to begin with.

Retrospective Evaluations

Real-time evaluations and holdout samples are two approaches to assessment of forecasting accuracy. Retrospective evaluation is a third. Here, you define a target month, say the most recent December. Then you record the forecasts for the target month that were made one month ago, two months ago, three months ago, and so forth. Subtracting each forecast from the actual December value gives you the error in a forecast made so many months prior. So-called backtracking grids or waterfall charts are used to display the retrospective forecast errors. An example can be seen at www.mcconnellchase.com/fd6.shtml.

It would be a good sign if the errors diminish as you approach the target month.

The retrospective evaluation, like the rolling-origin evaluation, allows you to group errors by lead-time. You do this by repeating the analysis for different target months and then collecting the forecast errors into one month before, two months before, and so forth. If your replenishment cycle is short, you need go back only a few months prior to each target.

Accuracy Metrics

The core of virtually all accuracy metrics is the difference between what the model forecast and the actual data point. Using A for the actual and F for the forecast, the difference is the forecast error.

The forecast error can be calculated as A – F (actual minus forecast) or F – A (forecast minus actual). Most textbooks and software present the A – F form, but there are plenty of fans of both methods. Greene and Tashman (2008) summarize the preferences between the two forms. Proponents of A – F cite convention—it is the more common representation—while advocates of F – A say it is more intuitive, in that a positive error F > A represents an overforecast and F < A an underforecast. With A – F, an overforecast is represented by a negative error, which could be confusing to some people.

However, the form really doesn't matter when the concern is with accuracy rather than bias. Accuracy metrics are calculated on the basis of the difference between actual and forecast without regard to the direction of the difference. The directionless difference is called the absolute value of the error. Using absolute values prevents negative and positive errors from offsetting each other and focuses your attention on the size of the errors.

In contrast, metrics that assess bias—a tendency to misforecast in one direction—retain the sign of the error (+ or –) as an indicator of direction. Therefore, it is important to distinguish metrics that reveal bias from those that measure accuracy or average size of the errors.

Taboo #6: Failing to distinguish bias from accuracy, thus confounding error size with error direction.

The presence and severity of bias is more clearly revealed by a graph rather than a metric.

Pearson (2007) shows you how to create a Prediction-Realization Diagram. This single graphic reveals whether your forecasts are biased (and in what direction), how large your errors are (the accuracy issue), and if your forecasts are better than a naïve benchmark. Seeing all this in one graphic reveals patterns in your forecast errors and insights into how to improve your forecasting performance.

Classification of Accuracy Metrics

Hyndman (2006) classifies accuracy metrics into 4 types, but here I'm going to simplify his taxonomy into 3 categories:

1. Basic metrics in the original units of the data (same as Hyndman's scale dependent)
2. Basic metrics in percentage form (same as Hyndman's percentage error)
3. Relative-error metrics (Hyndman's relative and scale-free metrics)

I use the term *basic metric* to describe the accuracy of a set of forecasts for a single item from a single procedure or model. In a basic metric, *aggregation* is not an issue; that is, we are not averaging errors over many items.

In contrast to basic metrics, *relative-error* metrics compare the accuracy of a procedure against a designated benchmark procedure.

Aggregate-error metrics can be compiled from both basic and relative-error metrics.

Basic Metrics in the Original Units of the Data

Basic metrics reveal the average size of the error. The "original units" of the data will normally be volume units (# cases, # widgets) or monetary units (value of orders or sales).

The principal metric of this type is the *mean of the absolute errors,* symbolized normally as the MAD (mean absolute deviation) or MAE (mean absolute error). Recall that by "absolute" we mean that negative errors are not allowed to offset positive errors (that is, over- and underforecasts do not cancel). If we permitted negatives to offset positives, the result could well be an average close to zero, despite large errors overall.

A MAD of 350 cases tells us that the forecasts were off by 350 cases on the average.

An alternative to the MAD (MAE) that prevents cancellation of negatives and positives is the squared-error metric, variously called the RMSE (root mean square error), the standard deviation of the error (SDE), or standard error (SE). These metrics are more popular among statisticians than among forecasters, and are a step more challenging to interpret and explain. Nevertheless, they remain the most common basis for calculations of safety stocks for inventory management, principally because of the (questionable) tradition of basing safety-stock calculations on the bell-shaped Normal distribution.

Taboo #7: Failing to calculate the absolute (or squared) values of the errors, inadvertently allowing negative errors to cancel positive errors.

MAPE: The Basic Metric in Percentage Form

The percentage version of the MAD is the MAPE (the mean of the absolute percentage errors).

A MAPE of 3.5% tells us that the forecasts were off by 3.5% on the average.

There is little question that the MAPE is the most commonly cited accuracy metric, because it seems so easy to interpret and understand. Moreover, since it is a percentage, it is scale free (not in units of widgets, currency, etc.) while the MAD, which is expressed in the units of the data, is therefore scale dependent.

A scale-free metric has two main virtues. First, it provides perspective on the size of the forecast errors to those unfamiliar with the units of the data. If I tell you that my forecast errors average 175 widgets, you really have no idea if this is large or small; but if I tell you that my errors average 2.7%, you have some basis for making a judgment.

Secondly, scale-free metrics are better for aggregating forecast errors of different items. If you sell both apples and oranges, each MAD is an average in its own fruit units, making aggregation silly unless the fruit units are converted to something like cases. But even if you sell two types of oranges, aggregation in the original data units will not be meaningful when the sales volume of one type dominates that of the other. In this case, the forecast error of the lower-volume item will be swamped by the forecast error of the higher-volume item. (If 90% of sales volume is of navel oranges and 10% of mandarin oranges, equally accurate procedures for forecasting the two kinds will yield errors that on average are 9 times greater for navel oranges.)

Clearly, the MAPE has important virtues. And, if both MAD and MAPE are reported, the size of the forecast errors can be understood in both the units of the data and in percentage form.

Still, while the MAPE is a near-universal metric for forecast accuracy, its drawbacks are poorly understood, and these can be so severe as to undermine the forecast accuracy assessment.

MAPE: The Issues

Many authors have warned about the use of the MAPE. A brief summary of the issues:

- Most companies calculate the MAPE by expressing the (absolute) forecast error as a percentage of the actual value A. Some, however, prefer a percentage of the forecast F; others, a percentage of the average of A and F; and a few use the higher of A or F. Greene and Tashman (2009) present the various explanations supporting each form.
- The preference for use of the higher of A or F as the denominator may seem baffling; but, as by Hawitt (2010), this form of the MAPE may be necessary if the forecaster wishes to report "forecast accuracy" rather than "forecast error." This is the situation when you wish to report that your forecasts are 80% accurate rather than 20% in error on the average.
- Kolassa and Schutz (2007) describe three potential problems with the MAPE. One is the concern with forecast bias, which can lead us to inadvertently prefer methods that produce lower forecasts; a second is with the danger of using the MAPE to calculate aggregate error metrics across items; and the third is the effect on the MAPE of intermittent demands (zero orders in certain time periods). The authors explain that all three concerns can be overcome by use of an alternative metric to the standard MAPE called the MAD/MEAN ratio. I have long felt that the MAD/MEAN ratio is a superior metric to the MAPE, and recommend that you give this substitution serious consideration.

- The problem posed by intermittent demands is especially vexing. In the traditional definition of the MAPE—the absolute forecast error as a percentage of the actual A—a time period of zero orders (A = 0) means the error for that period is divided by zero, yielding an undefined result. In such cases, the MAPE cannot be calculated. Despite this, some software packages report a figure for the "MAPE" that is potentially misleading. Hoover (2006) proposes alternatives, including the MAD/MEAN ratio.
- Hyndman's (2006) proposal for replacing the MAPE in the case of intermittent demands is the use of a scaled-error metric, which he calls the mean absolute scaled error or MASE. The MASE, he notes, is closely related to the MAD/MEAN ratio.
- Another issue is the aggregation problem: What metrics are appropriate for measurement of aggregate forecast error over a range (group, family, etc.) of items. Many companies calculate an aggregate error by starting with the MAPE of each item and then weighting the MAPE by the importance of the item in the group, but this procedure is problematic when the MAPE is problematic. Again, the MAD/MEAN ratio is a good alternative in this context as well.

Taboo #8: Reporting a MAPE for intermittent data as well as for other situations in which this metric is problematic.

Relative Error Metrics

The third category of error metrics is that of relative errors, the errors from a particular forecast method in relation to the errors from a benchmark method. As such, this type of metric, unlike basis metrics, can tell you whether a particular forecasting method has improved upon a benchmark. Hyndman (2006) provides an overview of some key relative-error metrics including his preferred metric, the MASE.

The main issue in devising a relative-error metric is the choice of benchmark. Many software packages use as a default benchmark the errors from a naïve model, one that always forecasts that next month will be the same as this month. A naïve forecast is a no-change forecast (another name used for the naïve model is the random walk). The ratio of the error from your forecasting method to that of the error from the naïve benchmark is called the relative absolute error. Averaging the relative absolute errors over the months of the forecast period yields an indication of the degree to which your method has improved on the naïve.

Of course, you could and should define your own benchmark; but then you'll need to find out if your software does the required calculations. Too many software packages offer limited choices for accuracy metrics and do not permit variations that may interest you. More generally, the problem is that your software may not support best practices.

A relative-error metric not only can tell you how much your method improves on a benchmark; it provides a needed perspective for bad data situations. Bad data usually means high forecast errors, but high forecast errors do not necessarily mean that your forecast method has failed. If you compare your errors against the benchmark, you may find that you've still made progress, and that the source of the high error rate is not bad forecasting but bad data.

Taboo #9: Failing to report a relative-error metric and hence offering no perspective on the degree to which your forecasting method improves on an appropriate benchmark.

Benchmarking and Forecastability

Relative-error metrics represent one form of benchmarking, that in which the forecast accuracy of a model is compared to that of a benchmark model. Typically, the benchmark is a naïve model, one that forecasts "no change" from a base period.

Two other forms are more commonly employed. One is to benchmark against the accuracy of forecasts made for similar products or under similar conditions. Frequently, published surveys of forecast accuracy (from a sample of companies) are cited as the source of these benchmarks. Company names of course are not disclosed. This is external benchmarking.

In contrast, internal benchmarking refers to comparisons of forecasting accuracy over time, usually to determine whether improvements are being realized.

External Benchmarking

Kolassa (2008) has taken a critical look at these surveys and questions their value as benchmarks. Noting that "comparability" is the key in benchmarking, he identifies potential sources of incomparability in the product mix, time frame, granularity, and forecasting process. This article is worth careful consideration for the task of creating valid benchmarks.

Taboo #10: Relying on benchmarks from external surveys without giving detailed attention to the possible areas of incomparability.

Internal Benchmarking

Internal benchmarking is far more promising than external benchmarking, according to Hoover (2009) and Rieg (2008). Rieg develops a case study of internal benchmarking at a large automobile manufacturer in Germany. Using the MAD/MEAN ratio as the metric, he tracks the changes in forecasting accuracy over a 15-year period, being careful to distinguish organizational changes, which can be controlled, from changes in the forecasting environment, which are beyond the organization's control.

Hoover provides a more global look at internal benchmarking. He first notes the obstacles that have inhibited corporate initiatives in tracking accuracy. He then presents an eight-step guide to the assessment of forecast accuracy improvement over time.

Taboo #11: Failing to create a process for tracking forecast accuracy changes over time.

Forecastability

Forecastability takes benchmarking another step forward. Benchmarks give us a basis for comparing our forecasting performance against an internal or external standard. However, benchmarks do not tell us about the potential accuracy we can hope to achieve.

Forecastability concepts help define achievable accuracy goals.

Catt (2009) begins with a brief historical perspective on the concept of the data-generating process, the underlying process from which our observed data are derived. If this process is largely deterministic—the result of identifiable forces—it should be forecastable. If the process is essentially random—no identifiable causes of its behavior—it is unforecastable. Peter uses six data series to illustrate these fundamental aspects of forecastability. Now the question is what metrics are there to assess forecastability.

Several books, articles, and blogs have proposed the coefficient of variation as a forecastability metric. The coefficient of variation is the ratio of some measure of variation (e.g., the standard deviation) of the data to an average (normally the mean) of the data. It reveals something about the degree of variation around the average. The presumption made is that the more variable (volatile) the data series, the less forecastable it is; conversely, the more stable the data series, the easier it is to forecast.

Catt demonstrates, however, that the coefficient of variation does not account for behavioral aspects of the data other than trend and seasonality, and so has limitations in assessing forecastability. A far more reliable metric, he finds, is that of approximate entropy, which measures the degree of disorder in the data and can detect many patterns beyond mere trend and seasonality.

Taboo #12: Assessing forecastability on the basis of the coefficient of variation.

Yet, as Boylan (2009) notes, metrics based on variation and entropy are really measuring the stability-volatility of the data and not necessarily forecastability. For example, a stable series may nevertheless come from a data-generating process that is difficult to identify and hence difficult to forecast. Conversely, a volatile series may be predictable based on its correlation with other variables or upon qualitative information about the business environment. Still, knowing how stable-volatile a series is gives us a big head start, and can explain why some products are more accurately forecast than others.

Boylan argues that a forecastability metric should supply an upper and lower bound for forecast error. The upper bound is the largest degree of error that should occur, and is normally calculated as the error from a naïve model. After all, if your forecasts can't improve on simple no-change forecasts, what have you accomplished? On this view, the relative-error metrics serve to tell us if and to what extent our forecast errors fall below the upper bound.

The lower bound of error represents the best accuracy we can hope to achieve. Although establishing a precise lower bound is elusive, Boylan describes various ways in which you can make the data more forecastable, including use of analogous series, aggregated series, correlated series, and qualitative information.

Taboo #13: Failing to seek more forecastable series, especially when forecast errors on the product in question are high.

Kolassa (2009) compares the Catt stability metric with the Boylan forecastability bounds. He sees a great deal of merit in the entropy concept, pointing out its successful use in medical research, quantifying the stability in a patient's heart rate. However, entropy is little understood in the forecasting community and is not currently supported by forecasting software. Hopefully, that will change, but he notes that we do need more research on the interrelation of entropy and forecast-error bounds.

These articles do not provide an ending to the forecastability story, but they do clarify the issues and help you avoid simplistic approaches.

Costs of Forecast Error

Forecast accuracy metrics do not reveal the financial impact of forecast error, which can be considerable. At the same time, we should recognize that improved forecast accuracy does not automatically translate into operational benefits (e.g., improved service levels, reduced inventory costs). The magnitude of the benefit depends upon the effectiveness of the forecasting and the planning processes. Moreover, there are costs to improving forecast accuracy, especially when doing so requires upgrades to systems, software, and training.

How can we determine the costs of forecast error and the costs and benefits of actions designed to reduce forecast error? A good starting point is the template provided by Catt (2007a). The cost of forecast error (CFE) calculation should incorporate both inventory costs (including safety stock) and the costs of poor service (stockouts).

The calculation requires (1) information or judgment calls about marginal costs in production and inventory, (2) a forecast-error measurement that results from a statistical forecast, and (3) the use of a statistical table (traditionally the Normal Distribution) to translate forecast errors into probabilities of stockouts.

The potential rewards from a CFE calculation can be large. First, the CFE helps guide decisions about optimal service level and safety stock, often preventing excessive inventory. Additionally, CFE calculations could reveal that systems upgrades may not be worth the investment cost.

Taboo #14: Making service-level, safety-stock, and systems-upgrade decisions without a careful calculation of the cost of forecast error.

Clarifications and enhancements to this CFE template are offered by Boylan (2007) and Willemain (2007). Boylan recommends that service-level targets be set strategically—at higher levels of the product hierarchy—than tactically at the item level. John also shows how you can get around the absence of good estimates of marginal costs by creating tradeoff curves and applying sensitivity analysis to cost estimates.

Willemain explains that the use of the normal distribution is not always justifiable, and can lead to excessive costs and poor service. Situations in which we really do need an alternative to the normal distribution—such as the bootstrap approach—include service parts, and short and intermittent demand histories. He also makes further suggestions for simplifying the cost assumptions required in the CFE calculation.

Taboo #15: Relying exclusively on normal distributions to optimize inventory levels and calculate the CFE.

Catt's (2007b) reply is to distinguish the cost inputs that can usually be extracted from the accounting system from those that require some subjectivity. He concurs with Boylan's recommendation of the need for sensitivity analysis of the cost estimates and shows how the results can be displayed as a CFE surface plot. Such a plot may reveal that the CFE is highly sensitive to, say, the inventory carrying charge, but insensitive to the service level.

Software could and should facilitate the CFE calculation; however, Catt sadly notes that he has yet to find a package that does: "Vendors often promise great benefits but provide little evidence of them."

And this leads us to our final taboo:

Taboo #16: Failing to question whether your software is up to date and embeds best practices.

REFERENCES

Boylan, J. (2007). Key assumptions in calculating the cost of forecast error. *Foresight: International Journal of Applied Forecasting* 8, 22–24.

Boylan, J. (2009). Toward a more precise definition of forecastability. *Foresight: International Journal of Applied Forecasting* 13, 34–40.

Catt, P. (2007a). Assessing the cost of forecast error: A practical example. *Foresight: International Journal of Applied Forecasting* 7, 5–10.

Catt, P. (2007b). Reply to "Cost of Forecast Error" commentaries. *Foresight* 8, 29–30.

Catt, P. (2009). Forecastability: Insights from physics, graphical decomposition, and information theory. *Foresight: International Journal of Applied Forecasting* 13, 24–33.

Greene, K., and Tashman, L. (2008). Should we define forecast error as E = F – A or E = A – F? *Foresight* 10, 38–40.

Greene, K., and Tashman, L. (2009). Percentage Error: What Denominator? *Foresight* 12, 36–40.

Hawitt, D. (2010), Should you report forecast error or forecast accuracy? *Foresight* 19, Summer 2010, p. 46.

Hoover, J. (2006). Measuring forecast accuracy: Omissions in today's forecasting engines and demand planning software. *Foresight: International Journal of Applied Forecasting* 4, 32–35.

Hoover, J. (2009). How to track forecast accuracy to guide forecast process improvement. *Foresight* 14, 17–23.

Hyndman, R. (2006). Another look at forecast-accuracy metrics for intermittent demand. *Foresight* 4, 43–46.

Kolassa, S., and Schütz, W. (2007). Advantages of the MAD/MEAN ratio over the MAPE. *Foresight: International Journal of Applied Forecasting* 6, 40–43.

Kolassa, S. (2008). Can we obtain valid benchmarks from published surveys of forecast accuracy? *Foresight* 11, 6–14.

Kolassa, S. (2009). How to assess forecastability. *Foresight: International Journal of Applied Forecasting* 13, 41–45.

Pearson, R. (2007). An expanded prediction-realization diagram for assessing forecast errors. *Foresight* 7, 11–16.

Rieg, R. (2008). Measuring improvement in forecast accuracy, a case study. *Foresight: International Journal of Applied Forecasting* 11, 15–20.

Tashman, L., and Hoover, J. (2000). Diffusion of forecasting principles through software. In J. S.Armstrong (ed.), *Principles of Forecasting* 651–676.

Willemain, T. (2007). Use of the normal distribution in calculating the cost of forecast error. *Foresight: International Journal of Applied Forecasting* 8, 25–26.

3.2 HOW TO TRACK FORECAST ACCURACY TO GUIDE FORECAST PROCESS IMPROVEMENT*

Jim Hoover

While considerable attention has been paid to the measurement of forecast accuracy for individual items at particular points in time, it is also important that an organization measure and track its aggregate forecast accuracy. Jim Hoover notes that tracking aggregate forecast accuracy over the range of SKUs provides insight into your organization's overall forecasting process. Aggregate accuracy metrics help identify systemic changes in your forecast process, either from intentional improvement efforts or as a result of environmental forces.

However, relatively few firms track forecast accuracy over time. Apparent obstacles include data storage difficulties, outdated technology, inability to agree on appropriate metrics, and lack of impetus from the forecast process. The key steps involve determining the appropriate (a) forecast accuracy metric, (b) level of aggregation, (c) process attributes for storage, (d) targets for accuracy improvement, and (e) weights to be applied to targeted SKUs.

Hoover concludes that retaining key attributes from your forecasting process provides a "forecasting autopsy," with explanations for failing to meet forecast accuracy targets. This can be an important aid in identifying the routes to improved forecast accuracy.

Introduction

One of the more important tasks in supply-chain management is improving forecast accuracy. Because your investment in inventory is tied to it, forecast accuracy is critical to the bottom line. If you can improve accuracy across your range of SKUs, you can reduce the safety-stock levels needed to reach target fill rates.

I have seen a great deal of information in the forecasting literature on measuring forecasting accuracy for individual items at a point in time but see very little attention paid to the issues of tracking changes in forecasting accuracy over time, especially for the aggregate of items being forecast. *Foresight* has begun to address this topic with a case study from Robert Rieg (2008).

In practice, the portion of firms tracking aggregated accuracy is surprisingly small. Teresa McCarthy and colleagues (2006) reported that only 55% of the companies they surveyed believed that forecasting performance was being formally evaluated. When I asked the same question at a recent conference of forecasting practitioners, I found that approximately half of the participants indicated that their company tracked forecast accuracy as a key performance indicator; less than half reported that financial incentives were tied to forecast-accuracy measurement.

* This article originally appeared in *Foresight: The International Journal of Applied Forecasting* (Summer 2009), and appears here courtesy of the International Institute of Forecasters.

Obstacles to Tracking Accuracy

Why aren't organizations formally tracking forecast accuracy? One reason is that forecasts are not always stored over time. Many supply-chain systems with roots in the 1960s and 1970s did not save prior-period forecasts because of the high cost of storage in that era. Technology advances have reduced storage costs and, while the underlying forecast applications have been re-hosted on new systems, they have not been updated to retain prior forecasts, thus forfeiting the possibility of tracking performance over time.

A second reason is that saving the history in a useful manner sometimes requires retention of the original customer-level demand data. These are the data that can later be rebuilt into different levels of distribution center activity, when DCs are added or removed. This additional requirement creates a much larger storage challenge than saving just the aggregated forecasts.

Third, there are companies that haven't settled on a forecast-accuracy metric. While this may seem to be a simple task, the choice of metric depends on the nature of the demand data. For intermittent demands, popular metrics such as the Mean Absolute Percentage Error (MAPE) are inappropriate, as pointed out in Hoover (2006).

Finally, some companies don't have processes in place that factor forecast-accuracy metrics into business decisions. So they lack the impetus to track accuracy.

Multistep Tracking Process

A process for effective tracking of forecasting accuracy has a number of key steps, as shown in Figure 3.1.

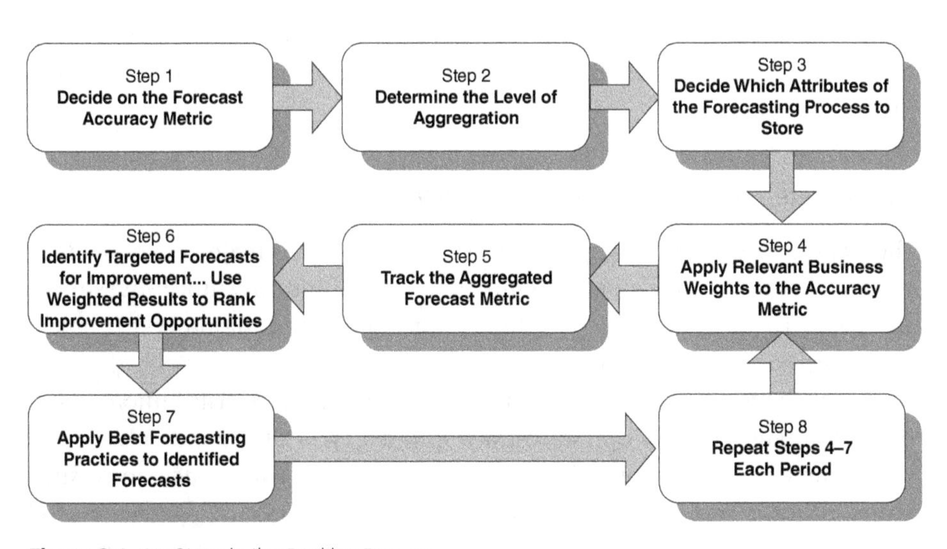

Figure 3.1 Key Steps in the Tracking Process

Step 1. Decide on the Forecast-Accuracy Metric

For many forecasters, the MAPE is the primary forecast-accuracy metric. Because the MAPE is scale-independent (since it is a percentage error, it is unit free), it can be used to assess and compare accuracy across a range of items. Kolassa and Schutz (2007) point out, however, that this virtue is somewhat mitigated when combining low- and high-volume items.

The MAPE is also a very problematic metric in certain situations, such as intermittent demands. This point was made in a feature section in *Foresight* entitled "Forecast-Accuracy Metrics for Inventory Control and Intermittent Demands" (Issue 4, June 2006). Proposed alternatives included the MAD/Mean ratio, a metric which overcomes many problems with low-demand SKUs and provides consistent measures across SKUs. Another metric is the Mean Absolute Scaled error, or MASE, which compares the error from a forecast model with the error resulting from a naïve method. Slightly more complex is GMASE, proposed by Valentin (2007), which is a weighted geometric mean of the individual MASEs calculated at the SKU level. Still other metrics are available, including those based on medians rather than means and using the percentage of forecasts that exceed an established error threshold.

In choosing an appropriate metric, there are two major considerations. The metric should be scale-independent so that it makes sense when applied to an aggregate across SKUs. Secondly, the metric should be intuitively understandable to management. The popularity of the MAPE is largely attributable to its intuitive interpretation as an average percentage error. The MAD-to-Mean is nearly as intuitive, measuring the average error as a percent of the average volume. Less intuitive are the MASE and GMASE.

I would recommend the more intuitive metrics, specifically MAD-to-Mean, because they are understandable to both management and forecasters. Using something as complicated as MASE or GMASE can leave some managers confused and frustrated, potentially leading to a lack of buy-in or commitment to the tracking metric.

Step 2. Determine the Level of Aggregation

The appropriate level of aggregation is the one where major business decisions on resource allocation, revenue generation, and inventory investment are made. This ensures that your forecast-accuracy tracking process is linked to the decisions that rely on the forecasts.

If you have SKUs stored both in retail sites and in a distribution center (DC), you will have the option to track forecast error at the individual retail site, at the DC, or at the overall aggregate level. If key business decisions (such as inventory investment and service level) are based on the aggregate-level SKU forecasts and you allocate that quantity down your supply chain, then you should assess forecast accuracy at the aggregate level. If you forecast by retail site and then aggregate the individual forecasts up to the DC or at the overall SKU aggregate, then you should be measuring forecasting accuracy at the individual site level. Again, the point is to track accuracy at the level where you make the important business decisions.

Additionally, you should consider tracking accuracy across like items. If you use one service-level calculation for fast-moving, continuous-demand items, and a second standard for slower- and intermittent-demand items, you should calculate separate error measures for the distinct groups.

Table 3.1 illustrates how the aggregation of the forecasts could be accomplished to calculate an average aggregate percent error for an individual time period.

Step 3. Decide Which Attributes of the Forecasting Process to Store

There are many options here, including:

- the actual demands
- the unadjusted statistical forecasts (before override or modifications)
- when manual overrides were made to the statistical forecast, and by whom
- when outliers were removed
- the method used to create the statistical forecast and the parameters of that method
- the forecaster responsible for that SKU
- when promotions or other special events occurred
- whether there was collaboration with customers or suppliers
- the weights applied when allocating forecasts down the supply chain

Table 3.1 Calculation of an Aggregate Percent Error

SKUs at Store Location 1	History Current Period	Forecast for Current Period	Error (History – Forecast)	Absolute Error	Absolute Percent Error
SKU 1	20	18	2	2	10.0%
SKU 2	10	15	–5	5	50.0%
SKU 3	50	65	–15	15	30.0%
SKU 4	5	2	3	3	60.0%
SKU 5	3	8	–5	5	166.7%
SKU 6	220	180	40	40	18.2%

Average Error = 55.8%

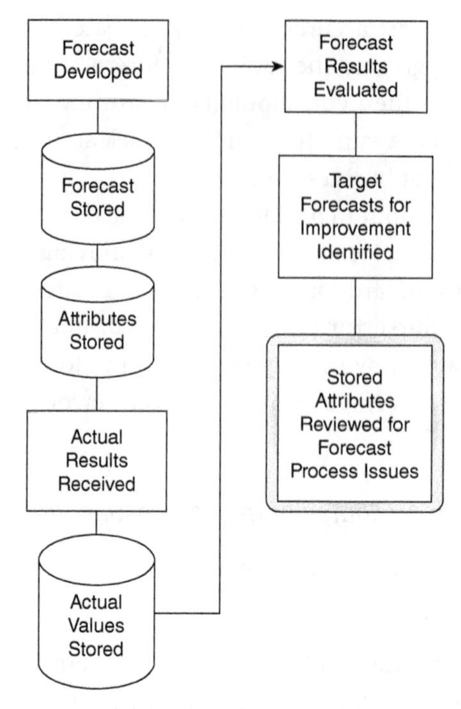

Figure 3.2 Flowchart for Storing Attributes of a Forecasting Process

Choosing the right attributes facilitates a *forecasting autopsy,* which seeks explanations for failing to meet forecast-accuracy targets. For example, it can be useful to know if forecast errors were being driven by judgmental overrides to the statistical forecasts. To find this out requires that we store more than just the actual demands and final forecasts.

Figure 3.2 presents a flowchart illustrating the sequence of actions in storing key attributes. Please note that the best time to add these fields is when initially designing your accuracy-tracking system. It is more difficult and less useful to add them later, it will cost more money, and you will have to baseline your forecast autopsy results from the periods following any change in attributes. It is easier at the outset to store more data elements than you think you need, rather than adding them later.

Step 4. Apply Relevant Business Weights to the Accuracy Metric

George Orwell might have put it this way: "All forecasts are equal, but some are more equal than others." The simple truth: You want better accuracy when forecasting those items that, for whatever reason, are more important than other items.

The forecast-accuracy metric can reflect the item's importance through assignment of weights. Table 3.2 provides an illustration, using inventory holding costs to assign weights.

Table 3.2 Calculating a Weighted Average Percent

SKUs at Store Location 1	History Current Period	Forecast for Currant Period	Error (History-Forecast)	Absolute Error	Absolute Percent Error	Cost of Item	Inventory Holding Cost	Percentage of Total Holding Costs	Weighted APE Contribution
SKU 1	20	18	2	2	10.0%	$50.00	$900.00	5.3%	0.5%
SKU 2	10	15	–5	5	50.0%	$50.00	$750.00	4.4%	2.2%.
SKU 3	50	65	–15	15	30.0%	$25.00	$1,625.00	9.6%	2.9%
SKU 4	5	2	3	3	60.0%	$5.00	$10.00	0.1%	0.0%
SKU 5	3	8	–5	5	166.7%	$15.00	$120.00	0.7%	1.2%
SKU 6	220	180	40	40	18.2%	$75.00	$13,500.00	79.9%	14.5%

Weighted summary APE calculated from individual weights applied to SKU's based on holding costs

Summarized Monthly APE = 21.4%

Unweighted MAPE = 55.8%

As shown in this example, SKUs 3 and 6 have the larger weights and move the weighted APE metric down from the average of 55.8% (seen in Table 3.1) to 21.4%.

Use the weighting factor that makes the most sense from a business perspective to calculate your aggregated periodic forecast-accuracy metric. Here are some weighting factors to consider:

- Inventory holding costs
- Return on invested assets
- Expected sales levels
- Contribution margin of the item to business bottom line
- Customer-relationship metrics
- Expected service level
- "Never out" requirements (readiness-based)
- Inventory

Weighting permits the forecaster to prioritize efforts at forecast-accuracy improvement.

Step 5. Track the Aggregated Forecast-Accuracy Metric over Time

An aggregate forecast-accuracy metric is needed by top management for process review and financial reporting. This metric can serve as the basis for tracking process improvement over time. Similar to statistical process-control metrics, the forecast-accuracy metric will assess forecast improvement efforts and signal major shifts in the forecast environment and forecast-process effectiveness, both of which require positive forecast-management action.

Figure 3.3 illustrates the tracking of a forecast-error metric over time. An improvement process instituted in period 5 resulted in reduced errors in period 6.

Step 6. Target Items for Forecast Improvement

Forecasters may manage hundreds or thousands of items. How can they monitor all of the individual SKU forecasts to identify those most requiring improvement? Simply put, they can't, but the weighting factors discussed in Step 4 reveal those items that have the largest impact on the aggregated forecast-accuracy metric (and the largest business effect). Table 3.3 illustrates how to identify the forecast with the biggest impact from the earlier example.

You can see that SKU 6 has the largest impact on the weighted APE tracking metric. Even though SKU 4 has the second-highest error rate of all of the SKUs, it has very little effect on the aggregated metric.

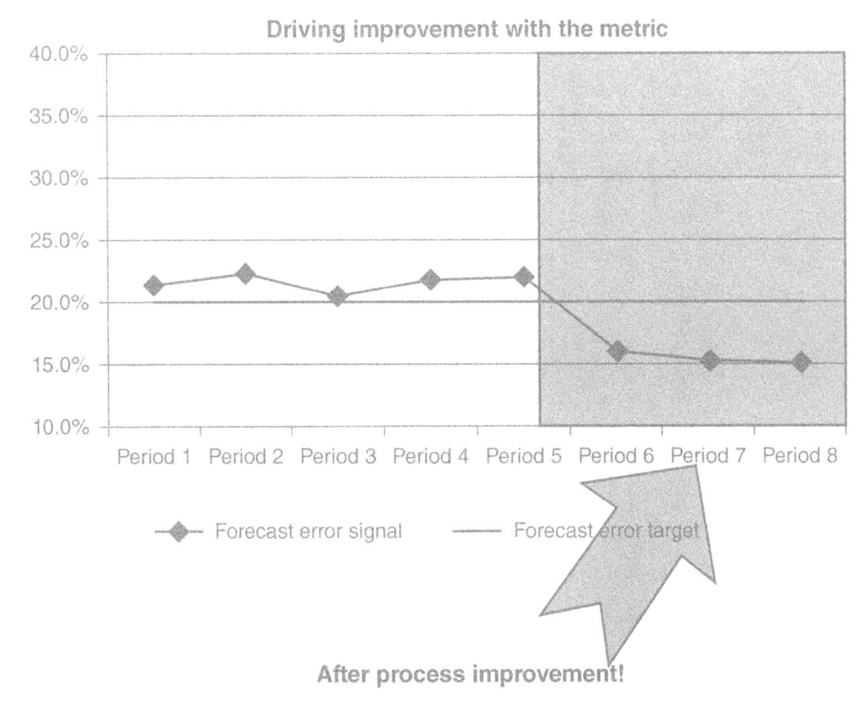

Figure 3.3 Illustration of a Tracking Signal

Step 7. Apply Best Forecasting Practices

Once you have identified those items where forecast improvement should be concentrated, you have numerous factors to guide you. Did you:

- Apply the principles of forecasting (Armstrong, 2001)?
- Try automatic forecasting methods and settings?
- Analyze the gains or losses from manual overrides?
- Identify product life-cycle patterns?
- Determine adjustments that should have been made (e.g., promotions)?
- Evaluate individual forecaster performance?
- Assess environmental changes (recession)?

As Robert Reig reported in his case study of forecast accuracy over time (2008), significant changes in the environment may radically affect forecast accuracy. Events like the current economic recession, the entry of new competition into the market space of a SKU, government intervention (e.g., the recent tomato salmonella scare), or transportation interruptions can all dramatically change the accuracy of your forecasts. While the change might not be the forecaster's "fault," tracking accuracy enables a rapid response to deteriorating performance.

Table 3.3 Targets for Forecast Improvement

SKUs at Store Location 1	History Current Period	Forecast for Currant Period	Error (History – Forecast)	Absolute Error	Absolute Percent Error	Cost of Item	Inventory Holding Cost	Percentage of Total Holding Costs	Weighted APE Contribution
SKU 1	20	18	2	2	10.0%	$50.00	$900.00	5.3%	0.5%
SKU 2	10	15	–5	5	50.0%	$50.00	$750.00	4.4%	2.2%
SKU 3	50	65	–15	15	30.0%	$25.00	$1,625.00	9.6%	2.9%
SKU 4	5	2	3	3	60.0%	$5.00	$10.00	0.1%	0.0%
SKU 5	3	8	–5	5	166.7%	$15.00	$120.00	0.7%	1.2%
SKU 6	220	180	40	40	18.2%	$75.00	$13,500.00	79.9%	14.5%

Step 8. Repeat Steps 4 through 7 Each Period

All of the factors in Step 7 form a deliberative, continuous responsibility for the forecasting team. With the proper metrics in place, forecasters can be held accountable for the items under their purview. Steps 4–7 should be repeated each period, so that the aggregated forecast-accuracy metric is continually updated for management and new targets for improvement emerge.

Conclusions and Recommendations

Forecast accuracy has a major impact on business costs and profits. The forecasting process must be evaluated by individual and aggregated forecast-accuracy metrics. Tracking these metrics over time is critical to driving process improvement.

See if your company has included forecast accuracy as a key performance indicator for management. If it has not, create a plan to begin recording accuracy at the aggregated level, and sell the idea to management. Build a tracking database that saves the key attributes of the forecasting process. Doing so will permit forecasting autopsies, which drive improvement efforts and prioritization of forecaster workload. See if you have weighted the forecasts to include the relative business impact, and make sure you have a structured approach to improving the individual and aggregated forecast accuracy over time. The data gathered in a good tracking process should lead to any number of improved business outcomes.

REFERENCES

Armstrong, J. S. (ed.) (2001). *Principles of Forecasting*. Boston: Kluwer Academic Publishers.

Hoover, J. (2006). Measuring forecast accuracy: Omissions in today's forecasting engines and demand planning software. *Foresight: International Journal of Applied Forecasting* 4, 32–35.

Kolassa, S., and W. Schütz (2007). Advantages of the MAD/Mean ratio over the MAPE. *Foresight: International Journal of Applied Forecasting* 6, 40–43.

McCarthy, T., D. Davis, L. Glolicic, and J. Mentzer (2006). The evolution of sales forecasting management: A 20-year longitudinal study of forecasting practices. *Journal of Forecasting* 25, 303–324.

Rieg, R. (2008). Measuring improvement in forecast accuracy, a case study. *Foresight: International Journal of Applied Forecasting* 11, 15–20.

Valentin, L. (2007). Use scaled errors instead of percentage errors in forecast evaluations. *Foresight: International Journal of Applied Forecasting* 7, 17–22.

3.3 A "SOFTER" APPROACH TO THE MEASUREMENT OF FORECAST ACCURACY*

John Boylan

In a 2010 letter to the editor of *Foresight*, David Hawitt suggested that forecast managers would be more receptive to hearing about forecast accuracy rather than forecast error. Hawitt argued that reporting (for example) a 40% average error might generate "knee-jerk reactions and the creation of unrealistic goals." But reporting 60% accuracy might stimulate executive thinking about "What can we do to improve this?"

Hawitt's letter generated a series of commentaries, including a different angle from Mark Little (2011): "Rather than attempt to express accuracy in a form executives think they understand, it may be better to focus on the improvements in business outcomes (the KPIs) that result through better forecasts."

In this article, John Boylan portrays the discussion in terms of the different perspectives of academics and practitioners. He attempts to reconcile these positions through the lens of Soft Systems Methodology (SSM)—an approach described in the book *Learning for Action* (Checkland and Poulter, 2006).

The first step in this approach is to gain organizational commitment to accuracy metrics, with agreement on written definitions by key stakeholders. The appropriate metrics depend on the context of use and needs of the users. It is clear that forecasting researchers and practitioners have different needs and perspectives on forecast accuracy. But their viewpoints can be reconciled and synthesized.

SSM encourages managers to gain greater understanding of effectiveness and accuracy measures that are the most appropriate for their organization. While SSM can be quite demanding of the managers who participate in this approach, Boylan contends that it allows for genuine growth in understanding as well as ownership of metrics that have been agreed on by management. SSM holds the promise of tying forecast accuracy metrics to the needs and perspectives of the organization.

The Complement of Mean Absolute Percent Error

Recently, I was invited to talk on new developments in forecasting to a Supply-Chain Planning Forum of a manufacturing company with facilities across Europe. I had met the group supply-chain director previously, but not the senior members of his team. To get better acquainted, I arrived on the evening before the forum.

In informal discussion, it soon became clear that forecast-accuracy measurement was a hot topic for the company. Documentation was being written on the subject, and the managers thought my arrival was very timely. I made

* This article originally appeared in *Foresight: The International Journal of Applied Forecasting* (Fall 2011), and appears here courtesy of the International Institute of Forecasters.

a mental note to add some more slides on accuracy measurement and asked if they had already prepared some draft documentation. They had, and this was duly provided for me just before I turned in for the night.

In the documents, there was a proposal to define forecast accuracy (FA) as the complement of mean absolute percentage error (MAPE):

$$FA = 100\% - MAPE$$

where MAPE is found by working out the error of each forecast as a percentage of the actual value (ignoring the sign if the error is negative), and then calculating the overall mean. If the value of FA was negative, it would be forced to zero, to give a scale of 0 to 100.

What would your advice be?

Forecast Researchers and Practitioners: Different Needs and Perspectives

I know how some feel about this topic, as there's been a recent discussion thread on forecast accuracy in the International Institute of Forecasters "Linked In" group. Keenan Wong, demand-planning analyst at Kraft Food, Toronto, wondered, "If 1 – Forecast Error gives me forecast accuracy, does 1 – MAPE give me mean absolute percent accuracy?" The question sparked a lively discussion, with over 20 comments at the time of this writing. I want to focus on just two, as they summarize the tensions in my own mind:

1. Len Tashman responded: "Both forms of the '1 minus' offer only very casual meanings of accuracy. Technically, they mean nothing—and 1 – MAPE is frequently misunderstood to mean the percentage of time the forecast is on the mark."
2. Alec Finney commented: "A very powerful way of defining forecast accuracy is to agree on a written definition with key stakeholders. Ultimately, it's not about formulae, numerators, denominators, etc., but about an easy-to-understand, transparent indicator."

Both of these comments contain significant truths, and yet they come from very different perspectives. Can these viewpoints possibly be reconciled? I believe that they can.

A good starting point is a comment by Hans Levenbach, also from the discussion group: "Accuracy needs to be defined in terms of the context of use, with practical meaning in mind for users." I think it is instructive to look at the needs of two groups of users—forecasting researchers and forecasting practitioners—to see how they are similar and how they vary.

The first requirement for the forecasting researcher is that accuracy metrics should not be unduly influenced by either abnormally large or small observations (outliers). If they are so influenced, then research results do not generalize to other situations. Instead, the results would depend on the vagaries of outliers being present or absent from datasets. This is an example of where the needs of researchers and practitioners coincide. The practitioner may not need to generalize from one collection of time series to another, but does need to generalize from findings in the past to recommendations for the future.

A second requirement for the forecasting researcher is scale independence. After the first M-Competition, which compared a range of forecasting methods on 1,001 real-world time-series, it was found that the overall results according to some measures depended very heavily on less than 1% of the series, typically those with the highest volumes. From a researcher's perspective, this is a real issue: Again, the results may not generalize from one collection of time series to another. Researchers typically get around this problem by dividing errors by actual values (or means of actual values). Thus, an error of 10% for a very low-volume item receives the same weight as an error of 10% for a very high-volume item.

This is a good example of where the needs of researchers and practitioners may not coincide. The practitioner is likely to say that the forecast error of a high-value, high-volume item should not receive the same weight as the forecast error of a low-value, low-volume item. (Exceptions arise when the forecast accuracy of a low-value item is important because its availability allows the sale of a related high-value item.) Consideration of value-related importance of forecast accuracy has led some practitioners to seek alternative measures, such as weighted MAPEs.

This discussion leads me to two conclusions:

1. When designing forecast-accuracy measures for practical application, we should not ignore the insights that have been gained by forecasting researchers.
2. Nevertheless, the requirements of forecasting researchers and practitioners are not identical. We must begin with the needs of the practitioner when choosing an error measure for a particular practical application.

The Soft Systems Approach

An insightful way of looking at forecasting-systems design is through the lens of Soft Systems Methodology (SSM), an approach developed principally by Peter Checkland. It is well known in the UK operational research community, but less so in other countries. A good introduction can be found in the book *Learning for Action* (Checkland and Poulter, 2006).

A summary of the SSM approach, in the context of forecasting systems, is shown in Figure 3.4.

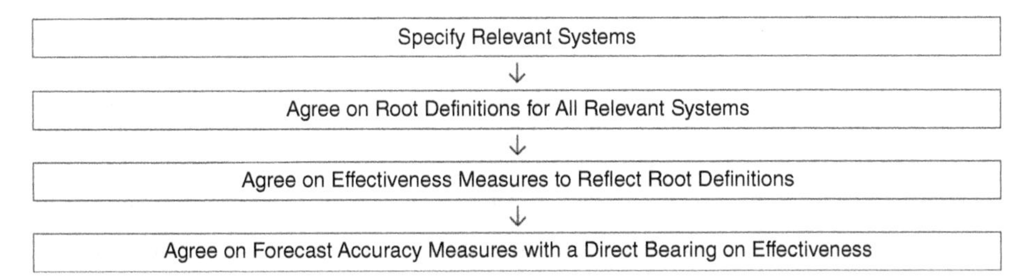

Figure 3.4 Soft Systems Methodology Applied to Forecasting

Relevant Systems and Root Definitions

SSM starts by asking a group of managers, "What relevant systems do you wish to investigate?" This simple question is worth pondering. I was involved in a study a decade ago (Boylan and Williams, 2001) in which the managers concluded there were three systems of interest: (i) HR Planning System; (ii) Marketing Planning System; and (iii) Financial Planning System. It then became clear to the managers that all three systems need the support of a fourth system, namely a Forecasting System.

SSM requires managers to debate the intended purpose of systems and to describe the relevant systems in a succinct *root* definition. The managers agreed that the root definition for HR Planning would be:

> *A system, owned by the Board, and operated out of Corporate Services, which delivers information about production and productivity to team leaders, so that new employees can be started at the right time to absorb forecasted extra business.*

Root definitions may appear bland, rather like mission statements. However, the main benefit is not the end product but the process by which managers debate what a system is for, how it should be informed by forecasts, and then come to an agreement (or at least some accommodation) on the system and its purpose. In the HR planning example, the implication of the root definition is that planning should be informed by forecasts of *extra business, production,* and *productivity*. The root definition was a product of its time, when demand was buoyant, but could be easily adapted to take into account more difficult market conditions, when decisions need to be made about not replacing departing employees or seeking redundancies.

Effectiveness Measures and Accuracy Measures

The root definition offers a guide not only to the required forecasts, but also to the purpose of the forecasts. For HR planning, the purpose was "so that new employees can be started at the right time to absorb forecasted extra business." In Soft Systems Methodology, this statement of purpose helps to specify the metrics by which the system should be measured, in three main categories:

1. **System effectiveness** measures whether the system is giving the desired effect. In the example, the question is whether the HR planning system enables extra business to be absorbed. Appropriate effectiveness metrics would reflect the managers' priorities, including measures like "business turned away," "delays in completing business orders," and "cost of employees hired." These measures are influenced by forecast accuracy and have been described as "accuracy implication metrics" (Boylan and Syntetos, 2006).
2. **System efficiency** measures the cost of resources to make the system work (strictly, the ratio of outputs to inputs). This has received relatively little attention in the forecasting literature but is an important issue for practitioners. Robert Fildes and colleagues (2009) found that small adjustments had a negligible effect on the accuracy of computer-system-generated forecasts. The proportion of employee time spent on such small adjustments would offer a useful measure of efficiency (or inefficiency!).
3. **System efficacy** measures whether the system works at an operational level. In our HR example, efficacy measures would include the timeliness and accuracy of forecasts. The accuracy metrics should be chosen so that they have a direct bearing on the system-performance measures. The exact relationship between forecast accuracy measures and effectiveness measures often cannot be expressed using a simple formula. However, computer-based simulations can help us understand how different error metrics can influence measures of system effectiveness.

It is sometimes asked why measures of forecast accuracy are needed if we have measures of system effectiveness. After all, it's the business impact of forecasts that is most important to the practitioner. While this is true, forecast accuracy is vital for diagnosis of system problems. Suppose we find that additional staff is being taken on, but not quickly enough to absorb the new business. Then we can turn to measures such as the mean error (which measures forecast bias) to see if the forecasts are consistently too low, and whether another forecast method would be able to detect and predict the trend more accurately.

In a supply chain context, the first type of monitor often relates to stockholding or service-level measures. These may be expressed in terms of total system cost or service-level measures such as fill rates, reflecting the priorities of the company. When system performance begins to deteriorate in terms of these metrics, then diagnosis is necessary. If the reason for poorer system performance relates to forecasting, rather than ordering policy, then we need to examine forecast accuracy. Suppose that stock levels appear to be too low, with too many stock-outs, and that the system is based on order-up-to levels set at the 95% quantile of demand, calculated from forecasts of the mean and standard deviation of demand. A diagnostic check of forecast accuracy relating to these quantities may reveal why the quantile estimates are too low, and remedial action can be taken.

Using a Structured Approach in Practice

I should stress that Soft Systems Methodology is just one structured approach that can be used by managers to think through their needs and to specify forecast-accuracy measures accordingly. Others are available, too. The main benefit of a participative, structured approach is to encourage managers to gain greater understanding of effectiveness measures and forecast-accuracy measures that are most appropriate for their organization.

Let's return here to our quotations from Len Tashman and Alec Finney. They both have understanding at the heart of their comments. Len is concerned about managers' misunderstanding of metrics, and Alec wants to promote easy-to-understand indicators. From my experience, the greater the participation by managers in the high-level designs of systems, the better their understanding.

Soft Systems Methodology is quite demanding and challenging of the managers who participate in the process. They must agree on the relevant systems, hammer out written root definitions, and specify measures of system effectiveness. This requires open debate, which may or may not be facilitated by an independent party familiar with SSM. The stage of debating metrics of forecast accuracy poses an additional challenge: understanding how accuracy metrics have a bearing on effectiveness. If the managers are already savvy in such matters, they will be ready to face this additional challenge. If not, it may be beneficial to use a facilitator who is an expert in forecasting methods and error metrics. The facilitator should desist from playing a dominant role, but be well placed to challenge the specification of measures that would be unduly affected by outliers, suffer from "division by zero" problems, or have other technical shortcomings.

This approach allows for genuine growth in understanding and ownership of measures that have been agreed on by managers, as suggested by Alec. The involvement of an expert facilitator will avoid the sort of problems highlighted by Len.

Postscript: Advice on the Complement of MAPE

Returning to the incident prompting these reflections, I thought long and hard about how to advise a company intending to use the "Complement of MAPE" as its error measure. There was insufficient time to go back to first principles, and to ask them to specify the relevant systems, root definitions, and measures of effectiveness. It would be inappropriate for me, as a visiting speaker not acting in a full consulting capacity, to propose a set of alternative measures, especially without the necessary background of the systems supported by the company's forecasts. Still, I felt that I should not let the proposed measure go unchallenged.

In my talk, I gave examples where the forecast error was so large as to be greater than the actual value itself. I asked if this was realistic for some stock-keeping units in the company and was assured that it was. I then pointed out that using their definition would result in a forecast accuracy of zero, whether the error was just greater than the actual value or far exceeded it. This gave the group pause, and they are currently reviewing their metrics.

My recommendation for this company—indeed, for any company—is not to adopt standard recommendations such as "use Mean Absolute Percentage Error." Rather, by working backwards from first principles, involving the key stakeholders in the process, it should be possible to agree on system-effectiveness measures that are relevant to the company and, in turn, to forecast-error measures that have a direct bearing on system effectiveness.

REFERENCES

Boylan J. E., and A. A. Syntetos (2006). Accuracy and accuracy-implication metrics for intermittent demand. *Foresight* 4 (Summer), 39–42.

Boylan, J. E., and Williams, M. A. (2001). Introducing forecasting and monitoring systems to an SME: The role of Soft Systems Methodology. In M. G. Nicholls, S. Clarke, and B. Lehaney (Eds.), *Mixed-Mode Modelling: Mixing Methodologies for Organizational Intervention.* Dordrecht: Kluwer Academic Publishers.

Checkland, P., and J. Poulter (2006). *Learning for Action: A Short Definitive Account of Soft Systems Methodology and Its Use for Practitioners, Teachers and Students.* Hoboken, NJ: John Wiley & Sons.

Fildes, R. A., P. Goodwin, M. Lawrence, and K. Nikolopoulos (2009). Effective forecasting and judgmental adjustments: An empirical evaluation and strategies for improvement in supply-chain planning. *International Journal of Forecasting* 25, 3–23.

Hawitt, D. (2010). Should you report forecast error or forecast accuracy? *Foresight* 18 (Summer), 46.

Hoover, J., and M. Little (2011). Two commentaries on forecast error vs. forecast accuracy. *Foresight* 18 (Spring), 45–46.

3.4 MEASURING FORECAST ACCURACY*

Rob Hyndman

Drawing from his online textbook *Forecasting: Principles and Practice* (coauthored with George Athanasopoulos), Rob Hyndman explains the use of Training and Test sets for evaluating forecasting performance.

A common "worst practice" is to select forecasting models based solely on their fit to the history that was used to construct them. Unscrupulous consultants or forecasting software vendors can impress customers with models that closely (or even perfectly) fit their history—yet fit to history provides little indication of how well the model will forecast the future.

Hyndman shows how forecast model development can be improved by dividing history into "training data" (used to estimate the model), and "test data" (used to evaluate forecasts generated by the model). (These terms have the same meaning as "fit set" and "test set" respectively, the terms used in the Tashman article.) When there is sufficient history, about 20% (the most recent observations) should be "held out" to serve as test data. For shorter time series, Hyndman illustrates the method of *time series cross-validation*, in which a series of training and test sets are used.

Everyone wants to know how accurate their forecasts are. Does your forecasting method give good forecasts? Are they better than the competitor methods?

There are many ways of measuring the accuracy of forecasts, and the answers to these questions depends on what is being forecast, what accuracy measure is used, and what data set is used for computing the accuracy measure. In this article, I will summarize the most important and useful approaches.

Training and Test Sets

It is important to evaluate forecast accuracy using genuine forecasts. That is, it is invalid to look at how well a model fits the historical data; the accuracy of forecasts can only be determined by considering how well a model performs on new data that were not used when estimating the model. When choosing models, it is common to use a portion of the available data for testing, and use the rest of the data for estimating (or "training") the model. Then the testing data can be used to measure how well the model is likely to forecast on new data.

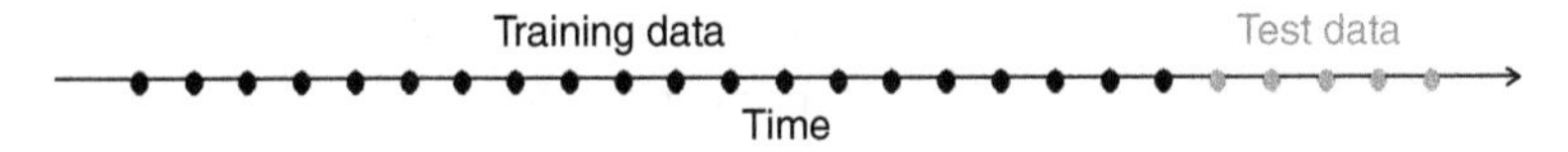

Figure 3.5 A time series is often divided into training data (used to estimate the model) and test data (used to evaluate the forecasts).

* This article is based on Section 2.5 of *Forecasting: Principles and Practice* by Rob J. Hyndman and George Athanasopoulos, available online at www.otexts.org/fpp/2/5, and used with permission.

The size of the test data set is typically about 20% of the total sample, although this value depends on how long the sample is and how far ahead you want to forecast. The size of the test set should ideally be at least as large as the maximum forecast horizon required.

The following points should be noted:

- A model that fits the data well does not necessarily forecast well.
- A perfect fit can always be obtained by using a model with enough parameters.
- Overfitting a model to data is as bad as failing to identify the systematic pattern in the data.

Some references describe the test data as the "hold-out set" because these data are "held out" of the data used for fitting. Other references call the training data the "in-sample data" and the test data the "out-of-sample data."

Forecast Accuracy Measures

Suppose our data set is denoted by $y_1, \ldots, y_T$, and we split it into two sections: the training data $(y_1, \ldots, y_N)$ and the test data $(y_{N+1}, \ldots, y_T)$. To check the accuracy of our forecasting method, we will estimate the parameters using the training data, and forecast the next $T - N$ observations. These forecasts can then be compared to the test data.

The h-step-ahead forecast can be written as $\hat{y}_{N+h|N}$. The "hat" notation indicates that it is an estimate rather than an observed value, and the subscript indicates that we are estimating $\hat{y}_{N+h}$ using all the data observed up to and including time N.

The forecast errors are the difference between the actual values in the test set and the forecasts produced using only the data in the training set. Thus

$$e_t = y_t - \hat{y}_{t|N} \quad \text{for } t = N+1, \ldots, T.$$

Scale-Dependent Errors

These errors are on the same scale as the data. For example, if y_t is sales volume in kilograms, then e_t is also in kilograms. Accuracy measures that are based directly on e_t are therefore scale-dependent and cannot be used to make comparisons between series that are on different scales.

The two most commonly used scale-dependent measures are based on the absolute errors or squared errors:

$$\text{Mean absolute error: MAE} = \text{mean}(|e_i|),$$

$$\text{Root mean squared error: RMSE} = \sqrt{\text{mean}(e_i^2)}.$$

When comparing forecast methods on a single data set, the MAE is popular as it is easy to understand and compute.

Percentage Errors

The percentage error is given by $p_t = 100e_t/y_t$. Percentage errors have the advantage of being scale-independent, and so are frequently used to compare forecast performance between different data sets. The most commonly used measure is:

$$\text{Mean absolute percentage error: MAPE} = \text{mean}(|p_t|).$$

Measures based on percentage errors have the disadvantage of being infinite or undefined if $y_t = 0$ for any observation in the test set, and having extreme values when any y_t is close to zero.

Another problem with percentage errors that is often overlooked is that they assume a scale based on quantity. If y_t is measured in dollars, or kilograms, or some other quantity, percentages make sense. On the other hand, a percentage error makes no sense when measuring the accuracy of temperature forecasts on the Fahrenheit or Celsius scales, because these are not measuring a quantity. One way to think about it is that percentage errors only make sense if changing the scale does not change the percentage. Changing y_t from kilograms to pounds will give the same percentages, but changing y_t from Fahrenheit to Celsius will give different percentages.

Scaled Errors

Scaled errors were proposed by Hyndman and Koehler (2006) as an alternative to using percentage errors when comparing forecast accuracy across series on different scales. A scaled error is given by $q_t = e_t/Q$ where Q is a scaling statistic computed on the training data. For a nonseasonal time series, a useful way to define the scaling statistic is the mean absolute difference between consecutive observations:

$$Q = \frac{1}{N-1}\sum_{j=2}^{N}|y_j - y_{j-1}|.$$

That is, Q is the MAE for naïve forecasts computed on the training data. Because the numerator and denominator both involve values on the scale of the original data, q_t is independent of the scale of the data. A scaled error is less than one if it arises from a better forecast than the average naïve forecast computed on the training data. Conversely, it is greater than one if the forecast is worse than the average naïve forecast computed on the training data. For seasonal time series, a scaling statistic can be defined using seasonal naïve forecasts:

$$Q = \frac{1}{N-m} \sum_{j=m+1}^{N} \left| y_j - y_{j-m} \right|.$$

The mean absolute scaled error is simply

$$\text{MASE} = \text{mean}(|q_j|) = \text{MAE}/Q.$$

The value of Q is calculated using the training data because it is important to get a stable measure of the scale of the data. The training set is usually much larger than the test set, and so allows a better estimate of Q.

Example: Australian Quarterly Beer Production

Figure 3.6 shows forecasts for quarterly Australian beer production (data source: Australian Bureau of Statistics, Cat. No. 8301.0.55.001). An ARIMA model was estimated on the training data (data from 1992 to 2006), and forecasts for the next 14 quarters were produced. The actual values for the period 2007–2010 are also shown.

The forecast accuracy measures are computed in Table 3.4. The scaling constant for the MASE statistic was $Q = 14.55$ (based on the training data 1992–2006).

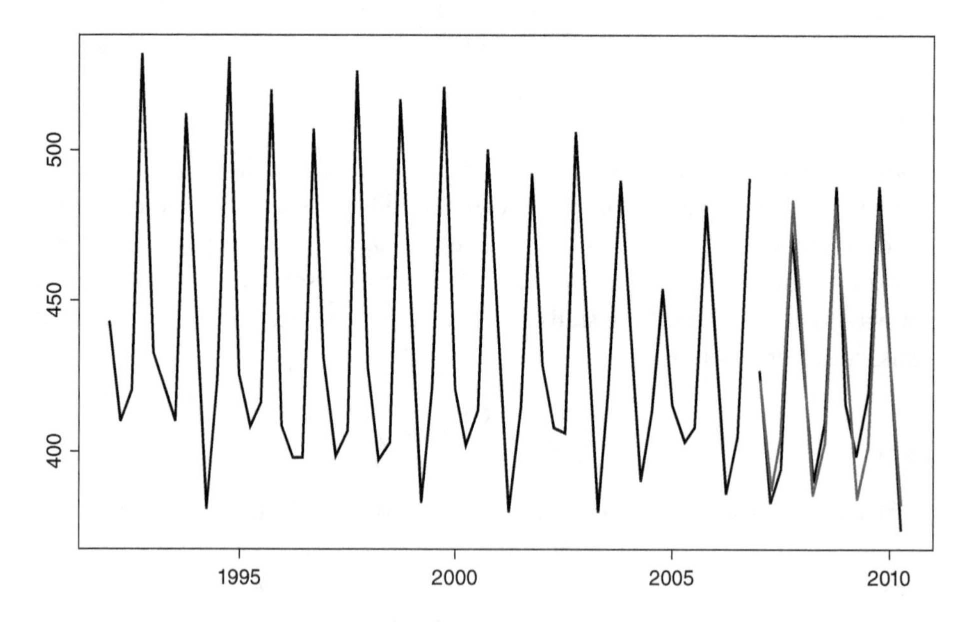

Figure 3.6 Forecasts of Australian quarterly beer production using an ARIMA model applied to data up to the end of 2006. The thin line shows actual values (in the training and test data sets) while the thick line shows the forecasts.

Table 3.4 Accuracy Measures Computed from ARIMA Forecasts for the 14 Observations in the Test Data

	Actual	Forecast	Error	Percent Error
2007 QI	427	423.69	3.31	0.78
2007 Q2	383	386.88	-3.88	-1.01
2007 Q3	394	404.71	-10.71	-2.72
2007 Q4	473	483.59	-10.59	-2.24
200S QI	420	423.81	-3.81	-0.91
200S Q2	390	385.42	4.58	1.17
200S Q3	410	403.25	6.75	1.65
2008 Q4	488	482.13	5.87	1.20
2009 QI	415	422.35	-7.35	-1.77
2009 Q2	398	383.96	14.04	3.53
2009 Q3	419	401.79	17.21	4.11
2009 Q4	488	480.67	7.33	1.50
2010 QI	414	420.89	-6.89	-1.66
2010 Q2	374	382.50	-8.50	-2.27
MAE			7.92	
RMSE			8.82	
MAPE				1.89%
MASE			0.54	

Time-Series Cross-Validation

For short time series, we do not want to limit the available data by splitting some off in a test set. Also, if the test set is small, the conclusions we draw from the forecast accuracy measures may not be very reliable. One solution to these problems is to use *time-series cross-validation.*

In this approach, we use many different training sets, each one containing one more observation than the previous one. Figure 3.7 shows the series of training sets (in black) and test sets (in gray). The forecast accuracy measures are calculated on each test set and the results are averaged across all test sets (adjusting for their different sizes).

A variation on this approach focuses on a single forecast horizon for each test set. Figure 3.8 shows a series of test sets containing only one observation in each case. Then the calculation of accuracy measures is for one-step forecasts, rather than averaging across several forecast horizons.

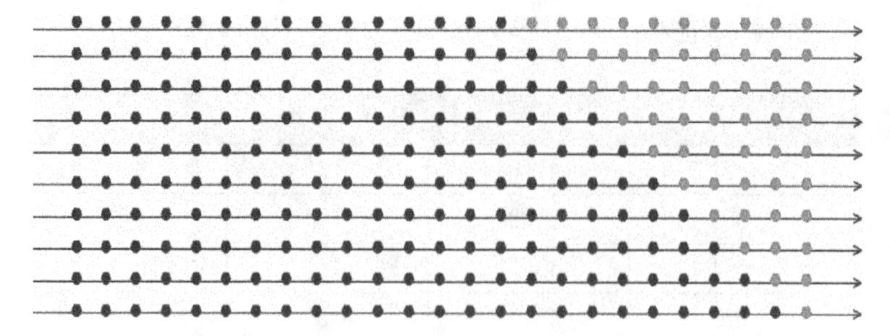

Figure 3.7 In time series cross-validation, a series of training and test sets are used. Each training set (black) contains one more observation than the previous one, and consequently each test set (gray) has one fewer observations than the previous one.

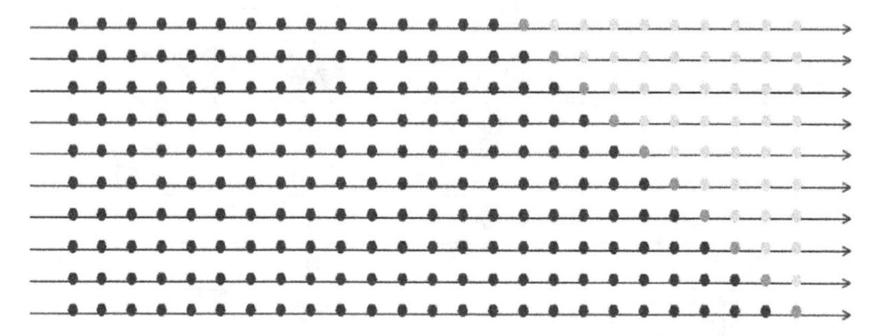

Figure 3.8 Time-series cross-validation based on one-step forecasts. The black points are training sets, the gray points are test sets, and the light-gray points are ignored.

In any of these cross-validation approaches, we need a minimum size for the training set because it is often not possible to do any meaningful forecasting if there is not enough data in the training set to estimate our chosen model. The minimum size of the training set depends on the complexity of the model we want to use.

Suppose k observations are required to produce a reliable forecast. Then the process works as follows:

1. Select the observation at time $k + i$ for the test set, and use the observations at times $1, 2, \ldots, k + i - 1$ to estimate the forecasting model. Compute the error on the forecast for time $k + i$.
2. Repeat the above step for $i = 1, 2, \ldots, T - k$ where T is the total number of observations.
3. Compute the forecast accuracy measures based on the errors obtained.

This procedure is sometimes known as evaluation on a "rolling forecasting origin" because the "origin" $(k + i - 1)$ at which the forecast is based rolls forward in time.

With time-series forecasting, one-step forecasts may not be as relevant as multistep forecasts. In this case, the cross-validation procedure based on a rolling forecasting origin can be modified to allow multistep errors to be used. Suppose we are interested in models that produce good h-step-ahead forecasts:

1. Select the observation at time $k + h + i - 1$ for the test set, and use the observations at times 1, 2, . . . , $k + i - 1$ to estimate the forecasting model. Compute the h-step error on the forecast for time $k + h + i - e$.
2. Repeat the above step for $i = 1, 2, \ldots, T - k - h + 1$ where T is the total number of observations.
3. Compute the forecast accuracy measures based on the errors obtained. When $h = 1$, this gives the same procedure as outlined above.

Example: Australian Quarterly Beer Production

To illustrate the above procedure (for one-step forecasts only), we will use the Australian beer data again, with an ARIMA model estimated for each training set. We will select a new ARIMA model at each step using the Hyndman–Khandakar (2006) algorithm, and forecast the first observation that is not in the training data. The minimum size of the training data is set to $k = 16$ observations, and there are $T = 74$ total observations in the data. Therefore, we compute $58 = 74 - 16$ models and their one-step forecasts. The resulting errors are used to compute some accuracy measures:

To calculate the MASE we need to compute the scaling statistic Q, but we do not want the value of Q to change with each training set. One approach is to compute Q using all the available data. Note that Q does not affect the forecasts at all, so this does not violate our rule of not using the data we are trying to forecast when producing our forecasts. The value of Q using all available data is $Q = 13.57$, so that MASE = 11.14/13.57 = 0.82. This shows that, on average, our forecasting model is giving errors that are about 82% as large as those that would be obtained if we used a seasonal naïve forecast.

Notice that the values of the accuracy measures are worse now than they were before, even though these measures are computed on one-step forecasts and the previous calculations were averaged across 14 forecast horizons. In general, the further ahead you forecast, the less accurate your forecasts should be. On the other hand, it is harder to predict accurately with a smaller training

Table 3.5 Error Measures Calculated on One-Step Forecasts Computed Using a Time-Series Cross-Validation Beginning with 16 Observations in the Training Data, and Finishing with 73 Observations in the Training Data

MAE	11.14
RMSE	14.66
MAPE	2.57%

set because there is greater estimation error. Finally, the previous results were on a relatively small test set (only 14 observations) and so they are less reliable than the cross-validation results, which are calculated on 58 observations.

Conclusions

- Always calculate forecast accuracy measures using test data that was not used when computing the forecasts.
- Use the MAE or RMSE if all your forecasts are on the same scale.
- Use the MAPE if you need to compare forecast accuracy on several series with different scales, unless the data contain zeros or small values, or are not measuring a quantity.
- Use the MASE if you need to compare forecast accuracy on several series with different scales, especially when the MAPE is inappropriate.
- Use time series cross-validation where possible, rather than a simple training/test set split.

REFERENCES

Hyndman, R. J., and G. Athanasopoulos (2012). *Forecasting: Principles and Practice.* OTexts. http://otexts.com/fpp.

Hyndman, R. J., and Y. Khandakar (2008). Automatic time series forecasting: The forecast package for R. *Journal of Statistical Software* 26(3), 1–22.

Hyndman, R. J., and A. B. Koehler (2006). Another look at measures of forecast accuracy. *International Journal of Forecasting* 22(4), 679–688.

3.5 SHOULD WE DEFINE FORECAST ERROR AS $e = F - A$ OR $e = A - F$?*

Kesten Green and Len Tashman

The definition of forecast error is the subject of a seemingly perpetual debate. The question is posed in online chat groups, discussed in classrooms and conferences, and pontificated upon in blogs and articles. In order to resolve the debate and provide a definitive answer, Kesten Green and Len Tashman report results of a survey to members of the International Institute of Forecasters (IIF).

Green and Tashman asked one question: Should forecast error be defined as (a) error = actual – forecast or (b) error = forecast – actual? Although the responses were about evenly divided (so the debate remains unresolved), this article provides a useful summary of the arguments for and against each alternative.

---

* This article originally appeared in *Foresight: The International Journal of Applied Forecasting* (Summer 2008), and appears here courtesy of the International Institute of Forecasters.

The Issue

Suppose we forecast sales of 900 units for the month just gone (F), and actual sales (A) were recorded as 827 units. The difference between the two figures, 73 units, is the magnitude of the forecast error.

One way to express the forecast error is as A minus F ($A - F$), which yields an error of:

$$e = 827 - 900 = -73\text{units}.$$

Alternatively, the forecast error can also be expressed as F minus A ($F - A$). Using this formulation, the forecast error for the month just gone is:

$$e = 900 - 827 = +73\text{units}.$$

Does it matter which formula we use?

The Survey

In March of this year, Kesten Green sent the following message to the membership of the International Institute of Forecasters (IIF):

Dear All,

How should "forecast error" be defined? A Google Scholar search for "error 'forecast minus actual'" and for the reverse formulation turns up 51 and 46 hits respectively—almost a tie.

I asked a small sample of senior IIF members (two) whether they prefer to define forecast error as $A - F$ or as $F - A$, and why. Again, opinion was divided, with one preferring the $A - F$ definition as derived from the basic statistical model formulation of $A = F + e$, while the other preferred the more intuitively appealing $F - A$ whereby a positive error means that the forecast was too high.

I'd like to know what you think: Which do you prefer, and why?

Regards,

Kesten

By the time of writing, eleven responses had been received, with more than half preferring to calculate error as $A - F$.

Respondents who preferred $F - A$ all reasoned that it was more intuitive that a positive error represented an over-forecast and a negative error an under-forecast. $F - A$ is also more consistent with concepts of bias.

Respondents who preferred the $A - F$ formulation argued that statistical convention, ease of statistical calculation, investment in software that adhered to statistical convention, and plain pragmatism provided justification. Two fans of $A - F$ also suggested that this version is intuitive when assessing performance against a budget or plan, because a positive value indicates that a budget has been exceeded or a plan has been surpassed.

Here is an edited sampling of the individual responses:

Support for $A - F$

1. Can't say I've ever thought of "why," since the statistical measure is always $A - F$, with the basic idea being:

$$A = \text{forecast model} + \text{forecast error}.$$

This basic concept provides the justification. Obviously, there is no mathematical reason why it could not be forecast model minus forecast error, but that would be more complex and therefore not sensible.

2. I use Actual minus Forecast. I am a pragmatist and do not believe there is a right answer—merely a need to settle the answer by convention. I am saying that there is, as a matter of fact, no basis for finding a right answer, and seeking one is fruitless; thus the need for a convention. Of course, all of us will be attached to the method we frequently use and will easily find justifications for its correctness.

3. In statistical terms, the forecast is an expected value. A deviation in statistical computations is actual minus mean or other expected value. Thus, error = $A - F$ is consistent with standard statistical calculations, actual minus mean.

In planning and control settings, the sign of the deviation can be important in the context of a negative feedback control loop.

There are other explanations; however, none preclude the opposite definition, but an additional operation (subtraction) would be necessary to make e = $F - A$ operable in the planning and control settings.

4. In seismology, where the sign of prediction error does matter (model) forecasted travel time comes with "–," i.e., we use error = $A - F$. Effectively, when actual seismic wave arrives before the time predicted by model we have negative travel time residual (error).

5. I agree that $A - F$ is counterintuitive in that a positive error means that a forecast was too low.

However, $A - F$ makes sense for people using forecasts to set budgets or make plans (e.g., a positive value would show that the budget or plan has been exceeded).

Exponential smoothing corrects for its past errors. In its specification $A - F$ arguably makes life a bit simpler as we have $F_{t+1} = F_t$ + alpha * error, rather than $F_{t+1} = F_t$ – alpha * error, which may be a bit more difficult to explain.

In regression, fitted residuals and forecast errors are measured in the same way if we stick to $A - F$. If we were also to start using $F - A$ for residuals, then the whole of regression analysis and its associated software would need to be revised.

6. I use $A - F$, and I do feel this is the mathematically correct answer. [Respondent #5] has already provided an excellent defense of this position, so I won't bother to elaborate further.

But since both formulae appear to be commonly used, how does a forecaster communicate a signed forecast error to someone else?

Obviously, if both parties know the convention being used, then there is not an issue. Unfortunately, I feel that even if the participants in this discussion were to decide upon a convention, it is unlikely to be universally adopted in the near future. So what's a forecaster to do when confronted with having to communicate a signed forecast error to someone who is ignoring this thread? I would suggest that we teach our students to use the words "overforecasted" and "underforecasted."

Stating "I overforecasted by 200 units" is unambiguous, and conveys the same information as "my forecast error was −200" (to an $A - F$ type like me).

7. I think that $A - F$ makes a lot more sense; as in common financial terms, F would be budget (B) and a positive Actual minus Budget would be over budget while a negative would be under budget.

Support for $F - A$

1. The one advantage of $F - A$ is that it fits intuition that a positive error is an over-forecast and a negative error an underforecast.

2. I would prefer and use forecast error as $F - A$ since it is easy to explain that positive bias means forecast is higher than actual and negative bias means forecast is lower than actual.

3. It makes intuitive sense to express error in the same way that bias is interpreted, i.e., $F - A$, where positive indicates "over."

More important: From a business point of view, it only really matters that you track it against history as a relative point of reference to gauge improvement (or not). So it's really up to the users.

Most error (not bias) measures discard the sign in favor of working with absolute or standardized data, so the effect is minimal there.

4. When I'm in a training session and one of the students says, "My error was too high (or too big or too positive)," this means that it was the forecast that was too high; forecast bigger than the observed value means that the error in popular vernacular is positive.

If, on the other hand, he says his error was very negative, then what he means to say is that the forecast was lower than the observed value. In common vernacular, the reference point is the observed value and the forecast is compared to it, either too high or too low, either too positive or too negative.

Mathematically, it's better (or easier or more consistent) to use $A = F + e$ for the few in the human race who believe that mathematical propositions are more reasonable (or scientific, or structured). To understand what this means—that $F = A + e$ doesn't work very well for mathematical formulations—I had to go to graduate school.

3.6 PERCENTAGE ERROR: WHAT DENOMINATOR?*

Kesten Green and Len Tashman

In a second survey of IIF members, Green and Tashman asked another frequently discussed (but unresolved) question: What should the denominator be when calculating percentage error (Actual, Forecast, or something else)?

Although a majority of respondents favored using the Actual as denominator, 29% favored something else. Preferred alternatives included:

- Max (*F*,*A*)—assures that percent error is always scaled between 0 and 100%.
- Mean (*F*,*A*)—results in what is known as symmetric MAPE (sMAPE).
- Average of Actuals—results in a MAD/Mean type of measure.
- Absolute average of period-over-period differences in the data—results in MASE.

While this survey does not definitely resolve the question, it shares the valuable reasoning and insights of the respondents.

The Issue

This is our second survey on the measurement of forecast error. We reported the results of our first survey in the Summer 2008 issue of *Foresight* (Green and Tashman, 2008). The question we asked in that survey was whether to define forecast error as Actual minus Forecast ($A - F$) or Forecast minus Actual ($F - A$). Respondents made good arguments for both of the alternatives.

In the current survey, we asked how *percentage forecast error* should be measured. In particular: What should the denominator be when calculating percentage error (See Figure 3.9)?

We posed the question to the *International Institute of Forecasters* discussion list as well as to *Foresight* subscribers, in the following way:

The first two options in the questionnaire have each been used when calculating the mean absolute percentage error (MAPE) for multiple forecast periods. The first option is the more traditional form.

One popular alternative to using either A or F as the denominator is to take an average of the two: $(A + F)/2$. Calculated over multiple forecast periods, this measure is most commonly called the symmetric MAPE (sMAPE) and has been used in recent forecasting competitions to compare the accuracy of

* This article originally appeared in *Foresight: The International Journal of Applied Forecasting* (Winter 2009), and appears here courtesy of the International Institute of Forecasters.

To calculate a percentage error, it is better to use...

	(Check or write in)
1. The actual value (A) as the denominator	[ ]
2. The forecast (F) as the denominator	[ ]
3. Neither (A) nor (F) but some other value	[ ]

I recommend my choice of denominator, because:____

Figure 3.9 Survey Question

forecasts from different methods. See, for example, www.neural-forecasting-competition.com/index.htm.

Survey Results

We received 61 usable responses: 34 of these (a majority of 56%) preferred option 1, using the Actual as the denominator for the percentage error; 15% preferred option 2, using the Forecast as the denominator; while 29% chose option 3, something other than the actual or the forecast.

One respondent wrote: *"For our company, this issue led to a very heated debate with many strong points of view. I would imagine that many other organizations will go through the same experience."*

*Option 1: Percentage Error = Error / Actual * 100*

Of the 34 proponents of using the Actual value for the denominator, 31 gave us their reasons. We have organized their responses by theme.

A. The Actual is the forecaster's target.

Actual value is the forecast target and therefore should represent the baseline for measurement.

The measure of our success must be how close we came to "the truth."

Actual is the "stake in the ground" against which we should measure variance.

Since forecasting what actually happened is always our goal, we should be comparing how well we did to the actual value.

We should measure performance against reality.

B. The Actual is the only consistent basis for comparing forecast accuracy against a benchmark or for judging improvement over time.

Actual is the only acceptable denominator because it represents the only objective benchmark for comparison.

Without a fixed point of reference quantity in the denominator, you will have trouble comparing the errors of one forecast to another.

You want to compare the forecast to actuals and not the other way around. The actuals are the most important factor. It drives safety stock calculations that are based on standard deviation of forecast error calculations that use actuals as the denominator.

Forecast error is measured here as (Actual – Forecast)/Actual, for comparability to other studies.

C. The Actuals serve as the weights for a weighted MAPE.

Using the Actuals is more consistent for calculating a weighted average percentage error (WAPE) for a group of SKUs or even for the full product portfolio. Using actual value as denominator is providing the weight for the different SKUs, which is more understandable—one is weighting different SKUs based on their actual contribution. If we use F (forecast), this means we will weigh them based on the forecast—but this can be challenged as subjective. Someone may calculate the single SKU accuracy based on F as denominator, and then weigh according to Actual sales of each SKU, but this unnecessarily complicates the formula.

D. The Actual is the customary and expected denominator of the MAPE.

I would argue that the standard definition of "percent error" uses the Actual. The Actual is used without any discussion of alternatives in the first three textbooks I opened, it is used in most forecasting software, and it is used on Wikipedia (at least until someone changes it).

If you are creating a display that reads "percent error" or "MAPE" for others to read without further explanation, you should use Actual—this is what is expected.

Actual is the generally used and accepted formula; if you use an alternative, such as the Forecast, you might need to give it a new name in order to avoid confusion.

E. Use of the Actual gives a more intuitive interpretation.

If the forecast value is > the actual value, then the percentage error with the forecast in the denominator cannot exceed 100%, which is misleading. For example, if the Actual is 100 and the Forecast is 1,000, the average percentage error with Actual is 900% but with Forecast is only 90%. (Ed. note: See Table 3.6 (1a) for an illustrative calculation.)

The reason is pragmatic. If Actual is, say, 10 and Forecast is 20, most people would say the percentage error is 100%, not 50%. Or they would say forecast is twice what it should have been, not that the actual is half the forecast.

Table 3.6 Illustrative Calculations

A	F	Absolute Error	% Error with A	% Error with F	Avg A&F	% Error w/Avg
1a. If the Forecast exceeds the Actual, the % error cannot exceed 100%						
100	200	100	100%	50%	150	67%
100	1000	900	900%	90%	550	164%
100	10000	9900	9900%	99%	5050	196%
1b. Illustration of the symmetry of the sMAPE						
100	50	50	50%	100%	75	67%
50	100	50	100%	50%	75	67%
1c. When the Actual equals zero, use of sMAPE always yields 200%						
0	50	50	#DIV/0!	100%	25	200%
0	100	100	#DIV/0!!	100%	50	200%

By relating the magnitude of the forecast error to an Actual figure, the result can be easily communicated to non-specialists.

From a retail perspective, explaining "overforecasting" when Forecast is the denominator seems illogical to business audiences.

F. Using the Forecast in the denominator allows for manipulation of the forecast result.

Utilizing the Forecast as the benchmark is subjective and creates the opportunity for the forecaster to manipulate results.

Use of the Actual eliminates "denominator management."

Using Forecast encourages high forecasting.

G. Caveats: There are occasions when the Actual can't be used.

Use of Actual only works for non-0 values of the Actual.

If you are trying to overcome difficulties related to specific data sets (e.g., low volume, zeroes, etc.) or biases associated with using a percentage error, then you may want to create a statistic that uses a different denominator than the Actual. However, once you do so, you need to document your nonstandard definition of "percentage error" to anyone who will be using it.

For me, the Actual is the reference value. But in my job I deal with long-term (5–10 years+) forecasts, and the Actual is seldom "actually" seen. And since you're asking this question, my suspicion tells me the issue is more complicated than this.

*Option 2: Percentage Error = Error / Forecast * 100*

Eight of the 9 respondents who preferred to use the Forecast value for the denominator provided their reasons for doing so. Their responses fell into two groups.

A. Using Forecast in the denominator enables you to measure performance against forecast or plan.

For business assessment of forecast performance, the relevant benchmark is the plan—a forecast, whatever the business term. The relevant error is percent variation from plan, not from actual (nor from an average of the two).

For revenue forecasting, using the Forecast as the denominator is considered to be more appropriate since the forecast is the revenue estimate determining and constraining the state budget. Any future budget adjustments by the governor and legislature due to changing economic conditions are equal to the percentage deviations from the forecasted amounts initially used in the budget. Therefore, the error as a percent of the forecasted level is the true measure of the necessary adjustment, instead of the more commonly used ratio of (actual – forecast)/actual.

It has always made more sense to me that the forecasted value be used as the denominator, since it is the forecasted value on which you are basing your decisions.

The forecast is what drives manufacturing and is what is communicated to shareholders.

You are measuring the accuracy of a forecast, so you divide by the forecast. I thought this was a standard approach in science and statistics.

If we were to measure a purely statistical forecast (no qualitative adjustments), we would use Actual value (A) as the denominator because statistically this should be the most consistent number. However, once qualitative input (human judgment) from sales is included, there is an element that is not purely statistical in nature.

For this reason, we have chosen to rather divide by forecast value (F) such that we measure performance to our forecast.

B. The argument that the use of Forecast in the denominator opens the opportunity for manipulation is weak.

The politicizing argument is very weak, since the forecast is in the numerator in any case. It also implies being able to tamper with the forecast after the fact, and that an unbiased forecast is not a goal of the forecasting process.

*Option 1 or 2: Percentage Error = Error / [Actual or Forecast: It Depends] * 100*

Several respondents indicated that they would choose *A* or *F*, depending on the purpose of the forecast.

Actual, if measuring deviation of forecast from actual values. Forecast, if measuring actual events deviated from the forecast.

If the data are always positive and if the zero is meaningful, then use Actual. This gives the MAPE and is easy to understand and explain. Otherwise we need an alternative to Actual in the denominator.

The actual value must be used as a denominator whenever comparing forecast performance over time and/or between groups. Evaluating performance is an assessment of how close the forecasters come to the actual or "true" value. If forecast is used in the denominator, then performance assessment is sullied by the magnitude of the forecasted quantity.

If Sales and Marketing are being measured and provided incentives based on how well they forecast, then we measure the variance of the forecast of each from the actual value. If Sales forecast 150 and Marketing forecast 70 and actual is 100, then Sales forecast error is (150–100)/150 = 33% while Marketing forecast error is (70–100)/70 = 43%. When Forecast is the denominator, then Sales appears to be the better forecaster—even though their forecast had a greater difference to actual.

When assessing the impact of forecast error on deployment and/or production, then forecast error should be calculated with Forecast in the denominator because inventory planning has been done assuming the forecast is the true value.

*Option 3: Percentage Error = Error / [Something Other Than Actual or Forecast] * 100*

One respondent indicated use of Actual or Forecast, whichever had the higher value. No explanation was given.

Three respondents use the average of the Actual and the Forecast.

Averaging actual and forecast to get the denominator results in a symmetrical percent-error measure. (See Table 3.6 (1b) for an illustration, and the article by Goodwin and Lawton (1999) for a deeper analysis of the symmetry of the sMAPE.)

There likely is no "silver bullet" here, but it might be worthwhile to throw into the mix using the average of F and A—this helps solve the division-by-zero issues and helps take out the bias. Using F alone encourages high forecasting; using A alone does not deal with zero actuals. (Ed. note: Unfortunately, the averaging of A and F does not deal with the zero problem. When A is zero, the division of the forecast error by the average of A and F always results in a percentage error equal to 200%, as shown in Table 3.6 (1c) and discussed by Boylan and Syntetos [2006].)

I find the corrected sMAPE adequate for most empirical applications without implying any cost structure, although it is slightly downward biased. In company scenarios, I have switched to suggesting a weighted MAPE (by turnover, etc.) if it is used for decision making and tracking.

Four respondents suggest use of some "average of Actual values" in the denominator.

Use the mean of the series. Handles the case of intermittent data, is symmetrical, and works for cross section. (This recommendation leads to use of the MAD/Mean, as recommended by Kolassa and Schutz [2007].)

My personal favorite is MAD/Mean. It is stable, even for slow-moving items, it can be easily explained, and it has a straightforward percentage interpretation.

A median baseline, or trimmed average, using recent periods, provides a stable and meaningful denominator.

I prefer a "local level" as the denominator in all the error % calculations. (Ed. note: The local level can be thought of as a weighted average of the historical data.) When using Holt-Winters, I use the level directly, as it is a highly reliable indication of the current trading level of the time series. In addition, it isn't affected by outliers and seasonality. The latter factors may skew readings (hence, interpretations) dramatically and lead to incorrect decisions.

With other types of forecasting—such as multivariate—there's always some "local constant" that can be used. Even a median of the last 6 months would do. The main problem that arises here is what to do when this level approaches zero. This—hopefully—does not happen often in any set of data to be measured. It would rather point, as a diagnostic, to issues other than forecasting that need dire attention.

Two Respondents Recommend that the Denominator Be the Absolute Average of the Period-Over-Period Differences in the Data, Yielding a MASE (Mean Absolute Scaled Error)

The denominator should be equal to the mean of the absolute differences in the historical data. This is better, for example, than the mean of the historical data, because that mean could be close to zero. And, if the data are nonstationary (e.g., trended), then the mean of the historical data will change systematically as more data are collected. However, the mean of the absolute differences will be well behaved, even if the data are nonstationary, and it will always be positive. It has the added advantage of providing a neat, interpretable statistic: the MASE. Values less than 1 mean that the forecasts are more accurate than the in-sample, naïve, one-step forecasts. (See Hyndman, 2006.)

Mean absolute scaled error, which uses the average absolute error for the random walk forecast (i.e., the absolute differences in the data).

REFERENCES

Boylan, J., and A. Syntetos (2006). Accuracy and accuracy-implication metrics for intermittent demand. *Foresight: International Journal of Applied Forecasting* 4, 39–42.

Goodwin, P., and R. Lawton (1999). On the asymmetry of the symmetric MAPE. *International Journal of Forecasting* 15, 405–408.

Green, K. C., and L. Tashman (2008). Should we define forecast error as $e = F - A$ or $e = A - F$? *Foresight: International Journal of Applied Forecasting* 10, 38–40.

Hyndman, R. (2006). Another look at forecast-accuracy metrics for intermittent demand. *Foresight: International Journal of Applied Forecasting* 4, 43–46.

Kolassa, S., and W. Schutz (2007). Advantages of the MAD/MEAN ratio over the MAPE. *Foresight: International Journal of Applied Forecasting* 6, 40–43.

3.7 PERCENTAGE ERRORS CAN RUIN YOUR DAY*

Stephan Kolassa and Roland Martin

While mean absolute percent error (MAPE) or one of its variants is the most commonly used forecasting performance metric, it has many recognized weaknesses. For example, when we compute the absolute percent error the usual way, as

$$\text{APE} = |\,\text{Forecast} - \text{Actual}\,| \,/\, \text{Actual}$$

APE is undefined when Actual = 0, a particular problem when the historical demands are intermittent. It can also lead to huge percent error values when Actual is very small compared to the size of the error.

Stephan Kolassa and Roland Martin now alert us to yet another danger. They show how you can be led astray if you use the MAPE to select a best forecasting method or to reward forecast accuracy. Minimizing the MAPE is often not a good idea.

There are some good reasons why MAPE and its variants are the most widespread error metrics used by forecasting practitioners: They are intuitive and can be used to assess accuracy for both individual products and across product groups. But one important problem that has not received adequate attention arises when the MAPE is used as the basis for comparisons. MAPE rewards methods that systematically underforecast, especially for series that fluctuate widely.

Kolassa and Martin provide a clever, easy to understand illustration of the problem, by rolling dice (actually a single die). Their example reveals how forecasts chosen on the basis of lowest MAPE can be seriously biased on the low side.

So why should management care? Because if the sole job objective of their forecasters is to minimize MAPE, and those forecasters are smart enough to do the math, the forecasters will purposely forecast too low—perhaps leading to chronic inventory shortages and poor customer service.

* This article originally appeared in *Foresight: The International Journal of Applied Forecasting* (Fall 2011), and appears here courtesy of the International Institute of Forecasters.

Introduction

The accuracy of forecasts needs to be measured in order to decide between different forecasting models, methods, or software systems or even to decide whether monies for forecast improvements will be well spent. Many different forecast accuracy metrics are available, each with its own advantages and disadvantages.

In supply chain forecasting, where we usually forecast demands, orders or sales, the most common accuracy measurement is the absolute percentage error (APE)—the percentage gap between the actual demand and the forecast of it for one time period. When we average the APEs across time periods, we obtain the MAPE, the mean absolute percentage error.

If y_i represents actual demands by time period or by item and associated forecasts, the APE of an individual forecast is

$$\mathrm{APE_i} = \frac{|\hat{y}_i - y_i|}{y_i},$$

and the MAPE of these forecasts is the mean of the APEs,

$$\mathrm{MAPE} = \frac{1}{\mathrm{N}}\sum_{i=1}^{N}\mathrm{APE_i} = \frac{1}{N}\sum_{i=1}^{N}\frac{|\hat{y}_i - y_i|}{y_i}.$$

The APE/MAPE yields an easy interpretation of the error as a percentage of the actual value. As such, it is scale free (not measured in units or currency) and thus can be used to compare forecasting accuracy on time series with different sales levels. These two advantages have led to the MAPE being the best known and most widely used key performance indicator in supply chain forecasting, at least among practitioners.

The MAPE is also used to compare different forecasting methods, to decide between different forecasting software packages in a *forecasting competition* or to measure a forecaster's performance. In all these cases, the MAPE allows such comparisons to be made across the multiple products or services to be forecast. In contrast, scaled error metrics such as the MAD—the mean absolute deviation—cannot provide a basis for comparison between items measured in different units.

However, the MAPE has shortcomings. For instance, it is undefined if one or more of the actual demands are zero, and it explodes if there are demands which are very small compared to the forecast, even though these demands may be outliers, and the forecast may be sensible.

One consequence of these problems is that choosing among options based on which has the lowest MAPE will likely lead to forecasts that are badly biased on the low side. This downward bias is usually not what the forecast user expects or wants. Even a user who has little knowledge of statistics usually expects the forecasts to be "on target," not systematically too high or too low but on average close to the actual values.

This problem is poorly understood both among academic forecasters and practitioners in industry and retail. One reason is that it is difficult to explain the concept of bias and the problem of biased forecasts to nontechnical consulting clients—and most consumers of forecasts as well as managers overseeing forecasters are nontechnical. Consequently, it appears difficult to counterbalance the (obvious) benefits of the MAPE—easy interpretability and scale freeness—with its (less obvious) drawbacks, leading to what we believe to be an overreliance on the MAPE.

So we devised a simple experiment to better explain the problem to nonexperts, one that might be of interest to other practitioners, as well as academic forecasters in consulting or teaching engagements.

All the claims made below can be proved rigorously. Please refer to our white paper (Kolassa and Martin, 2011) for the details.

Rolling Dice

The Basic Demonstration

Take a standard six-sided die and tell the audience that you are going to simulate demands by rolling this die. Explain that the die roll could represent natural variations in demand for an item with no trend, seasonality, or causal factors to influence sales. The die rolls can stand for successive monthly demands of a single product, or for the demands for multiple products during a single month.

Ask the audience what the "best" forecast for the die roll would be. A favorite, almost certainly, would be 3.5—this is the expected value of the die roll: That is, if we roll the die often enough, the result will average 3.5, and over- and underforecasts will be roughly equal. In addition, the audience will understand that using the same forecast for each die roll makes sense, instead of having different forecasts for the first, the second, the third roll, etc.

Tell the audience that you will now compare the forecast of 3.5 to a forecast of 2 and see which has the better (lower) MAPE. It should be obvious that a forecast of 2—far below the expected value of 3.5—makes little sense.

Roll the die (even better, have someone from the audience roll the die) ten times and record the "demands" generated. Calculate the MAPEs of a forecast of 3.5 and of a forecast of 2. What you will find is that, in about 80% of cases, the MAPE for a forecast of 2 will be lower than the MAPE for a forecast of 3.5.

Thus, if we select forecasts based on the MAPE, we would wind up with a biased and probably worthless forecast of 2 instead of an unbiased forecast of 3.5. This should convince the audience that selections based on the MAPE can lead to counterintuitive and problematic forecasts.

Note that we still have a 20% chance that a forecast of 3.5 will yield a MAPE lower than a forecast of 2. If this happens, the audience could be confused about our point. But there is a way to deal with this by slightly bending the rules. Instead of rolling exactly ten times, we can use a stopping rule to determine the number of rolls. When rolling the die, keep a running tally (without telling the audience). Start with 0. If the die roll is 1, subtract 9 from the tally. If the roll is 2, subtract 4. On a rolled 3, add 1, on a 4, add 3, on a 5, add 2, and on a 6, add 2. Only stop rolling the die if the tally is negative.

The Problem with the MAPE

Where does the problem with the MAPE come from? A percentage error explodes if the actual value turns out to be very small compared to the forecast. This, in turn, stems from the inherent asymmetry of percentage errors for under- vs. overforecasts. The most extreme illustration of this asymmetry is that the average percentage error (APE) for an underforecast must be between 0 and 100%—while the APE for an overforecast can easily exceed 100% by far.

For instance, we know that 3.5 on average is the correct forecast for our die roll. If the actual die face turns out to be 2, the forecast of 3.5 yields an APE of 75%. On the other hand, if the actual die face is 5, the APE of our forecast is only 30%. Thus, the APE will differ widely depending on whether we over- or underforecast, even though the absolute error of the forecast is the same in both cases, namely 1.5.

If we for now concentrate only on the outcomes 2 and 5, since 2 and 5 are equally likely actual outcomes (as in throwing dice), we expect an APE of 52.5% (the average of 75% and 30%) on average to result from our forecast of 3.5. What happens if we reduce the forecast slightly to 3? An actual of 2 now yields an APE of 50% (down from 75%), while an actual of 5 yields an APE of 40% (up from 30%). Thus, the improvement in the APE with respect to a low actual was 25%, while the deterioration in APE with respect to a high actual is only 10%. On average, reducing the forecast from 3.5 to 3 will therefore reduce the expected APE from 52.5% to 45%. If our goal is to minimize the APE, we will therefore prefer a forecast of 3 to 3.5—even although 3 is biased downward.

Suppose we have a very good forecasting team that delivers unbiased forecasts, i.e., forecasts that are not systematically too high or too low. If this forecasting team has its yearly performance bonus depend on the MAPE it achieves, we now know that it can improve its MAPE by adjusting its forecasts downward. The resulting forecasts will not be unbiased any more (and thus, probably be worse for downstream planning), but the MAPEs will be lower. Thus, the MAPE will lead to biased forecasts, especially for time series that vary a lot relative to the average—i.e., where there is a high coefficient of variation. In this case, we will see many demands that are a small fraction of the mean, and the MAPE will again lead to forecasts that are biased low.

Is Bias Ever Desirable?

In some cases it may appear that a biased forecast is what the user wants. Normally, we prefer to have too much stock on hand rather than too little, since unsatisfied demands are usually more costly than overstocks. This could be taken to mean that we should aim at forecasts that are higher than the expected value of sales. Conversely, in stocking very perishable and expensive items, such as fresh strawberries, a supermarket would rather go out of stock in mid-afternoon than risk having (expensive) overstock at the end of the day, which would need to be thrown away. In this situation, one could argue that we really want a forecast that errs on the low side (i.e., is biased downward).

And while choosing a forecasting method to minimize the MAPE will lead to downward biased forecasts, doing so to minimize overstock is mistaken. The degree of underforecasting that results from minimizing the MAPE may not correspond to a specifically desired degree of bias. It is much better practice to aim for an unbiased point forecast and for understanding the distribution of demand, from which one can extract a forecast and safety stock that is consistent with the supply chain cost factors. This leads to considering the loss function and a "Cost of Forecast Error" calculation (Goodwin, 2009).

Variants of the APE

A recent survey reported in *Foresight* (Green and Tashman, 2009) found that practitioners use a variety of variants of the APE in order to deal with some of its shortcomings. Do any of these variants reward unbiased forecasts? That is, in the case of rolling the die, does a forecast of 3.5 lead to the lowest APE-type metric?

Variant 1: Using the Forecast Rather than the Actual in the Denominator

While one usually calculates the APE by dividing the absolute forecasting error by the actual value, it is quite common among practitioners to use the forecast instead of the actual as the denominator This "APE with respect to the forecast" (APEf) can also lead to strongly biased forecasts, but this time the forecasts are biased upward, and by the same amount as forecasts obtained by minimizing the standard APE are biased downward.

For our roll of the die, the forecast that minimizes this variant of the APE is 5 (see Table 3.7 and Figure 3.10). Forecasters who understand this but are incentivized to minimize this variant of the APE may engage in "denominator management" (Gilliland, 2010).

Table 3.7 Variants of the APE and the Forecast Yielding the Minimal Expected Error When Rolling a Standard Six-Sided Die

APE Variant	Formula	Forecast That Minimizes the Expected Error in Rolling Dice
Original APE	$\frac{\lvert\hat{y}-y\rvert}{y}$	2
APEf (APE with respect to the forecast)	$\frac{\lvert\hat{y}-y\rvert}{\hat{y}}$	5
sAPE (Symmetric APE)	$\frac{\lvert\hat{y}-y\rvert}{\frac{1}{2}(\hat{y}+y)}$	4
maxAPE (Max of Actual and Forecast)	$\frac{\lvert\hat{y}-y\rvert}{\max\{\hat{y},y\}}$	4
tAPE (Truncated APE)	$\min\left\{\frac{\lvert\hat{y}-y\rvert}{y},1\right\}$	3

Variant 2: Using the Average of the Actual and Forecast—the sAPE

A second variant is the sAPE, which stands for "symmetric APE" and is calculated by using the average of the forecast and the actual for the denominator of the percentage error measurement. The sAPE has been recommended as a remedy to the asymmetry of the APE in dealing with over- vs. underforecasts (O'Connor and colleagues, 1997; O'Connor and Lawrence, 1998; Makridakis and Hibon, 2000).

However, the nature of the sAPE's symmetry is not always understood. While the sAPE is symmetric with regard to the forecast and the actual being exchanged, it is not symmetric with regard to over- and underforecasts for the same actual: For a given actual demand, an underforecast and overforecast of the same amount will yield a different sAPE (Goodwin and Lawton, 1999; Koehler, 2001).

Regarding its potential to select unbiased forecasts, the sAPE lies between the APE (which biases low) and the APEf (which biases high): The sAPE-optimal forecast for a die roll is 4, leading to a slight upward bias, but all forecasts between 3 and 4 are similar in expected sAPE. Thus, the sAPE seems to make the best of a bad situation and may be a better choice than either the "normal" APE or the APEf.

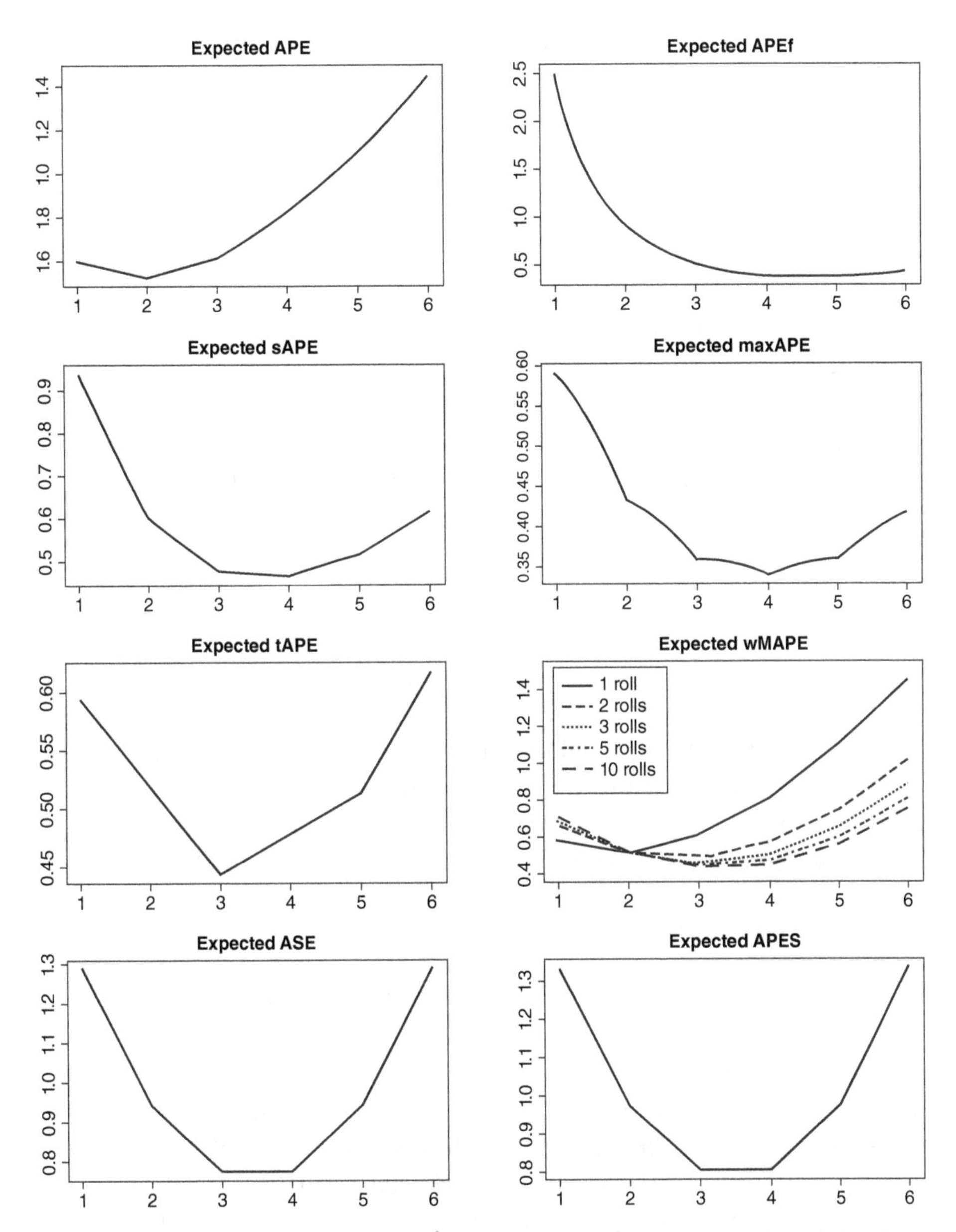

Figure 3.10 Expected Percentage Errors When Rolling a Standard Six-Sided Die, for Variations in APE

Variant 3: Using the Maximum of the Actual and Forecast

Using the maximum of the forecast and the actual as the denominator of the APE was suggested by David Hawitt (2010) as a way of providing an error metric that ranges between 0 and 100%. For our roll of the die, the forecast that yields the lowest "maxAPE" is 4, which is a slight upward bias. Thus, the maxAPE is better than using either the forecast or the actual in the denominator, similar to the sAPE.

Variant 4: Truncating the Maximum Percentage Error at 100%

As discussed above, while the APE of an underforecast can be at most 100%, there is no upper limit to the APE for an overforecast. Jim Hoover (2011) has recommended that the possible explosion of the APE for overforecasts be prevented by truncating the APE at 100%. Thus, the truncated APE (trAPE) will never be above 100%, no matter how badly we overforecast.

This does not completely eliminate the problem of bias. For the roll of the die, the forecast that yields the best trAPE is 3, a slight downward bias. More problematically, we lose discriminatory power—forecasts of 5 and 50 for an actual of 2 both yield a percentage error of 100%, although an extreme overforecast of 50 will probably have far more serious consequences than a lower overforecast of 5.

Alternatives to the APE and Its Variants

The problems with the APE and the variants described in the previous section can be reduced in one of two ways: Either choose a denominator that is independent of both the forecast and the actual value in the forecast horizon, or average the percentage errors in a way that minimizes the problem.

The ASE and the APES

An example of the first approach was suggested by Hyndman and Koehler (2006). Divide an absolute forecasting error by the mean absolute error (across the sample time periods used to build the forecasting model) of a random walk model. The random walk model forecasts each demand as unchanged from the previous time period. The resulting statistic is the absolute scaled error (ASE). Alternatively, Billah and colleagues (2006) suggested dividing the absolute error by the in-sample standard deviation (APES).

Both of these metrics are really the absolute error of the forecast, scaled by some factor that is independent of the forecasts or the actuals in the evaluation period. As the expected absolute error is minimized by an unbiased forecast as long as errors are symmetric, these two measures are too. For the roll of the die, the forecast that yields the lowest expected scaled error is 3.5, right on target.

Weighted MAPEs and the MAD/MEAN

The second approach is to average the percentage errors across forecasting periods (or multiple time series) by a weighted average, using the corresponding actual demands as weights. This contrasts with the (unweighted) MAPE and the variants discussed in the prior section which all are averaged without weights. In fact, a very short calculation shows that the weighted MAPE (wMAPE) is equivalent to dividing the mean absolute error (MAD or MAE) of the forecasts by the mean of the actuals in the forecast period (Kolassa and Schütz, 2007). The result is the ratio: MAD/Mean. If we summarize a large number of APEs, the wMAPE's denominator will thus tend toward the expectation of the actual, i.e., 3.5 and be less and less influenced by the actual realizations encountered, which will reduce but not eliminate the problem of bias.

All these measures are still scale free and lead to natural interpretations of the error as a percentage: of the in-sample random walk MAD, of the in-sample standard deviation, or of the mean of the actuals during the evaluation period. The wMAPE still rewards biased forecasts but to a lesser degree than the MAPE. Moreover, its interpretation as a percentage of averaged actuals makes it attractive and easy to understand. Thus, although these alternative measures are conceptually slightly more complicated than the MAPE, they have a good chance of adoption by forecast users who understand the problems the MAPE suffers from.

Conclusion

We have given a simple illustration, suitable for non-technical audiences, of one of the main problems of the MAPE as a forecast quality measure: It systematically rewards biased forecasts. We recommend that forecasters examine the time series they are asked to forecast and counsel students, users, or consulting clients against using the MAPE as a Key Performance Indicator if the series fluctuates strongly. Rolling dice as explained above may help others understand the problem with the MAPE.

Instead, one of the alternatives described above should be used, ideally combined with some measure of the cost of forecast error. In the end, using KPIs to assess forecast quality without considering how the forecast will be used in subsequent processes will quite probably lead to perverse incentives. Thus, quality control of forecasts should always entail understanding what the forecasts will be used for.

REFERENCES

Billah, B., M. L. King, R. D. Snyder, and A. B. Koehler (2006). Exponential smoothing model selection for forecasting. *International Journal of Forecasting* 22(2), 239–247.

Gilliland, M. (2010). *The Business Forecasting Deal*. Hoboken, NJ: John Wiley & Sons.

Goodwin, P. (2009). Taking stock: Assessing the true cost of forecast error. *Foresight: International Journal of Applied Forecasting* 15 (Fall), 8–11.

Goodwin, P., and R. Lawton (1999). On the asymmetry of the symmetric MAPE. *International Journal of Forecasting* 15(4), 405–408.

Green, K., and L. Tashman (2009). Percentage error: What denominator. *Foresight: International Journal of Applied Forecasting* 12 (Winter), 36–40.

Hawitt, D. (2010). Should you report forecast error or forecast accuracy? *Foresight: International Journal of Applied Forecasting* 18 (Summer), 46.

Hoover, J. (2011). Commentary on forecast error vs. forecast accuracy. *Foresight: International Journal of Applied Forecasting* 21.

Hyndman, R. J., and A. B. Koehler (2006). Another look at measures of forecast accuracy. *International Journal of Forecasting* 22(4), 679–688.

Koehler, A. B. (2001). The asymmetry of the sAPE measure and other comments on the M3-Competition. *International Journal of Forecasting* 17(4), 570–574.

Kolassa, S., and R. Martin (2011). Rolling dice: A simple illustration of the bias induced by minimizing the MAPE. White Paper No. 08, SAF AG, Tägerwilen, Switzerland.

Kolassa, S., and W. Schütz (2007). Advantages of the MAD/Mean ratio over the MAPE. *Foresight* 6 (Spring), 40–43.

Makridakis, S., and M. Hibon (2000). The M3-Competition: Results, conclusions and implications. *International Journal of Forecasting* 16(4), 451–476.

O'Connor, M., and M. Lawrence (1998). Judgmental forecasting and the use of available information. In G.Wrightand P.Goodwin (Eds.), *Forecasting with Judgment* (pp. 65–90). Hoboken, NJ: John Wiley & Sons.

O'Connor, M., W. Remus, and K. Griggs (1997). Going up—going down: How good are people at forecasting trends and changes in trends? *Journal of Forecasting* 16(3), 165–176.

3.8 ANOTHER LOOK AT FORECAST-ACCURACY METRICS FOR INTERMITTENT DEMAND*

Rob Hyndman

Some traditional measurements of forecast accuracy are unsuitable for intermittent-demand data because they can give infinite or undefined values. Rob Hyndman summarizes these forecast accuracy metrics and explains their potential failings. He also introduces a new metric—the mean absolute scaled error (MASE)—which is more appropriate for intermittent-demand data. More generally, he believes that the MASE should become the standard metric for comparing forecast accuracy across multiple time series.

Per his summary, Hyndman notes there are four types of forecast-error metrics:

- Scale-dependent metrics such as the mean absolute error (MAE or MAD)
- Percentage-error metrics such as the mean absolute percent error (MAPE)
- Relative-error metrics, which average the ratios of the errors from a designated method to the errors of a naïve method

---

* This article originally appeared in *Foresight: International Journal of Applied Forecasting* (June 2006), and appears here courtesy of the International Institute of Forecasters.

- Scale-free error metrics, which express each error as a ratio to an average error from a baseline method

For assessing accuracy on a single series, Hyndman prefers MAE because it is easiest to understand and compute. However, MAE cannot be compared across series because it is scale dependent; it makes no sense to compare accuracy on different scales.

He notes that percentage errors have the advantage of being scale independent, so they are frequently used to compare forecast performance between different data series. But measurements based on percentage errors have the disadvantage of being infinite or undefined if there are zero values in a series, as is frequent for intermittent data.

In regard to relative-error metrics, these are also scale independent. However, when the errors are small, as they can be with intermittent series, use of the naïve method as a benchmark is no longer possible because it would involve division by zero.

Hyndman's new scale-free error metric is called the mean absolute scaled error (MASE). MASE can be used to compare forecast methods on a single series and also to compare forecast accuracy between series. This metric is well suited to intermittent-demand series because it never gives infinite or undefined values.

Introduction: Three Ways to Generate Forecasts

There are three ways we may generate forecasts (F) of a quantity (Y) from a particular forecasting method:

1. We can compute forecasts from a common origin t (for example, the most recent month) for a sequence of forecast horizons $F_{n+1}, \ldots, F_{n+m}$ based on data from times $t = 1, \ldots, n$. This is the standard procedure implemented by forecasters in real time.
2. We can vary the origin from which forecasts are made but maintain a consistent forecast horizon. For example, we can generate a series of one-period-ahead forecasts $F_{1+h}, \ldots, F_{m+h}$ where each F_{j+h} is based on data from times $t = 1, \ldots, j$. This procedure is done not only to give attention to the forecast errors at a particular horizon but also to show how the forecast error changes as the horizon lengthens.
3. We may generate forecasts for a single future period using multiple data series, such as a collection of products or items. This procedure can be useful to demand planners as they assess aggregate accuracy over items or products at a location. This is also the procedure that underlies forecasting competitions, which compare the accuracy of different methods across multiple series.

While these are very different situations, measuring forecast accuracy is similar in each case. It is useful to have a forecast accuracy metric that can be used for all three cases.

An Example of What Can Go Wrong

Consider the classic intermittent-demand series shown in Figure 3.11. These data were part of a consulting project I did for a major Australian lubricant manufacturer.

Suppose we are interested in comparing the forecast accuracy of four simple methods: (1) the historical mean, using data up to the most recent observation; (2) the *naïve* or random-walk method, in which the forecast for each future period is the actual value for this period; (3) simple exponential smoothing; and (4) Croston's method for intermittent demands (Boylan, 2005). For methods (3) and (4) I have used a smoothing parameter of 0.1.

I compared the *in-sample* performance of these methods by varying the origin and generating a sequence of one-period-ahead forecasts—the second forecasting procedure described in the introduction. I also calculated the *out-of-sample* performance based on forecasting the data in the hold-out period, using information from the fitting period alone. These out-of-sample forecasts are from one to twelve steps ahead and are not updated in the hold-out period.

Table 3.8 shows some commonly used forecast-accuracy metrics applied to these data. The metrics are all defined in the next section. There are many infinite values occurring in Table 3.8. These are caused by division by zero. The undefined values for the naïve method arise from the division of zero by zero. The only measurement that always gives sensible results for all four of the forecasting methods is the MASE, or the mean absolute scaled error. Infinite, undefined, or zero values plague the other accuracy measurements.

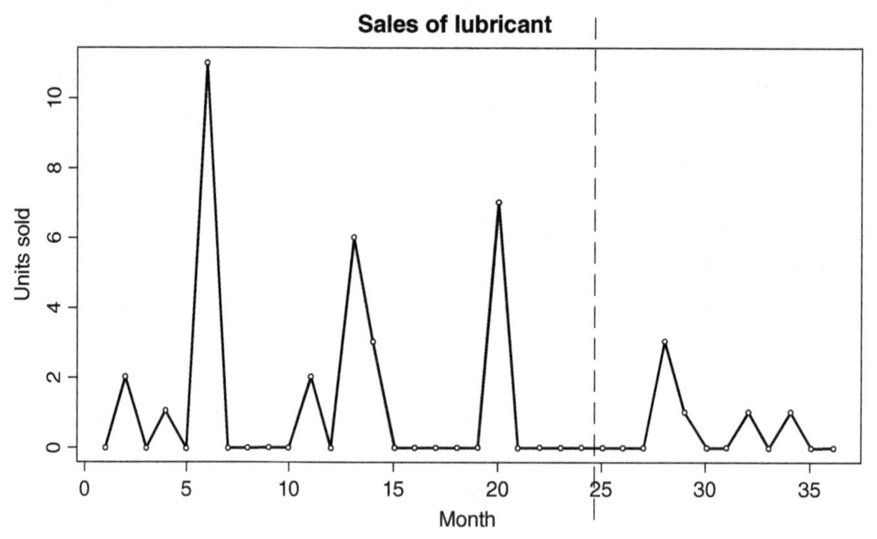

Data source: Product C in Makridakis et al. (1998, chapter 1). The vertical dashed line indicates the end of the data used for fitting and the start of the holdout set used for out-of-sample forecasting.

Figure 3.11 Three Years of Monthly Sales of a Lubricant Product Sold in Large Containers

Table 3.8 Forecast-Accuracy Metrics for Lubricant Sales

		Mean		Naïve		SES		Croston	
		In	Out	In	Out	In	Out	In	Out
GMAE	Geometric Mean Absolute Error	1.65	0.96	0.00	0.00	1.33	0.09	0.00	0.99
MAPE	Mean Absolute Percentage Error	∞	∞	—	—	∞	∞	∞	∞
sMAPE	Symmetric Mean Absolute	1.73	1.47	—	—	1.82	1.42	1.70	1.47
	Percentage Error								
MdRAE	Median Relative Absolute Error	0.95	∞			0.98	∞	0.93	∞
GMRAE	Geometric Mean Relative Absolute Error	∞	∞	—	—	∞	∞	∞	∞
MASE	Mean Absolute Scaled Error	0.86	0.44	1.00	0.20	0.78	0.33	0.79	0.45

In this particular series, the out-of-sample period has smaller errors (is more predictable) than the in-sample period because the in-sample period includes some relatively large observations. In general, we would expect out-of-sample errors to be larger.

Measurement of Forecast Errors

We can measure and average forecast errors in several ways:

Scale-Dependent Errors

The forecast error is simply, $e_t = Y_t - F_t$, regardless of how the forecast was produced. This is on the same scale as the data, applying to anything from ships to screws. Accuracy measurements based on e_t are therefore scale-dependent.

The most commonly used scale-dependent metrics are based on absolute errors or on squared errors:

$$\text{Mean Absolute Error (MAE)} = \text{mean}(|e_t|)$$

$$\text{Geometric Mean Absolute Error (GMAE)} = \text{gmean}(|e_t|)$$

$$\text{Mean Square Error (MSE)} = \text{mean}(e_t^2)$$

where *gmean* is a geometric mean.

The MAE is often abbreviated as the MAD ("D" for "deviation"). The use of absolute values or squared values prevents negative and positive errors from offsetting each other.

Since all of these metrics are on the same scale as the data, none of them are meaningful for assessing a method's accuracy across multiple series.

For assessing accuracy on a single series, I prefer the MAE because it is easiest to understand and compute. However, it cannot be compared between series because it is scale dependent.

For intermittent-demand data, Syntetos and Boylan (2005) recommend the use of GMAE, although they call it the GRMSE. (The GMAE and GRMSE are identical; the square root and the square cancel each other in a geometric mean.) Boylan and Syntetos (2006) point out that the GMAE has the flaw of being equal to zero when any error is zero, a problem which will occur when both the actual and forecasted demands are zero. This is the result seen in Table 3.8 for the naïve method.

Boylan and Syntetos claim that such a situation would occur only if an inappropriate forecasting method is used. However, it is not clear that the naïve method is always inappropriate. Further, Hoover indicates that division-by-zero errors in intermittent series are expected occurrences for repair parts. I suggest that the GMAE is problematic for assessing accuracy on intermittent-demand data.

Percentage Errors

The percentage error is given by $p_t = 100e_t / Y_t$. Percentage errors have the advantage of being scale independent, so they are frequently used to compare forecast performance between different data series. The most commonly used metric is

$$\text{Mean absolute percentage error (MAPE)} = \text{mean}(|p_t|)$$

Measurements based on percentage errors have the disadvantage of being infinite or undefined if there are zero values in a series, as is frequent for intermittent data. Moreover, percentage errors can have an extremely skewed distribution when actual values are close to zero. With intermittent-demand data, it is impossible to use the MAPE because of the occurrences of zero periods of demand.

The MAPE has another disadvantage: It puts a heavier penalty on positive errors than on negative errors. This observation has led to the use of the "symmetric" MAPE (sMAPE) in the M3-competition (Makridakis and Hibon, 2000). It is defined by

$$\text{sMAPE} = \text{mean}(200 * |Y_t - F_t| / (Y_t + F_t))$$

However, if the actual value Y_t is zero, the forecast F_t is likely to be close to zero. Thus the measurement will still involve division by a number close to zero. Also, the value of sMAPE can be negative, giving it an ambiguous interpretation.

Relative Errors

An alternative to percentages for the calculation of scale-independent measurements involves dividing each error by the error obtained using some benchmark method of forecasting. Let $r_t = e_t/e_t^*$ denote the relative error where e_t^* is the forecast error obtained from the benchmark method. Usually the benchmark method is the naïve method where F_t is equal to the last observation. Then we can define

$$\text{Median relative absolute error (MdRAE)} = \text{median}(|r_t|)$$

$$\text{Geometric mean relative absolute error (GMRAE)} = \text{gmean}(|r_t|)$$

Because they are not scale dependent, these relative-error metrics were recommended in studies by Armstrong and Collopy (1992) and by Fildes (1992) for assessing forecast accuracy across multiple series. However, when the errors are small, as they can be with intermittent series, use of the naïve method as a benchmark is no longer possible because it would involve division by zero.

Scale-Free Errors

The MASE was proposed by Hyndman and Koehler (2006) as a generally applicable measurement of forecast accuracy without the problems seen in the other measurements. They proposed scaling the errors based on the *in-sample* MAE from the naïve forecast method. Using the naïve method, we generate one-period-ahead forecasts from each data point in the sample. Accordingly, a scaled error is defined as

$$q_t = \frac{e_t}{\frac{1}{n-1}\sum_{i=2}^{n}|Y_i - Y_{i-1}|}$$

The result is independent of the scale of the data. A scaled error is less than one if it arises from a better forecast than the average one-step, naïve forecast computed in-sample. Conversely, it is greater than one if the forecast is worse than the average one-step, naïve forecast computed in-sample.

The mean absolute scaled error is simply

$$\text{MASE} = \text{mean}(|q_t|)$$

The first row of Table 3.9 shows the intermittent series plotted in Figure 3.11. The second row gives the naïve forecasts, which are equal to the previous actual values. The final row shows the naïve-forecast errors. The denominator of q_t is the mean of the shaded values in this row; that is the MAE of the naïve method.

Table 3.9 Monthly Lubricant Sales, Naïve Forecast

	In-sample	Out-of-sample
Actual Y_t	02010100002063000070000	000310010100
Naïve forecast $\hat{Y}_t$	0201010000206300007000	000000000000
Error $\lvert Y_t - \hat{Y}_t \rvert$	2211110002263300077000	000310010100

The only circumstance under which the MASE would be infinite or undefined is when all historical observations are equal.

The in-sample MAE is used in the denominator because it is always available and it effectively scales the errors. In contrast, the out-of-sample MAE for the naïve method may be zero because it is usually based on fewer observations. For example, if we were forecasting only two steps ahead, then the out-of-sample MAE would be zero. If we wanted to compare forecast accuracy at one step ahead for 10 different series, then we would have one error for each series. The out-of-sample MAE in this case is also zero. These types of problems are avoided by using in-sample, one-step MAE.

A closely related idea is the MAD/Mean ratio proposed by Hoover (2006) which scales the errors by the in-sample mean of the series instead of the in-sample mean absolute error. This ratio also renders the errors scale free and is always finite unless all historical data happen to be zero. Hoover explains the use of the MAD/Mean ratio only in the case of in-sample, one-step forecasts (situation 2 of the three situations described in the introduction). However, it would also be straightforward to use the MAD/Mean ratio in the other two forecasting situations.

The main advantage of the MASE over the MAD/Mean ratio is that the MASE is more widely applicable. The MAD/Mean ratio assumes that the mean is stable over time (technically, that the series is "stationary"). This is not true for data that show trend, seasonality, or other patterns. While intermittent data are often quite stable, sometimes seasonality does occur, and this might make the MAD/Mean ratio unreliable. In contrast, the MASE is suitable even when the data exhibit a trend or a seasonal pattern.

The MASE can be used to compare forecast methods on a single series, and, because it is scale-free, to compare forecast accuracy across series. For example, you can average the MASE values of several series to obtain a measurement of forecast accuracy for the group of series. This measurement can then be compared with the MASE values of other groups of series to identify which series are the most difficult to forecast. Typical values for one-step MASE values are less than one, as it is usually possible to obtain forecasts more accurate than the naïve method. Multistep MASE values are often larger than one, as it becomes more difficult to forecast as the horizon increases.

The MASE is the only available accuracy measurement that can be used in all three forecasting situations described in the introduction, and for all forecast methods and all types of series. I suggest that it is the best accuracy metric for intermittent demand studies and beyond.

REFERENCES

Armstrong, J. S., and F. Collopy (1992). Error measures for generalizing about forecasting methods: Empirical comparisons. *International Journal of Forecasting* 8, 69–80.

Boylan, J. (2005). Intermittent and lumpy demand: A forecasting challenge. *Foresight: International Journal of Applied Forecasting* 1, 36–42.

Boylan, J., and A. Syntetos (2006). Accuracy and accuracy-implication metrics for intermittent demand. *Foresight: International Journal of Applied Forecasting* 4, 39–42.

Fildes, R. (1992). The evaluation of extrapolative forecasting methods. *International Journal of Forecasting* 8, 81–98.

Hoover, J. (2006). Measuring forecast accuracy: Omissions in today's forecasting engines and demand-planning software. *Foresight: International Journal of Applied Forecasting* 4, 32–35.

Hyndman, R. J., and A. B. Koehler (2006). Another look at measures of forecast accuracy. *International Journal of Forecasting* 22(4), 679–688.

Makridakis, S., and M. Hibon (2000). The M3-competition: Results, conclusions and implications. *International Journal of Forecasting* 16, 451–476.

Makridakis, S. G., S. C. Wheelwright, and R. J. Hyndman (1998). *Forecasting: Methods and Applications*, 3rd ed. New York: John Wiley & Sons.

Syntetos, A. A., and J. E. Boylan (2005). The accuracy of intermittent demand estimates. *International Journal of Forecasting* 21, 303–314.

3.9 ADVANTAGES OF THE MAD/MEAN RATIO OVER THE MAPE*

Stephan Kolassa and Wolfgang Schütz

Stephan Kolassa and Wolfgang Schütz provide a careful look at the ratio MAD/Mean, which has been proposed as a substitute metric for the MAPE in the case of intermittent demand series. They explain how MAD/Mean can be viewed as a weighted mean of absolute percentage errors and thus as a weighted alternative to MAPE. They describe several advantages of MAD/Mean to the MAPE, including applicability to inventory decisions, absence of bias in method selection, and suitability for series with intermittent as well as near-zero demands.

The authors observe that for many types of time series, the MAD/Mean is equivalent to a weighted MAPE (WMAPE). For inventory decisions in the face of widely fluctuating demands, method selection based on the WMAPE is more sensible than method selection based on the ordinary MAPE.

---

* This article originally appeared in *Foresight: The International Journal of Applied Forecasting* (Spring 2007), and appears here courtesy of the International Institute of Forecasters.

As noted in Kolassa and Martin above, using the MAPE as a criterion for method selection can bias the selection in favor of methods that issue low forecasts. Method selection based on the MAD/Mean does not introduce bias.

Kolassa and Schütz also suggest that, in the case of intermittent series when the MAPE can no longer be used, the MAD/Mean, the MASE, and the Percentage Better are attractive alternatives.

The MAD, the MAPE, and the MAD/Mean

In selecting and evaluating forecasting methods, metrics to assess the accuracy of forecasts are essential. One of the best-known and most intuitive metrics is the mean absolute deviation (MAD; Figure 3.12), also called the mean absolute error (MAE). The MAD is the arithmetic mean of the absolute differences between the forecast and the true demand over the forecasting horizon.

Apart from its role in comparing forecasting methods, the MAD has a direct application in inventory control systems. A frequently used inventory control policy is the order-up-to policy, in which one orders sufficient product to satisfy forecast demand plus an appropriate safety margin. One simple way to calculate this safety margin is to multiply historical (or exponentially smoothed) MADs with a prespecified safety stock factor.

However, the MAD suffers from a serious shortcoming when we wish to compare forecasting methods across a group of series: Because it is a scaled metric, it is not comparable across series. A forecast with a MAD of 10 is quite accurate when the mean of the true demands is 100, but much less so if the mean is 10. Thus, the MAD cannot be meaningfully averaged over different time series. To do so would be tantamount to comparing apples and oranges.

One alternative and well-known metric that can be used to compare accuracy across series is the Mean Absolute Percentage Error (MAPE, Figure 3.13). The absolute error between the forecast and true value is calculated, a relative error is computed by dividing the absolute error by the true demand, and finally these relative errors are averaged over the periods of the forecast horizon.

A MAPE of 20% tells us that on average our forecasts over- or underestimate the true values by 20%. The MAPE has the critical advantage of being scale-free: An error of 1 with a true demand of 10 yields a MAPE of 10%, just as an error of 10 with a true demand of 100. This allows the comparison of MAPEs across multiple time series with different levels.

$$MAD = \frac{1}{T}\sum_{t=1}^{T} \left| True_t - Forecast_t \right|$$

Figure 3.12 Calculation of the Mean Absolute Deviation (MAD)

$$MAPE = \frac{1}{T}\sum_{t=1}^{T} \left| \frac{True_t - Forecast_t}{True_t} \right|$$

Figure 3.13 Calculation of the Mean Absolute Percentage Error (MAPE)

$$\frac{MAD}{Mean} = \frac{\frac{1}{T}\sum_{t=1}^{T}|True_t - Forecast_t|}{\frac{1}{T}\sum_{t=1}^{T}True_t}$$

Figure 3.14 Calculation of the MAD/Mean

However, when there are zeroes in the data series, as is the case for intermittent demands, the MAPE cannot be calculated (Hoover, 2006). An alternative metric to compare the accuracy of methods across series is the ratio of the MAD to the mean of the series, MAD/Mean (Figure 3.14).

We may have MAD = 10 and Mean= 100, and MAD = 1 and Mean = 10 for two series, but both are forecast with comparable accuracy, and in both cases, we have MAD/Mean = 10%. Not only is the MAD/Mean comparable across series but it can be calculated for intermittent series as well. We discuss this case in our final section.

The MAD/Mean Ratio as a Weighted MAPE

Recall that the MAPE is simply the mean of the absolute percentage errors. The MAD/Mean, however, can be viewed as a weighted analog of the MAPE: a weighted mean of the APEs, where each APE is weighted by the corresponding true value (Figure 3.15). In this way, MAD/Mean can be called a weighted MAPE, or WMAPE for short. As the classical MAPE sets absolute errors in relation to the actual values, the WMAPE considers percentage errors and again weighs them by actual values. Thus, the WMAPE is a generalization of the ordinary MAPE.

The MAD/Mean or WMAPE avoids a problem inherent in the MAPE when forecasting for inventories in face of widely fluctuating demands. If the demand for an item is either 10 or 100 units per period, a 10% MAPE means lost sales (if the forecast was too low) or storage requirements (if the forecast was too high) of either 1 or 10 units per period. The inventory implications of 1 vs. 10 unit errors are very different. In this situation, the MAD remains important to draw attention to large absolute errors associated with large demands. As Figure 3.16 shows, the WMAPE calculation gives high weight to high demands, and therefore errors associated with high demands are given greater influence on the WMAPE than are errors corresponding to smaller demands.

$$\frac{MAD}{Mean} = \frac{\frac{1}{T}\sum_{t=1}^{T}|True_t - Forecast_t|}{\frac{1}{T}\sum_{t=1}^{T}True_t} = \frac{1}{\sum_{t=1}^{T}True_t}\sum_{t=1}^{T}\left[True_t \times \underbrace{\frac{|True_t - Forecast_t|}{True_t}}_{=APE_t}\right]$$

Figure 3.15 MAD/Mean as a Weighted Mean of APEs

$$\frac{MAD}{Mean} = \frac{\frac{1}{T}\sum_{t=1}^{T}\left|True_{const} - Forecast_t\right|}{\underbrace{\frac{1}{T}\sum_{t=1}^{T}True_{const}}_{=True_{const}}} = \frac{1}{T}\sum_{t=1}^{T}\frac{\left|True_{const} - Forecast_t\right|}{True_t} = MAPE$$

Figure 3.16 For Constant True Demands, WMAPE = MAPE

Thus, the WMAPE takes widely fluctuating demands into account. What does the picture look like when the actual values exhibit little fluctuation? In the case of constant actual values, WMAPE simply turns into the ordinary MAPE (Figure 3.16), and for actual values with low fluctuations, the difference is small, emphasizing that the MAD/Mean, or WMAPE, is a generalization of the MAPE.

The Issue of Forecast Bias

Armstrong (1985) notes another problem with the MAPE, that an underforecast error can be no larger than 100% while an overforecast error has no upper bound. For example, a forecast of 0 will have an APE of 100% for any nonzero demand, while the APE can be larger than 100% for forecasts that overshoot the true demand. Thus, methods generating lower forecasts will tend to produce lower MAPEs, and selecting a method based on MAPE will favor methods that supply lower forecasts.

In contrast, selecting methods on the basis of MAD/Mean does not lead to bias. Assume that we are dealing with a deseasonalized and detrended series where the values are uniformly distributed between 10 and 50, as in Figure 3.17. Because we are considering a single series, minimizing the MAD/Mean is the same as minimizing the MAD.

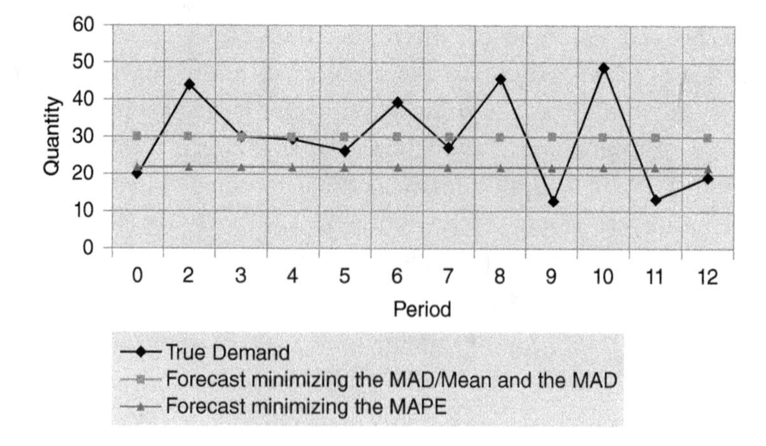

Figure 3.17 Forecasts Minimizing the MAPE and MAD/Mean

One could reasonably call a forecast of 30 the "best" forecast, and a constant forecast of 30 leads to MAD/Mean ratio of 34%. There is no other constant forecast that achieves a lower MAD/Mean. However, if we focus on the MAPE, we would select a constant forecast of 22 rather than 30. With the forecast of 22, the MAPE is 39% while, with a forecast of 30, the MAPE is 46%. Thus, when we minimize the MAPE, 22 is a "better" forecast than 30, which runs counter to our intuition. The MAD/Mean is much closer to our intuitive understanding of forecast accuracy.

The MASE

In an earlier issue of *Foresight,* Rob Hyndman (2006) examines another error measure that is scale free, the Mean Absolute Scaled Error (MASE; see Figure 3.18). To calculate a MASE, you divide the MAD during the forecasting period by the MAD attained on the historical sales from a naive forecasting method that simply projects today's demands to the next period. Because it is scale-free, the MASE can be averaged across series, and it remains suitable for intermittent demands.

Hyndman writes that MAD/Mean has a disadvantage in that the mean of the series may not be stable, e.g., if the series exhibits a trend or a seasonal pattern. The MASE, in contrast, captures the trend or seasonality in the series and is thus more suitable to measure errors for trended or seasonal series.

One feature of the MASE that may need getting used to is using the in-sample MAD of the naive method as the denominator. As Hyndman (2006) explains, this in-sample MAD is always available and more reliably non-zero than any out-of-sample measures. However, a consequence of the in-sample MAD in the denominator of the MASE is that the MASE is vulnerable to outliers or structural breaks in the historical time series. Thus the MASE of two time series with identical forecasts and identical true demands during the forecast horizon will differ if the two series differed in their historical demands. While it is easy to understand and explain to users that forecasts depend on historical behavior of time series, it may be harder to communicate the dependence of the MASE metric on the historical data.

The MASE is thus a slightly more complicated metric to interpret. Having only recently been introduced, it is not yet widely reported in forecasting

$$MASE = \frac{\frac{1}{T}\sum_{t=1}^{T} \left| True_t - Forecast_t \right|}{\frac{1}{H}\sum_{t=-H+1}^{0} \left| True_t - True_{t-1} \right|}$$

Figure 3.18 Calculation of the Mean Absolute Scaled Error (MASE)

software. It will be interesting to see whether the MASE will be accepted by forecasting software developers and reported in future forecasting software releases.

The Case of Intermittent Series

Intermittent demand occurs when some time periods exhibit zero demand, as is common in daily, weekly, and even monthly orders for SKUs such as spare parts and fashion items. Intermittent demands not only pose significant challenges to forecasting methods (Boylan, 2005) but also undermine traditional accuracy metrics, such as the MAPE. (See the series of illuminating articles on the topic in *Foresight* 4, 2006.) Indeed, whenever the true values during some periods are zero, the MAPE is mathematically undefined, since we would need to divide the error by zero. Hence, the MAPE loses its value as a metric in situations of intermittent demand.

As Hoover (2006) points out, many commercial software packages report a "MAPE" even when the true values of the series contain zeros, although the MAPE is undefined in this case. The software does this by simply excluding periods with zero sales. Needless to say, this software-calculated MAPE does not reflect the true errors of a forecast.

On the other hand, both MAD/Mean and MASE are well-defined for forecasts of intermittent demand series, so long as not every demand is zero (in which case the Mean would also be zero and MAD/Mean would entail a division by zero). Still another option for intermittent demands is the Percentage Better metric (Boylan, 2005).

Many demand series are not intermittent but contain occasional values very close to zero. For a near-zero demand, a small error in absolute terms can translate into a large percentage error, which can make the MAPE explode. For example, in a demand series that normally fluctuates between 10 and 20 units per period, an error of 5 units in one period becomes an APE of 25–50%. However if demand dropped to 1 unit in a period, a 5-unit error would yield an APE of 500% and would lead to a sharply increased MAPE. In such circumstances the MAD/Mean is a safer alternative in that it is less sensitive to errors on demands close to zero. Still another attractive option is to calculate the median of the absolute percentage errors (MdAPE, see Armstrong and Collopy, 1992) but MdAPEs are not typically reported in forecasting software.

We should note that, when applied to intermittent demands, the MAD/Mean ratio, while still defined, can no longer be viewed as a WMAPE. Indeed, Figure 3.15 shows that once again divisions by zero would occur in this interpretation. Nevertheless, it remains a useful metric for intermittent demands.

Recap

In conclusion, the ratio MAD/Mean has many advantages to recommend it to forecasting practitioners. It can be interpreted as a weighted alternative to ordinary MAPE for non-intermittent series. It is very close to the MAPE for demands with a low degree of fluctuation, but is better than the MAPE at taking large fluctuations into account. It avoids a bias in the method-selection process that afflicts the MAPE. And it remains useful for intermittent series, in contrast to the MAPE.

REFERENCES

Armstrong, J. S. (1985). *Long-Range Forecasting*, 2nd ed. New York: John Wiley & Sons. http://www.forecastingprinciples.com/Long-Range%20Forecasting/contents.html.

Armstrong, J. S., and F. Collopy (1992). Error measures for generalizing about forecasting methods: Empirical comparisons. *International Journal of Forecasting* 8, 69–80.

Boylan, J. E. (2005). Intermittent and lumpy demand: A forecasting challenge. *Foresight: International Journal of Applied Forecasting* 1, 36–42.

Hoover, J. (2006). Measuring forecast accuracy: Omissions in today's forecasting engines and demand planning software. *Foresight: International Journal of Applied Forecasting* 4, 32–35.

Hyndman, R. J. (2006). Another look at forecast accuracy metrics for intermittent demand. *Foresight: International Journal of Applied Forecasting* 4, 43–46.

3.10 USE SCALED ERRORS INSTEAD OF PERCENTAGE ERRORS IN FORECAST EVALUATIONS*

Lauge Valentin

Lauge Valentin, a forecasting director for the LEGO Group, presents a case for abandoning percentage errors when evaluating forecasts and replacing them by scaled errors. Scaled errors, such as the MASE introduced above, express the size of a forecast error in relation to the average error from a benchmark method. He describes how the shift from percentage errors to scaled errors was motivated by his company's need for an accuracy statistic that would lend itself to benchmarking across product groups. Valentin shows how scaled error measures are used at LEGO for evaluating forecasting performance.

But accuracy statistics based on scaled errors, such as the mean absolute scaled error (MASE), can fail to point out bad forecasts when the benchmark forecasts are very bad. In this circumstance, Valentin suggests calculating a cumulative error statistic to use in conjunction with the MASE. Finally, converting the MASE to an index makes the scaled-error concept easier to understand and can therefore improve its chances of acceptability by management.

*This article originally appeared in *Foresight: The International Journal of Applied Forecasting* (Summer 2007), and appears here courtesy of the International Institute of Forecasters.

Evaluating Forecasts in the LEGO Group

Percentage errors have been the intuitive basis for evaluating forecasts. When you want to know how good a forecast is, you ask, "By how many percentage points is the forecast off?" To evaluate a set of forecasts, percentage errors are averaged, giving us statistics such as the mean absolute percentage error (MAPE).

Although intuitive, the use of percentage errors is problematic. In this article I will build the case for abandoning use of percentage errors in forecast evaluations and replacing them by scaled errors.

Let's first define the terms error measurements and accuracy statistic (Figure 3.19). Error measurements form the basis for an accuracy statistic. The simplest way to measure an error is to calculate the difference between the actual and the forecast. This measurement can be expressed as a percentage of the actual (a percentage error), as a ratio to the error measurement from a benchmark method (a scaled error), or other alternatives. An accuracy statistic is a calculation that takes all of the error measurements into account. The usual way of doing this is to calculate the average of the error measurements.

In 2006, I began work on a forecasting performance index for the LEGO Group that could form the basis for forecasting evaluation at the item level. We wanted the index to be based on error measurements that had the following properties:

- **Symmetrical**. Overforecasting and underforecasting would be equally penalized.
- **Unidirectional**. The larger the forecast error, the larger the value of the error measurement.
- **Comparable**. Evaluations of forecast errors at different levels should be directly comparable and hence valid for benchmarking.

Comparability is the key to benchmarking. If an error index is comparable across business units, it allows the forecasting performance of different branches of the forecasting organization to be compared. In turn, analysts in the branches can learn from each other's successes and failures.

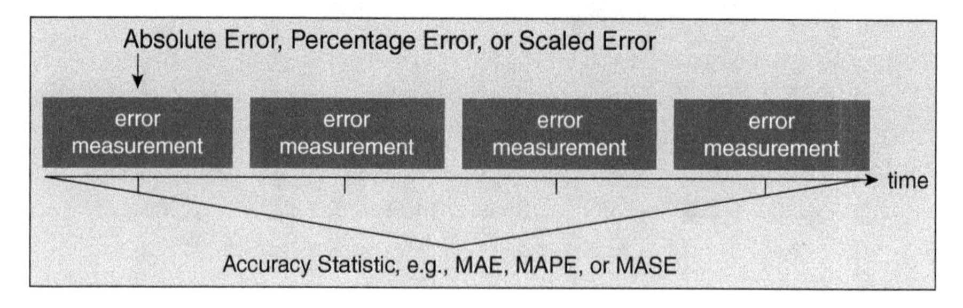

Figure 3.19 Error Measurement and Accuracy Statistics

Initially, we had believed that percentage errors, as used in the MAPE, were a suitable choice. According to Mentzer and Kahn (1995), the MAPE is the most widely used forecast accuracy statistic. However, we began to realize that percentage errors were problematic in some respects and we eventually abandoned them in favor of scaled error measurements.

Problems with Percentage Errors

The drawbacks of percentage error measurements are threefold: asymmetry, ambiguity, and instability.

Asymmetry. Percentage errors are bound on the low side, since the maximum error in an under forecast is 100%. But on the high side there is no limit to the percentage error. Hence, over forecasts and under forecasts are measured across different scales.

Ambiguity. A percentage error shows the relationship between the forecast and the actual value, not the size of the error. It is not possible to determine whether an error in one period is better or worse than an error in the next period by studying the percentage error. The problem is that the denominator in the percentage error changes from period to period. As we shall see, this ambiguity prevents measurements from being unidirectional and comparable.

Instability. Percentage errors are undefined when the actual is zero, which can occur when demands are intermittent. Hoover (2006) discusses this problem in detail. Moreover, percentage errors can explode if the actual value is very close to zero.

Example of Asymmetry

The error asymmetry occurs because under forecasting is penalized less than over forecasting. Both calculations below reflect an absolute error of 50, but the percentage errors differ widely. In the first calculation, the actual is 50 and the forecast is 100; in the second, the actual is 100 and the forecast is 50.

$$abs(PE) = \frac{abs(50 - 100)}{50} = 100\%$$

$$abs(PE) = \frac{abs(100 - 50)}{100} = 50\%$$

To deal with the asymmetry, studies such as the M3-Competitions (Makridakis and Hibon, 2000) have used a symmetric variant of the percentage error: sPE for symmetric percentage error. In an sPE measurement, the denominator is not the actual value but the average of the actual and the forecast. With this measurement, the same absolute error (50 in the above example) yields the same sPE. But the interpretation of the sPE is not as intuitive as the percentage errors.

$$abs(sPE) = \frac{abs(50-100)}{(50+100)/2} \approx 67\%$$

$$abs(sPE) \approx \frac{abs(100-50)}{(100+50)/2} \approx 67\%$$

The accuracy statistic based on the sPE measurements is called the sMAPE.

Example of Ambiguity

When you have an actual of 50 in one period and a forecast of 450, you have an 800% error.

However, if you have an actual of 5,000 pieces in the next period, a forecast of 600 will be evaluated as an 88% error.

$$abs(PE) = \frac{abs(5000-600)}{5000} = 88\%$$

The size of the error in the second period is much larger at 4,400 than the error of 400 in the first period; but this is not evident from the percentages. If we did not know the actual values, we would conclude that the error in the first period is a more serious error than the error in the second.

The conclusion is that in order for the percentage errors to be unidirectional, the actual values must have approximately the same level, which is not the case in the industry in which the LEGO Group operates.

Example of Instability

When the actual in one period is a very small value, the percentage error "explodes." For example, when the actual is 1 and the forecast is 100.

$$abs(PE) = \frac{abs(1-100)}{1} = 9{,}900\%$$

The sPE is less explosive, since the actual is averaged with the forecast.

$$abs(sPE) = \frac{abs(1-100)}{(1+100)/2} \approx 196\%$$

When there is a period of zero demand, the percentage error cannot be calculated for this period, and the sPE is of no help since it will always be equal to 200%.

$$abs(PE) = \frac{abs(0-5)}{0} = undefined$$

$$abs(sPE) = \frac{abs(0-5)}{(0+5)/2} = 200\%$$

Hoover (2006) proposed an alternative to the MAPE for small volume items: the MAD/Mean ratio. The MAD/Mean is an example of an accuracy statistic that is based on scaled error measurements. Kolassa and Schütz (2007) show that the MAD/Mean ratio can often be interpreted as a weighted MAPE, and that it overcomes many of the shortcomings of the MAPE. But as I explain in the next section, scaling can be done in a different way, one that better facilitates the benchmarking of forecasting performance.

Scaled Errors

The concept of scaled errors was introduced by Hyndman and Koehler (2006) and summarized for *Foresight* readers by Hyndman (2006). As opposed to percentage errors, scaled errors are formed by dividing each forecast error by a figure that represents the scale of the time series, such as its mean. Alternatively the denominator can represent the mean absolute error MAE from a benchmark forecasting method (b).

$$SE = E\ /MAE_b$$

Scaled Error SE: Error in Relation to the MAE of a Benchmark Method

Hyndman-Koehler called their accuracy statistic based on scaled error measurements the MASE, for mean absolute scaled error:

$$MASE = mean(|SE|)$$

MASE: Average (Arithmetic Mean) of the Scaled Errors

Their particular benchmark method is the naïve, which assumes that the forecast for any one period is the actual of the prior period. As Pearson (2007) notes in his accompanying article in this issue of *Foresight*, the naïve is the standard benchmark against which the accuracy of a particular forecast method is evaluated.

The use of the naïve as the benchmark, however, can be inappropriate for seasonal products, providing a benchmark that is too easy to beat. In this case, analysts sometimes use a seasonal naïve benchmark—essentially a forecast of no change from the same season of the prior year. However, for products with less than a 1-year life span, the seasonal naïve benchmark cannot be used. Many seasonal LEGO products have short life spans. So we decided to keep things simple and use the standard naïve method for all products, including the seasonal ones.

A MASE = 1 indicates that the errors from a forecast method on average are no better or worse than the average error from a naïve method. A MASE less than 1 means there has been an improvement on the naïve forecasts and a MASE greater than 1 reflects forecast errors that are worse on average than those of the naïve.

For the denominator of the MASE, Hyndman and Koehler use the MAE of the fitting error; that is the in-sample error, rather than the out-of-sample errors. In the LEGO Group, however, there is no distinction between in-sample and out-of-sample in time series because the forecast methods used are not statistical but judgmental; we use the entire data series for evaluation. In this context, the MASE is equivalent to the ratio of the MAE from the judgmental forecasts to the MAE of the naïve forecasts.

The MASE is independent of scale and has the property of comparability, which enables benchmarking. Hyndman (2006) shows that the MASE works well for intermittent demand products, when the MAPE and sMAPE break down, and it does not explode when the actual values drop close to zero.

Table 3.10 compares scaled and percentage errors for two periods in which the levels of both the actual values and the forecast values are widely divergent. In Period 1, the actual volume is 600 but falls to 10 in period 2. The LEGO forecasts were 900 for Period 1 (we overshot by 300) and 300 for Period 2 (we overshot by 290). The naïve forecast was 50 for Period 1—this was the volume in the period prior to Period 1—and 600 in Period 2 (the actual volume in Period 1).

Table 3.10 Percentage vs. Scaled Errors

PERIOD	1	2	MEAN STATISTICS
Actual volume	600	10	Mean = 305
LEGO forecast	900	300	
Naïve forecast	50	600	
Abs(E) of LEGO forecast	300	290	295 (MAD or MAE)
Abs(E) of Naive forecast	550	590	570 (MAD or MAE)
Abs(PE) of LEGO forecast	50%	2900%	MAPE = 1,475 %
Abs(sPE) of LEGO forecast	40%	187%	sMAPE = 114 %
Scaled error of LEGO forecast	300/ 570 = 0.53	290/570 = 0.51	MASE = 0.52
MAD/Mean of LEGO forecast			MAD/Mean = 0.97

The absolute percentage error in Period 2 (2900%) is much larger than that in Period 1 (50%) despite the fact that the absolute errors in the LEGO forecast are about the same (290 and 300). In addition, the percentage error in Period 2 exploded due to the small actual value. Hence the MAPE of near 1500% is essentially useless.

In contrast, the scaled errors—the errors divided by the MAE of the naïve method—are proportional to the absolute size of the error, because they are scaled with a constant, which is the MAE = 570 of the naïve method. We see that the error in the first period is only slightly larger than the error in the second period. The MASE indicates that the LEGO forecasts improved on the naïve forecasts—the LEGO forecast errors were slightly more than half (0.52) of the average error of the naïve method.

The MAD/Mean can be viewed as a special case of a MASE in which the benchmark method is not the naïve method but a method that forecasts all values as equal to the mean of the time series. However, the naïve forecast is the standard benchmark, which provides us with a natural definition of good or bad performance. Hence the MASE comes with built-in benchmarking capabilities, which means that the MASE always can be used as a performance indicator.

The GMASE

In the LEGO Group, we seek to compare forecasting performance between product groups: We ask if the forecasting performance in one group of products is better or worse than the forecasting performance in another group of products. Within any product group, individual product turnover varies, and products with a higher turnover are more important to LEGO Group revenues. So in calculating a forecasting accuracy statistic for a product group, we assign weights to each product based on turnover. It is necessary to calculate a weighted average of the MASEs within groups.

For each product within a group, we calculate the MASE and assign a weight. Then we calculate a weighted average of the individual-product MASEs to obtain a group-average MASE. But in taking the product-group average, we believe it makes mathematical sense to calculate a geometric mean rather than an arithmetic mean. The MASE is a statistic based on ratios—each scaled error is a ratio—and geometric means are more appropriate as averages of ratios. Hence, our product-group average MASE is a weighted geometric mean of scaled errors. We call it the GMASE. Like the MASE, a GMASE = 1 indicates that the forecasts are no more accurate than the naïve forecasts.

Suppose we have a group with two products and that the MASE is 0.05 for product 1 and 20 for product 2. In this example, the performance of the first forecast is 20 times better than the naïve method and the performance of the second forecast is 20 times worse than the naïve method. What is the average

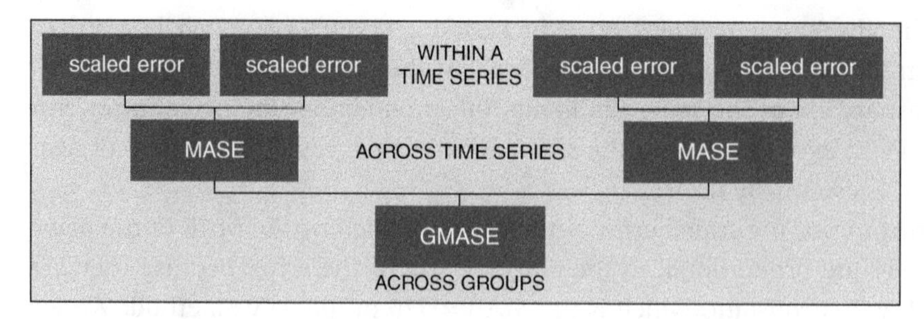

Figure 3.20 GMASE as an Average of Individual Product MASEs

forecasting performance? If you take an arithmetic mean of the two MASEs, you would obtain a result of approximately 10: (20+0.05)/2, which would signify that the forecasting performance is, on average, 10 times worse than the naïve method. Use of the geometric mean, however, yields the sensible result of 1, Sqrt(20 * 0.05), indicating that forecasting performance was no better or worse than the naïve on average.

Figure 3.20 summarizes the sequence of calculations leading to the GMASE.

The Problem of Bad Forecasts

The MASE may fail to recognize a forecast that is clearly bad when the benchmark forecast is even worse. In other words, it can turn a blind eye to some unacceptable forecasts. Our solution follows the advice offered by Armstrong (2001), to use multiple accuracy statistics.

We developed a simple segmentation technique that flags those bad forecasts that have acceptable MASE evaluations. We do so by calculating a pair of statistics: the MASE and the AFAR (Accumulated Forecast to Actual Ratio). The AFAR is defined as the ratio of the sum of the forecasts to the sum of the actual values. It is an indicator of bias toward over forecasting (AFAR > 1) or under forecasting (AFAR < 1). An AFAR ratio of 2, for example, signifies that the cumulative forecast is twice as large as the cumulative actual, a severe bias of over forecasting.

$$AFAR = \frac{Forecast_1 + Forecast_2 + \cdots + Forecast_n}{Actual_1 + Actual_2 + \cdots Actual_n}$$

AFAR: Accumulated Forecast to Actual Ratio

Note that the AFAR is reset once a year, in order to avoid potential effects from the previous year's bias.

In the LEGO Group, we initially chose the bounds 0.75 to 1.5 to define an acceptable range for the AFAR. This is illustrated in Figure 3.21 for a sample of data.

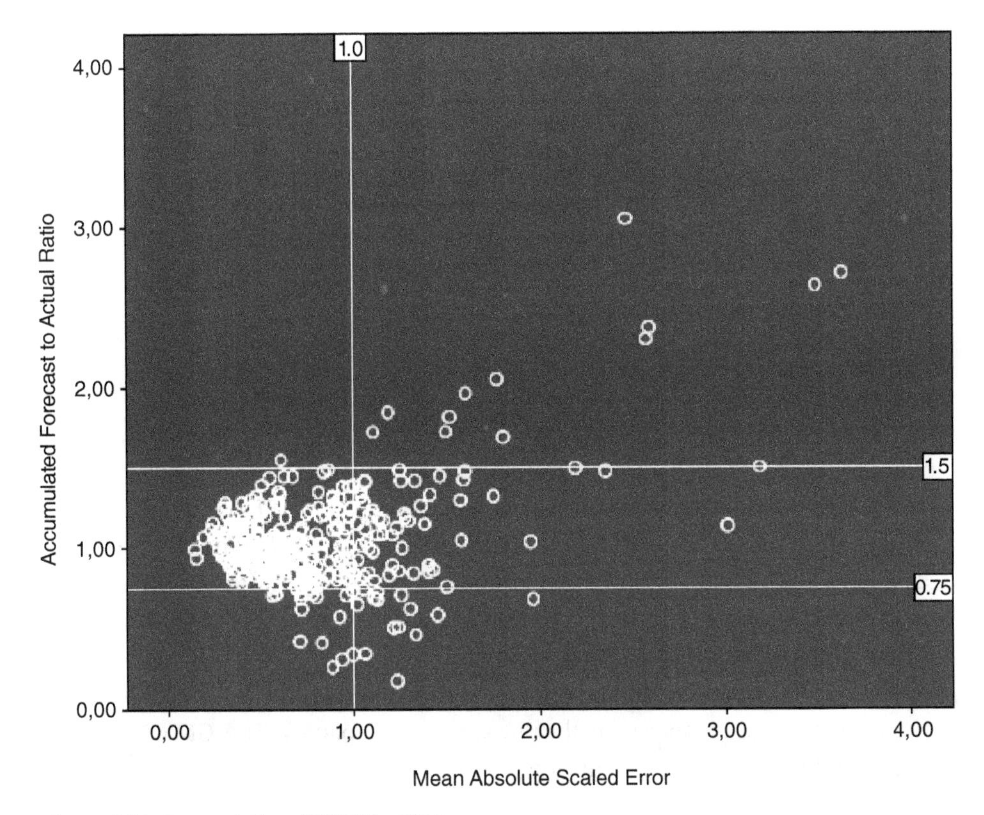

Figure 3.21 Segmentation of MASE by AFAR

- The AFAR cuts the chart in 3 parts. One horizontal line is set where the ratio is 1.5 and one where the ratio is 0.75. The middle part is defined as the acceptable range. Of course these ranges can be set to whatever is desired.
- The MASE cuts the chart in 2 parts. The vertical line represents the case where MASE = 1. A MASE less than one is considered acceptable. A MASE greater than one is not.
- Forecasts in the middle-left sector are within the acceptable range; that is, the bias is not unacceptable and the accuracy is superior to that of the benchmark method.

For these sample data, 81% were acceptable, 19% unacceptable.

The segmentation can get more detailed as illustrated in Figure 3.22.

Perspectives for Intercompany Benchmarking

The MASE and the GMASE are used in the LEGO Group for intracompany benchmarking. The business units compete for the best evaluation. This allows the business units to exchange ideas for improvements and to diagnose good and bad behaviors.

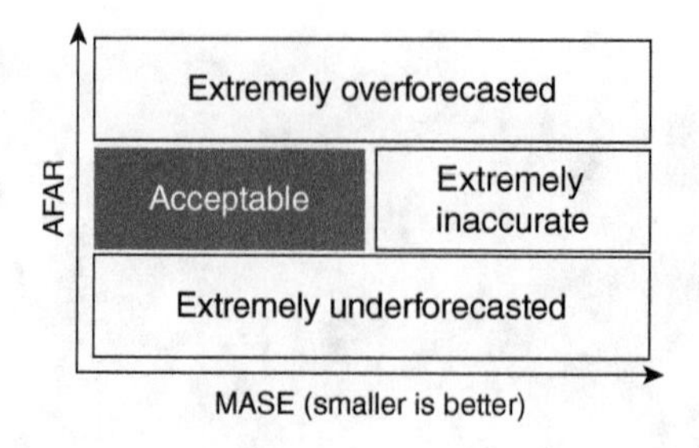

Figure 3.22 Advanced Segmentation of MASE

The GMASE can also be used for intercompany benchmarking, which would reveal whether the forecasting performance in Company X is better or worse than in Company Y. Using a statistic based on MAPE for this purpose is not prudent. For one, consider comparing a company that tends to over forecast with a company that tends to under forecast: The result is an unfair comparison, since the asymmetry property of percentage errors gives the under forecasting company a potential advantage.

The LEGO Group would be interested in knowing how its average forecasting performance compares to that in similar companies. The GMASE can be used for this kind of benchmarking.

How to Make MASE and GMASE Management Friendly

There is a risk in using unfamiliar statistics like MASE and GMASE in presentations to management, who may distrust statistics they view as exotic. Statistics based on percentage errors have the virtue that they are intuitive for people who don't work with the details. Statistics based on scaled errors are not so intuitive.

What is the solution? Perhaps the second most common medium for business measurements, after percentages, is an index.

When interpreting an index, you only need to know whether larger is better or worse (the direction of the index) and what the index value of 100 signifies.

The MASE and the GMASE can easily be turned into indices. We have created an index we call the LEGO Forecasting Performance Index (LFPI). Its avowed purpose is to hide the technical bits of the MASE and the GMASE from the sight of the managers.

The index is simply 100 times the MASE or the GMASE, rounded to the nearest integer. If the index is greater than 100, the forecasts are less accurate than those of the benchmark. If the index is smaller than 100, the forecasts improve upon the benchmark. We show managers an LFPI Barometer as a nice graphical representation. See Figure 3.23. The initial reception in the LEGO Group has been very favorable.

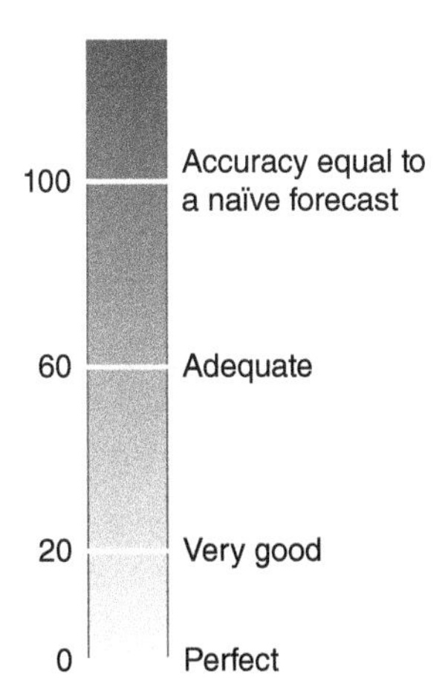

Figure 3.23 The LFPI Barometer

Summary

Percentage error statistics are not adequate for evaluating forecasts in the LEGO Group. Instead, we introduced statistics based on scaled errors, since they are symmetrical, unidirectional, and comparable. We calculate the mean absolute scaled error, MASE, for each product and a geometric mean of weighted MASEs for each product group. We convert the MASE and GMASE statistics into indices for presentations to management.

To deal with situations in which the benchmark forecast is so bad it turns a blind eye to bad forecasts, we calculate an accumulated forecast to actual ratio, AFAR. In conjunction with a MASE, the AFAR defines a region of acceptable forecasts—those with low bias and accuracy that improves on the benchmark method.

REFERENCES

Armstrong, J. S. (Ed.) (2001). *Principles of Forecasting—A Handbook for Researchers and Practitioners*. Boston: Kluwer Academic Publishers.

Hoover, J. (2006). Measuring forecast accuracy: Omissions in today's forecasting engines and demand planning software. *Foresight: International Journal of Applied Forecasting* 4, 32–35.

Hyndman, R. J. (2006). Another look at forecast-accuracy metrics for intermittent demand. *Foresight: International Journal of Applied Forecasting* 4, 43–46.

Hyndman, R. J., and A. B. Koehler (2006). Another look at measures of forecast accuracy. *International Journal of Forecasting* 23, 679–88.

Kolassa, S., and W. Schütz (2007). Advantages of the MAD/Mean ratio over the MAPE *Foresight: International Journal of Applied Forecasting* 6, 40–43.

Makridakis, S., and M. Hibon (2000). The M3-Competition: Results, conclusions and implications. *International Journal of Forecasting* 16, 451–476.

Mentzer, J. T., and K. B. Kahn (1995). Forecasting technique familiarity, satisfaction, usage, and application. *Journal of Forecasting* 14, 465–476.

Pearson, R. (2007). An expanded prediction-realization diagram for assessing forecast errors. *Foresight: International Journal of Applied Forecasting* 7, 11–16.

3.11 AN EXPANDED PREDICTION-REALIZATION DIAGRAM FOR ASSESSING FORECAST ERRORS*

Roy Pearson

Nearly 50 years ago, Henri Theil (perhaps best known for his Theil's U statistic) proposed the prediction-realization diagram (PRD). In this article, Roy Pearson resurrects the PRD to depict the degree to which a method correctly forecasts the direction of change. Roy extends the PRD to provide a more comprehensive picture of forecasting performance.

Theil's original PRD compared forecasts with the actual changes that were realized. His diagram emphasizes an element of accuracy that is not accounted for in traditional metrics—the accuracy with which you forecast the correct direction of change. Roy expands on the original diagram to incorporate evaluation of whether the forecasts are improvements on the standard benchmark of naïve (no-change) forecasts.

A PRD is a good complement to measures of error size, such as MAPE. The PRD of your forecasts quickly shows if you've got the direction of change right, if you've overestimated or underestimated the changes, and if your forecasts were better than no-change predictions. Also, seeing a plot of all of the outcomes reveals patterns in your errors, providing insights about what you can do to improve your accuracy and credibility.

Pearson suggests adding a table summarizing the forecast error distribution and quantifying the patterns shown in the diagram. He also points out that while the PRD is a useful addition to the forecaster's personal accuracy dashboard, you may not want to include it in forecast reports to management. The reason: A naïve (no-change) forecast beats most forecasters more often than we'd expect. Management may soon realize that such forecasts are much cheaper to produce than ours.

Introduction

A very useful tool to add to your forecast accuracy dashboard is the prediction-realization diagram [PRD] devised over 40 years ago by Henri Theil (Theil, 1966, pp. 19–26). This diagram tells you, quickly and comprehensively, how your predicted changes compare with the actual results. In my expanded version, the PRD charts 17 categories of outcomes, showing the size and direction of the errors and whether the forecasts were more accurate than those produced by a naïve (no-change) model.

The PRD can be set up in Excel as a custom, user-defined chart and then used to visualize patterns in the outcomes for up to about 50 forecasts.

The Prediction-Realization Plot

The PRD plots the actual percentage changes on the horizontal axis and the predicted percentage changes on the vertical axis (Figure 3.24).

*This article originally appeared in *Foresight: The International Journal of Applied Forecasting* (Summer 2007), and appears here courtesy of the International Institute of Forecasters.

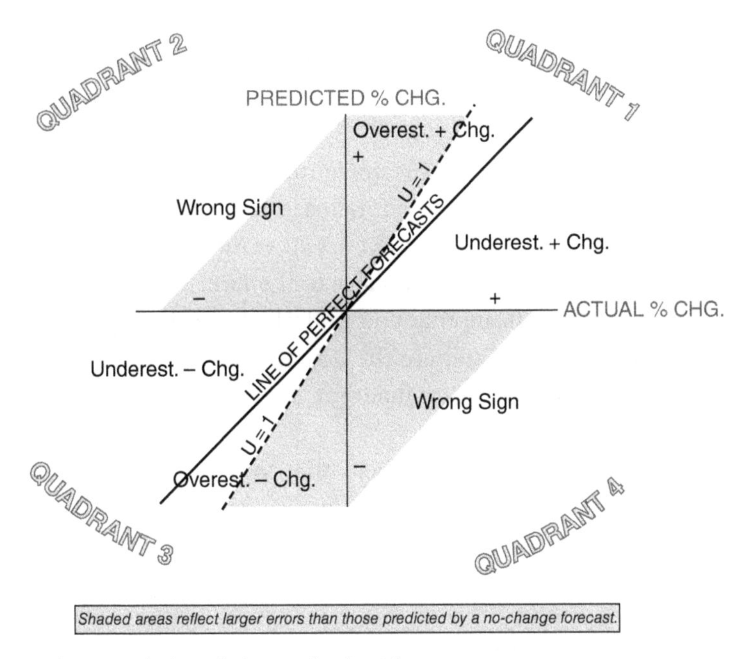

Figure 3.24 The Expanded Prediction-Realization Diagram

The 45° line through the origin is the line of perfect forecasts (LoPF). Points on this line reflect forecasts that predicted the actual changes without error.

I have added another line, labeled $U = 1$. This line has a slope of two times the actual change. Predictions falling on this line have the same error as predictions from a no-change forecast, which is frequently referred to as a naïve or naïve 1 forecast. Points along the horizontal axis (other than the origin itself) also are outcomes where $U = 1$, since the forecaster is predicting no change, exactly the same as a naive forecast.

Henri Theil created the U statistic, which he called the *inequality coefficient* (Theil, 1966, pp. 26–29), a scale-free ratio that compares each error produced by a forecast method with that produced by a naïve method. If the two errors are equal, Theil's U is equal to 1. When the forecasts are perfect, $U = 0$. When $U < 1$, your forecasts are more accurate than those of the naïve model, and when $U > 1$, your errors are larger than those of a no-change forecast.

You can find the U formula in most forecasting textbooks. However, its weakness is that U is undefined if all of the actual percentage changes are zero. Hyndman (2006) has proposed an alternative form of the statistic, the MASE (mean absolute scaled error), which avoids this weakness, but requires knowing the in-sample errors for the naïve forecast method. Still another alternative form is the GMASE (geometric mean absolute scaled error) proposed by Valentin (2007).

In Figure 3.24, the shaded areas represent the region where $U > 1$, the region you hope will not contain your forecasts. Your goal is for U to be small, at least less than 1 and preferably less than 0.5. At this point your efforts will have reduced the error to less than half of the error that would have resulted from the naïve forecast.

I have labeled the four quadrants in Figure 3.24. Points falling in Quadrant 1 indicate that the actual change is an increase and that you correctly forecast an increase. However, within Quadrant 1 you want your forecast point to be below the $U = 1$ line and of course as close to the LoPF as possible. Quadrant 1 points below the LoPF indicate that you underforecast the amount of change.

Now look at Quadrant 3, where the actual change is a decrease, and you have forecast a decrease. Within Quadrant 3, you want the outcomes to be above the $U = 1$ line.

Points in Quadrants 2 and 4 reveal that you have forecast the wrong direction of change—either you forecast an increase when a decrease actually occurred (Quadrant 2) or a decrease when an increase actually occurred (Quadrant 4).

The 17 Possible Outcomes

This expanded PRD above contains more information than is described in most textbooks, including Theil (1966) and Levenbach and Cleary (2006, pp. 177–178). In Theil's original version—without the $U = 1$ line—there were 13 possible outcomes. In my expanded version, which includes the $U = 1$ line, there are 17 possible outcomes for any forecast: 5 each in Quadrants 1 and 3, 1 each in Quadrants 2 and 4, and 5 falling on the axes. The 4 added outcomes result from identifying in Quadrants 1 and 3 whether U values for the predicted increases or decreases were >, <, or = to 1.

Zero error occurs in only 3 of the 17 possibilities (in italics below), while there are 10 ways your forecast error can be equal to or worse than that of a no-change forecast. If getting the direction right is what counts most, 11 (including a no-change forecast) of the 17 reveal that the direction of change was predicted correctly. Table 3.11 provides a summary.

For any points lying along the horizontal axis, Theil's $U = 1$. As the outcomes move toward the LoPF, U declines toward zero. Moving beyond the LoPF, U increases again, reaching 1 when the predicted percentage change is equal to two times the actual and then rising above 1 and remaining above 1 throughout Quadrants 2 and 4.

Predicted Changes vs. Predicted Levels

Any outcome on the line of perfect forecasts indicates that the forecast predicted the actual percentage change without error. These points also imply

Table 3.11 The 17 Possible Forecast Outcomes

Quadrant 1: Correctly Predicted Increase
Correct Direction, Underestimated % Change, but U<1
Correct Direction, Correct % Change (U=0)
Correct Direction, Overestimated % Change, but U<1
Correct Direction, Overestimated % Change, and U=I
Correct Direction, Overestimated % Change, and U<1

Quadrant 3: Correctly Predicted Decrease
Correct Direction, Underestimated % Change, but U<1
Correct Direction, Correct % Change (U=0)
Correct Direction, Overestimated % Change, but U<1
Correct Direction, Overestimated % Change, and U=I
Correct Direction, Overestimated % Change, and U>1

Quadrants 2 and 4: Mispredicted the Direction of Change
Quadrant 2: Incorrectly Predicted an Increase, U>1
Quadrant4: Incorrectly Predicted a Decrease, U>1

Outcomes on the Axes
Correctly Predicted No Change (Point is on the Origin), U undefined, but counted as U=0
Predicted No Change but Increase Occurred (Point is on the horizontal axis), U=I
Predicted No Change but Decrease Occurred (Point is on the horizontal axis), U=I
Predicted Increase but No Change Occurred (Point is on the vertical axis), U is undefined, but counted as U>1
Predicted Decrease but No Change Occurred (Point is on the vertical axis), U is undefined, but counted as U>1

that the forecast also predicted the level of the variable without error. For any outcome above the LoPF, the forecast overestimated the level, and for any outcome below the LoPF, the forecast underestimated the level.

Strictly speaking, that analysis holds only if the predicted percentage change, as well as the actual percentage change, had the previous actual value as the denominator. For published predicted percentage changes made before the base actual values were known (or revised), that will not be the case—but the distortion will be minimal if errors in estimating the base value are small.

Applying the PRD to Energy Price Forecasts

The points in Figure 3.25 are 25 one-year-ahead energy-price forecasts, five forecasts for each of five types of fuel. The overall U for the 25 forecasts is 0.74, indicating that the forecast errors were smaller than those of the naïve forecast. The figure shows the forecasted changes by year, which is appropriate if you wish to see when particular errors occurred.

Figure 3.26 shows the same forecasts plotted by category instead of by year, to see how the forecasts for the individual series compare.

Both figures show at a glance that the forecasts underestimated the actual price changes most of the time (20 out of 25 forecasts). From Figure 3.25, we can see that all five forecasts for 2000 and for 2003 were too low, and all five forecasts for 2004 erroneously predicted a decrease in energy prices when in

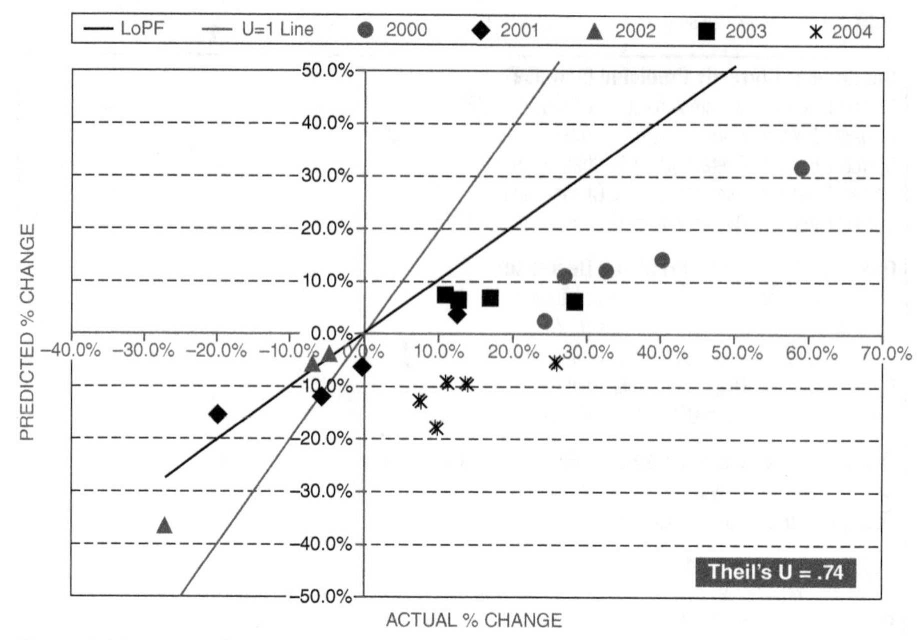

Figure 3.25 Energy Price Forecasts, by Year 2000–2004

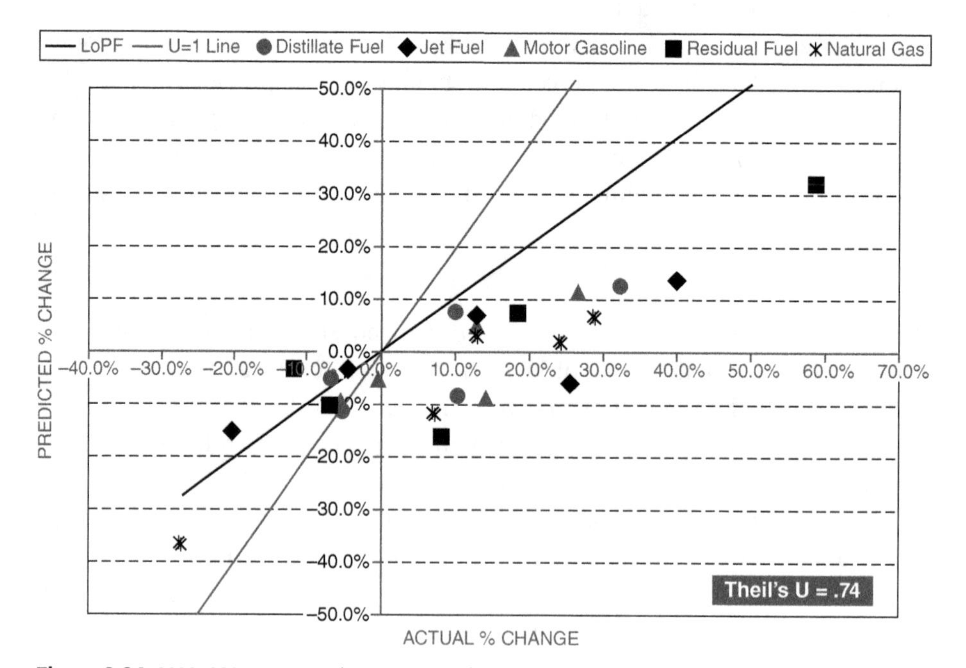

Figure 3.26 2000–2004 Energy Price Forecasts, by Type

fact they rose. The year 2002 was the best year for forecasting, with all five forecasts close to the LoPF.

For me, what stands out is the need to explore why the forecasts had the wrong sign in 2004, and how, in the future, you could avoid the general tendency to underestimate energy price increases.

In Figure 3.26, no group of the five forecasts for any one type of fuel is off to itself, clustered away from the other forecasts, so the types of errors do not appear to be unique for any one fuel category.

Table 3.12 shows a useful numerical way to summarize the plots on energy price forecasts. The prediction-realization section at the left side of the table is the prediction-realization table used by Theil (Ibid., pp. 361–363) to describe how well the forecaster predicted direction. The ideal distribution is for all forecasts to be in the diagonal from upper left to lower right, in which case the row sums for the predictions will be identical to the column sums for the realizations. The actual outcomes here show that when an increase was forecasted, that was the correct direction (reading across the row). A forecast user could treat a predicted increase as useful information about the probable direction of change. However, when a decrease was predicted (which was over half the time), it frequently was the wrong direction. If I were the forecast user, I would not place high faith in this forecaster being right when predicting a decrease.

Theil's prediction-realization table does not identify where correct predictions of an increase or decrease fell with respect to the $U = 1$ line. Some with correct direction still could have larger errors than those produced by a naïve forecast. Adding the section with the distribution relative to the U values completes the picture. Here the distribution of the U values shows all predicted increases had $U < 1$, enhancing their credibility. However, Theil's U was greater than 1 for one-half of the predicted decreases, accounting for all 28% of the outcomes where the predictions were no better than those of a no-change forecast. In sum, seeing the forecast distributions summarized in tables points out the asymmetry between forecasting increases and decreases, which the forecaster needs to correct before the two types of forecasts will be equally credible.

Payroll Employment Forecasts: The Difficulty of Improving on a Naïve Forecast

The points in Figure 3.27 are 30 forecasts for nonagricultural payroll employment in the U.S. and five of its Census regions. The $U = 1.21$ tells us that the overall error is 21% higher than if we had always predicted no-change. The actual values were taken from the following year's forecast report (before future benchmark revisions).

Table 3.12 Distribution of the 25 Energy Price Forecasts by Direction and *U* Values

	REALIZATION			
PREDICTION	INCREASE	NO CHANGE	DECREASE	
Increase	44.0%	0.0%	0.0%	44.0%
No Change	0.0%	0.0%	0.0%	0.0%
Decrease	20.0%	0.0%	36.0%	56.0%
	64.0%	0.0%	36.0%	100.0%
	INCREASE	NO CHANGE	DECREASE	
Correct Sign	44.0%	0.0%	36.0%	80.0%

	THEIL'S U				
PREDICTION	U=0	U<1	U=1	U>1	
Increase	0.0%	44.0%	0.0%	0.0%	44.0%
No Change	0.0%		0.0%		0.0%
Decrease	0.0%	28.0%	0.0%	28.0%	56.0%
	0.0%	72.0%	0.0%	28.0%	100.0%

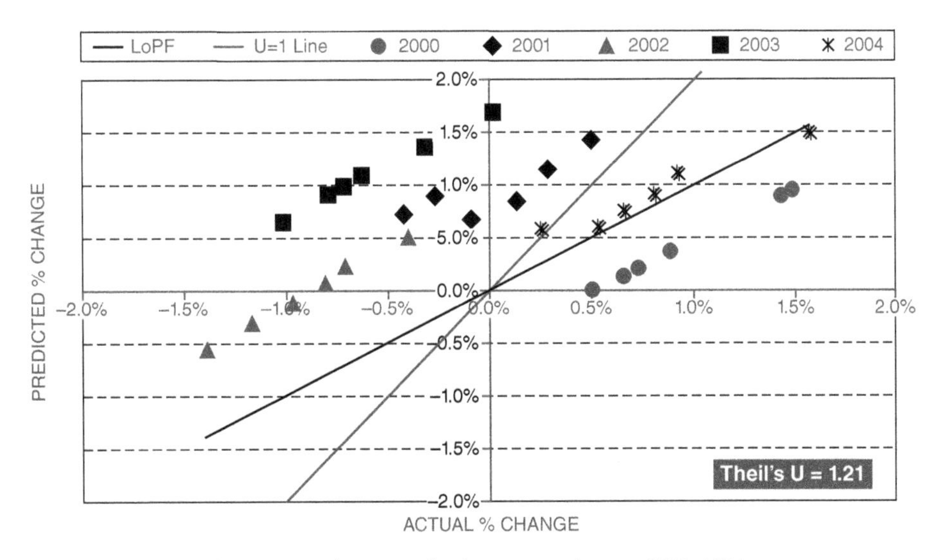

Figure 3.27 U.S. and Eastern Regions Payroll Job Forecasts, by Year 2000–2004

A major weakness in these forecasts is the substantial number that falls in Quadrant 2, predictions of increases when decreases occurred. In addition, several points (5) are in Quadrant 1 above the $U = 1$ line: forecasted increases more than twice as large as the actual increases.

By year, we see that the 2004 forecasts were very accurate ($U = .22$), and the 2000 forecasts were relatively good, even though the increases were underestimated. However, in 2001 and 2003, all forecast errors were worse than those provided by no-change forecasts (calculated *U*'s were well above 2).

Table 3.13 shows in this case the forecasts of increases were not very credible. When an increase was predicted, decreases frequently occurred; and being wrong on the sign or size of predicted increases caused over half (53%) of the 30 forecasts to be worse than those from a no-change forecast. By comparison, the prediction of a decrease was more credible. To me, the chart and table indicate a substantial bias toward forecasting job increases.

The overall U statistic was much smaller for the energy price forecasts ($U = .74$) than for the payroll employment forecasts ($U = 1.21$). A reason is revealed by looking at the scales for the actual changes in the two diagrams. The annual fuel price changes have been much larger than those for payroll employment. If you plotted the employment forecasts in the energy price chart, the employment forecasts would show up as a small solid blob at the origin.

For variables with small percentage changes, a naïve (no-change) forecast will yield low percent errors, making it a real challenge to beat. Hence a *U* close to or even above 1 is a disappointment but not startling. For such variables, the forecaster's main contribution may be to provide insight about the future direction of change, instead of the amount, and to focus on a forecasting

Table 3.13 Distributions of the 30 Employment Forecasts by Direction and *U* Values

	REALIZATION			
PREDICTION	INCREASE	NO CHANGE	DECREASE	
Increase	50.0%	0.0%	36.7%	86.7%
No Change	0.0%	0.0%	0.0%	0.0%
Decrease	3.3%	0.0%	10.0%	13.3%
	53.3%	0.0%	46.7%	100.0%
	INCREASE	NO CHANGE	DECREASE	
Correct Sign	50.0%	0.0%	10.0%	60.0%

	THEIL'S U				
PREDICTION	U=0	U<1	U=1	U>1	
Increase	0.0%	33.3%	0.0%	53.3%	86.7%
No Change	0.0%		0.0%		0.0%
Decrease	0.0%	10.0%	0.0%	3.3%	13.3%
	0.0%	43.3%	0.0%	56.7%	100.0%

process that predicts direction well, such as leading indicator approaches. If you can avoid outcomes in Quadrants 2 and 4, giving wrong directional signals, your prediction of an increase or decrease will be much more credible.

Summary and Recommendation

The prediction-realization diagram shows at a glance how well you did in getting the direction right. For me, that feature alone makes the PRD a worthwhile component of my accuracy dashboard, using either my expanded version here or Theil's original version.

The common measures of forecast error reported for rolling out-of-sample forecasts in most software packages, such as mean absolute percent error and mean absolute deviation, reveal only magnitude of error, offering no information about direction. The PRD thus is a useful addition to the error-magnitude statistics, worth trying in your personal accuracy dashboard.

I say personal dashboard, because you may not wish to include it in forecast reports to management, especially with the Theil's U information. A no-change forecast beats most forecasters (including me) on the size of the error more often than we forecasters expect, and management will realize that such forecasts are much cheaper to produce than ours.

The summary tables here are relatively simple ones. You can customize them as you see fit to include more information about the nature and quality of your forecasts. Two versions with more emphasis on the direction of change are in Pearson et al. (2000), evaluating establishment forecasts of employment three-months-ahead, where no-change was the actual outcome 30% of the time.

REFERENCES

Hyndman, R. J. (2006). Another look at forecast-accuracy metrics for intermittent demand. *Foresight: International Journal of Applied Forecasting* 4 (June 2006), 43–46.

Levenbach, H., and J. P. Cleary (2006). *Forecasting: Practice & Process for Demand Management.* Belmont, CA: Thomson Brooks/Cole.

Pearson, R. L., G. W. Putnam, and W. K. Almousa (2000). The accuracy of short-term employment forecasts obtained by employer surveys: The State of Illinois experience. Federal Forecasters Conference 2000 Papers and Proceedings, District of Columbia: U.S. Department of Education Office of Educational Research and Improvement.

Theil, H. (1966). *Applied Economic Forecasting*. Amsterdam: North-Holland Publishing.

Valentin, L. (2007). Use scaled errors instead of percentage errors in forecast evaluations. *Foresight: International Journal of Applied Forecasting* 7 (June 2007), 17–22.

3.12 FORECAST ERROR MEASURES: CRITICAL REVIEW AND PRACTICAL RECOMMENDATIONS*

Andrey Davydenko and Robert Fildes

Andrey Davydenko and Robert Fildes augment the discussion of forecasting performance metrics with a critical review of existing metrics for measuring error across many series (e.g., SKU level data). This review is necessary, they observe, because the forecasting function is often evaluated using inappropriate measures, with the consequence of misleading results.

As a practical consideration, forecasting performance metrics should be robust (showing good performance across a wide range of data) and easy to interpret (understood not just by professional forecasters, but by business managers and executives as well). Davydenko and Fildes systematize the well-known problems with existing measures and identify additional limitations. They compare the existing measures and a new one, across three years of monthly sales data for a fast-moving consumer goods (FMCG) manufacturer.

A key finding of this study is that different metrics can lead to different conclusions being drawn from the same data. For their FMCG data, some measures show that judgmental overrides improved the forecast, while other measures show the overrides made the forecast worse. It is therefore important to have a clear understanding of the statistical properties of any error measure being used. Inappropriate measures can have severe consequences, such as leading to the selection of inappropriate forecasting models.

1. Introduction

The choice of a measure to assess the accuracy of forecasts across time series is of wide practical importance, since the forecasting function is often evaluated using inappropriate measures distorting the link to economic performance (Armstrong and Fildes, 1995). Despite the continuing interest in the topic, the choice of the most suitable measure still remains controversial. Due to their statistical properties, popular measures do not always ensure easily interpretable results when applied in practice (Hyndman and Koehler, 2006). Surveys show that the proportion of firms tracking the aggregated accuracy is surprisingly small (55% as reported by McCarthy et al., 2006). One apparent reason for this is the inability to agree on appropriate accuracy metrics (Hoover, 2006).

We look at the behaviors of commonly used measures when measuring accuracy across many series (e.g., when dealing with SKU-level data). After identifying the desirable properties of an error measure (including robustness and ease of interpretation), we show that traditional measures may lead to confusing and even misleading results. Some popular measures (such as the popular, mean absolute percentage error: MAPE) are extremely vulnerable to outliers. Limitations of popular error measures have been widely discussed

* This article was adapted from (Davydenko and Fildes, 2014), which is an extended and revised version of (Davydenko and Fildes, 2013).

(e.g., see Hyndman and Koehler, 2006). Here we systemize well-known problems and identify a number of additional important limitations of existing measures that have not yet been given enough attention.

Hyndman and Koehler (2006) proposed the MASE (mean absolute scaled error) to overcome the problems of percentage-based measures by scaling errors using the MAE (mean absolute error) of a naïve forecast. We show that MASE (i) introduces a bias toward overrating the performance of the benchmark as a result of arithmetic averaging and (ii) is vulnerable to outliers as a result of dividing by small benchmark MAEs. So even the latest measures have serious disadvantages.

To overcome the above difficulties, we propose an enhanced measure that shows an average relative improvement under linear loss. In contrast to MASE, our measure averages relative MAEs using the weighted geometric mean.

Our empirical analysis uses SKU-level data containing statistical forecasts and corresponding judgmental adjustments. We look at the task of measuring the accuracy of such adjustments. Some studies of accuracy of judgmental adjustments have produced conflicting results (e.g., Fildes et al., 2009; Franses and Legertee, 2010, with one arguing that judgmental adjustments add value with the other concluding the opposite). This is an important issue for organizations in managing their demand planning function. Different measures were applied to different data and this led to different conclusions. Several studies reported an interesting picture where adjustments improved MdAPE, while harming MAPE (Fildes et al., 2009; Trapero et al., 2011). These confusing results require better understanding about what lies behind different error measures. We discuss the appropriateness of various measures used and demonstrate the use of the measure we recommend.

The next section describes the data employed for empirical illustrations. Section 3 illustrates the limitations of well-known measures. Section 4 introduces the enhanced measure. Section 5 contains the results of applying different measures. The concluding section summarizes our findings and offers recommendations as to which of the different measures can be employed safely.

2. Data

We employ monthly data from a fast-moving consumer goods (FMCG) manufacturer collected over three years. For each SKU and each month we have:

1. The one-step-ahead forecast computed automatically by a software system (the system forecast);
2. The corresponding judgmentally adjusted forecast obtained from experts after their revision of the statistical forecast (Fildes et al., 2009) (the final forecast); and
3. Actual sales (actuals).

In total, our data contain 412 series and 6,882 observations. The data are representative for companies dealing with many series of different lengths relating to different SKUs. The frequency of zero demand and zero error observations for our data was not high. However, our further discussion will also consider situations when small counts and zeroes occur frequently, as is common with intermittent demand.

3. Critical Review of Existing Measures

3.1 Desirable Properties

What are the properties of an ideal error measure? There have been different attempts in literature to identify the most important properties by which the adequacy of an error measure should be judged. In particular, Fildes (1992) justifies the properties of interpretability and sensitivity to outliers (robustness).

Some authors (e.g., Zellner, 1986) argue that the criterion by which we evaluate forecasts must correspond to the criterion by which we optimize our estimates when producing forecasts. In other words, if we optimize our estimates using some given loss function, we must use the same loss function for empirical evaluation in order to find out which model is better.

Typically, if our density forecast is symmetric, fitting a statistical model gives forecasts optimal under both linear and quadratic loss. However, if we log-transform series and then transform back forecasts by exponentiation, we get forecasts that are optimal only under linear loss. If we use another loss, we must first obtain the density forecast, and then adjust our estimate given our specific loss function (see examples of doing this in Goodwin, 2000).

Given the above consideration, we will focus on evaluating the accuracy in terms of the symmetric linear loss. Let's assume we want to empirically compare two methods and find out which method is better. If we have only one time series, it seems natural to use a mean absolute error (MAE). Also, MAE is attractive as it is simple to understand and calculate (Hyndman, 2006). Potentially, MAE has the following limitation: Absolute errors follow a highly skewed distribution with a heavy right tail, which means that MAE is not robust (in other words, it is a highly inefficient estimate). But there is a more important problem: When comparing accuracy across series, MAE becomes unsuitable as it is not scale-independent—it is a case of comparing apples and oranges.

In this paper we address the question of how to adequately represent forecasting performance under symmetric linear loss when measuring accuracy across many time series. We aim for the following properties: (1) easy-to-interpret, (2) robust, (3) applicable in a wide range of settings (e.g., allows zero errors or forecasts/actuals, negative forecasts/actuals, etc.), (4) informative (i.e., brings valuable information), (5) uses the same loss function that was used for optimization and producing forecasts, and (6) scale-independent.

3.2 Percentage Errors

Although MAPE is very popular, it has many problems:

- **Problem 1: Zero and negative actuals cannot be used.** MAPE is therefore unsuitable for intermittent demand data.
- **Problem 2: Extreme percentages.** The sample mean of APEs due to the skewed and diffuse distribution gives a highly inefficient estimate and is severely affected by extreme cases. The distribution of APEs for our data is illustrated by Figure 3.28. APEs are often larger than 100%. Such extremes do not allow for a meaningful interpretation since corresponding forecasting errors are not necessarily very harmful or damaging in practice. Large percentages often arise merely due to the relatively low actual values. Due to the large influence of outliers the sample mean in a highly skewed distribution becomes inefficient. In other words, for highly skewed distributions it can take a very big sample size before the most likely value of the sample mean approaches the true population mean (Fleming, 2008).
- **Problem 3: MAPE-based comparisons do not reflect accuracy in terms of a symmetric loss.** Percentage errors put a heavier penalty on positive errors than on negative errors when the forecast is taken as fixed. This leads to a serious bias when trying to average APEs using the arithmetic mean. Kolassa and Schutz (2007) provide the following example. Assume that we have a series containing values distributed uniformly between 10 and 50. If we are using a symmetrical loss, the best forecast would be 30. However, a forecast of 22 produces better MAPE. Thus, MAPE is not indicative of accuracy in terms of a symmetric loss even for a single series.
- **Problem 4: Misleading when errors correlate with actuals.** The comparison of forecasting performance based on percentage errors can give misleading results when the improvement in accuracy correlates with actual value on the original scale (Davydenko and Fildes, 2013).

Various improvements have been proposed in the literature (see Table 3.14), but none of them solves the problems.

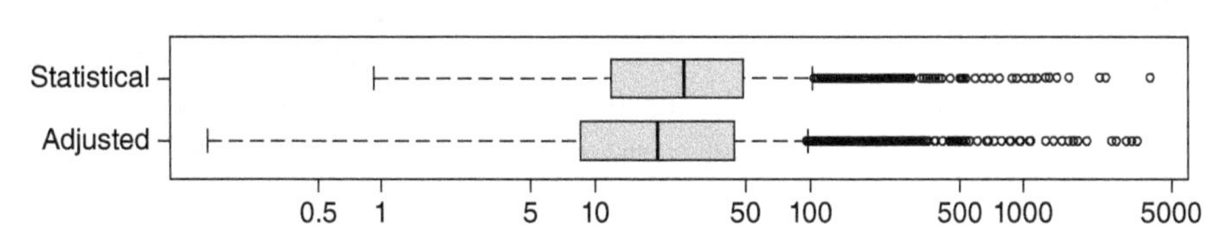

Figure 3.28 Box-plot for APEs (log scale)

Table 3.14 Proposed Improvements

Trimmed/Winsorized MAPE	This approach aims to improve robustness, but introduces another problem. Since the distribution of APEs is non-symmetric, the use of trimmed or Winsorized means makes the resulting estimates biased (they do not reflect the MAPE value). Moreover, this does not solve problems 1, 3, and 4.
Symmetric MAPE, SMAPE	As shown in literature, SMAPE does not solve problem 2 at all (Goodwin & Lawton, 1999). In fact, this approach does not solve any of the above problems whatsoever. The only correct approach to average ratios is through the use of logarithms (Fleming & Wallace, 1986), but see the next comments.
Geometric mean APE, GMAPE	This is equivalent to the mean of log-transformed APEs as suggested by (Swanson et al., 2000). This solves problems 2 and 3, but does not solve problems 1 and 4. Also, zero errors are not allowed.
MdAPE	MdAPE-based comparisons are not easily interpretable, especially when forecasting methods have different shapes of error distributions. Essentially, MdAPE is a special case of the trimmed MAPE and has the corresponding disadvantages. The sample median of APEs is resistant to the influence of extreme cases, but is insensitive to large errors even if they are not outliers or extreme percentages. This means that MdAPE will not show the best method in terms of the linear loss. Additionally, the sample median of APEs is a biased estimate of the population median of APEs, and the bias depends on the sample size. It is also difficult to assess statistical significance of differences in accuracy when using MdAPEs.

3.3 Relative Errors (REs)

Well-known RE-measures include mean relative absolute error (MRAE), median relative absolute error (MdRAE), and geometric mean relative absolute error (GMRAE).

When averaging benchmark ratios, the geometric mean has the advantage over the arithmetic mean (Fleming and Wallace, 1986). The geometric mean produces rankings that are invariant to the choice of the benchmark. Suppose method A is compared with method B. Let method A be used as the benchmark and the arithmetic mean of absolute REs indicates that method B is superior. Then, if method B is used as a benchmark instead of method A, the arithmetic mean can indicate that now method A is superior. Such results are ambiguous and can lead to confusion in their interpretation. Of the measures based on REs, GMRAE is the only measure that has the property of not changing the ranking depending on what method is used as the benchmark. But GMRAE has its limitations:

- **Problem 1: Zero errors are not allowed.** When using intermittent demand data, the use of relative errors becomes impossible due to the frequent occurrences of zero errors (Hyndman, 2006).
- **Problem 2: GMRAE generally does not reflect changes in accuracy under linear or quadratic loss.** For instance, for a particular time series GMAE can compare methods in favor of a method producing errors with a heavier tailed-distribution, while for the same series MAE or MSE can suggest the opposite ranking.

Consider the following example. Suppose that for a particular time series, method A produces errors e_t^A that are independent and identically distributed variables following a heavy-tailed distribution. More specifically, let e_t^A follow the t-distribution with $v = 3$ degrees of freedom: $e_t^A \sim t_v$. Also, let method B produce independent errors that follow the normal distribution: $e_t^B \sim N(0,3)$. Let method B be the benchmark method. It can be shown analytically that the variances for e_t^A and e_t^B are equal (methods have the same performance under quadratic loss): $\mathrm{Var}(e_t^A) = \mathrm{Var}(e_t^B) = 3$. However, GMRAE shows method A as better than method B: GMRAE ≈ 0.69.

Thus, even for a single series, a statistically significant improvement of GMRAE is not equivalent to a statistically significant improvement under quadratic or linear loss.

3.4 Percent Better

A simple approach to compare forecasting accuracy of methods A and B is to calculate the percentage of cases when method A was closer to actual than method B. This measure, known as *percent better* (PB), was recommended by some authors as a fairly good indicator (e.g., Chatfield, 2001). It has the advantage of being immune to outliers and scale-independent. Although PB seems to be easy to interpret, the following important limitations should be taken into account:

- **Problem 1: PB does not show the magnitude of changes in accuracy** (Hyndman and Koehler, 2006). Thus, it becomes hard to assess the consequences of using one method instead of another.
- **Problem 2: PB does not reflect changes under linear loss.** As was the case for the GMRAE, we can show that if shapes of error distributions are different for different methods, PB becomes nonindicative of changes under linear loss even for a single series.
- **Problem 3: Many equal forecasts lead to confusing results.** When methods A and B frequently produce equal forecasts (this often happens

with intermittent demand data), obtaining PB < 50% is not necessarily a bad result. But, without additional information, we cannot draw any conclusions about the changes in accuracy.

3.5 Scaled Errors

When forecasts are produced from varying origins but with a constant horizon, the MASE is calculated as

$$q_{i,t} = \frac{e_{i,t}}{\text{MAE}_i^{\text{b}}}, \text{MASE} = \text{mean}\left(\left|q_{i,t}\right|\right),$$

where $e_{i,t}$ is forecasting error for period t for time series i, $q_{i,t}$ is the scaled error, and MAE_i^{b} is the in-sample MAE of naïve forecast for series i.

It is possible to show that, in this scenario, MASE is equivalent to the weighted arithmetic mean of relative MAEs, where the number of available values of $e_{i,t}$ is used as the weight:

$$\text{MASE} = \frac{1}{\sum_{i=1}^{m} n_i} \sum_{i=1}^{m} n_i r_i, \ r_i = \frac{\text{MAE}_i}{\text{MAE}_i^{\text{b}}},$$

where m is the total number of series, n_i is the number of available values of $e_{i,t}$ for series i, MAE_i^{b} is the MAE of the benchmark forecast for series i, and MAE_i is the MAE of the forecast being evaluated against the benchmark.

- **Problem 1: Bias toward overrating the benchmark.** As noted previously, the arithmetic mean is not appropriate for averaging observations representing relative quantities. In such situations the geometric mean should be used instead. As a result of using the arithmetic mean of r_i, equation (1) introduces a bias toward overrating the accuracy of a benchmark forecasting method. In other words, the penalty for bad forecasting becomes larger than the reward for good forecasting.

  For example, suppose that the performance of some forecasting method is compared with the performance of the naïve method across two series ($m = 2$), which contain equal numbers of forecasts and observations. For the first series, the MAE ratio is $r_1 = 1/2$, and for the second series, the MAE ratio is the opposite: $r_2 = 2/1$. The improvement in accuracy for the first series obtained using the forecasting method is the same as the reduction for the second series. However, averaging the

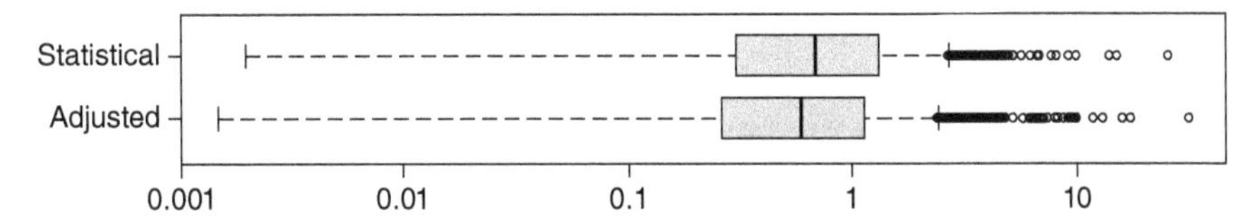

Figure 3.29 Box-plot for Absolute Scaled Errors (log scale)

ratios gives MASE = $\frac{1}{2}(r_1 + r_2) = 1.25$, which indicates that the benchmark method is better. While this is a well-known point, its implications for error measures, with the potential for misleading conclusions, are widely ignored.

- **Problem 2: Skewed, heavy-tailed, left-bounded distribution.** In addition to the above effect, the use of MASE (like MAPE) may result in unstable estimates, as the arithmetic mean is severely influenced by extreme cases arising from dividing by relatively small values (see Figure 3.29). In case of MASE, outliers occur when dividing by relatively small benchmark MAEs. Such MAEs are likely to appear in short series. At the same time, attempts to trim or Winsorize MASE lead to biased results.

Thus, while the use of the standard MAPE has long been known to be flawed, the newly proposed MASE also suffers from some of the same limitations, and may also lead to an unreliable interpretation of the empirical results.

3.4 MAD/MEAN Ratio

In contrast to the MASE, the MAD/MEAN ratio assumes that the forecasting errors are scaled by the mean of series actuals instead of by the in-sample MAE of naïve forecast. This reduces the risk of dividing by a small denominator (see Kolassa and Schutz, 2007), however:

- **Problem 1: MAD/MEAN assumes stable mean.** Hyndman (2006) notes that the MAD/MEAN ratio assumes the series mean is stable over time, which may make it unreliable when the data exhibit trends or seasonal patterns.
- **Problem 2: Outliers.** Figure 3.30 shows that the MAD/MEAN scheme is prone to outliers for the dataset we consider here. Again, attempts to trim/Winsorize lead to biases. Generally, MAD/MEAN ratio introduces the risk of producing unreliable estimates that are based on highly skewed left-bounded distributions.

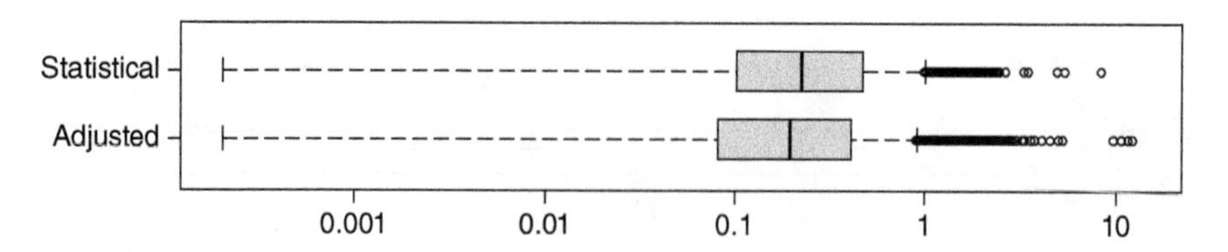

Figure 3.30 Box-plot for Absolute Scaled Errors Found by the MAD/MEAN Scheme (log scale)

4. Recommended Scheme for Measuring the Accuracy of Point Forecasts across Many Series

To ensure a reliable evaluation of forecasting accuracy under symmetric linear loss, we recommend using the following scheme. Suppose we want to measure the accuracy of h-step-ahead forecasts produced with some forecasting method A across m time series. Firstly, we need to select a benchmark method. This, in particular, can be the naïve method. Let n_i denote the number of periods for which both the h-step-ahead forecasts and actual observations are available for series i. Then the accuracy measurement procedure is as follows:

1. For each time series i in $1...m$
   a. Calculate the relative MAE as $r_i = \frac{\text{MAE}_i^A}{\text{MAE}_i^B}$, where MAE_i^A and MAE_i^B denote out-of-sample h-step-ahead MAEs for method A and for the benchmark, respectively.
   b. Calculate the weighted log relative MAE as $l_i = n_i \ln r_i$.
2. Calculate average relative MAE:

$$\text{AvgRelMAE} = \exp\left(\frac{1}{\sum_{i=1}^{m} n_i} \sum_{i=1}^{m} l_i\right).$$

   If there is evidence for a nonnormal distribution of l_i, use the following procedure to ensure more efficient estimates:
   a. Find the indices of l_i that correspond to the 5% of largest and 5% of lowest values. Let R be a set that contains the remaining indices.
   b. Calculate trimmed AvgRelMAE:

$$\text{AvgRelMAE}^{\text{trimmed}} = \exp\left(\frac{1}{\sum_{i \in R} n_i} \sum_{i \in R} l_i\right).$$

3. Assess the statistical significance of changes by testing the mean of l_i against zero. For this purpose, the Wilcoxon's one-sample signed rank test can be used (assuming that the distribution of l_i is symmetric, but not necessarily normal). If the distribution of l_i is nonsymmetric, the

binomial test can be used to test the median of l_i against zero. If the distribution has a negative skew, then it is likely that the negative median will indicate negative mean as well.

Notes

(a) In theory, the following effect may complicate the interpretation of AvgRelMAE. Let $e_{i,t}^{A}$ be error from method A for series i and time period t. Let $e_{i,t}^{B}$ be error from the benchmark. If the kurtosis of the distribution of $e_{i,t}^{A}$ differs from that of the distribution of $e_{i,t}^{B}$, then $\ln r_i$ becomes a biased estimate of $\ln\left(E\left|e_{i,t}^{A}\right| / E\left|e_{i,t}^{B}\right|\right)$. In fact, when $n_i = 1$ for each i, the AvgRelMAE becomes equivalent to the GMRAE, which has the limitations described in Section 3.3. However, in practice this effect usually becomes negligible when $n_i > 5$. If necessary, well-known correction methods for ratio estimators can be used to improve the measure.

(b) If the distribution of absolute errors is heavily skewed, MAE becomes a very inefficient estimate of the expected value of the absolute error. A productive way to improve the efficiency of estimates without introducing substantial bias is to use asymmetric trimming. See, for example (Alkhazeleh and Razali, 2010) for the details of how this can be done.

(c) In step 2, the optimal trim depends on the shape of the distribution of l_i. Our experiments suggest that the efficiency of the trimmed mean is not highly sensitive to the choice of the trim level. Any trim between 2% and 10% gives reasonably good results. Generally, when the underlying distribution is symmetrical and heavy-tailed relative to Gaussian, the variance of the trimmed mean is quite a lot smaller than the variance of the sample mean. Therefore, we highly recommend the use of the trimmed mean for symmetrical distributions.

5. Results of Empirical Evaluation

The results of applying the measures described above are shown in Table 3.15. When calculating the AvgRelMAE we used statistical forecast as the benchmark.

For the empirical dataset, the analysis has shown that judgmental adjustments improved accuracy in terms of the AvgRelMAE, but for the same dataset, a range of well-known error measures, including MAPE, MdAPE, GMRAE, MASE, and the MAD/MEAN ratio, indicated conflicting results. The analysis using MAPE, MASE, and the MAD/MEAN was affected by the highly skewed underlying distribution.

The AvgRelMAE result shows improvements from both positive and negative adjustments, whereas, according to MAPE and MASE, only negative adjustments improve the accuracy. For the whole sample, adjustments

Table 3.15 Accuracy of Adjustments According to Different Error Measures

Error Measure	Positive Adjustments		Negative Adjustments		All Nonzero Adjustments	
	Statistical Forecast	Adjusted Forecast	Statistical Forecast	Adjusted Forecast	Statistical Forecast	Adjusted Forecast
MAPE, % (untrimmed)	**38.85**	61.54	70.45	**45.13**	**47.88**	56.85
MAPE, % (2 % trimmed)	**30.98**	40.56	48.71	**30.12**	**34.51**	37.22
MdAPE, %	25.48	**20.65**	23.90	**17.27**	24.98	**19.98**
GMRAE	1.00	**0.93**	1.00	**0.70**	1.00	**0.86**
GMRAE (5 % trimmed)	1.00	**0.94**	1.00	**0.71**	1.00	**0.87**
MASE	**0.97**	0.97	0.95	**0.70**	0.96	**0.90**
Mean (MAD/Mean)	**0.37**	0.42	0.33	**0.24**	**0.36**	0.37
Mean (MAD/Mean) (5 % trimmed)	**0.34**	0.35	0.29	**0.21**	0.33	**0.31**
AvgRelMAE	1.00	**0.96**	1.00	**0.71**	1.00	**0.90**
AvgRelMAE (5 % trimmed)	1.00	**0.96**	1.00	**0.73**	1.00	**0.89**
Avg. improvement based on AvgRelMAE	0.00	**0.04**	0.00	**0.29**	0.00	**0.10**

improve the MAE of statistical forecast by 10%, on average. Positive adjustments are less accurate than negative adjustments and provide only minor improvements. To assess the significance of changes in accuracy in terms of MAE, we applied the two-sided Wilcoxon test to test the mean of the weighted relative log-transformed MAEs against zero. The p-value was < 0.01 for the set containing the adjustments of both signs, < 0.05 for only positive adjustments, and $< 2.210^{-16}$ for only negative adjustments.

6. Conclusions

Since analyses based on different measures can lead to different conclusions, it is important to have a clear understanding of the statistical properties of any error measure used. We showed that in practice many well-known error measures become inappropriate. The consequences of a poor choice of error measure are potentially severe: The wrong statistical method can be chosen to underpin the demand forecasting activity. In addition, there can easily be misjudgments as to the value added that demand planners are making to forecasting accuracy, whether collectively or individually.

In order to overcome the disadvantages of existing measures, we recommend the use of the average relative MAE (AvgRelMAE) measure, which is calculated as the geometric mean of relative MAE values.

In practice, the adoption of a new error measure may present difficulties due to organizational factors. If the organization insists on using percentages, we recommend using geometric mean APE instead of MAPE because it helps overcome some of the problems, as described in Section 3.2. And it remains interpretable, a crucial organizational requirement.

REFERENCES

Alkhazaleh, A. M. H., and A. M. Razali (2010). New technique to estimate the asymmetric trimming mean. *Journal of Probability and Statistics* doi:10.1155/2010/739154.

Armstrong, J. S., and R. Fildes (1995). Correspondence on the selection of error measures for comparisons among forecasting methods. *Journal of Forecasting* 14, 67–71.

Chatfield, C. (2001) *Time-series Forecasting*. Boca Raton, FL: Chapman & Hall.

Davydenko, A., and R. Fildes (2013). Measuring forecasting accuracy: The case of judgmental adjustments to SKU-level demand forecasts. *International Journal of Forecasting* 29, 510–522.

Davydenko, A., and R. Fildes (2014). Measuring forecasting accuracy: Problems and recommendations (by the example of SKU-level judgmental adjustments). In *Intelligent Fashion Forecasting Systems: Models and Applications* (pp. 43–70). Berlin: Springer Berlin Heidelberg.

Fildes, R. (1992). The evaluation of extrapolative forecasting methods. *International Journal of Forecasting* 8, 81–98.

Fildes, R., P. Goodwin, M. Lawrence, and K. Nikolopoulos (2009). Effective forecasting and judgmental adjustments: An empirical evaluation and strategies for improvement in supply-chain planning. *International Journal of Forecasting* 25, 3–23.

Fleming, G. (2008). Yep, we're skewed. *Variance* 2, 179–183.

Fleming, P. J., and J. J. Wallace (1986). How not to lie with statistics: The correct way to summarize benchmark results. *Communications of the ACM* 29, 218–221.

Franses, P. H., and R. Legerstee (2010). Do experts' adjustments on model-based SKU-level forecasts improve forecast quality? *Journal of Forecasting* 29, 331–340.

Goodwin, P., and Lawton, R. (1999). On the asymmetry of the symmetric MAPE. *International Journal of Forecasting* 4, 405–408.

Goodwin, P. (2000). Improving the voluntary integration of statistical forecasts and judgment. *International Journal of Forecasting* 16, 85–99.

Hyndman, R. J. (2006). Another look at forecast-accuracy metrics for intermittent demand. *Foresight: International Journal of Applied Forecasting* 4, 43–46.

Hyndman, R., and A. Koehler (2006). Another look at measures of forecast accuracy. *International Journal of Forecasting* 22, 679–688.

Kolassa, S., and W. Schutz (2007). Advantages of the MAD/MEAN ratio over the MAPE. *Foresight: International Journal of Applied Forecasting* 6, 40–43.

McCarthy, T. M., D. F. Davis, S. L. Golicic, and J. T. Mentzer (2006). The evolution of sales forecasting management: A 20-year longitudinal study of forecasting practice. *Journal of Forecasting* 25, 303–324.

Trapero, J. R., R. A. Fildes, and A. Davydenko (2011). Nonlinear identification of judgmental forecasts at SKU-level. *Journal of Forecasting* 30, 490–508.

Zellner, A. (1986). A tale of forecasting 1001 series: The Bayesian knight strikes again. *International Journal of Forecasting* 2, 491–494.

3.13 MEASURING THE QUALITY OF INTERMITTENT DEMAND FORECASTS: IT'S WORSE THAN WE'VE THOUGHT!*

Steve Morlidge

In what he calls the *numerator problem*, Steve Morlidge adds yet another performance metric challenge when dealing with intermittent demand.

Using simple examples of an intermittent series, Morlidge points out that absolute error metrics (like MAD or MAPE) can lead us to make nonsensical forecasts. Specifically, if at least 50% of the time periods are zero, then the average absolute error is minimized when the forecast in *every period* is zero. (Of course, using zero forecasts to drive replenishment decisions will result in poor customer service.) The implication is that we cannot use absolute error metrics like MAD and MAPE for forecast model selection or to judge the quality of our intermittent demand forecasts.

After examining and rejecting several existing approaches to the numerator problem, Morlidge proposes a new metric, the bias-adjusted mean absolute error (BAMAE). BAMAE combines two separate components—the bias and the dispersion of forecast error—and thereby properly reflects the manner in which forecast error has an impact on inventory levels. He shows how this metric leads to a more appropriate evaluation of forecasting performance for intermittent demand. And it has the added advantage of being applicable to situations of normal (nonintermittent) demands as well.

Introduction

In most businesses, there are products that do not register a sale in every period, a fact that complicates the lives of forecasters. Many practitioners are aware that intermittent demand needs to be forecast in a different way from normal demand, using methods like Croston's. (See Boylan (2005) for a tutorial introduction to the forecasting of intermittent demand.)

Indeed, forecasters often realize it is tricky to apply conventional forecasting metrics like MAPE (mean absolute percentage error) in this area, because of the small or zero denominator in the equation. But few will be aware that

* This article originally appeared in *Foresight: The International Journal of Applied Forecasting* (Spring 2015), and appears here courtesy of the International Institute of Forecasters.

the problem goes deeper than this: Conventional accuracy metrics like MAD (mean absolute deviation) and MAPE can give misleading signals about forecasting performance and steer us to select poor models; this has potentially severe implications for inventory management, where forecasts are used to drive replenishment orders in a supply chain.

The Problems with Intermittent Demand

Intermittent demand has always presented problems for forecasters.

The main difficulty arises because the data that forecasters rely on to make predictions are sparse: Periods with positive values are often separated by a number of periods with zero values. As a result, it is difficult to identify trends and other patterns. And because it is also difficult to estimate which periods in the future will register some activity and which will be empty, most forecasters don't even try; instead, they seek to forecast an average (mean) value over time.

Many businesses deal almost exclusively in products that exhibit intermittent patterns of demand, and even those with more consistent demand patterns will encounter this problem if the choice is made to use narrower time buckets (e.g., weekly or even daily) for forecasting.

The difficulty in forecasting intermittent demand is compounded by the problem of measuring the quality of the results. It has long been recognized that intermittent levels of demand undermine the usefulness of traditional forecast error metrics, like MAPE. Because the denominator in the MAPE is the actual demand, a zero denominator will yield an infinite value for this metric. This is the denominator problem. In his 2006 article in *Foresight*, Jim Hoover describes just how poorly software solutions deal with the problem, some of which exclude the periods of zero actual demand for the MAPE calculation.

Suggestions to address this problem include:

- A **denominator-adjusted MAPE** (DAM), in which each period of zero demand is represented by a 1, as if one unit had been demanded (Hoover, 2006). Still, with a small quantity in the denominator, small absolute errors can translate into extremely large percentage errors, exploding the MAPE, thus giving a distorted picture of forecast accuracy.
- Substituting the **MAD/MEAN** for the MAPE (Kolassa and Schütz, 2010). The two are similar in interpretation: While the MAPE is the mean of the absolute percentage errors, the ratio MAD/MEAN is the mean absolute error as a percentage of mean demand. However, in the MAD/ MEAN, periods of zero actual demand are averaged in the denominator with the positive demands of other periods, avoiding the exploding MAPE.

- Using the **mean absolute scaled error** (MASE) in lieu of the MAPE (Hyndman, 2006). The MASE differs from the MAPE in that it calculates the forecast errors made as a percent of the in-sample (rather than forecast) errors from a naive model. It is similar to the MAD/ MEAN in that both use the MAD in the numerator. The denominator elements of the MAD/MEAN, however, are the actual demands and not the errors from the naïve model.
- The **relative absolute error** metric (Morlidge, 2013) is similar to the MASE, but uses the naïve error as the denominator from the same range of periods as the numerator—the range, as applied, being the out-of-sample (i.e., the forecast) periods.

All of these MAPE alternatives work by changing the denominator so that zeros do not explode the metric.

And there is an even bigger problem than this, one that has largely escaped the notice of practitioners and researchers: the numerator problem.

The Numerator Problem

To understand the numerator problem, consider this simple example of an intermittent demand series.

Take the sequence of demands shown in Table 3.16.

What is the best forecast for this sequence?

On average, it would be best to forecast the mean = 3 for each period, since total demand over the 5 periods is 15 units. And, as shown in Table 3.17, the average absolute error for this forecast is 3.6.

But look what happens if we make what seems to be an unthinkable forecast: zero for each period, an example proposed by Teunter and Duncan (2009). As shown in Table 3.18, the average absolute error is now just 3.0!

Table 3.16 An Example of Intermittent Demand

Period 1	Period 2	Period 3	Period 4	Period 5	Mean
0	5	0	10	0	3.0

Table 3.17 Errors Associated with a "Perfect" Forecast

	Period 1	Period 2	Period 3	Period 4	Period 5	Mean
Actual	0	5	0	10	0	3.0
Unbiased Forecast	3	3	3	3	3	3.0
Absolute Error	3	2	3	7	3	3.6

Table 3.18 Errors Associated with a Zero Forecast

	Period 1	Period 2	Period 3	Period 4	Period 5	Mean
Actual	0	5	0	10	0	3.0
Zero Forecast	0	0	0	0	0	0.0
Absolute Error	0	5	0	10	0	3.0

So it appears that the zero forecast is better than that which correctly forecasts the mean demand of 3.0. This would be true regardless of how large the nonzero demands were in periods 2 and 5. How can this be?

The reason we get these apparently nonsensical results is because of a fundamental misconception: Most of us probably assume that the average absolute forecast error metric (MAD) will guide us to select the best forecast method, the one that gives us a forecast closest to the mean demand pattern. But alas, this is not the case: instead of guiding us to the mean of a distribution, it guides us to the median, which is the most common value in the intermittent demand series. If more than half of all periods exhibit zero demand, then the median will be zero.

So the average absolute error metric optimizes on the median—not the mean—of the probability distribution. The mean and the median are the same if the probability distribution is symmetric—like the normal distribution—but not if the distribution is skewed, as is the case with intermittent demand series: If 50% or more of the values are zero, the "optimum forecast" will be a forecast of zero, irrespective of the size of the nonzero values.

As you would suppose, the consequences of the numerator problem can be significant.

The main implication for forecasting practitioners is that it means we cannot judge how good our intermittent demand forecasts actually are by using metrics like the MAD or MAPE. And it also means that we cannot rely on forecast algorithm selection methods that use the absolute error, when it comes to selecting the best forecast model.

Given this problem, one that is well known to statisticians (Hanley et al., 2001; Syntetos and Boylan, 2005), it will probably surprise practitioners to discover that the majority of academic research into different methods for forecasting intermittent demand—where the consequences are most acute—uses absolute error measures to analyze the results. Indeed, it has recently been suggested that this may be the reason why there has been so little consistency in the findings of research in this area (Teunter and Duncan, 2009).

Solutions to the Numerator Problem

Since no business that has a significant number of products displaying intermittent demand can ignore the problem, what are the solutions?

Table 3.19 Squared Errors for the Forecasts in Tables 3.17 and 3.18

	Period 1	Period 2	Period 3	Period 4	Period 5	MSE
Actual	0	5	0	10	0	3.0
Unbiased Forecast = 3	9	4	9	49	9	16.0
Zero Forecast	0	25	0	100	0	25.0

A good solution should generate a forecast that optimizes on the *mean demand*—not median demand. At a practical level, it is also important that the chosen metric is simple to calculate and easy to understand and explain. It should also work for ordinary (nonintermittent) demand since it is impractical to have different metrics for the two classes of demand, particularly since the dividing line between them is not easy to define.

Use the Mean Squared Error (MSE)

One option is to compare methods using mean squared error instead of the mean absolute error. As shown in Table 3.19, use of the MSE for the intermittent series in Table 3.16 would have correctly selected the best forecast of mean demand (3.0) rather than the median of 0. The MSE for this unbiased forecast is 16.0, while that for the zero forecast is 25.0.

While this metric correctly finds the unbiased forecast at the mean (3) to be better than the zero forecast at the median (0), it comes with a major concern. Because of the squaring of errors, the MSE gives great if not extreme weight to "faraway" errors, with the potential to create a distorted impression of the impact of forecast error on the business (excessive safety stock). This is a particular problem for intermittent demand series, which are by definition more volatile than "normal" data series and carry greater risk of outliers.

Direct Measurement of Inventory Costs and Service Levels

Another option involves measuring the impact of error on inventory or service levels directly (Teunter and Duncan, 2009; Wallstrom and Segerstedt, 2010). Doing so, however, is complicated and problematic since the relationship between error and the business impact will vary from product to product.

For example, the business impact of overforecasting will be very high if the product is perishable (e.g., fresh salads) or the cost of production is high (e.g., personal computers). In these circumstances, the impact of forecast error on stock levels is the primary concern. If the margin on a product is high or it is not perishable, and there is a risk of losing sales to competition, then the business is likely to be very sensitive to underforecasting (e.g., ice cream). Here, the impact of error on service levels is the most significant factor.

As a result, to measure the business impact of forecast error directly in a satisfactory manner, one needs a way of recognizing those product characteristics that matter. It would be desirable to find a single metric that enables us to strike a balance between different types of impact—for example, the tradeoff between the cost of higher stocks with the benefits of having a better service level.

Lastly, while it is easy enough to add up error to arrive at a measure of forecast quality for a group of products, it is less easy to do the same for a metric such as service level, particularly if different products have different target service levels.

Mean-Based Error Metric

Some authorities (Wallstrom and Segerstedt, 2010; Kourentzes, 2004; Prestwich and colleagues, 2014) have proposed calculating forecast errors by comparing a forecast with the series mean over a range of actual values rather than the actual for each period.

This has the merit of simplicity and solves the denominator problem (unless every period demand is zero). However, while it successfully captures how well a forecast reflects the actual values on average—that is, it effectively measures bias—it ignores how far adrift the forecast is on a period-by-period basis. In effect, it assumes that all deviations from the mean demand represent noise.

This view can lead us astray when forecasts are equally biased, as the highly simplified example in Table 3.20 demonstrates.

Both forecasts are similarly biased over the range (both overforecast by an average of 1). Using this mean-based metric, however, the flat forecasts (= 4) look

Table 3.20 Comparing Forecasts to the Mean Can Create a Misleading Impression of Forecast Performance

	Parted 1	Period 2	Period 3	Period 4	Period 5	Mean
Actual	0	5	0	10	0	3.0
Biased (Flat) Forecast	4	4	4	4	4	4.0
Net Error	4	–1	4	–6	4	1.0
Absolute Error vs. Mean	1	1	1	1	1	1.0
Biased (Better) Forecast	0	8	0	12	0	4.0
Net Error	0	3	0	2	0	1.0
Absolute Error vs. Mean	3	5	3	9	3	4.6

significantly better because they are consistently close to the period average. On the other hand, the bottom set of forecasts looks mediocre (the absolute error against the mean being 4.6 compared to 1 for the first forecast) despite better capturing the period-by-period change in the demand pattern. The relative superiority of this bottom set of forecasts can be demonstrated without working through the detailed safety stock calculations: In the case of the flat forecasts, additional safety stock would need to be held to avoid stockouts in periods that were underforecast (periods 2 and 4).

The Bias-Adjusted Error

The approach I propose involves separately measuring the two components of forecast error—bias and dispersion of error—and then appropriately combining them. Minimizing bias is important because it ensures that, over time, we will not have consistently too much or too little stock on hand to meet demand. Dispersion of error has a direct impact on the safety stock needed to meet service-level targets.

In contrast, conventional metrics lump together bias and dispersion because they measure variation of the errors from zero, rather than from the mean of the errors. It can be enlightening to distinguish and separately report these two components:

- First, calculate bias by the mean net error (MNE).
- Second, calculate the magnitude of variation of error around the MNE.
- Finally, add the MNE (expressed in absolute terms) and dispersion measurement.

Table 3.21 illustrates the calculations. The appendix has a fuller explanation of the calculation method.

In these calculations, I've assumed that the bias and variation components of error are of equal importance, so they can simply be added together. Of course, weights can be assigned to represent the relative importance of bias and variation.

By disaggregating the error calculation into a bias component and variation component, we ensure that the resulting metric picks a forecast pattern with a lower or lowest sum of bias and variation. In this example, the second forecast is now correctly identified as a better fit than the constant forecast at the mean of 4.

For completeness, we show the bias-adjusted error for the zero forecasts in the lowest frame in Table 3.21. The ME is –3, reflecting the tendency to underforecast by a total of 15 units and mean value of 3. Variation about this mean averages 3.6 units, and so adding the mean bias and variation yields a bias-adjusted error of 6.6 units, clearly inferior to the other two sets of forecasts.

Table 3.21 The Bias-Adjusted Error Metric Correctly Reflects Both Bias and Variation

	Period 1	Period 2	Period 1	Period 4	Period 5	Mean
Actual	0	5	0	10	0	3.0
Mean Forecast	4	4	4	4	4	4.0
Net Error	4	–1	4	-6	4	1.0
Variation	3	2	3	7	3	3.6
Bias Adjusted Error (absolute net error + variation)						4.6
Better Forecast	0	8	0	12	0	4.0
Net Error	0	3	0	2	0	1.0
Variation	1	2	1	1	I	1.2
Bias Adjusted Error (absolute net error + variation)						2.2

Bias-adjusted error therefore successfully measures the error associated with intermittent demand forecasts in a meaningful manner, thereby solving the numerator problem—the biggest problem that most practitioners didn't even realize they had!

To aggregate error metrics across products, we need a scale-free metric: To this end, the bias-adjusted error can serve as the numerator over any denominator that is not exploded by a sequence of zeros, such as the mean of the actual demand. Doing so yields a metric formally analogous to the MAD/MEAN—except that, while the MAD does not adjust for bias, the bias-adjusted variation metric builds this adjustment in.

While the bias-adjusted variation metric provides a solution to the numerator problem arising from intermittent demands, it has the added advantage of readily generalizing to situations of normal demand.

Conclusion

The bias-adjusted error metric solves the numerator problem experienced when measuring the performance of intermittent demand forecasts, a problem that has dogged academic work for many years. It is also relatively straightforward for forecasting practitioners to calculate and explain to their clients—and, as already mentioned, it properly reflects the manner in which forecast error has an impact on inventory levels. In principle, this means that it should be possible to apply it to the calculation of error where there is no intermittency of demand.

Appendix

How to Calculate Bias-Adjusted Mean Absolute Error

The formula for bias-adjusted mean absolute error (BAMAE) is calculated as follows, where *t* is a period, *n* the number of periods, and *e* the error (forecast less the actual value):

Step 1: calculate bias (mean error):

$$\text{Bias(ME)} = \sum_{t-1}^{n} e_t / n$$

Step 2: calculate variation (mean absolute error excluding bias):

$$\text{Variation (MAUE)} = \sum_{t-1}^{n} |e_t - \text{ME}| / n$$

Step 3: calculate BAMAE by adding bias expressed in absolute terms to the variation:

$$\text{BAMAE} = \text{MAUE} + |\text{ME}|$$

REFERENCES

Boylan, J. (2005). Intermittent and lumpy demand: A forecasting challenge. *Foresight* 1 (June 2005), 36–42.

Hanley, J., L. Joseph, R. Platt, M. Chung, and P. Belisle (2001). Visualizing the median as the minimum-deviation location. *The American Statistician* 55 (2), 150–152.

Hoover, J. (2006). Measuring forecast accuracy: Omissions in today's forecasting engines and demand-planning software. *Foresight* 4 (June 2006), 32–35.

Hyndman R. J. (2006). Another look at forecast accuracy metrics for intermittent demand. *Foresight* 4 (June 2006), 43–46.

Kolassa, S., and Schutz, W. (2010). Advantages of the MAD/MEAN ratio over the MAPE. *Foresight* 6 (Spring 2007), 40–43.

Kourentzes, N. (2014). On intermittent demand model optimization and selection. *International Journal of Production Economics* 156, 180–190.

Morlidge, S. (2013). How good is a "good" forecast? Forecast errors and their avoidability. *Foresight* 30 (Summer 2013), 5–11.

Prestwich, S., R. Rossi, A. Trim, and B. Hench, (2014). Mean-based error measures for intermittent demand forecasting. *International Journal of Production Research* 52 (August), 6782–6791.

Syntetos, A., and J. Boylan (2005). The accuracy of intermittent demand forecasts. *International Journal of Forecasting* 21, 303–314.

Teunter, R., and L. Duncan (2009). Forecasting intermittent demand: A comparative study. *Journal of the Operational Research Society* 60 (3), 321–329.

Wallstrom, P., and A. Segerstedt (2010). Evaluation of forecasting error: Measurements and techniques for intermittent demand. *International Journal of Production Economics* 128, 625–630.

3.14 MANAGING FORECASTS BY EXCEPTION*

Eric Stellwagen

In the ideal world, every statistical forecast would be reviewed for plausibility. But the reality, in a world where companies may need to produce millions of forecasts (e.g., by store / item / week for a retailer), nobody can afford to hire an army of forecast analysts.

Eric Stellwagen identifies the situations where monitoring forecasts is necessary, such as when a forecast changes dramatically from the previous planning cycle or when forecasts diverge widely from actuals. He points out some common misuses of exception reporting, such as when a forecast error is large simply because of the high-volume of the series (so the percentage error is still relatively small) or the error may be large simply because of the high volatility and unforecastability of the series—not because the forecasting model is doing a poor job.

There is an obvious tradeoff between the size of the threshold and the cost or effort to make the manual reviews. Low thresholds will generate more "false positives"—after review, no changes are needed. But high thresholds will generate fewer "true positives" where a change should be made, but it does not appear in the exception report. To handle the tradeoff, Stellwagen suggests categorizing your series by importance, using lower thresholds for high-value items, and higher thresholds for the low-value items.

Human review of a statistically generated forecast is an important step in the forecast process. Ideally, every statistical forecast should be inspected for plausibility. At times, the sheer volume of the forecasts being generated precludes exhaustive individual inspection. In these instances, exception reports are an effective tool to help you sift through the forecasts and focus on the items where human attention is most needed.

What Is an Exception Report?

An exception report compares a value "A" to a value "B" and creates an entry for every item where the difference between A and B exceeds a defined threshold. In the example (Table 3.22), an exception report lists all items where the current forecast for the next month has changed by more than 25% compared to the last forecast generated for the same period. Reviewing exception reports is essentially a form of monitoring. In this example, the report allows us to immediately spot items for which our forecasts have changed significantly and thus human attention may be warranted.

* This article was adapted from *Forecasting 101: Managing Forecasts by Exception* by Eric Stellwagen, originally published in The Forecast Pro Blog, 3/12/2014, and is reprinted with permission.

Table 3.22 Sample Exception Report

Total	Category	Customer	SKU	Lower Bound	Upper Bound	Date	Forecast	Archive Period(1)	Deviation	% Deviation
Total	Cakes	Food-King	CA-20-01	–25%	25%	2009-Jul	6,185	3,375	2,810	83%
Total	Cakes	Stuff-Mart	CO-20-01	–25%	25%	2009-Jul	1,916	4,958	(3,042)	-61%
Total	Cakes	Sids-Club	LF-20-02	–25%	25%	2009-Jul	10,599	7,187	3,412	47%
Total	Muffins	Stuff-Mart	COR-12-11	–25%	25%	2009-Jul	6,545	4,800	1,745	36%
Total	Cakes	Food-King	CH-20-01	–25%	25%	2009-Jul	11,774	18,187	(6,413)	–35%
Total	Cakes	Food-King	CO-20-01	–25%	25%	2009-Jul	11,204	14,974	(3,770)	–25%

Monitoring forecasts to spot potential problems prior to finalizing the numbers is a very common application of exception reporting. Typically, the forecasts would be monitored against previously generated forecasts (as in the above example) or against historic values (e.g., against the last historic point or the same period last year).

Another application of exception reporting is to monitor forecasts that you've generated in the past against what actually happened. This allows you to spot problem areas where changes in your forecasting approach might be considered.

Some forecasters monitor within-sample error statistics such as the MAPE and MAD. This type of exception reporting is often misused by individuals who assume that large within-sample errors indicate poor forecasting models—usually they don't. More commonly, large within-sample errors reflect the scale and volatility of the data rather than the accuracy of the forecasting model. Highly volatile data sets always generate large within-sample errors because they are volatile—not because the forecasting model is doing a poor job. Similarly, high-volume series generate larger MADs (unit errors) than low-volume series because they are higher volume—not because the forecasting model is inferior. Thus, monitoring within-sample statistics can be useful to understand the scale and volatility in the data, but since it is not monitoring the actual forecasts, it is not very useful in terms of finding potentially poor forecasts where action may be needed.

How Do I Select the Thresholds?

An important consideration when running exception reports is setting proper values for the thresholds. Let's consider our previous example, where we set the exception thresholds to flag any forecast that changed by more than 25%.

Clearly, if we had selected a lower threshold (say, 10%), we would have generated more exceptions, and if we had selected a higher threshold (say, 50%), we would have generated fewer exceptions. Thus, the thresholds control the sensitivity of the monitor (i.e., how many exceptions are detected) and by extension, the number of forecasts that will need to be manually reviewed.

When forecasters manually review the forecast for an item on an exception report they either decide that the forecast is not acceptable and change it, or they decide that the forecast is acceptable and leave it as is. Items that fall into the latter category are sometimes referred to as false positives (i.e., they were flagged as exceptions; however, no action was required).

Lowering the threshold values will generate more exceptions and a higher fraction of these exceptions will be false positives. There is a cost to lower thresholds—reviewing additional false positives requires time and resources and does not improve the final forecasts. On the other hand, there is also a benefit to lower thresholds—they can generate additional true positives where taking action improves forecast accuracy and saves money. Thus, the thresholds need to be set to values that balance the cost of reviewing the false positives with the cost of missing true positives. This is usually accomplished by some up-front experimentation to understand the relationship between the size of the thresholds and the number of false positives generated.

It should also be noted that thresholds should rarely be "one-size-fits-all." High-value items warrant lower thresholds (and thus more weeding through false positives) than low-value items, by virtue of the higher cost of missing the true positives. A good practice is to categorize your items based on their importance and vary the thresholds for your different categories accordingly.

3.15 USING PROCESS BEHAVIOR CHARTS TO IMPROVE FORECASTING AND DECISION MAKING*

Martin Joseph and Alec Finney

In addition to the efforts of academic researchers, there is a lot of interesting and important new work being done by industry forecasting practitioners. Among these are Martin Joseph and Alec Finney, who studied the application of statistical process control (SPC) methods during long careers at the pharmaceutical company, AstraZeneca.

In this article, Joseph and Finney extend the ideas of quality thought leader Donald Wheeler into business forecasting and planning. While Wheeler's book, *Understanding Variation: The Key to Managing Chaos,* is not about business forecasting, its scathing critique of management reporting and misinterpretation of data delivers a valuable lesson on the application of SPC methods to business decision making. Joseph and Finney build upon this lesson.

The objective of SPC is to distinguish "normal" variation in the output of a process from a signal that the process is changing—and possibly out of control. The authors show how process behavior charts (PBCs) can be extended from their original applications in quality control to time series of sales histories and forecasts.

A key observation is that most companies manage their businesses by means of tabular reports. Yet tables of data, rather than graphical visualizations, can leave the important information (upon which decisions need to be made) indistinguishable from the unremarkable. PBCs provide a means to make this distinction.

The authors provide practical guidance on how to create appropriate charts (e.g., when there is trend in the data, as often observed when forecasting sales). They also show how to identify signals in the data, so that the forecaster will know when to act and when to avoid overreacting. They present three vignettes of situations that regularly occur in S&OP meetings and discuss how the PBCs provide a crucial context for deciding whether new actions are needed.

* This article was originally published in *Foresight: International Journal of Applied Forecasting* (Fall 2103), and appears here courtesy of the International Institute of Forecasters.

Introduction

We are presented with data every day. We look at the data for relevance, information, and, if we are lucky, insight. Our subsequent behaviors and the decisions we make are closely linked to the way we see that information. By adapting a proven technique from manufacturing process control we can present forecasting and planning data in a more understandable way, show meaningful context, and differentiate between noise and important signals.

Our discussion has four parts. The first, "Data to Information to Insight," shows the way reports have evolved from simple, tabulated data, through time series presentations—which provide some historical context—and finally to PBCs, which set the boundary conditions for detecting real change (signals) among the ever-present noise. From the original applications of PBCs in linear process control, we extend the technique to a trended process—making it suitable for much of our work in forecasting and planning.

The second part, "Control Limits and Signals of Change," shows how to create a PBC and use it to identify significant changes.

The third part, "Application of PBCs to Forecasting," shows how using PBCs can significantly improve forecast quality and target forecasting resources.

The fourth part, "Application of PBCs to Planning," consists of vignettes describing how PCBs provide focus and aid decision making set in an S&OP environment.

Data to Information to Insight

Data to Information

Most companies manage their businesses by means of tabular reports, often comparing one month, quarter, or year with the previous period as well as with their internal targets or budget. Figure 3.31 shows a simplified example; these data are used subsequently for most of our tables and charts.

These comparisons can mislead an organization because:

- Important information, upon which decisions need to be taken, cannot be distinguished from the unremarkable.
- The tabular format encourages binary comparisons: When only two data points are considered, historical or future context is ignored.
- The use of percentage differences can mislead, depending on the base—the reader's eye is naturally drawn to the largest number.
- There frequently is no accompanying narrative.

Period	Sales	Sales vs. SPLY	% Change vs. Previous Yr	Forecast	Budget	Sales vs. Budget	Sales vs. Budget
1	490650						
2	387210						
3	405720						
4	576210						
5	430630						
6	445260						
7	589230						
S	463170						
9	635730						
10	467160						
11	635940						
12	421020						
13	544320	53670	11		595257	50937	91%
14	659760	272550	70		624779	-34981	106%
15	594510	188790	47		654301	59791	91%
16	554190	-22020	-4	547500	683823	129633	81%
17	547500	116820	27	617813	713345	165845	77%
IS	602700	157440	35	688125	742868	140168	81%
19	817500	228270	39	758438	772390	-45110	106%
20	772320	309150	67	828750	801912	29592	96%
21	570270	-65460	-10	899063	831434	261164	69%
22	655830	188670	40	969375	860956	205126	76%
23	913410	277470	44	1039688	890478	-22932	103%
24	730000	122700	29	1110000	920000	190000	79%

Figure 3.31 A Tabular Management Report (SPLY = same period last year)

While tabular formats are commonplace, most organizations are also familiar with time series, a sequence of data points over time, usually plotted as simple line charts with or without trend as shown in Figure 3.32.

The time plot has clear advantages over the tabular style: It provides context while eliminating the temptation to make binary comparisons. However, it lacks boundary conditions that distinguish real change from background noise.

Information to Insight

Control Charts, otherwise known as Statistical Process Control Charts, Shewhart Charts, or Process Behavior Charts, have been in use since the

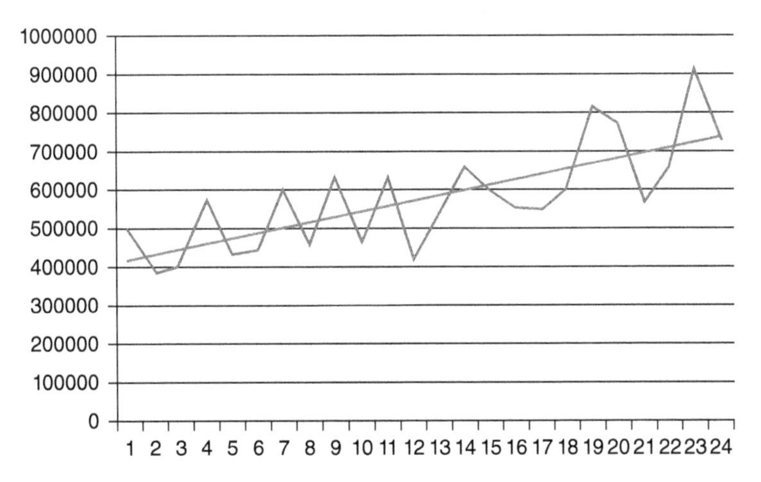

Figure 3.32 Time Series with Trend

1920s, particularly in the manufacturing arena. They have been a mainstay of the Six Sigma system of practices, originally developed by Motorola to eliminate process defects, and are latterly closely associated with lean manufacturing approaches. An example with upper and lower control limits is shown in Figure 3.33.

We like the term *process behavior charts* (PBCs) as most descriptive of the application of statistical process control techniques to sales, sales forecasting, and business planning processes. It is frequently human behavior that introduces bias and the confusion between forecasts and plans and between those plans and targets (Finney and Joseph, 2009).

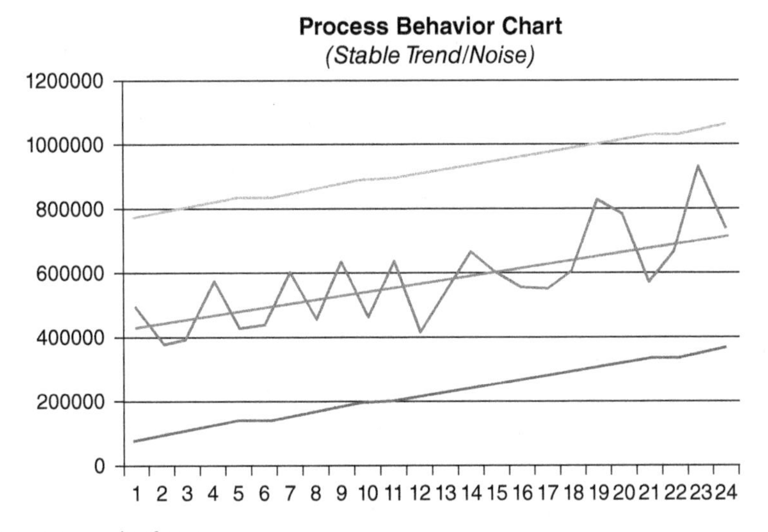

Figure 3.33 Example of a PBC

The published works of W. Edwards Deming, Walter Shewhart, and Donald J. Wheeler are familiar in the production setting but not in the commercial arena. Wheeler's book *Understanding Variation: The Key to Managing Chaos* (Wheeler, 2000) stimulated our thinking on the applications of statistical process control to forecasting and planning. Here are his key ideas, each of which we apply in this article:

- *Data have no meaning apart from their context.* PBCs provide this context both visually and in a mathematically "honest" way, avoiding comparisons between pairs of numbers.
- Before you can improve any system, you must listen to the *voice of the process*.
- There is a crucial distinction between *noise*, which is routine and is to be expected even in a stable process, and *signals*, which are exceptional and therefore to be interpreted as a sign of a change to the process. The skill is in distinguishing signal from noise, determining with confidence the absence or presence of a true signal of change.
- *PBCs work.* They work when nothing else will work. They have been developed empirically and thoroughly proven. They are not on trial.

In manufacturing, PBCs are employed mainly to display the outcomes of a process, such as the yield of a manufacturing process, the number of errors made, or the dimensions of what is produced. In this context, a signal identifies a deviation from a control number and indicates a potential concern. We have found that signals in sales data can indicate real changes in the commercial environment.

Control Limits to Distinguish Signals from Noise

Our focus is now on the application of PBCs to the forecasting process and the monitoring of sales. There are some unexpected benefits, too, which we will describe later.

The major innovation here involves the application of PBCs to trended data. Although doubtless done in practice, we are not aware of any publication covering the systematic application of PBCs to sales, forecasts, and planning in a business setting.

Control Limits

There are several methods described in the literature for calculating process control limits, and we have found that applying the experiential methods described in Wheeler's 2000 book will give organizations a very adequate platform to implement PBCs.

We have slightly modified Wheeler's method in order to allow for the trend in sales data. Wheeler calculates moving ranges from the absolute differences between successive sales data points; for example, for monthly data we'd

Month	Sales	Average Sales	Moving Range	Moving Range Average	UPL	LPL
1	490650	431566			706716	156415
2	387210	443763	103440	103440	718913	168612
3	405720	455960	18510	105247	731110	180809
4	576210	468157	170490	107054	743307	193007
5	430630	480354	145530	108861	755505	205204
6	445260	492551	14580	110668	767702	217401
7	589230	504749	143970	112475	779899	229598
S	463170	516946	126060	114282	792096	241795
9	635730	529143	172560	116089	804293	253993
10	467160	541340	168570	117896	816491	266190
11	635940	553537	168780	119703	828688	278387
12	421020	565735	214920	121510	840885	290584
13	544320	577932	123300	123317	853082	302781
14	659760	590129	115440	125123	865279	314979
15	594510	602326	65250	126930	877477	327176
16	554190	614523	40320	128737	889674	339373
17	547500	626721	6690	130544	901871	351570
IS	602700	638918	55200	132351	914068	363767
19	817500	651115	214800	134158	926265	375965
20	772320	663312	45180	135965	938463	388162
21	570270	675509	202050	137772	950660	400359
22	655830	687707	85560	139579	962857	412556
23	913410	699904	257580	141386	975054	424753
24	730000	712101	183410	145000	987251	436951

Figure 3.34 Data for Calculation of Upper and Lower Process Limits

calculate the differences, February minus January, March minus February, and so on. Figure 3.34 shows this applied to the sales data in Figure 3.31. The sequence of these absolute values is the moving range. We then calculate the moving range average and use this to calculate upper and lower process limits to represent the range of "normal variation" to be expected in the process. We use Wheeler's experiential factor of 2.66 (as opposed to others who use 3 σ) to calculate the upper and lower limits as follows:

$$\text{Upper process limit} = \text{Average sales} + (2.66 \times \text{Average moving range*})$$

$$\text{Lower process limit} = \text{Average sales} - (2.66 \times \text{Average moving range*})$$

* We use the average moving range at the start of the trend to avoid the complication of diverging process limits, which in our view only adds unnecessary complexity.

We now have the data in the correct format in the PBC and have introduced a set of controls that will help us distinguish signal from noise. What we need now is to be able to recognize signals as they appear.

Types of Signals

The literature also contains many examples of different criteria for identifying signals but in our experience the ones recommended by Wheeler (Types 1, 2, and 3) work well in practice. Examples of these are shown in Figure 3.35, Figure 3.36, and Figure 3.37.

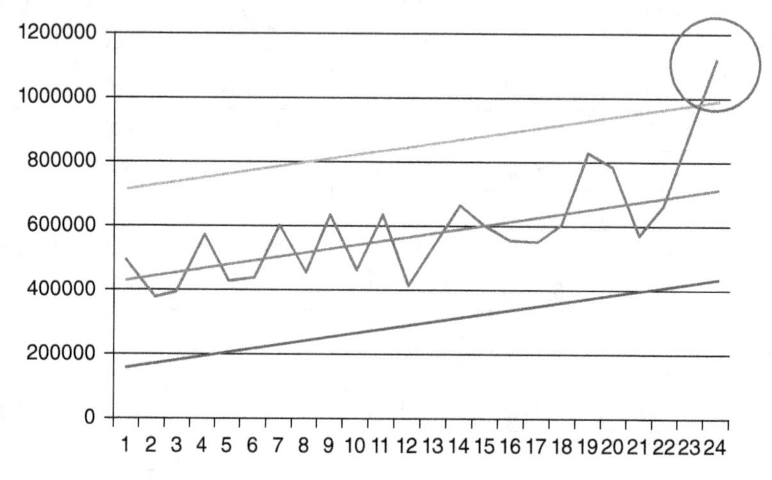

Figure 3.35 Type 1 Signal—Single Data Point Outside the Process Control Limits

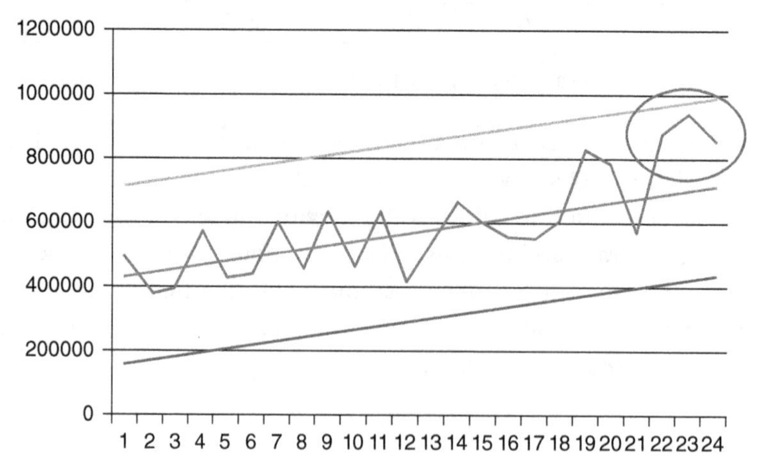

Figure 3.36 Type 2 Signal—Three or Four out of Four Consecutive Points Closer to One of the Limits than to the Trend

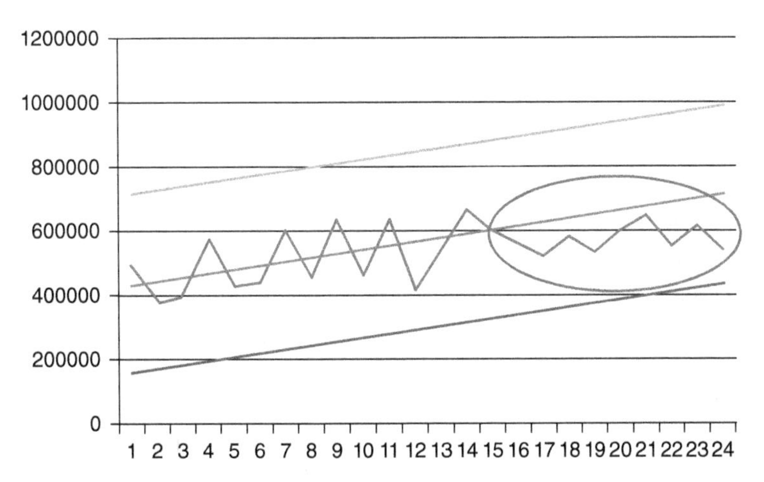

Figure 3.37 Type 3 Signal—Eight or More Successive Points Falling on the Same Side of the Trend

The framework of the PBC is now established, as are the types of signal we need to recognize. Before we can use the PBC as a forecasting tool, however, we need to understand the nature of the back data for all the items we wish to forecast.

The Historical Sales Data

First, it is necessary to specify what sales behavior is being evaluated: factory shipments or retail store sales, for example. We then examine the historical sales data in order to establish the current trend and the point at which it began. This analysis may well reveal historical changes to either or both the trend and the limits. As illustrated in Figure 3.38, identification of these signals enables analysis of the historic sales patterns for any item, product, or brand. A key component of the analysis is an understanding of the stability—the inherent volatility—of the item.

Stability Classification

Identification of these signals enables analysis of the historic sales patterns for any item, product, or brand. A key component of the analysis is

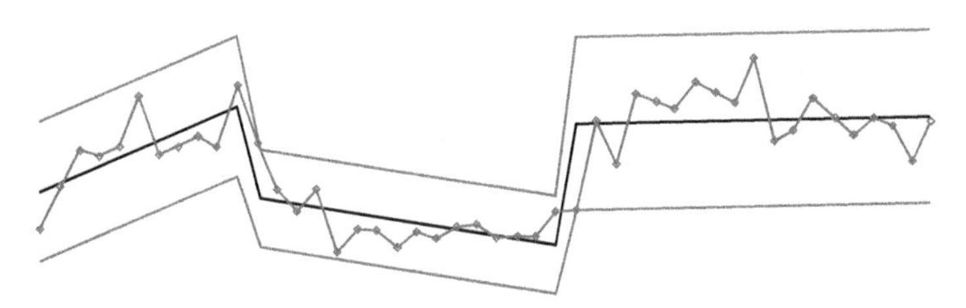

Figure 3.38 Illustrative Historical Sales Analysis

an understanding of the stability—the inherent volatility—of the item. The familiar bullwhip effect can introduce drastically different volatility at different stages in the supply chain (Gilliland, 2010, p. 31).

How do we define *stable?* First, we suggest accumulating 12 data points to provide a reliable identification of signals (although Wheeler suggests that useful average and upper and lower limits may be calculated with as few as 5 to 6 data points).

We classify items based on the stability as determined by the signals detected.

Insights

Group 1: Items determined to be stable (all values within the process limits) based on at least 12 data points

Group 2: Items that might be stable (no signals) but are not yet proven to be so because we have less than 12 data points within control limits

Group 3: Unstable items (those showing signals within the previous 12 data points)

In many industries, stable items represent the majority, typically 80% of the items, and include commercially important items. Unstable situations result from lack of data (including new products), sporadic data, or genuine rapid changes to product noise or trend caused by changes to the commercial environment.

When two or more years of stable data are available, PBCs can also detect seasonal patterns. Forecasts go awry if seasonality is present and not accounted for.

We could also create an archive or "library" of historical trends, rates of change to those trends, and similarly for noise levels ideally coupled with associated information on cause.

Application of PBCs to Forecasting

The three groups of items have to be treated differently for forecast generation.

Group 1: Stable Trend Items

These items are ideal for automated forecasting, which extrapolates the trend in the best-fitting way. Using PBCs, the trend and control limits can be "locked" after 12 points and then extrapolated. Only after a signal should they be "unlocked" and recalculated.

Since most organizations have statistical forecasting systems, generating these forecasts is essentially free. If there is no commercial intelligence about the items (for example, no known changes to competitive profile, pricing, resource levels), then there is no basis for tampering with the forecast. Indeed, such "tampering" may be wasted effort in that its forecast value added is zero or even negative (Gilliland, 2013). Organizations find it irresistible to "adjust" forecasts especially of business critical products in the light of progress against budgets or targets. Many organizations waste time and scarce resources making minor adjustments to forecasts (Fildes and Goodwin, 2007).

With the exception of adjustments for seasonality, there is no forecast value added if the amended forecasts still follow the trend and the individual point forecasts sit within the upper and lower process limits.

Group 2: Stable until Proved Otherwise

The approach to these items is essentially the same as for Group 1 except that we recommend a rolling recalculation of the trend and limits until 12 points have been accumulated. This results in periodic adjustments to the limits but signals are still evident. With the exception of some one-off type 1 signals, any signal occurring will indicate that items move to Group 3.

Group 3: Unstable

These are the "problem children" from a forecasting point of view. While there are statistical methods that attempt to deal with the problem children (e.g., Croston's method for intermittent data), it is our experience that software suppliers make exaggerated claims about the application of statistical methods to unstable data sets. Other techniques such as econometric methods (applied at a brand rather than SKU level) are often needed and are not within scope of this paper. In the absence of alternative valid forecasting methods we usually recommend handling the inherent uncertainty of these situations on a tactical basis, for example, by holding increased stock.

Applying PBCs for Decision Making

Now we are in a position to evaluate forecasts based on the context of sales history and with the aid of a library of what changes are reasonable.

Evaluating a New Marketing Plan

Figure 3.39 shows a situation in which a product manager has a new marketing plan the implementation of which he is convinced will increase market share. Using the very best methods available, let's say he produces a forecast that we label *most likely forecast*, or MLF.

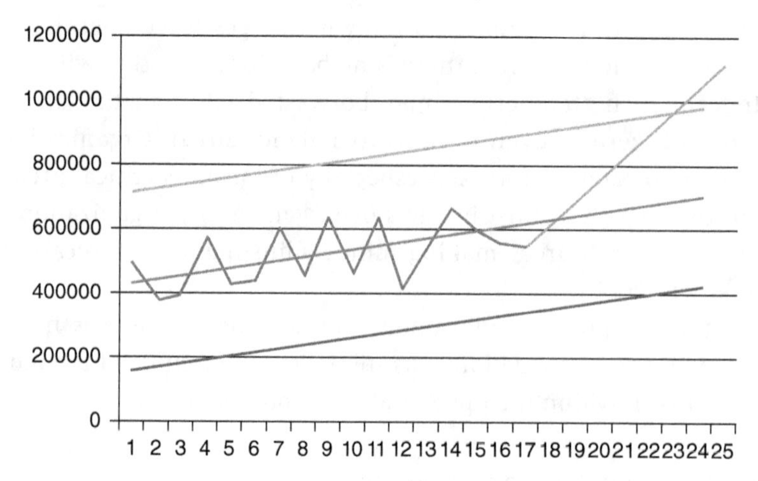

Figure 3.39 New Marketing Plan Forecast

If his projections are correct, we should expect a type 2 signal (three out of four consecutive points closer to one of the limits than they are to the average) by month 23.

Without the control limits to provide context, any departure of actual from trend will tend to elicit a response from the business. There should be no euphoria (or bonuses) if the sales track the existing trend to month 23, as this is within expected noise level!

However, if there is material market intelligence that projects that a signal will appear, use a new forecast and monitor closely—looking for the expected signal.

Adding a Budget or Target

Building on Figure 3.39, things get more interesting if we add a budget or target. We now have a discussion that is informed by historical trend and noise levels, the automatic extrapolative forecast, the forecast assumptions associated with the new marketing plan, and some context of historical trend changes from our reference library.

The PBC (Figure 3.40) can provide the transparency necessary to assess uncertainty in meeting the budget/target and appropriate acceptance of the level of risk. Businesses often use their budgets to set stretch targets and don't consider the inherent downside risk. Then along comes an ambitious marketing person who sees that sales might be below budget and who also is enthusiastic about the positive effect of his new plan (MLF). (We label this as MLF because it's the most likely forecast based on his rather optimistic assumptions!)

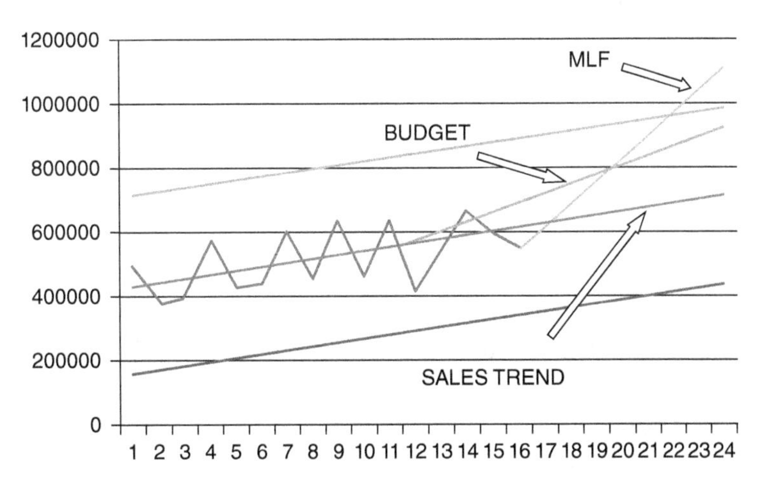

Figure 3.40 New Marketing Plan Forecast with Budget and Trend through Historical Sales

Bringing PBCs into S&OP and Other Planning Activities

PBCs have a valuable contribution to make in the sales and operations planning environment as well as in budget/business review setting. The classification of products into the three groups can help organizations decide tactics. (Group 2 (stable until proved otherwise) can be subsumed within Group 1 (stable) items until such time as instability is detected.)

We use the terms *business critical* and *non–business critical* to represent the importance of the item/brand to the business and consequently when reliable commercial intelligence is likely to be available.

Figure 3.41 offers a simplified tactical classification for S&OP deliberations.

	Business Critical Items	Non-critical Items
Stable Items (Group 1 & 2)	• Automate forecasting • Adjust forecast for marketing intelligence • Review exceptions in S&OP • Include exceptions in business review meeting	• Automate forecasting • Only critical issues reviewed in S&OP and business review meetings
Unstable Items (Group 3)	• Manual forecasting • Adjust forecast for marketing intelligence • Review all in S&OP • Include all in business review meeting	• Manual forecasting • Manage supply risk by stock • Only critical issues reviewed in S&OP and business review meeting

Figure 3.41 Tactical Classification for Decision Making

Here are three vignettes describing how PCBs provide focus and aid decision making in this simplified S&OP environment.

Item One: "We Had a Bad Month Last Month—We Need to Do Better."

By month 17 (Figure 3.42), there were two consecutive months of below-average sales. In previous S&OP meetings, this may have led to a search for the culprits, a beating and a message that implied the need to "continue the beatings until morale improves." Now there is context to understand what is really happening. First, the slightly lower month is within the control boundary conditions; it is not a signal. Second, there is not (at this time) any evidence of a potential trend change.

Figure 3.43 shows what happened to sales in the ensuing months: There was no change to the sales trend and the item remained stable with no signals!

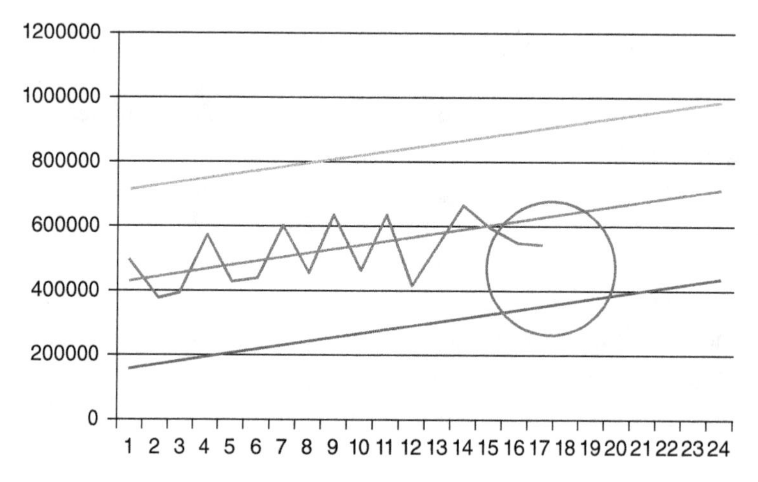

Figure 3.42 A Bad Month

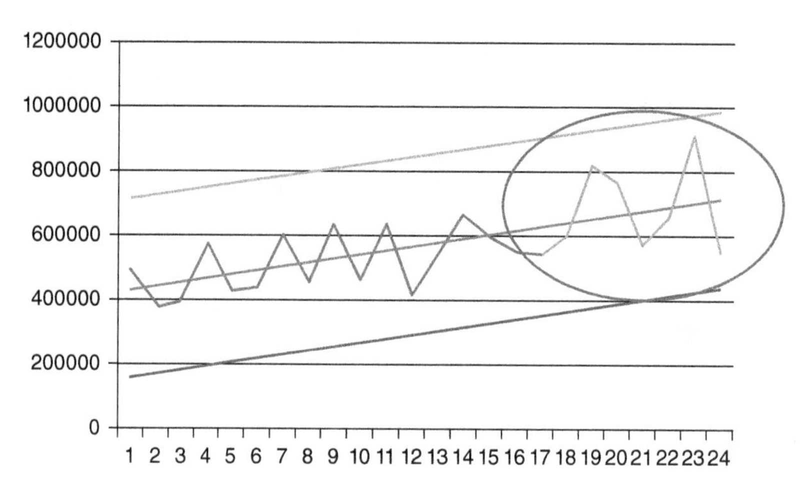

Figure 3.43 A Bad Month 2

Outcome using PBC: Maintain a watching brief and bring to next meeting. If the numbers are above the mean but within the limits, avoid the conclusion that there is a causal link between the beating and the improvement!

Item Two: "This Is a Type One Signal—What Shall We Do?"

In trying to understand why the signal occurred, we should first ask if the team knew of any reason for its appearance. It could have resulted from an unexpected (and maybe unforecasted) event like a one-off order or an out-of-stock. Competitor activity could provide the answer. If it were considered to be a singular event, then actions are identified as appropriate. Alternatively, if the signal was considered to be the start of a new trend, then forecasts should be amended to manage the risk associated with this change.

Outcome using PBC: The signal provides the basis for a discussion—not an unreasoned reaction to a potential change.

Item Three: "It Looks Like the Start of a Type 3 Signal—Do I Have to Wait for Eight Data Points?"

If one point appears above the average trend line, then there is no change to the trend—one point cannot constitute a change. If the next point is also above the average trend, then there is a 1 in 2 probability of this happening by chance. If we take this logic all the way to 8 successive points—the risk that this is not a signal of real change is less than 1 in 250. But intervention can take place at any time. The probability that 5 successive points will lie outside the control limits when there is no real signal is 1 in 32.

Outcome using PBC: PBC has given context, this time about the cost of missing an opportunity to act. But these signals should not always be seen as warnings—they highlight opportunities as well.

The outcome in these examples is better, more informed decision making. As Donald Wheeler says, "Process behavior charts work. They work when nothing else will work. They have been thoroughly proven. They are not on trial."

We have shown that they work equally well when applied to the sales forecasting and business-planning processes.

REFERENCES

Finney, A., and M. Joseph (2009). The forecasting mantra: An holistic approach to forecasting and planning. *Foresight* 12 (Winter).

Gilliland, M. (2010). *The Business Forecasting Deal.* Hoboken, NJ: John Wiley & Sons.

Gilliland, M. (2013). Forecast value added: A reality check on forecasting practices. *Foresight* 29 (Spring).

Goodwin, P., and R. Fildes (2007). Good and bad judgment in forecasting: Lessons from four companies. *Foresight* 8 (Fall).

Wheeler, D. J. (2000). *Understanding Variation: The Key to Managing Chaos*. Knoxville, TN: SPC Press.

3.16 CAN YOUR FORECAST BEAT THE NAÏVE FORECAST?*

Shaun Snapp

In this brief adaptation from his SCM Focus blog, Shaun Snapp adds another voice advocating for the use of naïve forecasts as the basis for performance comparison.

As a long-time practitioner and consultant in the forecasting field, Snapp notes that many companies fail to distinguish the performance of their software's statistical forecast versus manual adjustments. (They make this impossible to do, by storing just the "final" forecast in their system, and not tracking the statistical and override forecasts separately.)

Even worse, they fail to compare their final forecast to the ultimate baseline: doing nothing, and just using a naïve model to forecast. This article provides an appropriate segue into more thorough discussion of FVA analysis in the next chapter.

Background

In a recent article, I described how companies don't know how much they can improve their forecast accuracy (Snapp, 2012). In the article I described that companies find themselves in this position because they don't draw a distinction in their forecast accuracy measurements between manual adjustments and the system generated result.

However, there are other reasons for this problem as well. If we limit the discussion to just the statistical forecast, companies also don't know how much the forecasting models that they are using improve, or degrade, the forecast over the simplest model that they could use. This simple forecast model is called a naive forecast. A naive forecast can be simply the sales from the last period, a moving average, or for seasonal items, what was sold last year in the same period.

What to Expect?

The results of a naive forecast comparison are often surprising. When the naive forecast is tested against experts in the financial industry, the naive forecast often wins. In the article "History of the Forecasters" (Brooks and Grey, 2004),

* This article was adapted from the *SCM Focus* blog (March 15, 2012), http://www.scmfocus.com/demandplanning/2012/03/can-your-forecast-beat-the-naive-forecast/, and appears here courtesy of Shaun Snapp, managing editor at *SCM Focus*.

expert consensus opinion was compared against a naive forecast, and the very expensive Wall Street experts lost out to the naive forecast. A quote from this research is listed below:

> *Our analysis of semi-annual Treasury bond yield forecasts as presented in the Wall Street Journal shows that the consensus forecast is poor. Over the past 43 forecast periods, the consensus estimate of the yield change has been in the wrong direction 65% of the time. A naive forecast of the current yield results in 11% reduction in the standard derivation of forecast error.*

It has been proposed that beating a naive forecast is more difficult than most people generally assume.

> *Also, be aware that naïve forecasts can be surprisingly difficult to beat. When you report your results, they may be rather embarrassing to those participants who are failing to add value. Therefore, present the results tactfully. Your objective is to improve the forecasting process—not to humiliate anyone. You may also want to present initial results privately, to avoid public embarrassment for the non-value adders (Gilliland, 2008).*

People generally don't like admitting that there is no value to what they are doing, so they reflexively push back on the idea that the naive forecast can work better than their models.

If a forecast model cannot beat the naive forecast, or if can do so, but the effort put into creating the naive forecast is not worth the improvement, then the naive forecast should be used. Comparing a method against the naive forecast is how a forecast method is determined if it adds value. For instance, many people are very positive on Croston's as a method for improving lumpy demand forecasting. However, a number of tests have not shown that Croston's is more accurate than more simple methods.

How Long Should You Test the Naïve Forecast Against the Current Live Forecast?

Gilliland makes the additional point that one should give it time when evaluating a forecasting step.

> *The Forecast Value Added (FVA) approach is intended to be objective and scientific, so you must be careful not to draw conclusions that are unwarranted by the data. For example,*

> *measuring FVA over one week or one month does not provide enough data to draw any valid conclusions. Period to period, FVA will go up and down, and over short time frames FVA may be particularly high or low simply due to randomness. When you express the results . . . be sure to indicate the time frame reported, and make sure that time frame has been long enough to provide meaningful results.*

However, while this is necessary for many improvements made to the forecast, within statistical forecasting it's possible to turn the clock back and make a forecasting application think that it is six months prior to the current date. When this is done, a naive forecast can be compared against the forecast that was generated by the company versus the actuals to determine if the naive forecast performed better. However, what often cannot be accomplished is to be able to differentiate between the system generated forecasting and the naive forecast, because the manual changes are saved as the *final forecast*. When this comparison is being made, unless the system generated forecast is known, this test will not tell you if the naive forecast was inferior or superior to the system generated forecast, and that is a problem.

System Implications

In order to be able to perform a naive forecast the application must be able to create a forecast, and store it in a location that does not interact with the final forecast. This naive forecast can be created offline in the production application without affecting the live forecast. This naive forecast is therefore kept separate from the forecast (called the final forecast), which is sent to the supply planning system. It is not necessarily the best approach to perform the naive forecast in the same system as is used for production if that system is not a good prototype environment. It simply depends on the system that is being used.

This is essentially a forecast simulation, a term which is very rarely used with forecasting. (Note that scmfocus.com has an entire sub-blog dedicated to simulation.) However, it is increasingly apparent that in order to gain more knowledge of how to improve forecasting, companies must begin to perform forecasting simulations.

Conclusion

It is important to "baseline" the forecast by performing a naive forecast for all products because this allows the company to understand how much value is being added with the current forecasting process. It also helps provide an impression of how difficult the products are to forecast, and when a better forecasting method is applied, it can be understood how much value that method is adding to the forecast.

REFERENCES

Brooks, R., and J. B. Gray (2004). History of the forecasters. *Journal of Portfolio Management* 31(1), 113–117.

Gilliland, M. (2008). Forecast value added analysis: Step-by-step, SAS Institute whitepaper.

Snapp, S. (2012). How much can your forecast accuracy be improved? http://www.scmfocus.com/demandplanning/2012/02/how-much-can-your-forecasting-accuracy-be-improved/.

CHAPTER 4

Process and Politics of Business Forecasting

We all believe that business forecasting should be an objective, dispassionate, and scientific undertaking, and yet it is conducted within the often-politicized confines of an organization. Forecasters and decision makers can have biases and agendas that undermine forecast accuracy. With all the potential "game playing" in the process, you never know whom you can trust.

We begin this chapter with a look at forecast value added (FVA) analysis, an increasingly popular method for uncovering activities that fail to improve the forecasts. The unfortunate reality is that many common forecasting practices—even so-called *best practices*—may actually result in forecasts that are worse than doing nothing more than simply using the naïve no-change model. Steve Morlidge finds, for example, that half of the forecasts in his study failed to beat the naïve model forecasts.

Other articles in this chapter look at specific issues in forecast-process design: where to position the forecasting function, whether to hold face-to-face meetings, whether to include the sales force in the process, and how to set performance objectives. Various "worst practices" are identified, along with ways to provide a more *trustworthy* forecast that management will believe in and act on. We end this chapter with a look at the widely adopted process of sales and operations planning (S&OP)—how it can be applied in the retail industry, and its future direction.

4.1 FVA: A REALITY CHECK ON FORECASTING PRACTICES*

Michael Gilliland

Forecast value added (FVA) is the change in a forecasting performance metric that can be attributed to a particular step or participant in the forecasting process. Michael Gilliland has long advocated the use of FVA to determine whether the various activities in an organization's forecasting process are "adding value" by improving accuracy—or are worsening it. The concept turns attention away from the end result (the accuracy of the final forecast) to focus on the overall efficiency and effectiveness of the forecasting process.

FVA is computed by comparing the performance of sequential steps in the forecasting process. (A typical process might be Statistical Forecast → Analyst Adjustment → Consensus Forecast → Approved Forecast.) FVA assesses the effectiveness of adjustments to statistical forecasts, and ultimately to a naïve (no-change) forecast. Companies use FVA analysis to identify process waste—those steps that are failing to improve the forecast. Resources performing those non-value adding activities can be redirected to more productive activities, or eliminated.

---

* This article originally appeared in *Foresight: The International Journal of Applied Forecasting* (Spring 2013), and appears here courtesy of the International Institute of Forecasters.

It is recognized (see the Fildes and Goodwin article later on) that management "fiddling" with forecasts often makes them worse. FVA has caught on in many companies as an aid in identifying unnecessary or even harmful actions, resulting in a streamlined forecasting process—reducing the resources committed to forecasting—while simultaneously improving forecast accuracy.

Introduction

We all want our business practices to be effective, efficient, and certainly as waste-free as possible. No conscientious executive willingly squanders company resources on activities that have no benefit to customers or to the business's own bottom line. So when it comes to the practice of business forecasting, how do we know whether we are performing up to these standards?

A traditional forecasting performance metric, such as the MAPE, tells us the magnitude of our forecast error but little else. Knowing the MAPE of our forecasts does not tell us how efficient we were at achieving this level of error or how low an error would be reasonable to achieve. Nor does it tell us how our methods and processes perform compared to simpler alternatives. This is where forecast value added (FVA) steps in.

FVA analysis turns attention away from the end result (forecast accuracy) to focus on the overall effectiveness of the forecasting process. As the FDA will test a new drug for its safety and efficacy, FVA evaluates each step of the forecasting process to determine its net contribution. If the process step (such as a sophisticated statistical model or an analyst override) makes the forecast better, then it is "adding value" and FVA is positive. But if the effect of the step is inconclusive (we can't discern whether it is improving the forecast) or if it is making the forecast worse, then we can rightly question whether this step should even exist.

This article presents the basic data requirements and calculations for FVA analysis, along with sample report formats. It also examines some implementations by industry practitioners.

Calculating Forecast Value Added

Suppose we have this simple forecasting process:

Sales History → Forecasting Model → Statistical Forecast → Management Override → Final Forecast

In this common situation, historical sales information is read into forecasting software, where the history is modeled and the statistical forecast is generated. At that point, the forecast is reviewed and potentially adjusted, resulting in the "final forecast" that will be published and sent to downstream planning systems.

FVA is a measure of past performance. For each item being forecast, and for each time period in our history, we would need to gather:

- The Statistical Forecast
- The Final Forecast
- The Actual Value (e.g., actual sales)

If we have 100 items and have been forecasting them for the past 52 weeks, we would have 5,200 records in our data file, with the variables:

< ITEM WEEK STAT_FCST FINAL_FCST ACTUAL >

FVA is defined as:

> *The change in a forecasting performance metric that can be attributed to a particular step or participant in the forecasting process.*

In this simple example there are two process steps: the software's generation of the statistical forecast and the management's override resulting in the final forecast. A more elaborate process may have additional steps, such as a consensus or collaboration, and an executive approval.

In FVA analysis, there is also an implied initial step: generation of a naïve forecast. It is normal to use the random walk (no-change model) to generate the naïve forecast. This is easy to reconstruct from the historical data and can be added to our data file as a new variable:

< ITEM WEEK NAIVE_FCST STAT_FCST FINAL_FCST ACTUAL >

We compute FVA by comparing the performance of sequential steps in the forecasting process. Here, we would compute performance of the naïve, statistical, and final forecasts, and determine whether there was "value added" by these successive steps.

FVA doesn't care which traditional metric you are using to evaluate performance (although some flavor of MAPE is most common in industry). Results can be reported in the "stairstep" format shown in Figure 4.1. Rows represent sequential process steps, the second column shows the MAPE (or whatever performance metric is being used) for each step, and the right columns show pairwise comparisons between steps.

Note that a more elaborate process would have additional rows for the additional process steps and additional columns for the pairwise comparisons.

The stairstep report can be generated for each item being forecast, for item groupings, and for all items combined. Groupings are of interest when they have different demand patterns, use different forecasting processes, or are overseen

PROCESS STEP	MAPE	FVA vs NAÏVE_FCST	FVA vs STATFCST
NAÏVE FORECAST	50%		
STATISTICAL FORECAST	40%	10%	
FINAL FORECAST	42%	8%	-2%

Figure 4.1 Forecast Value Added "Stairstep" Report

by different forecast analysts. For example, a retailer might separate products with *everyday low pricing* from those with *high–low* (promotional) pricing to compare demand volatility, forecast accuracy, and FVA between the two groups.

Of course, over the thousands of items that may be forecast by a large organization, some of the observed FVA differences may be too small to be meaningful, or the observed difference may just be due to chance. One must be cautious in interpreting such a report and not jump to unwarranted conclusions or make rash process changes. Additional analysis can confirm that the observed difference is indeed "real" and not likely to be random.

How Organizations Are Using FVA

Our objective is to generate forecasts that are as accurate and unbiased as we can reasonably expect (given the nature of what we are trying to forecast), and also to do this as efficiently as possible. We can't completely control the level of accuracy achieved (since accuracy is ultimately limited by the forecastability of the behavior being forecast), but we can control the processes used and the resources we invest into forecasting.

S&OP thought leader Tom Wallace has called FVA "the lean-manufacturing approach applied to sales forecasting" (Wallace, 2011), and some organizations are using FVA in just this way: to identify process "waste." Activities that are failing to improve the forecast can be considered wasteful and resources committed to performing them can be redirected to more productive activities.

Practitioners have extended the FVA concept with new ways of analysis and reporting or have otherwise used FVA results to modify the way they do forecasting.

Newell Rubbermaid

Schubert and Rickard (2011) reported an analysis that found a positive 5% FVA in going from the naïve to the statistical forecast but a negative 2% FVA for judgmental overrides of the statistical forecasts. Realizing a limitation of the basic stairstep report—that important information may be buried in the "average FVA" reported for a group of items—they utilized histograms as in Figure 4.2 to show the distribution of FVA values across a product group.

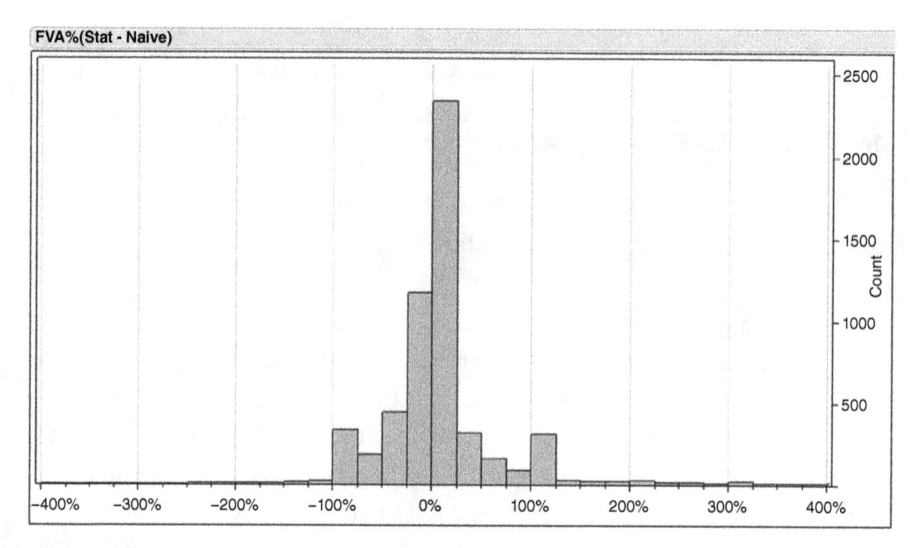

Figure 4.2 Statistical Forecast Value Added

Even though the statistical forecast was (on average) five percentage points more accurate than the naïve, for many items the statistical forecast did considerably worse, and these merited further attention. Likewise, the (not uncommon) finding that, on average, management overrides made the forecast worse provided opportunity for additional investigation and process tuning.

Tempur-Pedic

Eric Wilson (2008) oversaw a collaborative forecasting process wherein a baseline statistical forecast was manually updated with market intelligence, resulting in the final forecast. He used FVA analysis for visibility into the process and to identify areas for improvement.

With FVA, Wilson realized the best way to leverage the knowledge of salespeople was to appeal to their competitive nature. Instead of forcing them to adjust all statistical forecasts, he instead challenged them to "beat the nerd in the corner" by adding value to the nerd's computer-generated forecasts. This reduced frivolous forecast adjustments that were being made simply because of the requirement to make changes.

Amway

Mark Hahn (2011) used FVA in conjunction with analysis of forecastability to better understand and communicate what "good" performance is and what is realistic to achieve. He utilized monthly product-level reporting to determine the value added by analyst inputs and also identified instances where the statistical forecast was underperforming the naïve model.

Cisco

Fisher and Sanver (2011) reported on Cisco's use of FVA for accountability of the forecasting process and the people executing it. FVA was considered a simple and important metric for judging performance and appeared on the dashboards of Cisco's senior management. It showed the team where to put resources and where a naïve forecast suffices.

Which Naïve Model to Use?

In forecasting literature, the classic naïve model is the random walk or no-change model—our forecast for next period (and all future periods) is what we observed last period. In FVA analysis, the random walk can be the point of comparison for our forecasting process, the placebo against which we measure our process effectiveness.

The spirit of a naïve model is that it be something easily computed, with the minimal amount of effort and data manipulation, thus generating a forecast at virtually no cost, without requiring expensive computers or software or staffing. If our system and process cannot forecast any better than the naïve model on average, then why bother? Why not just stop doing what we are doing and use the naïve forecast?

The random walk may not be a suitable "default" model to use in situations where the existing forecasting process is not adding value. Suppose that forecasts are changing radically with each new period of actual values, producing instability in an organization's planning processes. For example, while a year ends with a strong week of 1,000 units sold, the naïve model would forecast 1,000 units per week through the next year, and the supply chain would have to gear up. However, if we only sell 100 units in week one of the new year, we would change our forecast to 100 units per week for the rest of the year, and gear the supply chain back down. This up and down could occur with each period of new actuals.

Supply-chain planners could not operate in an environment of such volatile forecasts and would end up tempering their actions around some "average" value they expect for the year. So rather than defaulting to a random walk when the forecasting process is not adding value, it may be better to default to another simple model which mitigates such up-and-down volatility (such as a moving average, seasonal random walk, or simple exponential smoothing). Just make sure this default model is performing better than the existing process and, hopefully, better than the random walk!

As a practical consideration, the default model should be included in the FVA stairstep report, so its performance can be monitored. In the unlikely event that it performs worse than a random walk, as long as it doesn't perform substantially worse, it has the advantage of providing stability to the downstream planning processes.

A Reality Check on Forecasting Practices

"Forecasting is a huge waste of management time."

We've heard this before—especially from management—but it doesn't mean that forecasting is pointless and irrelevant. It doesn't mean that forecasting isn't useful or necessary to run our organizations. And it doesn't mean that executives should neither care about their forecasting issues nor seek ways to improve them. It simply means that the amount of time, money, and human effort spent on forecasting is not commensurate with the amount of benefit achieved (the improvement in accuracy).

We spend far too much in organizational resources creating our forecasts, while almost invariably failing to achieve the level of accuracy desired. Instead of employing costly and heroic efforts to extract every last bit of accuracy possible, FVA analysis seeks to achieve a level of accuracy that is as good as we can reasonably expect, and to do so as efficiently as possible. FVA allows an organization to reduce the resources spent on forecasting and potentially achieve better forecasts—by eliminating process activities that are just making the forecast worse.

Remember: FVA analysis may not make you the best forecaster you can be—but it will help you to avoid becoming the worst forecaster you might be!

REFERENCE

Fisher, A., and M. Sanver (2011). Large-scale statistical forecasting for Cisco's high-tech demand patterns. INFORMS Conference on Business Analytics and Operations Research (April).

Hahn, M. (2011). Lean forecasting: How to get more bang for your forecasting buck. Best of the Best S&OP Conference (June).

Schubert, S., and R. Rickard (2011). Using forecast value added analysis for data-driven forecasting improvement. IBF Best Practices Conference (May).

Wallace, T. (2011). Forecasting: It's getting better. *BONEZONE* (June).

Wilson, J. E. (2008). How to speak sales. IBF Supply Chain Forecasting Conference (February).

4.2 WHERE SHOULD THE FORECASTING FUNCTION RESIDE?*

Larry Lapide

Among topics most frequently discussed by forecasting practitioners is where to place the forecasting function within an organization. Common locations include sales, marketing, finance, or strategic planning, or an area of operations / production / logistics / supply chain.

* This article originally appeared in *Journal of Business Forecasting* (Winter 2002–2003), and appears here courtesy of Dr. Chaman Jain, editor-in-chief.

Forecasting can also be a separate independent department—ostensibly to avoid the influence of these other groups.

Larry Lapide, a former industry analyst and long-time columnist for the *Journal of Business Forecasting*, suggests putting forecasting "in a department that will diligently execute an effective forecasting process in a way it needs to be conducted to ensure the best possible output." So instead of one right location for every company, Lapide lists criteria for evaluating a department's suitability, and identifies the pros and cons of each department.

Avoiding bias, politics, and personal agendas is a primary consideration, so a department must be *objective* to develop a good operational forecast. The forecasting group must have a solid *understanding of the business*, to know what drives demand. Forecasters should have sufficient *quantitative skills* to handle the statistical element of forecasting, and utilize the software. And they must have the *organizational skills* to run an effective forecasting process. The department that has the resources with these abilities may vary by industry.

While the correct location ultimately depends on the particulars within a company, Lapide's pro and con arguments for each department provide guidance for making the right choice.

The Fall 2002 *Journal of Business Forecasting* publication was a special issue on benchmarking. The publication covered a variety of benchmark data collected by the Institute of Business Forecasting (IBF) in a survey it conducted. One of the most interesting data sets I noticed dealt with results on where respondents stated their forecasting function resides. The results showed that across all industries polled the percent of companies where the forecasting function resides by department was:

Operations/Production	20%
Marketing	20%
Finance	14%
Sales	12%
Forecasting	10%
Logistics	9%
Strategic Planning	6%
Other	9%

While the data are certainly interesting, it is not insightful in helping a company determine where it should put its forecasting function. Essentially, it says: "Take your pick"! This type of inconclusive benchmarking result is the reason why I often talk about what is important in deciding in which department a forecasting group should reside.

On the face of it, my usual advice does not at first appear to be much help, because I take the opinion that it depends on a variety of factors, and that there is no one right answer for a company, generally speaking. The right answer to me is to put the forecasting function inside a department that will diligently execute an effective forecasting process in a way it needs to be conducted to ensure the best output possible—namely, the most accurate consensus forecast that can be developed and one that is used as the basis for all operational planning activities.

Executing an Effective Forecasting Process

Executing an effective operational forecasting process means setting up and adhering to a set of activities that enables the following to occur:

- A finalized demand forecast that incorporates a balanced mix of quantitative and qualitative data. The process should start with the development of a baseline forecast that is based on objective information, often developed using statistical forecasting methods to blend historical information with known factors about the future. The baseline forecast should then be adjusted to incorporate market intelligence.
- All stakeholder departments (such as Marketing, Sales, Operations, and Finance) provide the market intelligence that is used to adjust the baseline forecast to account for factors not incorporated into it.
- A consensus forecast is developed to which all stakeholder departments agree, as well as are accountable for in their respective ways. This further means that the consensus demand forecast is used as the basis for every department's operational planning—enabling a single number planning best practice.

As long as a department can successfully execute a forecasting process and enables the above to occur, it qualifies as a good place to put the forecasting function. Of course, if the forecasting function can accomplish this without being in any department, that is another option.

Evaluation Criteria

Not every department has all the qualifications for successfully conducting an effective demand planning process. There are evaluation criteria that can be used to assess whether a particular department fits the bill, as follows:

- **Objectivity**: A department needs to be objective to develop a good operational forecast. This manifests itself in being able to produce a set of forecasts that are based on facts and sound judgment, even if the department is heavily impacted by the forecasts generated. In addition, objectivity also derives from a department being a stakeholder that is impacted by customer demand. It also means a department needs to be open to valuable input from all stakeholder departments.

- **Business Understanding**: It is extremely important for a forecasting group to understand the nature of a business, especially in terms of what drives the dynamic nature of customer demand. Various drivers of demand need to be incorporated to develop a good forecast, so possession of this type of knowledge is essential to gathering inputs and synthesizing them to produce a good forecast.
- **Quantitative Skills**: The reality of forecasting is that it is quantitative in nature. A demand forecast may have to be produced for tens of thousands or millions of items, so the sheer scale of it means that computer skills are necessary. This requires a department to be somewhat "left-brained" and have an appreciation for quantitative and computer skills, in order to best leverage the capabilities of quantitative analysts.
- **Organization Skills**: One of the most critical criteria is the organization skills of the department. To run an effective forecasting process requires discipline and adherence to a process. This includes preparing for, leading, and doing follow-up for ongoing meetings, such as sales and operations planning (S&OP) meetings. It also includes publishing the demand forecast on time and ensuring that everyone has easy access to it for their own planning purposes.

Selecting a department in which to put the forecast function requires using the above criteria to assess which one is the best. Not all departments in a company meet the criteria, and which department is best often varies by industry.

The Pros and Cons of Departments

In industries, such as in Consumer Products and Pharmaceuticals, that are distribution-intensive in nature, there is a tendency to place the forecasting function in the Marketing department, since it may best understand future customer demand. However, in some companies there are a variety of reasons that may run counter to this placement of the forecasting function, including that their Marketing departments may not be objective enough or have the right quantitative skills to do the job.

Generally, here are some of the pro and con arguments for each department, as well as for creating a standalone forecasting department:

- **Standalone Forecasting Department**: The biggest reason for having a standalone forecasting department is that it can have a dispassionate, objective view of the company, as well as have the time and inclination to organizationally run a very effective forecasting process. In addition, it can be easily staffed with the appropriate quantitative skills needed. However, there is a significant downside to establishing a standalone group. As a non-stakeholder group it is not responsible for any operational processes that impact demand; therefore, will not have to take on any accountability for achieving a demand forecast. If not carefully managed, while this type of standalone group might get very efficient in developing and publishing forecasts, it may never develop a true understanding of the business and customers. This can lead to a tendency to develop forecasts in a vacuum without sufficient input from stakeholder organizations.

- **Marketing Department**: The biggest reason for putting the forecasting function in the Marketing department is that it has a very good understanding of future customer demands. It may or may not be objective enough depending on whether its performance goals are based on actual customer demand. There may be reluctance by the Marketing department to change to an operational forecast that is not aligned with its performance goals. In addition, this typically right-brained organization may lack the quantitative skills to do statistical forecasting and the computer skills to run the requisite software.
- **Production, Operations, or Logistics Department**: The biggest negative in putting the forecasting function into the Operations or Production department is that these organizations often do not get enough contact with customers to truly understand future demand. The Logistics department does have more contact with customers, but not with regard to their future needs. On the positive side, all these three left-brained organizations possess the quantitative skills to do statistical forecasting and the computer skills needed to run the requisite software. They are also disciplined enough to execute an effective forecasting process and are objective, because their operations and costs are highly dependent on future demand.
- **Sales Department**: Since the Sales department has the most contact with customers, this is a big plus in any argument assessing whether to put the forecasting function into it; as they should understand future customer needs the best. However, on other evaluation criteria the Sales department often falls short. Regarding objectivity, since sales reps are commissioned based on what they sell, they usually refuse to change operational forecasts to differ from their sales goals—so they often can't be objective. A Sales department may also lack the required quantitative skills needed and is often not interested in running a routine, structured forecasting process.
- **Finance Department**: Similar to the standalone Forecasting department, the best reason for putting the forecasting function into Finance is that this left-brained organization has the required quantitative skills and organizational discipline. The biggest negatives are that Finance has no direct contact with customers and customer demand does not directly impact its operations. Therefore, Finance usually understands customers the least among all other departments and is not held accountable for achieving the demand forecast. A concern relative to objectivity is that

Finance has an innate reluctance to change the operational forecasts that differ from the revenue forecasts incorporated into the financial budgets.

- **Strategic Planning Department**: Since the Strategic Planning department deals with long-term planning issues, it does not make sense in most companies to have the forecasting function to reside in it. Strategic Planning is more often about planning years in advance, in terms of developing strategic capital and resource plans, and is not really focused on forecasting to support tactical and operational activities. If the forecasting function is put into a Strategic Planning department, there will be a tendency for strategic revenue plans to become the operational forecasts, rather than the forecasts representing a true objective view of what will happen in the short and intermediate term. On the plus side, a Strategic Planning group usually has the quantitative and organizational skills needed to drive an effective forecasting process. However on the negative side, it usually does not understand shorter-term customer needs.

Conclusion

Table 4.1 summarizes the above pros and cons of putting the operational demand forecasting function into each department. As can be noted from the arguments made, there is no one department that is a clear-cut choice. That is, where the forecasting function should reside is highly dependent on a company and the industry it is in.

Table 4.1 Summary of Pros and Cons of Putting the Forecasting Function in Each Type of Department

Department	Objectivity	Business Understanding	Quantitative Skills	Organizational Skills
Standalone Forecasting	Objective, but not impacted by demand	No direct contact with customers	High level	High level of discipline
Marketing	Objective, but some bias from performance goals	Very good understanding of future customer needs	Low level	Moderate level of discipline
Production, Operations, and Logistics	Objective and impacted by demand	Little direct contact with customers	High level	High level of discipline
Sales	Bias from sales goals and commissions	Highest level of contact with customers	Low level	Less interest in running structured, routine processes
Finance	Objective, but some bias from budgeting and not impacted by demand	No direct contact with customers	High level	High level of discipline
Strategic Planning	Objective, but not impacted by demand and view is too long-term	No direct contact with customers	High level	High level of discipline

So what is the bottom line on where the forecasting function should reside in your company? As the benchmarking data shows, it depends. A good way to determine where the forecasting function should reside is to evaluate departmental competencies using the pros and cons arguments I've provided. In the final analysis, however, wherever your company decides to put it, make sure that the department has most of the characteristics needed to run an effective forecasting process—and more importantly, really wants to do it right!

4.3 SETTING FORECASTING PERFORMANCE OBJECTIVES*

Michael Gilliland

In two articles in Chapter 1, industry benchmarks for forecasting performance were shown to be untrustworthy. Yet industry benchmarks continue to be used to set forecasting performance objectives at many organizations.

In this article, Michael Gilliland provides five steps for setting appropriate objectives. He first rejects the common methods of benchmarks, improvement on past performance, and arbitrarily set goals, arguing that objectives must be based on the *forecastability* of what is being forecast.

A challenge is that we do not know the forecastability of future behavior. Forecastability may change over time, as for example, when a retailer switches from everyday low pricing to high–low pricing (which generates more volatile demand). Therefore, it is wrong to set specific numerical objectives for forecasting performance.

The solution, Gilliland suggests, is for the objective to be simply: Do no worse than the naïve "no-change" model. Beating the naïve model is not as easy as it sounds, but doing so indicates the forecasting process is at least "adding value" by making the forecast better. Reporting forecast accuracy in isolation, without comparison to the naïve model, may result in rewarding performance that is just making the forecast worse.

Setting forecasting performance objectives is one way for management to shine . . . or to demonstrate an abysmal lack of understanding of the forecasting problem. Inappropriate performance objectives can provide undue rewards (if they are too easy to achieve), or can serve to demoralize employees and encourage them to cheat (when they are too difficult or impossible). For example:

> Suppose you have the peculiar job of forecasting Heads or Tails in the daily toss of a fair coin. While you sometimes get on a hot streak and forecast

* This article was adapted from *The Business Forecast Deal* blog (September 4, 2014): http://blogs.sas.com/content/forecasting/2014/09/04/5-steps-to-setting-forecasting-performance-objectives-part-1/ and http://blogs.sas.com/content/forecasting/2014/09/04/5-steps-to-setting-forecasting-performance-objectives-part-2/.

correctly for a few days in a row, you also hit cold streaks, where you are wrong on several consecutive days. But overall, over the course of a long career, you forecast correctly just about 50% of the time.

If your manager had been satisfied with 40% forecast accuracy, then you would have enjoyed many years of excellent bonuses for doing nothing. Because of the nature of the process—the tossing of a fair coin—it took no skill to achieve 50% accuracy. (By one definition, if doing something requires "skill," then you can purposely do poorly at it. Since you could not purposely call the tossing of a fair coin only 40% of the time, performance is not due to skill but to luck. See Mauboussin (2012) for more thorough discussion of skill vs. luck.)

If you get a new manager who sets your goal at 60% accuracy, then you either need to find a new job or figure out how to cheat. Because again, by the nature of the process of tossing a fair coin, your long term forecasting performance can be nothing other than 50%. Achieving 60% accuracy is impossible.

So how do you set objectives that are appropriate for forecasting performance?

Five Steps for Setting Forecasting Performance Objectives

1. Ignore industry benchmarks, past performance, arbitrary objectives, and what management "needs" your accuracy to be.

Published benchmarks of industry forecasting performance are not relevant. This is addressed in Gilliland (2005) and more extensively by Kolassa (2008).

Previous forecasting performance may be interesting to know, but not relevant to setting next year's objectives. We have no guarantee that next year's data will be equally forecastable. For example, what if a retailer switches a product from everyday low pricing (which generated stable demand) to high–low pricing (where alternating on and off promotion will generate highly volatile demand). You cannot expect to forecast the volatile demand as accurately as the stable demand.

And of course, arbitrary objectives (like "All MAPEs < 20%") or what management "feels it needs" to run a profitable business, are inappropriate.

2. Consider forecastability . . . but realize you don't know what it will be next year.

Forecast accuracy objectives should be set based on the "forecastability" of what you are trying to forecast. If something has smooth and stable behavior, then we ought to be able to forecast it quite accurately. If it has wild, volatile, erratic behavior, then we can't have such lofty accuracy expectations.

While it is easy to look back on history and see which patterns were more or less forecastable, we don't have that knowledge of the future. We don't know, in advance, whether product X or product Y will prove to be more forecastable, so we can't set specific accuracy targets for them.

3. Do no worse than the naïve model.

Every forecaster should be required to take the oath, "First, do no harm." Doing harm is doing something that makes the results worse than doing nothing. And in forecasting, doing nothing is utilizing the naïve model (i.e., random walk, aka no-change model) where your forecast of the future is your most recent "actual" value. (So if you sold 50 last week, your forecast for future weeks is 50. If you actually sell 60 this week, your forecast for future weeks becomes 60, etc.)

You don't need fancy systems or people or processes to generate a naïve forecast—it is essentially free. So the most basic (albeit pathetic) minimum performance requirement for any forecaster is to do no worse than the naïve forecast.

4. Irritate management by not committing to specific numerical forecast accuracy objectives.

It is generally agreed that a forecasting process should do no worse than the naïve model. Yet in real life, perhaps half of business forecasts fail to achieve this embarrassingly low threshold (Morlidge, 2014). Since we do not yet know how well the naïve model will forecast next year, we cannot set a specific numerical accuracy objective. So next year's objective can only be "Do no worse than the naïve model."

If you are a forecaster, it can be reckless and career threatening to commit to a more specific objective.

5. Track performance over time.

Once we are into the new year and the "actuals" start rolling in each period, we can compare our forecasting performance to the performance of the naïve model. Of course, you cannot jump to any conclusions with just a few periods of data. But over time you may be able to discern whether you, or the naïve model, is performing better.

Always start your analysis with the null hypothesis:

$$H_0 : \text{There is no difference in performance.}$$

Until there is sufficient data to reject H_0, you cannot claim to be doing better (or worse) than the naïve model.

REFERENCES

Gilliland, M. (2005) Danger, danger: The perils of operational performance benchmarks. APICS e-News 5(23) (December 6).

Kolassa, S. (2008). Can we obtain valid benchmarks from published surveys of forecast accuracy? *Foresight: International Journal of Applied Forecasting* 20 (Fall).

Mauboussin, M. J. (2012). *The Success Equation: Untangling Skill and Luck in Business, Sports, and Investing*. Boston: Harvard Business Review Press.

Morlidge, S. (2014). Using relative error metrics to improve forecast quality in the supply chain. *Foresight: International Journal of Applied Forecasting* 34 (Summer), 39–46.

4.4 USING RELATIVE ERROR METRICS TO IMPROVE FORECAST QUALITY IN THE SUPPLY CHAIN*

Steve Morlidge

In his Chapter 1 article on the *avoidability* of forecast error, Steve Morlidge defined forecast accuracy in relation to the accuracy of naïve (no change) forecasts, and measured this by the relative absolute error (RAE). He showed that a reasonably performing forecasting process should have RAE between 0.5 and 1.0. (RAE less than 0.5 rarely occurs and can be considered a practical limit for the "best" you can expect to forecast. RAE above 1.0 means you are forecasting worse than the naïve model, i.e., negative FVA.) In this article, Morlidge continues his groundbreaking work by providing straightforward and practical guidance on where to focus forecasting-improvement efforts.

Morlidge's study of over 300,000 forecasts at eight supply chain companies uncovered a disturbing fact—half the forecasts had RAE > 1.0. In this article, he shows how relative error metrics can identify the best opportunities for improving forecast accuracy. His approach is based on (a) product volumes and variability and (b) a forecastability metric that assesses forecast accuracy in relation to the accuracy of a naïve forecast.

Noting that forecast quality can be improved in two ways—by better statistical models, and by better judgmental overrides—Morlidge segments the product portfolio via volume vs. RAE and volume vs. volatility (coefficient of variation) plots. He then identifies opportunity for improvement in each segment, and the appropriate improvement strategy. He also provides guidance for setting realistic targets by segment (a more sophisticated approach than Gilliland's "do no worse than the naïve model").

Introduction

"This is too wishy-washy. You will have to do something about this."

This was one among the many comments made by *Foresight* editors on receipt of my last article (Morlidge, 2014b). In it, I had detailed the results of the survey of nine sets of supply-chain forecasts drawn from eight businesses,

* This article originally appeared in *Foresight: The International Journal of Applied Forecasting* (Summer 2014), and appears here courtesy of the International Institute of Forecasters.

comprising over 300,000 data points in total. I measured the performance of all these forecasts using a relative absolute error (RAE) metric, where actual forecast error is compared to the simple "same as last period" naïve forecast error.

My purpose was to assess forecast quality in the supply chain by determining practical upper and lower bounds of forecast error—the lower bound representing the best accuracy that can be expected, the upper bound the worst that should be tolerated. My results—printed in the Spring 2014 issue of *Foresight*—showed that there were very few forecasts that had forecast errors more than 50% better than the naïve forecasts. Thus, for practical purposes, the lower bound of forecast error for the granular supply-chain data is an RAE of 0.5.

But also, and somewhat shockingly, I found that approximately 50% of the forecast errors were worse than those from the naïve forecasts, with an RAE > 1.0, the logical upper bound of forecast error. This is not a healthy situation: In principle, it should be easy to beat the naïve forecast. Failure to do so means that the forecast process is adding no value to the business. It also begs a couple of key questions: "What is causing this?" and, "What can be done about it?"

This was the issue that frustrated *Foresight* editors, and quite rightly so. Improving the craft of forecast measurement is laudable, but if nothing can be done with the results, then we have won no more than a Pyrrhic victory. No approach to measuring the quality of forecasts can, in itself, improve accuracy; it is a challenge for any measurement scheme, not just for RAE.

Therefore, in this current article, I will offer specifics on how to use the forecast-quality metric (RAE) in conjunction with product volumes to target efforts to improve forecast quality in the supply chain.

Before starting out on this quest, let me reprise some relevant points from my previous articles and explain their relevance to the task of forecasting in the supply chain.

Background

My motivation has been to discover the upper and lower bound—the worst and best levels—of forecast error and, in the process, produce a metric that can be used to make objective judgments about forecast quality.

The Upper Bound

The upper bound is easy to establish: There is no good reason why any set of forecasts should have larger errors on average than forecasts produced by the most primitive forecast conceivable—a naïve forecast that uses the prior period's actual as a forecast. This upper bound provides a benchmark against which forecast performance can be compared. A relative absolute error (RAE) of below 1.0 means that the average level of absolute errors from a forecast is lower than that of the naïve forecast; above 1.0 means that it is worse. But for practitioners working in the supply chain, the naïve forecast is more than a convenient benchmark.

Forecasting demand, and replenishing stock based on the demand forecast, is only economically worthwhile if it is possible to improve on the simple strategy of holding a fixed buffer (safety stock) and replenishing it to make good any withdrawals in the period. This simplistic replenishment strategy is arithmetically equivalent to using a naïve forecast (assuming no stockouts), since the naïve forecast is one of no change from our current level.

Safety Stock and Forecasting Value

The safety stock needed to meet a given service level is determined by our forecast errors. If the RAE of our forecasts is 1.0, yielding the same error on average as a naïve forecast, the buffer set by the naïve errors is appropriate. If our forecast has an RAE below 1.0, however, it means that the business needs to hold less stock than that indicated by the naïve. This is how forecasting adds value to a supply chain: The greater the level of absolute errors below those of the naïve forecast, the less stock is needed and the more value is added. Put simply, forecasting is not an end in itself; it is a means to an end, the end being a more efficient way of managing inventory (Boylan and Syntetos, 2006).

In order to assess the potential of a forecast to add more value (how much improvement it is possible to make), we need to be able to identify the lower bound of forecast error.

The Lower Bound

My first article in this series on forecastability included a demonstration of how the lower bound of error could be determined theoretically (Morlidge, 2013). It showed that the lower bound of forecast error is a product of

1. The level of random noise in a data series compared to the change in the signal, and
2. The volatility of the change in a signal. In the case of a signal with no trend, the theoretical lower bound of error was close to 30% below the naïve forecast, irrespective of the level of noise: i.e., an RAE of 0.7.

Trends, seasonal movements, and other systematic changes in the signal could theoretically lower (improve) the RAE further, but it was my speculation that the more changeable the signal is, the more difficult it is to forecast. In practical terms, I argued that it would be difficult for any forecast to better an RAE of 0.5, a hypothesis that was supported by my empirical work on supply-chain forecasts (Morlidge, 2014b).

The Practical Challenge

If 0.5 is accepted as a practical lower bound, then error in excess of an RAE of 0.5 is avoidable, while error below an RAE of 0.5 is unachievable and hence unavoidable. In principle, then, supply-chain forecasters should seek to drive RAE down as close to 0.5 as possible. However, they need to be mindful of the likelihood of increased difficulty of making incremental improvements the closer they get to the lower bound. Moreover, the value that forecasting generates for the business is related to the absolute amount of avoidable error, which is determined mainly by the product volume to be forecast. Hence analysts should be guided by the RAE weighted by volume, which is more meaningful as a measure of forecast performance than the unweighted average RAE.

With the requirement to forecast hundreds and often thousands of items by week or month, the practical challenges that supply-chain forecasters face are formidable. Some of these items can be volatile or intermittent, and may be affected by marketplace activity. In these situations, standard time-series methods cannot be used without adjustments and embellishments. Judgmental adjustments to statistical forecasts are therefore common (Goodwin and Fildes, 2007), and these are frequently based on input from people who are not forecasting experts. Worse, they may be motivated by "silo" concerns and pure self-interest (for example, submitting forecasts that are below target to ensure meeting a quota). Finally, forecasting software typically offers a bewildering array of methods and parameters and "black-box" automatic algorithm selection processes that (as demonstrated by other research) cannot always be relied on to produce acceptable results, even in controlled conditions (Morlidge, 2014).

Given the nature of these challenges, any approach to improving the quality of supply-chain forecasts must help practitioners:

1. Focus on those areas where the effort / reward ratio is most favorable;
2. Devise approaches that help identify the likely cause of problems and tailor strategies to solve them; and
3. Set realistic goals mindful of 1 and 2 above.

Focus the Efforts

Portfolio classification methods, such as "ABC," have been used extensively in inventory management as a way of helping practitioners develop differentiated approaches to the management of a portfolio, and to focus their efforts in those areas where they will be best rewarded (Synetos and colleagues, 2011).

One obvious way in which this approach could be applied to the challenge of forecast improvement is in helping practitioners target their efforts on those items with, at once, the poorest forecast performance (as measured by RAE weighted by volumes) and largest volumes.

This task will be easier if: (1) a large proportion of the opportunity (total amount of avoidable error in excess of 0.5 RAE) is concentrated in a small proportion of the product portfolio (true for our supply-chain data: approximately 20% of items contributed 80% of the avoidable error); and (2) forecast quality (RAE) is not strongly correlated with volume, as such a correlation might suggest that small-volume items are more difficult to forecast. In practice, we found this was not often the case, as large-volume products often did not have significantly lower RAE than low-volume products.

The first condition is the most important. A significant proportion of the opportunity (total amount of avoidable error) is typically concentrated in a small proportion of the product portfolio. For example, consider my previously used data comprising 11,000 items forecast in monthly buckets over a two-year period. Figure 4.3 plots these 11,000 items (each represented by a dot) on a chart where the *y*-axis shows the average volume and the *x*-axis marks forecast quality (RAE). (The volume axis uses a logarithmic scale so that the wide range of values can be displayed clearly, and so that any correlation between RAE and volume would be very obvious.) It is clear that no significant correlation exists in this case.

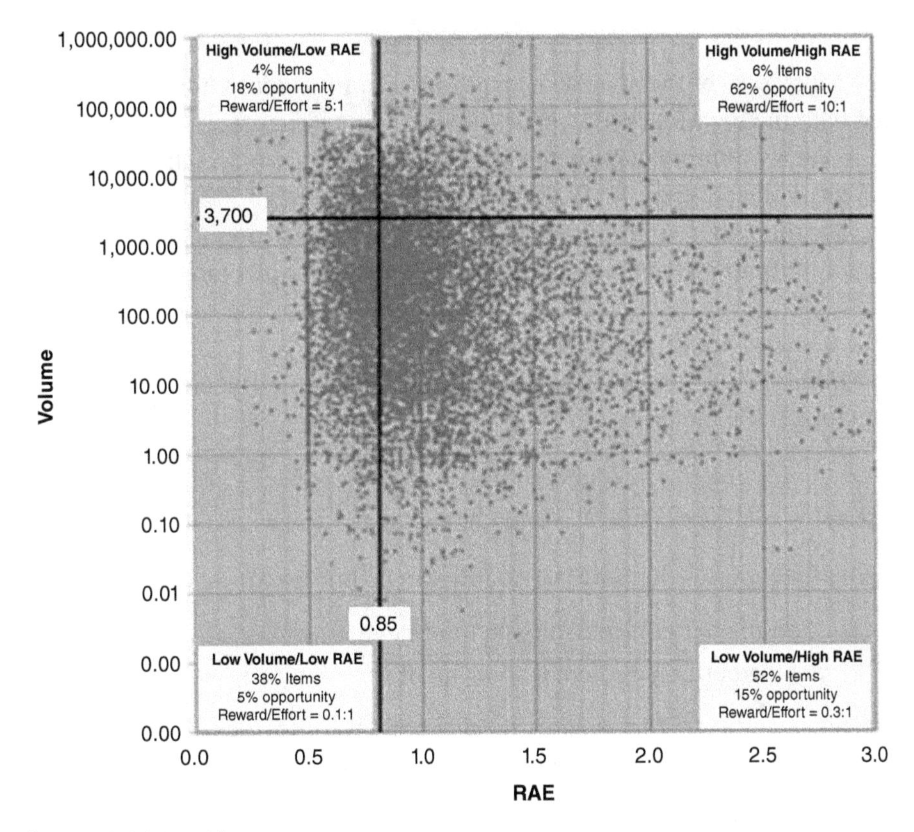

Figure 4.3 RAE vs. Volume

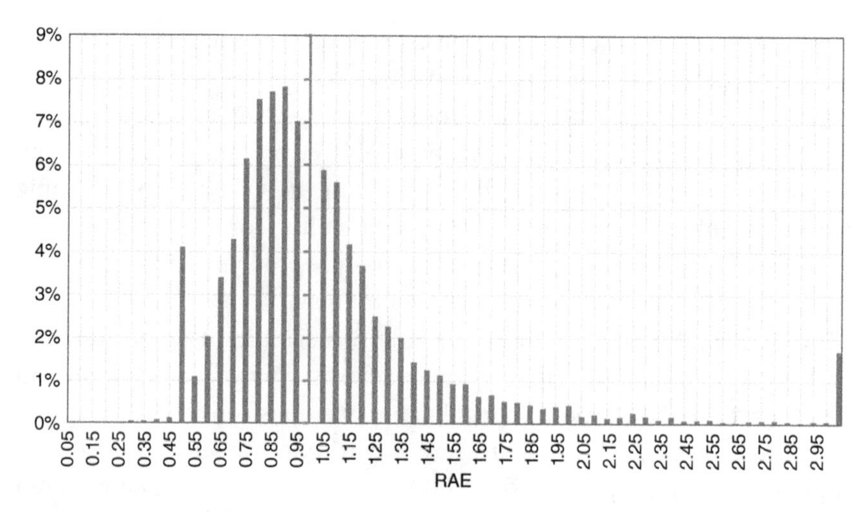

Figure 4.4 Distribution of RAE

The histogram below the chart, Figure 4.4, shows a large number of items with RAE in excess of 1.0 (about 40%), all of which could be avoided by using the naïve forecast (although in practice this should be the last resort) and very few below with RAE 0.5.

I have drawn separators in Figure 4.3 to distinguish four quadrants. This shows that 77% of the avoidable error (opportunity) comes from items associated with the high RAEs of 0.85 or above.

Accuracy improvement here should be relatively easy to achieve. Further, 80% of avoidable error is with the largest (by volume) 10% of the items. As a result, the "High Volume/High RAE" quadrant holds only 6% of the items but accounts for 62% of the opportunity, giving a very favorable effort/reward ratio. In this way, the focus of work to improve forecasting can be directed to those items where the greatest opportunities lie.

This leads to the next question: How do we identify the best approach for exploiting these opportunities?

Devise Improvement Strategies

There are two ways that forecast quality can be improved:

1. Choosing better forecasting methods; and
2. Making better judgmental adjustments.

This is a truism that applies to all items, but the trick is to match the improvement strategy with the right part of the portfolio.

The approach outlined here involves isolating those parts of the portfolio where, in principle, judgment can make a significant contribution to forecast quality, and then taking steps to ensure that such judgment is used judiciously. Outside this zone, the use of judgmental adjustments should be restricted; instead, effort must be focused on optimizing forecasting methods.

Figure 4.5 plots all the items in our sample portfolio on a second grid, which will help us select the most appropriate strategy to employ. This matrix is similar to the so-called ABC/XYZ approach used in the supply chain to help select the most appropriate replenishment and inventory policies.

As with the first classification grid, the *y*-axis represents volume and the horizontal line segregates the 20% of items that account for 80% of the avoidable error. However, here the *x*-axis records the coefficient of variation (CoV) of demand, which measures the volatility of the demand pattern. (I have calculated the CoV as the ratio of the mean absolute deviation—rather than standard deviation—to the arithmetic mean, a calculation that mitigates the impact of more extreme observations.)

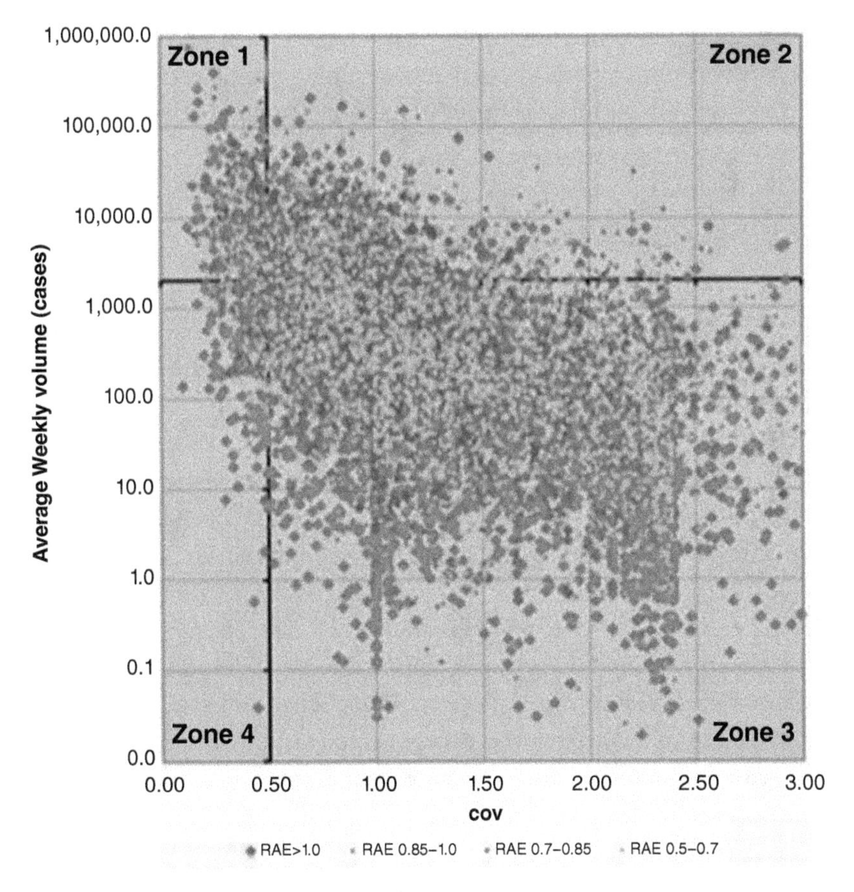

Figure 4.5 Volume vs. Volatility (CoV) of Forecast Items (Color codes distinguish forecast quality (RAE))

This approach is based on the reasonable assumption that, all things being equal, the less volatile the demand pattern (the lower the CoV), the easier it will be for forecasting methods to successfully pick up and forecast the signal in the data.

With lower CoVs, there is less chance that judgmental intervention will improve forecast quality. On the other hand, higher CoVs are more likely to be associated with data series heavily affected by sporadic events where relatively large judgmental interventions may be needed to improve statistical forecasts (Goodwin and Fildes, 2007).

The items are color-coded based on their RAE:

RAE > 1.0	= red
RAE 0.85 to 1.0	= amber
RAE 0.7 to 0.85	= green
RAE < 0.7	= blue

A cursory visual inspection of the chart suggests that there is considerable scope for improvement, based on the widespread scattering of red items. To maximize the opportunities for meaningful improvement, we must proceed in a structured, stepwise manner. This is my approach:

Priority 1: High-Volume/High-RAE Items

This is the part of the portfolio where the effort/reward ratio is most favorable, in that 6% of the items contribute 62% of the avoidable error. In Figure 4.5, these are (a) above the line and (b) coded with amber or red dots.

Some of these items are in Zone 1, where the COV is relatively low. For these the strategy should be to focus on refining the forecasting method (how data are cleansed, models selected, forecasts tracked), allowing judgmental adjustments to statistical forecasts only where the case for making a change is overwhelmingly favorable and the impact is likely to be significant (Goodwin and Fildes, 2007).

Zone 2 contains those items with a more volatile data pattern. Optimizing the forecasting method here is more difficult given the volatile nature of the data series and impact of one-off events. The focus in this zone should be on the effective use of judgment. The exception to this may be items with a well-defined seasonal pattern, which could be forecast statistically without manual intervention despite having a high CoV.

Zone 2 is the part of the portfolio where consensus forecasting techniques (statistical plus judgmental) are likely to add most value. That these items encompass a small proportion of the total number of items means that valuable management time can be focused very effectively. The success of these interventions can be quantified by measuring RAE before and after the consensus process, and using the forecast value added concept for the comparison (Gilliland, 2013). Since poor judgment is often manifest in consistent over- or underforecasting, managers should continuously monitor for bias.

Priority 2: High-Volume/Low-RAE Items

This second most interesting part of the portfolio comprised an additional 18% of the avoidable error. These items lie above the line and are color-coded green or blue. For the green items, I'd recommend the same approach followed for Priority 1; that is, improving the statistical forecasts while discouraging the application of judgment except for those items with a high CoV. Of course, it would not be worthwhile to work on the blue items, since they already have the very lowest RAE (lower than 0.7).

Priority 3: Low-Volume Items

In our sample, Zones 3 and 4 of the portfolio contain 90% of the items but only 20% of the avoidable error. Irrespective of the level of variation in the data series, they are unlikely to reward any efforts involved in a consensus forecasting process.

Instead, the focus should be using a very simple and conservative forecasting method, such as simple exponential smoothing (SES). The intermittent-demand items, which are most likely to be in Zone 3, should be forecast using SES or a variant of Croston's method (Synetos and colleagues, 2011). In some cases, where a data series approximates a random walk, the naïve model itself may be the best we can do. Perhaps these are not worth forecasting at all, using instead simple replenishment strategies or make-to-order (Boylan and Syntetos, 2006).

Setting Realistic Targets

Because the portfolio analysis is an exercise that will be carried out only periodically, it will be necessary to continuously track forecast quality (Hoover, 2009) to check that the hoped-for results are delivered and to identify when performance levels start to drop, necessitating another review. The key question, however, is, "What level of performance should we be aiming to achieve?" Clearly an RAE above 1.0 always flags a problem, and should be investigated (particularly if it is associated with a high-volume item), but what target should we be shooting for?

In a previous issue of *Foresight*, Sean Schubert suggests an approach based on the forecastability DNA of a product (Schubert, 2012), which takes account of factors other than the naïve forecast error. Here I propose adopting a similar approach by taking into account the volatility of the data series.

We have established that an RAE of 0.5 represents a practical lower limit of error in most cases. It would not be productive to adopt 0.5 as a target for small-volume items since the effort involved here probably could not be justified. For larger-volume items, Paul Goodwin has suggested a formula for setting sensible targets.

Goodwin's formulation is based on the assumption that the lowest RAEs are associated with the items with the most volatile signals, which are likely to be items with the highest CoV. This is counterintuitive: CoV is often considered to be a measurement of forecastability, with higher CoVs indicating more volatility and thus greater difficulty in achieving any given level of forecast accuracy. But, as shown in Figure 4.6, as the CoV increases, the weighted RAE tends to decline. Hence our argument is that we should set more stringent RAE targets for the higher CoV items.

The logic underpinning this argument is this: If the product is unforecastable—if the naïve forecast error is totally driven by noise—an RAE below 1.0 is unachievable. If there is a signal in the data (trend, seasonal, external factor), then the product is potentially forecastable, and the RAE should be expected to be better (lower) than 1.0. And we see here that lower CoV forecasts often perform very badly compared to the naïve, resulting in high RAEs.

Figure 4.6 plots the average and weighted-average RAE against CoV for our sample.

Figure 4.6 shows an increasing gap between the simple and weighted-average RAEs, reflecting that high-volume items/high-CoV items (i.e., those in Zone 2) have lower RAEs than those items with lower volumes.

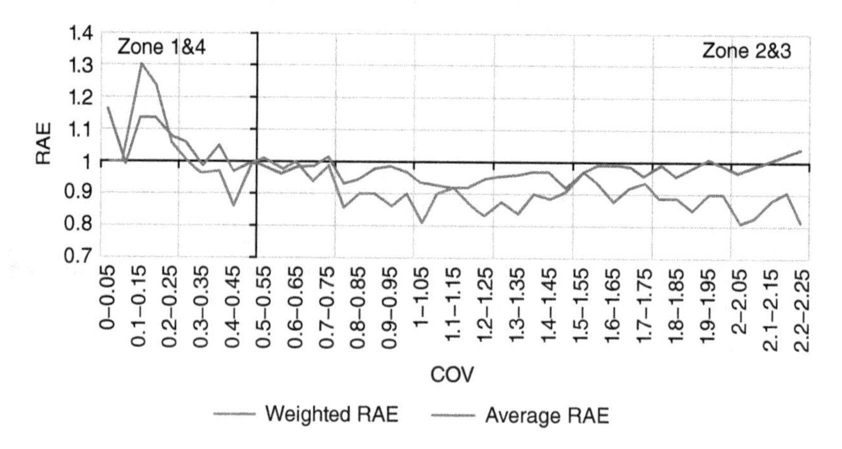

Figure 4.6 Average RAE Volatility (CoV)

Targets for High-CoV Items

Figure 4.6 results suggest that the target for Zone 2 items (high volume, high volatility) should be a relatively low RAE, while the target for items in Zone 3 (low volume, high volatility) should be less ambitious on the grounds that we quickly reach diminishing returns.

Targets for Low-CoV Items

In Zones 1 and 4 of Figure 4.5, which comprise items with low CoV, our intuition is to expect lower levels of forecast error than in Zones 2 and 3—that is, better RAE scores. Figure 4.6, however, shows that the lower the CoV, the worse the RAE (in this case, the RAE is significantly higher than 1.0). Also, there is no consistent difference between the simple and weighted-average RAEs, meaning that high-volume items have been forecast no better than low-volume items on average. What is causing this pattern is not clear—it may be the result of poorly judged manual interventions or overfitting of forecasting models—but whatever the cause, it is clearly unacceptable, and reasonable to expect better RAE scores for items in Zones 1 and 4 (though perhaps not as high as in Zone 2).

In summary, items in Zone 2 should have the most stretching targets since this is where the greatest scope exists to add value by manual intervention, and Zone 3 the least stretching because the low volumes make it unrewarding to expend the effort required to achieve good RAE scores. The targets for Zones 1 and 4 lie in between these extremes, but should be achievable with less effort because judgmental intervention is less likely to be needed.

Based on this analysis, I have proposed targets for items in each of these four zones in our sample, compared to the historic performance (Table 4.2). The scale of potential improvements is very significant: Avoidable forecast error (as measured by the weighted RAE) might perhaps be halved, with 71% of the total potential being contributed by 16% of the product portfolio. For the remaining 84% of items, the biggest contribution of this approach probably lies with the scope it gives to significantly reduce the amount of time and effort applied to forecasting them.

Table 4.2 Performance Targets and the Scale of Potential Improvement

	Percentage of Items	Current RAE	Target Range	Improvement Potential
Zone 1	3%	1.01	0.7–0.85	14%
Zone 2	13%	0.92	0.5–0.7	25%
Zone 3	7%	1.05	> 1.0	0%
Zone 4	77%	0.99	0.7–0.85	17%
Average	100%	0.97	**0.70**	55%

Conclusion

While it is unwise to make big claims based on one example, using RAE in conjunction with a small number of other easily calculated measures does appear to provide an objective and rational platform for constructing a set of forecast-improvement strategies tailored to a product portfolio. The goal is to maximize the overall benefit for a given level of effort.

Compared to a similar classification but based on conventional error metrics, RAE brings a number of benefits:

- It identifies where the greatest opportunities lie by quantifying the scope for improvement and where it is concentrated in the portfolio.
- It provides a quick and simple approach for dealing with items that are forecast poorly, and where the scope for improvement does not warrant the effort (the naïve forecast).
- It helps set meaningful goals, tailored to the nature of the product and the role it plays within a portfolio. These can be used to quantify the scope for improvement and track progress.

REFERENCES

Boylan, J., and A. Syntetos (2006). Accuracy and accuracy implications for intermittent demand. *Foresight: International Journal of Applied Forecasting* 4, 39–42.

Gilliland, M. (2013). FVA: A reality check on forecasting practices. *Foresight: International Journal of Applied Forecasting* 29 (Spring 2013), 14–19.

Goodwin, P., and R. Fildes (2007). Good and bad judgment in forecasting: Lessons from four companies. *Foresight: International Journal of Applied Forecasting* 8 (Fall 2007), 5–10

Hoover, J. (2009). How to track forecast accuracy to guide forecast process improvement. *Foresight: International Journal of Applied Forecasting* 14 (Summer), 17–23.

Morlidge, S. (2014a). Do forecasting methods reduce avoidable error? Evidence from forecasting competitions. *Foresight: International Journal of Applied Forecasting* 32 (Winter), 34–39.

Morlidge, S. (2014b). Forecastability and forecast quality in the supply chain. *Foresight: International Journal of Applied Forecasting* 33 (Spring), 26–31.

Morlidge, S. (2013). How good is a "good" forecast? Forecast errors and their avoidability. *Foresight: International Journal of Applied Forecasting* 30 (Summer), 5–11.

Schubert, S. (2012). Forecastability: A new method for benchmarking and driving improvement. *Foresight: International Journal of Applied Forecasting* 26 (Summer), 5–13.

Syntetos, A., J. Boylan, and R. Teutner (2011). Classification of forecasting and inventory. *Foresight: International Journal of Applied Forecasting* 20 (Winter), 12–17.

4.5 WHY SHOULD I TRUST YOUR FORECASTS?*

M. Sinan Gönül, Dilek Önkal, and Paul Goodwin

While we can never expect a forecast to be totally accurate, we do expect it to be based on the best use of available information, correctly applied methods, and justifiable assumptions. If we perceive the forecast to be a competent and honest expectation of future demand, we are more willing to trust it.

In this article, Sinan Gönül, Dilek Önkal, and Paul Goodwin examine the factors that instill trust in the work of the forecast providers. They find that misplaced incentives and *silo mentalities* create biases and mistrust that undermine the forecasting process. They share the latest research on steps to take that improve trust and reduce dysfunctional behavior in the forecasting function.

A key factor turns out to be perception of the goodwill of the forecast provider. If decision makers (or other "consumers" of the forecast) believe that the forecaster is striving to do his or her best to deliver reliable and accurate predictions, they are more likely to trust that source. However, forecast consumers will be less trusting if they perceive that the forecasts are influenced by the forecaster's biases or personal agenda.

Credible explanations are another key in building trust, effectively conveying the justification and rationale behind the forecasts. The keys are summarized into a list of behaviors and actions that make it more likely to earn trust.

The authors find that a benefit of trust is a reduction in forecast adjustments. This is good news, because adjustments consume time and resources. Other research (such as Fildes and Goodwin) has shown that adjustments frequently don't improve accuracy.

Introduction

Let's say you're sitting comfortably at your desk, sipping your coffee and preparing to plan your company's production levels for the following month. You begin first by examining the forecast report that's just been e-mailed to you. This report exhibits the predicted demand levels for the coming month. Suddenly a question pops into your head that, once there, just doesn't seem to want to go away: "Do I really trust these forecasts enough to base all my plans on these numbers?"

Trust and Forecasting

In everyday language, we use the word "trust" so frequently and casually that we sometimes forget what it actually means and entails. According to the *Oxford English Dictionary*, to "trust" something is to have a "firm belief in the

* This article originally appeared in *Foresight: The International Journal of Applied Forecasting* (Fall 2012), and appears here courtesy of the International Institute of Forecasters.

reliability and truth" of that thing. This implies that when we trust a forecast, we strongly believe the prediction is reliable and accurate.

But a mere strong belief is not enough to embrace the word's entire scope. Having that belief also means accepting certain consequences. For instance, when we use "trusted" forecasts and base our managerial decisions on them, we automatically shoulder the responsibility for those decisions, which includes admitting the possibility that these forecasts may be flawed. Of course, we would rarely expect any forecast—even one that we trust—to be totally accurate. We would, however, expect a trusted forecast to make the best use of available information, to be based on correctly applied methods and justifiable assumptions that are made explicit, and to be free of political or motivational biases (Gönül and colleagues, 2009). Overall, we would expect it to be a competent and honest expectation of future demand.

Trust, therefore, involves risk, because it makes us vulnerable to negative consequences if our trust is misplaced (Rousseau and colleagues, 1998).

The Determinants of Trust

What are the key factors that determine whether we should trust a forecast? There is general agreement among researchers that one factor is our perception of the goodwill of the forecast provider. If decision makers believe that the forecaster providing the predictions is striving to do his or her best to deliver reliable and accurate predictions, then we are more likely to trust that source. We will be less trusting if we perceive that the forecasts are influenced by the provider's agenda, which differs from ours.

For example, Adam Gordon (2008) discusses "future-influencing" forecasts that are used to try to achieve the future the forecast provider wants, rather than representing their genuine belief of what the future will hold. Forecasts by pressure groups that a new tax will drive companies out of business or that a new technology will treble cancer deaths may be of this type. Providers may also have other motivations. Within a company, forecasts provided by the marketing department may be perceived to be biased downwards so that the department looks good when sales regularly exceed forecasts (Goodwin, 1998).

If you are an intended recipient of a forecast, one indication that the forecast providers might share your agenda is their use of language which is familiar to you and free of jargon. In a study we recently concluded (Goodwin and colleagues, forthcoming), people trusted forecasts more when they were presented as "best case" and "worst case" values rather than as "bounds of a 90% prediction interval." In some situations, managers who are not mathematically inclined may be suspicious of forecasts presented using technical terminology and obscure statistical notation (Taylor and Thomas, 1982). Such a manager may respect the forecast provider's quantitative skills, but simultaneously perceive that the provider has no understanding of managers' forecasting needs—hence the manager distrusts the provider's forecasts.

Another critical factor is the perceived competence or ability of the forecast providers. In some cases, decision makers may prefer to entrust the job of forecast generation to professional forecasters, believing that they have more technical knowledge and insights. Sometimes this trust may be misplaced. People who confidently portray themselves as experts may be highly trusted—while an examination of their track record would reveal that, in fact, they may perform no better than chance (Tetlock, 2005).

In general, it appears that people just are not very good at assessing the competence of forecasters. A forecaster's reputation may be destroyed by one isolated bad forecast that people readily recall, even though the forecaster's overall accuracy is exemplary. In unfortunate contrast, one surprisingly accurate forecast of a major event that no one else foresaw will probably promote a poor forecaster to the status of a seer, thus eclipsing a record of wild inaccuracy (Denrell and Fang, 2010). If, for example, you correctly predicted the financial crisis of 2008, your forecasts are likely to be trusted without question, even if your past forecasting history suggests you generally have trouble foreseeing what day of the week follows Tuesday.

Of course, many forecasts originate from computers, not human beings. Do we trust computers more? It seems not. In a recent study (Önkal and colleagues, 2009), identical forecasts of stock market prices were presented to two groups of people, together with a graph depicting the stock price histories over time. One group was told that the forecasts emanated from a statistical algorithm, the other that they came from a financial expert (who, in fact, was the true source). When the groups were asked if they wanted to adjust the forecasts to make them more reliable, people made significantly larger changes to the forecasts that they thought came from the statistical algorithm—this despite the fact that the performance of experts in stock market forecasting is famously poor.

Future research is needed to see if attempting to give the computer systems human qualities, or creating a digital "persona," will improve trust perceptions. However, some research suggests that trust can be improved if the computer system provides an explanation of its forecast. Explanations have been a feature of expert systems since their inception (Önkal and colleagues, 2008). Through explanations, providers can convey their justification and rationale behind a given prediction, and through this information, users can build their perceptions about the competence, benevolence, and integrity of the forecasting source.

Researchers also observed (Gönül and colleagues, 2006) that the higher the perceived value of the explanations, the higher the level of acceptance of the forecast. Interviews with the users participating in these studies revealed that they enjoyed receiving explanations. The explanations provided "stories" that made the forecasts more "believable."

Trust and Adjustments to Provided Forecasts

Is the level of trust that people say they have in a set of forecasts (be they statistical or managerial) reflected in the way they treat these forecasts? Not surprisingly, it appears that greater levels of trust are associated with a decreasing tendency to adjust the forecasts.

However, the correlation is not perfect (Goodwin, forthcoming). Sometimes people may indicate a high level of trust and still go on to make big adjustments to the forecasts they receive. It seems that trust is only one factor determining forecast-adjustment behavior. This may be because separate and distinct mental processes are associated with assessing trust and judging the extent to which forecasts need to be adjusted (Twyman and colleagues, 2008). Trust assessments may originate from conscious and reflective thought processes and involve explicit thinking about whether we should trust what we are offered or not. On the other hand, when we make judgmental adjustments to forecasts there is plenty of evidence (Kahneman, 2011) that we unconsciously use heuristics—that is, intuitive *rules of thumb*. These may lead to different levels of adjustment, depending on the nature of the data we are given and the way it is presented. Whatever their cause, these discrepancies mean that people may treat two forecasts differently, even when they have told you they have the same level of trust in them.

The Need for Open Communication Channels

All these points indicate that communication between forecast users and forecast providers is critical. It is through open communication channels that users can express their expectations and receive cues to evaluate the prediction source in order to decide whether to trust or not to trust. The forecast providers might have benevolent intentions, might uphold similar principles, might be very skilled and experienced about generating predictions, and might indeed offer very accurate forecasts. But if they cannot effectively convey this information to their users and learn what the users are actually expecting, then all of these good qualities will be in vain.

Being transparent about general accuracy over a long period will reduce the tendency for users to make judgments on the basis of a single forecasting triumph or disaster. If this accuracy can be demonstrated relative to a reasonable benchmark, then so much the better. In very unpredictable situations, this will help to show that relatively high forecast errors are unavoidable and not a result of the forecaster's lack of competence. Being transparent about assumptions, and even presenting multiple forecasts based on different assumptions, will most likely reassure the user about the integrity of the provider.

Revealing previous assignments and giving information about groups or clients other than the current users might also be beneficial to demonstrating intentions of goodwill. By investigating the forecaster's client portfolio, the users of forecasts can find out what sort of people the provider is working with and has worked with in the past, which helps in formulating a picture of the values and principles that are important to the provider. However, more research is needed to find innovative ways through which communications between the two sides can be further enhanced, particularly where the forecasts are generated by statistical software.

Working to Earn Trust

So why should I trust your forecasts? The answer appears to lie in the quality of interaction and communication between the forecaster and the user. Getting this right is perhaps easier said than done, but remember these crucial points:

- Work to increase the forecast user's belief and confidence in the reliability and integrity of your forecasts, and you greatly increase the likelihood that the inevitable occasional forecast miscues will be seen as acceptable anomalies if viewed in the bigger picture.
- Affirm the forecast user's perception of your goodwill, not only by delivering the best, most accurate forecasts you can, but through reassuring the users that you share their motives and objectives and are not shoring up your own self-interest packaged as a forecast.
- Consider your audience, and take care to share information in language the forecast user is comfortable with, avoiding technical jargon and forecaster-speak wherever possible.
- Reassure the forecast user of your confidence in your systems and methods, while conveying the necessary degree of humility in your work by acknowledging that no forecaster ever gets it "right" every time.
- Be transparent about methodologies and increase user comfort levels by providing clear, cogent explanations of your forecasts.

- Let users review an honest history of your forecast accuracy levels that they can quickly assess and understand, preferably relative to reasonable benchmarks.
- Be forthcoming about your other current and past forecast clients or customers, as these relationships, by association, can help to convey to the forecast user a comforting and heartening sense of your own principles and values.

A tall order, yes—but get these priorities straight, and all the effort that you put into your forecasts is far less likely to be wasted on distrustful users. After all, creating and disseminating accurate forecasts is a hard enough job; the good news is that there are practical steps you can take to further a more trusting and trustful working environment with the people who use and depend on those forecasts.

REFERENCES

Denrell, J., and C. Fang (2010). Predicting the next big thing: Success as a signal of poor judgment. *Management Science* 56, 1653–1667.

Gönül, M. S., D. Önkal, and P. Goodwin (2009). Expectations, use and judgmental adjustment of external financial and economic forecasts: An empirical investigation. *Journal of Forecasting* 28, 19–37.

Gönül, M. S., D. Önkal, and M. Lawrence (2006). The effects of structural characteristics of explanations on use of a DSS. *Decision Support Systems* 42(3), 1481–1493.

Goodwin, P., M. S. Gönül, and D. Önkal (2013). Antecedents and effects of trust in forecasting advice. *International Journal of Forecasting* 29, 354–366.

Goodwin, P. (1998). Enhancing judgmental forecasting: The role of laboratory research. In Wright, G., and P. Goodwin (Eds.). *Forecasting with Judgment.* Chichester: John Wiley & Sons.

Gordon, A. (2008). *Future Savvy: Identifying Trends to Make Better Decisions, Manage Uncertainty, and Profit from Change*. New York: AMACOM.

Kahneman, D. (2011). *Thinking, Fast and Slow.* London: Allen Lane.

Önkal, D., P. Goodwin, M. Thomson, M. S. Gönül, and A. Pollock (2009). The relative influence of advice from human experts and statistical methods on forecast adjustments. *Journal of Behavioral Decision Making* 22, 390–409.

Önkal, D., M. S. Gönül, and M. Lawrence (2008). Judgmental adjustments of previously adjusted forecasts. *Decision Sciences* 39(2), 213–238.

Rousseau, D. M., S. B. Sitkin, R. S. Burt, and C. Camerer (1998). Not so different after all: A cross-discipline view of trust. *Academy of Management Review* 23, 393–404.

Taylor, P. F., and M. E. Thomas (1982). Short-term forecasting: Horses for courses. *Journal of the Operational Research Society* 33, 685–694.

Tetlock, P. E. (2005). *Expert Political Judgment.* Princeton: Princeton University Press.

Twyman, M., N. Harvey, and H. Harries (2008) Trust in motives, trust in competence: Separate factors determining the effectiveness of risk communication. *Judgment and Decision Making* 3, 111–120.

4.6 HIGH ON COMPLEXITY, LOW ON EVIDENCE: ARE ADVANCED FORECASTING METHODS ALWAYS AS GOOD AS THEY SEEM?*

Paul Goodwin

Complex models are good for fitting history. In fact, it is always possible to construct a model so complex that it *fits your time series history* perfectly. But does model complexity translate into more accurate *forecasts* of the future?

There is a large body of evidence that simpler models tend to forecast better than complex models—even if they don't fit the history as well as the complex model. Yet there is no shortage of new and increasingly complex models being published by forecasting researchers. Paul Goodwin argues that these researchers are justified in experimenting with difficult new methods. However, more than just publishing the new method, researchers should provide reliable evidence that the method can produce accurate forecasts under given sets of conditions. And they should compare accuracy of the method against appropriate benchmarks.

Goodwin cites several problematic articles where new methods were upheld by thin or even nonapplicable evidence. An excuse may be that these articles were published in journals not specializing in forecasting—so the editors may not be familiar with good forecasting principles and practice. Even so, Goodwin advises, "If the name of the method contains more words than the number of observations that were used to test it, then it's wise to put any plans to adopt the method on hold."

The Complexity Love Affair

Some forecasting researchers love complexity. Read their papers, and you just might begin to feel guilty that you haven't been integrating genetic fuzzy systems with data clustering to forecast sales in your company. If you are a long-term forecaster, you may be dreading the day when your boss finds out that you have not been using a neuro-fuzzy-stochastic frontier-analysis approach. Or perhaps you should take a whack at utility-based models, incorporating price forecasts based on an experience curve that has been fitted to your data using nonlinear least squares.

Of course, the world is a complex place, and intricate models may be needed to take into account the many factors that might have an impact on the demand for your product or your future costs. Hence, for reasons that seem obvious, forecasting researchers are justified in experimenting with difficult new methods, even if those methods would challenge most PhDs in math. However, there are two commonsense criteria that we should expect researchers to meet. First, they should provide reliable evidence that the methods they advocate can produce accurate forecasts under given sets of conditions.

* This article originally appeared in *Foresight: The International Journal of Applied Forecasting* (Fall 2011), and appears here courtesy of the International Institute of Forecasters.

Second, they should compare the accuracy of their methods with appropriate benchmarks.

Typical benchmarks would be simpler methods—to see if the extra complexity is justified—and existing methods that are currently in widespread use. Many research studies fail on both criteria.

A Case in Point

I recently reviewed for a journal a paper that recommends a technique to produce sales forecasts when there are few past observations: the analytic network process. This technique, which is based on relatively complex mathematics, allows experts to systematically structure their knowledge of the key drivers of sales with the aim of making their judgmental forecasts consistent and accurate. The paper's authors used this process to forecast the annual sales of printers in an Asian country. Their main finding was that the technique yielded forecasts with a percentage error of only 1.3%, which the researchers pointed out was minimal compared to the errors of six common statistical techniques that they had also applied to their data. This level of accuracy is highly impressive, of course, and it appeared to justify the considerable effort involved in applying the analytic network process.

However, a careful reading of the paper revealed a couple of problems. First, the statistical methods relied upon in the comparison were not designed to be used with the short time series studied. For example, their series exhibited a marked negative trend, which meant that moving averages and simple exponential smoothing could not be expected to give reliable forecasts. Instead, the obvious benchmark would have been experts' forecasts made without the benefit of the analytic network process. This would have indicated whether the method's complexity was worth the effort.

But that wasn't the most serious problem with the paper. It turned out that the researchers had only tested the accuracy of the methods on one sales figure. Their paper contained 33 pages of discussion and nine tables of results—two of which were 13-by-13 matrices containing figures to five decimal places. And yet the only evidence they provided in favor of their method was based on one number.

Proper Testing of Accuracy

Foresight Editor Len Tashman pointed out over a decade ago (Tashman, 2000) that forecasting methods need to be tested on a sufficient number of out-of-sample observations (i.e., observations that are unavailable to the method when it is fitted to the past data) to meet the criteria of adequacy and diversity. Adequacy applies when a method is tested on a sufficient number of observations from similar time series to enable the forecaster to draw reliable inferences about the performance of the forecasting method on such series. Diversity is achieved when testing is applied to series that are heterogeneous in both time period and nature, so that the forecaster can make an assessment of how effective the method is under a range of different circumstances.

Testing a model on out-of-sample observations is necessary because a close fit to past data does not guarantee accurate forecasts. Indeed, an improved fit to past data may be associated with poorer forecasts because the method is falsely seeing systematic patterns in the random movements in past data, and assuming that these will continue into the future. Forecasting accuracy is also not guaranteed even when a model is based on an internally consistent and rigorously tested theory (Clements and Hendry, 2008), so extensive out-of-sample testing is still highly advisable.

Inadequate Evidence

Despite these advisories, papers are still being published that draw big conclusions from small amounts of data. A recent article by Decker and Gnibba-Yakawa (2010) recommended that managers should use *utility-based models* to forecast the sales of high-technology consumer products (like CD and DVD players) in the years before the sales reach a peak. The models are elegant and well underpinned by economic theory. They allow forecasters to take into account factors like customers' expectations of falling prices (a common occurrence in marketing high-technology products) and network effects, where a product becomes more attractive as its user base grows due to the development and subsequent availability of complementary or supporting products (apps for smartphones, for example). The researchers reported that their models gave forecasts with a mean absolute percentage error of only 4.08%. It all looks very promising until you realize that this result is based on a total of just six holdout sales figures—three different products contributed only one, two, and three sales figures, respectively.

Or take a study by Zhu, Wang, Zhao, and Wang (2011) that proposed the use of a complex hybrid of methods (including moving averages and an adaptive particle-swarm optimization algorithm) to forecast electricity demand in China. They fitted their method to 57 past monthly observations and concluded that "our proposed model is an effective forecasting technique for seasonal time series with nonlinear trend." But their out-of-sample forecasts only covered the months from January to September of 2010. It is difficult to draw any conclusions about a method that is designed to handle seasonality when we have no forecasts for three months of the year.

It isn't hard to find other recent examples where complex, often computer-intensive methods are described in great detail but the recommendation to use the method is based on thin evidence. Significantly, these examples tend to be found in journals that do not specialize in forecasting, which may indicate that good forecasting principles and practices are having a hard time making inroads to other fields. For example, in the journal *Applied Soft Computing*, Azadeh and Faiz (2011) claim that the use of their "flexible integrated meta-heuristic framework based on an artificial neural network multilayer perceptron" would provide "more reliable and precise forecasting for policy makers" concerned with electricity supply. But they tested their method on just eight annual household electricity figures from Iran. On the basis of a mere two out-of-sample observations—China's natural gas consumption in 2007 and 2008—Xu and Wang (2010) concluded in the *Journal of Natural Gas Chemistry* that their "Polynomial Curve and Moving Average Combination Projection (PCMACP) model" can "reliably and accurately be used for forecasting natural gas consumption."

Conclusions

We should not be against complexity per se. Modern computing muscle gives us an unprecedented opportunity to apply more powerful techniques in pursuit of greater forecasting accuracy. Moreover, many of the techniques described above are a tribute to the inventiveness and intellectual caliber of the researchers who describe them. But for forecasters in the field, complexity can come at the cost of greater effort and time in preparing forecasts and a loss of credibility with senior managers. It is therefore vital that recommendations to use complex methods be supported with strong evidence about their reliability. If the name of a method contains more words than the number of observations that were used to test it, then it's wise to put any plans to adopt the method on hold.

REFERENCES

Azadeh, A., and Z. S. Faiz (2011). A meta-heuristic framework for forecasting household electricity consumption. *Applied Soft Computing* 11, 614–620.

Clements, M. P., and D. F. Hendry (2008). Economic forecasting in a changing world. *Capitalism and Society* 3: Issue 2, Article 1.

Decker, R., and K. Gnibba-Yakawa (2010). Sales forecasting in high-technology markets: a utility-based approach. *Journal of Product Innovation Management* 27,115–129.

Tashman, L. J. (2000). Out-of-sample tests of forecasting accuracy: An analysis and review. *International Journal of Forecasting* 16, 437–450.

Xu, G., and W. Wang (2010). Forecasting China's natural gas consumption based on a combination model. *Journal of Natural Gas Chemistry* 19, 493–496.

Zhu, S., J. Wang, W. Zhao, and J. Wang (2011). A seasonal hybrid procedure for electricity demand forecasting in China. *Applied Energy* 88, 3807–3815.

4.7 SHOULD THE FORECASTING PROCESS ELIMINATE FACE-TO-FACE MEETINGS?*

J. Scott Armstrong

When financial columnist James Surowiecki wrote *The Wisdom of Crowds*, he wished to explain the successes and failures of markets (an example of a "crowd") and to understand why the average opinion of a group is frequently more accurate than the opinions of most of the individuals in the group. In this expanded review of the book, Scott Armstrong asks a question of immediate relevance to forecasters: Are traditional face-to-face meetings an effective way to elicit forecasts from forecast crowds (i.e., teams)?

Armstrong doesn't believe so; quite the contrary, he writes that face-to-face meetings are a detriment to good forecasting practice and argues there are better alternatives. These include Markets, Nominal Groups, and Virtual Teams. Armstrong describes how these work, and reports the evidence on their value.

While there are familiar guidelines on how to run meetings effectively, Armstrong notes it is rare to find group leaders who use them. Traditional meetings persist partly because people falsely believe that they are necessary for aggregating opinions.

Some argue that face-to-face meetings are needed in certain contexts, such as when it is important to gain commitment to decisions, as in S&OP meetings (although Armstrong doesn't mention S&OP). However, evidence to back up these assertions is scarce. Armstrong concludes that traditional face-to-face meetings, which prevent forecasters from acting alone, yield poor decisions and inaccurate forecasts.

Introduction

Every week I hear people complain about meetings. What would happen to your organization if it became difficult to have face-to-face meetings? To this end, some organizations hold meetings in rooms without chairs. Some impose limits on the length of the session or the number of people who attend.

But what if an organization went further and penalized people for spending time in meetings? Or required that the meeting have a clear-cut payoff? As part of assessing the results, management could provide a visible taxi-style meter that uses attendees' billing rates to show the meeting's costs. Or what if management abolished face-to-face meetings entirely?

The Wisdom of Crowds

I have been thinking about the need for face-to-face meetings for some time now. Recently, I have been spurred on by *The Wisdom of Crowds* (Surowiecki,

---

* This article originally appeared in *Foresight: The International Journal of Applied Forecasting* (Fall 2006), and appears here courtesy of the International Institute of Forecasters.

2004), a delightful yet exasperating book. It is delightful because the writing is so clever and contains descriptions of interesting research studies, many of which were new to me; it is exasperating because it is not well organized, but the writing is so clever that one may not notice the gaps in logic. Nevertheless, the book's major conclusion is important:

Traditional meetings yield poor decisions and inaccurate forecasts.

Dave Barry summarized this conclusion in fewer words: "If you had to identify, in one word, the reason that the human race has not achieved, and never will achieve, its full potential, that word would be *meetings*." Apparently Barry's quote hit a nerve; a Google search for his conclusion turned up almost 600 relevant sites (out of 10,000 total sites) in July 2006.

The term *crowds* in the title of Surowiecki's *The Wisdom of Crowds* is unfortunate. He claims that the collective thinking of many individuals, when acting alone, contains wisdom. Crowds act together, and they do not have wisdom. A more descriptive title would have been *The Superiority of Combined Independent Anonymous Judgments*.

The book has been widely reviewed on Amazon, with comments from over 200 readers who have provided a bimodal ratings distribution. The negative reviewers fell into two classes: those who were upset at the basic conclusions and those who were upset at the gaps in logic. The experts priced this book at $25, but the crowd's price for a new copy in May 2006 was $10. If you enjoy books like *Who Moved My Cheese?* and Jack Welch's *Winning*, you are unlikely to enjoy *The Wisdom of Crowds*. But it will make you reconsider your assumptions about meetings. At least it had that strong effect on me.

Face-to-Face Meetings Could Be Effective

We do have guidelines on how to run meetings effectively. This was well summarized over four decades ago by Norman R. F. Maier. His research showed how group leaders could make effective use of people's information. His book (Maier, 1963) provides evidence-based principles for running meetings. Figure 4.7 provides a summary of guidelines that draws heavily on Maier's research.

Unfortunately, it is rare to find group leaders who use Maier's advice. In my 46-year career, I can remember only a handful of business students, academic administrators, or business executives who have run meetings effectively. Productive meetings are possible but rare.

Why do people persist in holding face-to-face meetings? First, we are social animals; many of us enjoy the interaction with others in a face-to-face setting.

- **Use time budgets**. Allocate time to discuss various topics and provide ample slack time.
- **Be problem centered**. Keep your discussion focused on a problem. Avoid looking for excuses or seeking to blame others.
- **Record suggestions**. Keep track of all suggestions for solving a problem or making sense of an issue so that each suggestion may be explored fully.
- **Explore**. Explore a number of suggestions for addressing an issue. Probing and evaluative questions can then be asked. How would that strategy work out? Do I understand the issue, or do I need to search out more information? Am I mistaken in my assumptions about the issue? What are the advantages or disadvantages of each proposal? Is there a way to combine suggestions to generate a better solution?
- **Protect people**. Protect individuals from personal attacks and criticism, especially if they present minority or divergent viewpoints. Avoid saying, 'That's a bad idea."
- **Understand and resolve differences**. Once ideas have been generated, encourage dissent. Understand differences of opinions within the group and attempt to resolve them.

Figure 4.7 Guidelines for Problem-Solving Meetings

Second, managers like the control that meetings give them over others; they can see that others are coming together at their commands. Third, people believe that meetings are effective; managers believe that they are doing something useful when they meet (although they often do not have the same opinion about meetings among their blue-collar workers).

A fourth reason is that people falsely believe that by merely aggregating opinions without a face-to-face meeting, one would get a decision or forecast that is only average. The scientist Sir Francis Galton dispelled such a belief in 1878. He showed that by averaging portraits of women, the resulting portrait was judged not average looking but rather more beautiful than all the component portraits. Larrick and Soll (2006), in a clever series of experiments, showed that among highly intelligent subjects (MBA students at INSEAD), most did not understand that the error of the group-average judgment is almost always smaller than the error of the average person in a group. More surprising to them was that the group-average judgment is sometimes better than the best judgment.

The Case Against Face-to-Face Meetings

Face-to-face meetings are expensive to schedule and run. They might involve travel costs or come at inconvenient times, when attendees are busy or tired. Time is wasted when people come late, talk about irrelevant topics, or leave early.

Meetings are also subject to many types of biases. How loudly do people talk? How deep are their voices? What do the people look like? How is the furniture arranged? How are people dressed? What is each person's body posture? Who has the power? How does the group leader guide the meeting? Does the group nurture dissent? Do people have preconceived positions on the topic at hand?

Some attendees are so concerned about what they want to say that they do not listen to what others are saying. Some are so intent on listening that they have no time to think. Some feel the need to restate their positions. Few people take notes; therefore they soon forget what happened in the meeting and are unable to develop useful action plans.

Not surprising then is the prevalence of studies showing that, compared with other methods of aggregating opinions (such as using the average of a set of independent judgments), the simple act of meeting face-to-face harms forecasting and decision making, although the people involved in these experiments typically do not believe the results.

Interestingly, the findings for forecasting and decision making are similar to those studies that involve groups generating creative ideas. As shown in the research review by Gallupe et al. (1991), individuals produce more creative suggestions than groups do, even if the groups are well run.

There are two conditions under which independent judgments should be combined. First, the experts must have useful information about the topic of interest; combining ignorance does not lead to wisdom. Second, participants must represent diversity of knowledge. The key word is *knowledge*. For example, it makes little sense to include experts because of differences in looks, heights, weights, religions, races, genders, and so on. In fact, Stewart's (2006) meta-analysis of 26 tests found a small negative relation between team members' demographic heterogeneity and group performance.

Decision making and forecasting can be improved to the extent that

- People state opinions independently, and
- Opinions are aggregated objectively, using a predetermined mechanical scheme.

The implication of the above research is that managers need to be creative in finding ways to use the knowledge effectively in a group while preventing members from meeting face-to-face. This will improve forecasting and decision making. It will also save time and money. Fortunately, modern technology has provided useful alternatives.

Alternatives to Face-to-Face Meetings: Markets, Nominal Groups, and Virtual Teams

There are a number of ways to implement alternatives to face-to-face meetings. I will discuss three: markets, nominal groups, and virtual teams.

Markets (Prediction Markets, Information Markets, or Betting Markets)

Experts and nonexperts alike bet on outcomes. These markets are common in finance and sporting events. People receive feedback only through prices and volume of trading.

In *The Wisdom of Crowds,* Surowiecki describes the use of markets for prediction. Their superiority has been shown by studies in financial markets since the 1920s. Although investors do not meet, they observe the outcomes of actions by others and draw on related information to make their decisions.

Outside of finance and sports, there have been few comparative studies on the value of prediction markets. The future looks promising, however. Surowiecki reports that some companies are using prediction markets for new-product sales. Since predictions for such problems are typically made in traditional meetings, I would expect prediction markets to produce more accurate forecasts.

I hope that *The Wisdom of Crowds* will lead some companies to consider the use of prediction markets. Technology should not pose a barrier. Some organizations will delegate a person to set up a betting market for sporting events.

Nominal Groups (Including Delphi)

In nominal groups, judgments are collected from a group of experts and are summarized by a group facilitator.

Surowiecki relied on suggestive and interesting (but indirect) evidence on the value of nominal groups. He failed to effectively use the wisdom of the crowds of forecasting researchers in his search for evidence on the value of simply combining judgments. In Armstrong (2001), I summarized 11 comparative empirical studies on the value of combining judgmental forecasts, which, to my knowledge, was an exhaustive listing of such studies. The median error of the group average in these studies was 12.2% less than that of the average expert's error.

The Delphi technique goes beyond nominal groups. It involves an anonymous collection of expert judgments by mail, Internet, or written responses. Feedback on the responses is provided to the experts, who then repeat this exercise for at least two rounds.

Rowe and Wright (2001) found that Delphi improved accuracy over traditional groups in five of the studies, harmed accuracy in one, and was inconclusive in two. Using an alternative benchmark, they found that it was more accurate than one-round expert surveys for 12 of 16 studies, with two ties and two cases in which Delphi was less accurate. For these 24 comparisons, Delphi improved accuracy in 71% of the cases and harmed it in 12%. I was unable to find any published studies that compared prediction markets with Delphi.

Freeware for Delphi is provided at forecastingprinciples.com. Usage of this freeware has increased substantially in recent years.

Virtual Teams

Virtual teams, enabled largely by the Internet, have several advantages. They allow for a freer flow of information than do markets or nominal groups. Members of virtual teams can use mail, e-mail, and websites. Phone calls are used only in emergencies, and conference calls are not used. These procedures remove some biases (for example, body language and modes of speech). They allow time for people to think before responding, and they provide a record of what was accomplished.

Despite the growing popularity of virtual teams, I was unable to find comparative studies on the value of these groups. However, based on related research summarized by Surowiecki, I expect that virtual teams would be much more effective than face-to-face groups, but less effective than prediction markets and Delphi. Consistent with this, Ganesan, Malter, and Rindfleisch (2005), in a study on new-product development, found that e-mail was superior to face-to-face meetings with respect to new-product creativity and development speed.

A Prediction Case

Can you predict the results of the following experiment? To solicit useful feedback on research studies, a group of 160 experts was provided with research papers, one paper per expert. The experts were randomly divided into two treatment groups. In group A, ten sets of eight experts participated in 80-minute meetings, where authors of the ten studies presented their papers and addressed questions. (Each group heard only one study.) In group B, each subject in the nominal groups of eight experts worked alone and without interruption for 80 minutes on one of the ten papers. These experts wrote comments in the margins of the papers. In effect, the intent was to have equal amounts of time spent on each paper. Which treatment, A or B, produced more useful suggestions? In which treatment did the authors of the study use the suggestions more effectively?

Unfortunately, there is little research to establish which of the mechanical methods of combining expert judgments are most creative, most accurate, least expensive, and most acceptable. For example, I have found that no published empirical comparisons have been made among prediction markets, Delphi, and virtual teams. In fact, the above study has not been conducted. Based on related research, however, I assume that Treatment B (nominal groups) would be superior to Treatment A (traditional groups) in terms of producing useful, accurate, and creative ideas. I also assume that, in Treatment B, the acceptance rate by the authors of the papers would be much higher.

Are Face-to-Face Meetings Useful Under Some Conditions?

The evidence against face-to-face meetings is extensive, and I have made no attempt to provide a complete summary here. I did, however, attempt to contact all authors whose work I cite in order to ensure that I have referenced the information properly. My primary concern is to find evidence that favors face-to-face meetings.

Are there conditions under which meetings contribute to forecasting or decision making? I speculate on three possibilities. The first is when the experts cannot read. The second is when very small groups, perhaps two people, may be able to work effectively. The third is when it is important to gain commitment to decisions. With respect to the third condition, one must be concerned not only with the quality of a decision but also with its acceptability. Would the feeling of involvement in a decision more likely lead to acceptance when the group has made a forecast or decision?

Some papers have suggested that meetings are useful when the situation is complex and the solutions are not obvious. While this suggestion has some intuitive appeal, tests of this concept have failed, according to Dennis and Kinney (1998). I doubt that such meetings are effective, given the evidence that (1) people can understand complex material better and faster when it is written (Chaiken and Eagly, 1976); (2) people in groups are poor at generating creative approaches; (3) many participants have difficulty performing complex analyses in the presence of others; and (4) groups are not tolerant of creative solutions.

Although I have circulated my paper for comments from e-mail lists and from other researchers, I have been unable to obtain evidence to support the use of face-to-face groups under these or any other conditions. Some people have responded with their opinions that meetings are useful or that many managers like meetings. There was one paper that provided promising results for face-to-face meetings, but the findings were not clear. Some people responded that they could not think of evidence favoring face-to-face meetings.

Such sessions may meet people's needs for socializing. Magne Jørgensen (personal communication) mentioned one company that did away with face-to-face meetings for their projects, replacing them with e-mail messages. To satisfy people's needs for meeting and talking, they sponsored social events.

Action Steps

Perhaps the first step is damage control. Reduce the number of meetings, the length of meetings, and the number of people invited. Post a chart on the group's homepage to track the people-hours (and their associated costs) that are consumed by the meetings. Ask the group leader to use Maier's guidelines for meetings. In addition, ask attendees to summarize the actions they have taken after each meeting.

If people in your organization do not know how to respond without meetings, you can bring them together in a room and then use structured procedures that simulate nominal groups, as described by Aiken and Vanjani (2003). For example, you could ask for a short "time-out" during a meeting and ask everyone to write his or her ideas. Software is available for conducting structured meetings, and these products have proved useful (Valacich et al., 1994) and have been gaining acceptance in organizations. For example, Briggs et al. (1998) reported that electronic brainwriting (individual idea generation) has been used by several million people in over 1,500 organizations around the world.

Individuals can also take action. My approach is to ask the person who calls a meeting to describe the problem and to inquire whether it would be useful to ask participants to provide written suggestions rather than to attend the meeting. The leader nearly always says yes and takes my proposal in a positive way. This approach makes it easier for people to absorb my suggestions and my reasoning while it reduces their desire to argue against me (because I am not there).

Conclusions

We rely heavily on face-to-face meetings, which are more expensive than alternative approaches, even though it is difficult to find evidence that supports their use. Although evidence-based principles exist for running face-to-face meetings effectively, they are used so rarely that we must turn to more practical solutions. In fact, a pattern of evidence suggests that prediction markets, nominal groups, and virtual teams allow for a more effective use of a group's collective wisdom. Technology has enhanced the value of these approaches.

REFERENCES

Aiken, M., and M. B. Vanjani (2003). Comment distribution in electronic poolwriting and gallery writing meetings. *Communications of the International Information Management Association* 3(2), 17–36.

Armstrong, J. S. (2001). Combining forecasts, in J. S. Armstrong (Ed.), *Principles of Forecasting*. Boston: Kluwer Academic Publishers, 417–439.

Briggs, R. O., J. F. Nunamaker Jr., and R. H. Sprague Jr. (1998). 1001 Unanswered research questions in GSS. *Journal of Management Information Systems* 14(3), 3–21.

Chaiken, S., and A. H. Eagly (1976). Communication modality as a determinant of message persuasiveness and message comprehensibility. *Journal of Personality and Social Psychology* 34, 605–614.

Dennis, A. R., and S. T. Kinney (1998). Testing media richness theory in new media: The effects of cues, feedback, and task equivocality. *Information Systems Research* 9(3), 256–274.

Gallupe, R. B., L. M. Bastianutti, and W. H. Cooper (1991). Unlocking brainstorms. *Journal of Applied Psychology* 76(1), 137–142.

Ganesan, S., A. J. Malter, and A. Rindfleisch (2005). Does distance still matter? Geographic proximity and new product development. *Journal of Marketing* 69, 44–60.

Larrick, R. P., and J. B. Soll (2006). Intuitions about combining opinions: Misappreciation of the averaging principle. *Management Science* 52, 111–127.

Maier, N. R. F. (1963). *Problem Solving Discussions and Conferences*. New York: McGraw-Hill. (Out of print, but used copies are available.)

Rowe, G., and G. Wright (2001). Expert opinions in forecasting: The role of the Delphi technique. In J. S. Armstrong (ed.), *Principles of Forecasting*. Boston: Kluwer Academic Publishers, 125–144.

Stewart, G. L. (2006). A meta-analytic review of relationships between team design features and team performance. *Journal of Management* 32, 29–54.

Surowiecki, J. (2004). *The Wisdom of Crowds*. New York: Doubleday.

Valacich, J. S., R. D. Alan, and T. Connolly (1994). Idea generation in computer-based groups: A new ending to an old story. *Organizational Behavior and Human Decision Processes* 57, 448–467.

Acknowledgments: Useful suggestions were provided by Monica Adya, Fred Collopy, Kesten Green, and Magne Jørgensen, as well as by *Foresight* editors.

4.8 THE IMPACT OF SALES FORECAST GAME PLAYING ON SUPPLY CHAINS*

John Mello

Game playing has been defined as the intentional manipulation of a forecasting process to gain personal, group, or corporate advantage. Summarizing the insights from his research on behaviors in the sales forecasting process, John Mello discusses the consequences of game playing for the company and its supply chain.

Mello identifies seven games: Enforcing, Filtering, Hedging, Sandbagging, Second Guessing, Spinning, and Withholding. He finds that certain organizational environments are conducive to game playing, especially conditions found in the reward systems, supply structures, and forecasting processes. But companies can discourage game playing by adjusting the ways they (a) reward employees, (b) manufacture goods and supply source materials, and (c) conduct their sales-forecasting activities. These remedies can improve forecasting performance.

* This article originally appeared in *Foresight: The International Journal of Applied Forecasting* (Spring 2009), and appears here courtesy of the International Institute of Forecasters.

Introduction

A well-established fact about forecasting is that the introduction of biases leads to inaccurate forecasts (Mentzer and Moon, 2005). One way that biases enter the picture is through forecast game playing, the intentional manipulation of forecasting processes to gain personal, group, or corporate advantage.

Adroit game players can win power, money, and other prizes by bending or breaking the rules of good forecasting practice. In the context of sales forecasting, game playing not only reduces the accuracy of a company's forecasts but can have deleterious impacts on company operations, and the operations of suppliers and customers as well.

My purpose here is to demonstrate the far-reaching effects of such sales-forecasting game playing on supply chains and to explore how companies can control the practice. I begin by describing various types of sales-forecasting games and their impact on the management of supply chains. I explore conditions that encourage game playing and conclude with recommendations to reduce or eliminate this practice in sales-forecasting processes.

The data for this study was obtained from audits conducted over a nine-year period by the Department of Marketing and Logistics at the University of Tennessee. I selected eleven audits that included firms in consumer packaged goods, major appliances, consumer electronics, home and garden supplies, beverages, food processing, and computer hard drives. Each audit typically involved interviews with 25–40 participants from forecasting, operations, production planning, marketing, sales, and senior-level positions, and addressed the company's sales-forecasting processes, issues, and competencies.

The Nature of Supply Chains

A supply chain has been defined as "all the organizations involved in the upstream and downstream flows of products, services, finances, and information from the ultimate supplier to the ultimate customer" (Mentzer et al., 2001, p. 2). The concept thus centers on the cross-company activities facilitating delivery of products and services to consumers. As Figure 4.8 indicates, products and services primarily flow downstream from suppliers, finances flow upstream in payment of products and services, and information travels in both directions across the various tiers of the chain. Supply chains frequently involve multiple firms at each tier, functioning more as a network of interacting companies than as a linear chain. One company's actions can affect many other companies along the chain. This highlights the importance of proper supply-chain management among interlinked companies.

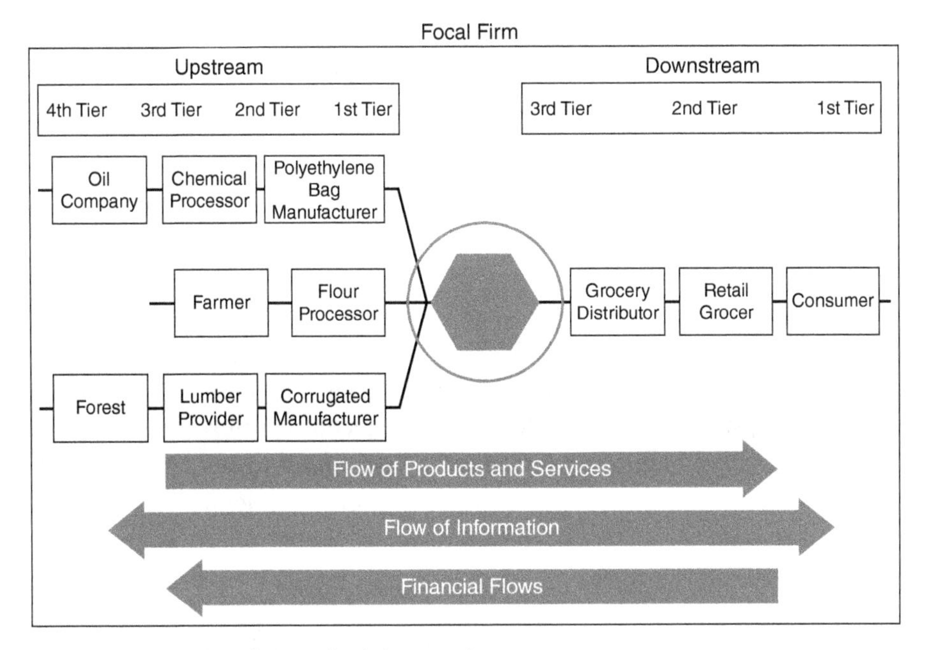

Figure 4.8 A Manufacturing Supply Chain Example

Due to the interdependence of companies in supply chains, any bias that enters into sales forecasts not only affects the company creating the forecast but also affects the operations of other companies along the chain. When individuals, groups, or companies "play games" with the sales-forecasting process, they hamper their own ability to operate effectively and potentially create far-reaching effects throughout the supply chain. It is important for companies to eliminate game-playing behaviors wherever they occur. The key here is honing our ability to identify the various forms of game playing that take place in sales forecasting.

Games People Play

During the course of this research, I observed a number of game-playing behaviors. My names for them are:

- Enforcing
- Filtering
- Hedging
- Sandbagging
- Second-guessing
- Spinning
- Withholding

In the following game definitions, the quotes are taken directly from the organizational participants who identified these behaviors.

> ***Enforcing**: Maintaining a higher forecast than actually anticipated sales, in order to keep forecasts in line with the organization's sales or financial goals.*

Enforcing is played when "taking the number down is not acceptable." In some companies, setting "stretch goals" is a tactic to motivate employees to exceed historical sales levels.

If forecasts fail to meet sales and financial goals, the numbers are changed to match the goals rather than reflect actual projections. Enforcing often occurs in a climate where employees feel there is "no option to not achieving sales goals." This precludes the reporting of forecasts that underachieve corporate goals and fosters "CYA" tactics: When forecasts simply reflect goals, no one needs to justify their forecast.

> ***Filtering**: Changing forecasts to reflect the amount of product actually available for sale in a given period.*

This game is used to mask capacity or supply issues. The supply functions are then able to "attain demand requirements," even though real demand is unattainable. Filtering occurs at a production planning level, where forecasts are changed within the master production schedule by manufacturing personnel. It happens in companies where healthy S&OP practices are absent or unenforced.

> ***Hedging**: Overestimating sales in order to secure additional product or production capacity.*

When production capacity shortages exist, field salespeople may use this game so that "the factory will have my stuff when I want it." Overestimating sales ensures that any potential "upside to the forecast" can be covered; it compensates for lack of manufacturing or supply flexibility and guarantees salespersons "will have plenty of inventory to meet their quotas at the end of the year." Other reasons for hedging include justifying higher budgets, seeking approval for advertising and promotions, asking for additional head-count, and selling new product development to senior management. Hedging is also used by customers when products from a supplier are in short supply or on allocation.

> ***Sandbagging**: Underestimating sales in order to set expectations lower than actually anticipated demand.*

Described by one participant as "gaming the quota" and by another as "skillful lying," this tactic sets sales quotas low in order to ensure they are exceeded, resulting in payment of bonuses and other compensation. Other reasons for sandbagging are found in the nature of the organization.

One participant described his firm as a "good news company" that encouraged overselling the forecast. In this environment, "if sales guys exceed their forecast there are high fives all around," but there are no penalties for forecasting inaccurately. Customer sandbagging occurs when customers associate forecasts with confirmed orders and are afraid of getting stuck with too much inventory.

> ***Second Guessing****: Changing forecasts based on instinct or intuition about future sales.*

Used when an individual or group mistrusts the forecasting process or has an "I know best" attitude. Production schedulers noted this game as an oft-used tactic. For example, one master scheduler described how she routinely changes forecasts because she feels that salespeople are "lowballing," yet she is the one who has to "live with the consequences" of excess inventories. Second-guessing is also used when individuals in power positions force changes to the forecast because they think they know their market better than anyone else in the company. An example discussed by several participants involved a vice president of sales who often "pulls numbers out of his hat" and orders changes to the forecast based on "gut feelings."

> ***Spinning****: Manipulating forecasts to obtain the most favorable reaction from individuals or departments in the organization.*

Spinning is used to "control the news cycle" in a company. One participant described his firm's salespeople as "very tactically focused" who give a "pie-in-the-sky forecast because that's what they think people want to hear." Another example is a sales director who asks her forecasters to "tell the truth and let her spin it" because she "knows how to hide certain numbers" that may not be well received by upper management. Spinning does not include legitimate management overrides of forecasts based on current data; it involves manipulation of the data in order to moderate the responses of higher-level managers who may react poorly to bad news.

> ***Withholding****: Refusing to share current sales information with other members of the organization.*

This game is used when news is good or bad. An example of withholding good news occurs when the sales force feels that it will sell well above the forecast but "put that information in their pocket" until they are sure sales will materialize. Withholding bad news is used as a protective mechanism because "no one wants to be the one to record bad news in the forecasting system." One participant commented, "For sales, it's a game of chicken. They keep forecasting the 'hockey stick' (a spike in demand at the end of a sales period corresponding to company sales goals) because they prefer to have just one screaming session with the boss" when sales don't materialize. Customer withholding often takes the form of refusal to share promotional plans or inventory policy changes with suppliers due to distrust of supply chain partners.

Unquestionably, these games bring bias into the forecasting process, degrading forecast accuracy. Most companies rely on accurate forecasting to help plan and execute procurement, manufacturing, and distribution operations. When individuals, groups, or companies intentionally play games with the forecast, they seriously hamper their own firm's ability to effectively perform these operations, inevitably disrupting the operations of other firms throughout the chain.

Consequences for the Supply Chain

Whether companies are in a make-to-stock, make- or assemble-to-order, or lean/just-in-time manufacturing environment, they attempt to match supply with demand so that adequate amounts are produced and delivered to the right place at the right time. Too little inventory results in production and distribution delays at customer locations; too much results in wasted money. When games are played with sales forecasts, demand signals are distorted, giving false information within and between firms. Such erroneous information can manifest itself in uncertainty, higher costs, and inter-firm behavioral dysfunction. Figure 4.9 depicts these outcomes and their relationships to specific game playing, both within a company and between customers and suppliers.

Greater Uncertainty in the Supply Chain

One serious result of game-playing bias is uncertainty within and between companies regarding how much supply is needed to meet demand.

Manufacturers and suppliers need to know what and how much to produce and how much manufacturing capacity is needed. In make-to-stock companies, businesses must decide where to store inventory, affecting warehousing and distribution space requirements. Companies also need volume information so they can select transportation modes and carriers with sufficient capacity to service customers.

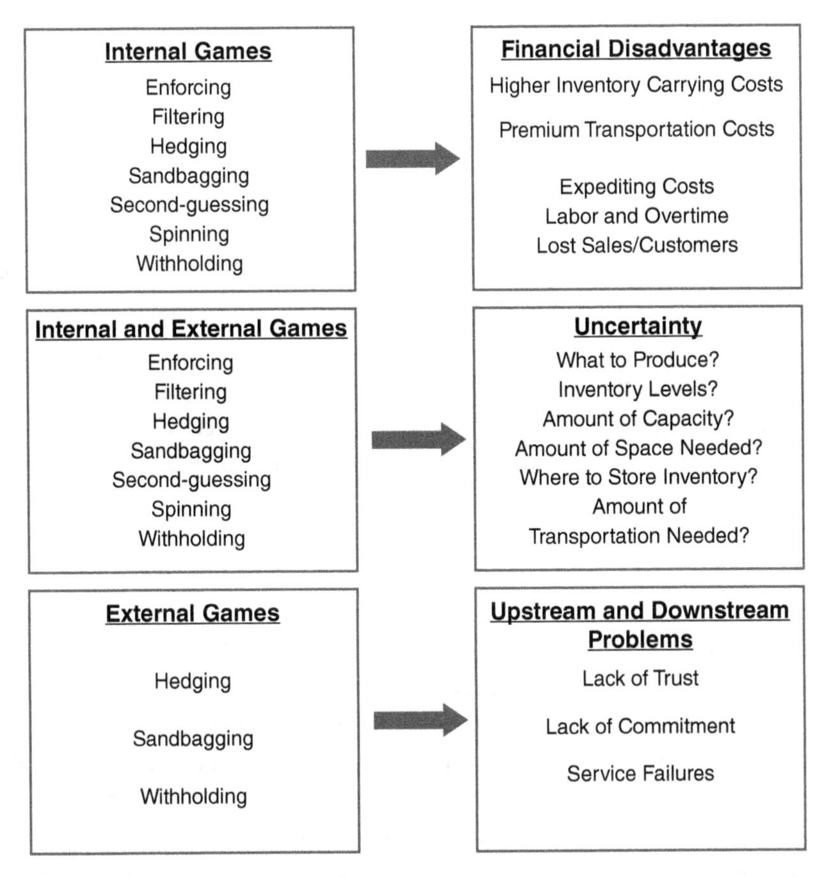

Figure 4.9 Sales Forecasting Games and Outcomes

These decisions must be made up and down the supply chain and are usually triggered by sales forecasts. Good decisions hinge on accurate and timely information. Bad decisions often result from biased information corrupted by game playing.

Hedging (overestimating sales in order to secure additional product or production capacity) sends a signal of higher-than-needed demand, which triggers surplus production of finished goods and excessive procurement of materials, components, and semi-finished items. The surplus travels up the supply chain, as suppliers react by passing unnecessary demand to their suppliers.

Sandbagging (underestimating sales in order to set expectations lower than anticipated demand) has the opposite effect: Manufacturing will schedule less than required volumes, and suppliers will do the same. When the higher volumes of sales materialize, there may not be sufficient time for the supply chain to react.

Withholding (refusing to share current sales information with other members of the organization) and other games that distort or delay the sharing of relevant information, prevent the supply chain from properly planning for and executing supply operations. The same result occurs when retail customers play games with manufacturers supplying their distribution centers and stores.

Excess Costs and Lost Sales

Primarily in make-to-stock companies, game playing results in excess cost from surplus inventory, expenses of expediting, and labor inefficiency. *Enforcing*, which substitutes sales goals for calculated forecasts, creates excess inventory as manufacturers gear up for demands unlikely to materialize. Likewise, *hedging* by retail customers or sales functions and *second-guessing* by executives or production planning force the procurement or production of "just-in-case" inventory that may be unnecessary in the sales period. *Withholding bad news* allows unwanted finished goods and supporting materials from suppliers to build up in the supply chain.

Excess labor costs throughout the supply are another liability, if manufacturing capacity is outstripped, if overtime is needed to meet production requirements, or if last-minute scheduling changes induce quality or rework problems or use of less cost-effective resources. Moreover, when excess inventory must be worked off and production slows, layoff expenses may ensue.

Excess labor costs also result from games that underestimate sales forecasts. *Sandbagging, second-guessing* (changing forecasts based on instinct or intuition about future sales) that the forecast is too high, and *withholding good news* all delay needed production volumes. As sales materialize and inventories drop below required volumes, manufacturing enters expedite mode. Production is ramped up, orders go out to suppliers, and companies all along the chain increase their production. The result is higher costs of overtime, premium transportation, and other expenses associated with expediting. Perhaps most seriously, if expedited production is unsuccessful, sales and even customers may be lost.

Upstream and Downstream Problems

When intentional overforecasting (hedging), underforecasting (sandbagging), or withholding sales, promotions, and other information affect upstream suppliers, these games can undermine the inter-firm trust and commitment essential to good supply chain management. Mistrust leads to second-guessing demand, resulting in excess inventories, customer service issues, and the costs associated with these problems. Mistrust grievously undermines the commitment to working closely together that is essential for companies to operate effective and efficient supply chains.

So game playing in sales forecasting causes serious problems not only within companies but throughout entire supply chains. Companies should strive to control, curtail, or eliminate the practice. To accomplish this, it is necessary to understand the conditions within firms that encourage, sustain, or tolerate game playing.

Conditions Fostering Game Playing

The conditions that compel individuals, groups, or businesses to play games with sales forecasts are often created and nurtured by the company. As shown in Figure 4.10, the three conditions that stand out as fostering game playing are reward structures, supply structures, and the sales-forecasting process itself.

Reward Structure

A company's priorities are established by how employees are rewarded. My research revealed certain aspects of reward structures tied to forecast game playing: the lack of accountability for forecast consequences, conflicting goals, and the lack of incentives for achieving forecasting accuracy.

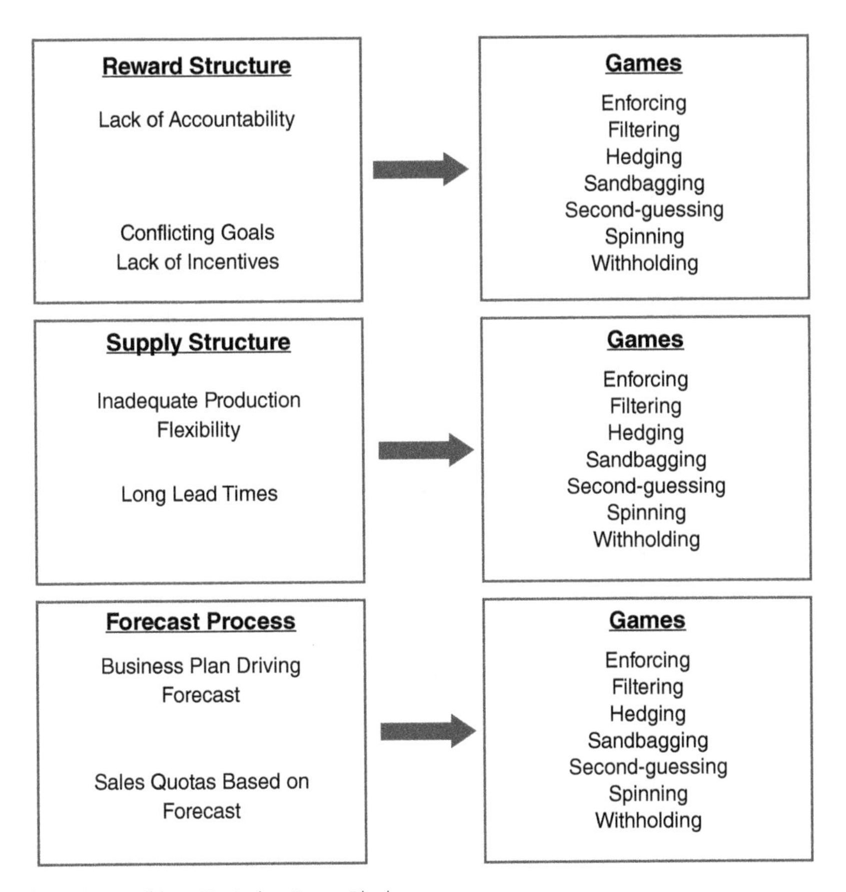

Figure 4.10 Conditions Fostering Game Playing

Lack of accountability is partly a consequence of the separation of responsibility for forecasting from the responsibility for customer service and inventory management. As one participant told us, "We haven't decided in this company who is responsible for excess inventory or being out of stock." Lack of accountability particularly enables hedging and sandbagging because there are no repercussions for the forecasters whose games drove excessive or inadequate inventory levels.

Conflicting goals between departments are what one participant likened to being "pushed and pulled by the objectives of different units." This climate fosters games such as hedging, sandbagging, second-guessing, and withholding, all of which work to the benefit of one department but against the objectives of other departments.

Then there are reward structures that lack incentives to forecast accurately, opening the door to sandbagging and hedging. "Underforecast during quota month, then overforecast the other months to make sure you get plenty of supply." "We never get in trouble for overforecasting."

Lack of incentives for forecasting accurately and lack of repercussions for poor forecasting enable employees to maximize circumstances that benefit themselves even if they harm the organization.

Supply Structure

One major contributor to game playing within a company is the lack of production flexibility/capacity. Production cannot always or immediately adapt to supply products in sufficient quantity and variety to meet demand. One participant explained, "We tend to overforecast because we aren't flexible in manufacturing, and we want to make sure our products are available." Another stated, "Salespersons get beat up when product is not available, so there is a push to have more inventory." Hedging and withholding knowledge of slow sales are used to ensure that particular products are available "just in case" sales materialize. Customers play these same games, particularly when products are on allocation and they know that only a percentage of their forecasts will be produced for them.

Long lead-times for finished goods and corresponding materials also encourage game playing. Increased use of offshore suppliers, by both retailers and manufacturers, has lengthened lead times and reduced flexibility of supply chains.

One company stated that "80% of items need to be ordered at least three months prior to production," with some materials having an even longer lead time. Knowing that response times are slow, people resort to hedging, filtering, and second-guessing the forecast to buffer spikes in demand and ensure adequate supplies. Compounding the lead time problem is that each retailer, manufacturer, and supplier in the supply chain has its own set of lead times.

The Forecasting Process Itself

The forecasting process itself can foster game playing. Forecasts tied to revenue or sales goals are unduly influenced by these goals, leading to games such as Enforcing and Spinning. Representative comments included "Corporate mandates forecasts," "Salespeople forecast what they need to sell, not what they think will sell," and "It would not be acceptable for me to forecast anything other than my targets."

When the forecasting process allows forecasts to be tied into sales quotas, salespeople are pressured to "play the quota games" of sandbagging and withholding, which often amounts to "lowballing" the forecast to influence the sales quota.

Forecast overrides are a third aspect of the problem with the forecasting process. When employees can override forecasts, it tempts people with an "I know best" attitude to make changes based on "gut feelings," which may not correspond to actual market conditions. This does not imply that numbers should never be changed, especially through legitimate processes such as S&OP. But when forecasts can be changed unilaterally without input from other stakeholders, principled forecasting methods are endangered. Paul Goodwin (2005) provides a prudent set of principles for when and how forecasts should be judgmentally adjusted.

How to Control Game Playing

In order for companies to reduce or eliminate game playing in their sales forecasting process, they need to address the conditions fostering these behaviors, those that are rooted in reward structures, supply structures, and the sales forecasting process itself.

Change the Reward Structure

Tie compensation to forecasting accuracy. When people are accountable for the results of their actions and rewarded accordingly, they have incentives to behave in desired ways. Therefore, those responsible for inputs to the forecast should have their compensation (base and bonus) tied in part to forecast accuracy. This discourages games such as hedging, sandbagging, and withholding that distort or prevent the flow of accurate information in forecasting processes.

Unify goals between supply and demand functions. Silo mentalities, turf battles, and suboptimization of functions occur in climates where functional areas compete rather than cooperate. When all functions are jointly responsible for customer service, inventory costs, and operational costs, the importance of accurate forecasting is heightened.

While this type of goal unification among functions is rare, it is a critical component of good supply-chain management. Game playing that exclusively benefits one's own functional area is drastically reduced.

Provide customers better incentives for forecasting accuracy. Offer preferred pricing or higher service levels to companies that forecast well. Stop conditioning customers to expect quarterly price breaks from low forecasts by varying timing of promotions and discounts.

Change the Supply Structure

Build more flexibility into production capabilities. When customers or salespersons think they cannot satisfy product demand due to manufacturing capacity or changeover issues, they naturally want to hedge by ordering or forecasting more than they need. When companies add capacity or capability to production operations, they help ensure adequate supply of products or materials, reducing or eliminating the temptation for hedging, filtering, withholding, and second-guessing in manufacturing. Some remedies include:

- Qualifying co-packers to make certain high-volume products
- Adding machine flexibility through purchasing general-purpose machines and equipment run by cross-trained employees (Coyle et al., 2009)
- Adding more production lines and facilities if long-range forecasts warrant
- Reducing changeover times and applying lean manufacturing techniques to get more flexibility out of existing capacity
- Reducing supplier lead times by selecting suppliers that are physically closer, have manufacturing flexibility, and work with reliable transportation carriers

Make a transition from an anticipation-based to a response-based supply chain. Anticipation-based supply chains make products to stock and wait for orders from customers; response-based supply chains take orders from customers, then make and ship the product. Response-based supply chains often use postponement strategies in which products are stored close to customers in a semi-completed state and finished to order. The highly reactive nature of this type of chain can help reduce or eliminate games like hedging, second-guessing, and withholding, since there is no need to build extra product to meet customer demands. Such a supply chain utilizes a partnership approach with suppliers and can include vendor-managed inventory systems (VMI); collaborative planning, forecasting, and replenishment (CPFR) programs; and other methods where forecasts and production schedules are shared and continually updated among supply-chain partners.

Change the Forecasting Process Itself

Delineate responsibilities and monitor performance. Clarifying forecast-accuracy targets, formalizing forecast-accuracy metrics, publishing accuracy achievements, performing root-cause analyses, analyzing the service level and inventory costs of forecast errors (see Catt, 2007), and having senior management monitor all this falls within an S&OP process.

Initiate a sales and operations planning (S&OP) process. S&OP is a cooperative, cross-functional effort that uses available market intelligence and key metrics to guide and synchronize demand and supply plans. The goal is a consensus forecast that provides a basis for action by all functions in a company, thus eliminating second-guessing and information withholding.

Build a collaborative planning, forecasting, and replenishment (CPFR) program with customers and suppliers. CPFR programs work toward developing a single forecast or production plan for an item, and sharing that forecast/plan with upstream suppliers. In order for CPFR to work, cooperation and honest information flow between companies are imperative (Coyle et al., 2009). Accurate data flow helps eliminate customer games such as hedging and withholding; there is less need for extra inventory to cover for uncertainty in the supply chain. The resulting saving in costs can be substantial (Boone and Ganeshan, 2008).

Keep sales forecasting separate from goal setting and quotas. Input from salespeople to the forecasting process is desirable, but discourage executives from pressuring forecasters to meet budget or sales targets. The forecasts should still be periodically compared to goals and quotas so that gaps can be dealt with through marketing programs, sales efforts, pricing, and other means.

Conclusion

Forecasting games take many forms. When individuals, groups, or companies play these games, the consequences reach well beyond the boundaries of a firm into the numerous tiers of a supply chain. An understanding of the conditions that foster game playing helps determine the actions companies can take to end these conditions. Controlling sales forecast game playing will almost certainly deliver a bigger payoff toward improving supply chain performance than will any new forecasting methodology.

REFERENCES

Boone, T., and R. Ganeshan (2008). The value of information sharing in the retail supply chain: Two case studies. *Foresight: International Journal of Applied Forecasting* 9, 12–17.

Catt, P. (2007). Assessing the cost of forecast error. *Foresight: International Journal of Applied Forecasting* 7, 5–10.

Coyle, J. J., C. J. Langley Jr., B. J. Gibson, R. A. Novack, and E. J. Bardi (2009). *Supply Chain Management: A Logistics Perspective*. Mason, OH: South-Western.

Goodwin, P. (2005). How to integrate managerial judgment with statistical forecasts. *Foresight: International Journal of Applied Forecasting*, 8–12.

Mentzer, J. T., and M. A. Moon (2005). *Sales Forecasting Management: A Demand Management Approach* (2nd ed.). Thousand Oaks, CA: Sage Publications.

Mentzer, J. T., W. DeWitt, J. S. Keebler, S. Min, N. W. Nix, C. D. Smith, and Z. G. Zacharia (2001). What is supply chain management? In J. T. Mentzer (ed.), *Supply Chain Management*. Thousand Oaks, CA: Sage Publications, 1–26.

4.9 ROLE OF THE SALES FORCE IN FORECASTING*

Michael Gilliland

It is widely assumed that the sales force should be engaged in the forecasting process. Salespeople are closest to the customer, the reasoning goes, so should be able to provide valuable insight on future customer demands. The only question is about how to secure sales force input—what system or process is best?

While involving salespeople in forecasting does seem like a good idea at first glance, Michael Gilliland poses a different question: Should we be soliciting sales force input at all? The problem, he asserts, is that the value of sale force input rests on three big assumptions:

1. Salespeople have the ability to accurately predict their customers' future buying behavior.
2. Salespeople will provide an honest forecast.
3. Improving customer-level forecasts will improve company performance.

Gilliland draws on his own and others' experience to identify the key issues in using sales force input to the forecasts. The answers are not black and white, but demonstrate the importance of thinking through how sales input should be provided, how to motivate reliable input, and how to judge the value to the organization.

Three Assumptions About Salespeople

A recurring question among business forecasters is how to incorporate input from the sales force. For example, from a recent LinkedIn discussion group:

> *My company is using Excel to do sales forecasting on a monthly basis, I am looking for a solution to automate the front part where salespeople will input their numbers directly in the system (instead of compiling different Excel spreadsheets currently). Please recommend a software that could automate this function.*

* This article originally appeared in *Foresight: The International Journal of Applied Forecasting* (Fall 2014), and appears here courtesy of the International Institute of Forecasters.

Involving salespeople in forecasting does indeed sound like a good idea. But the value of sales force engagement rests on three assumptions:

1. Salespeople have the ability to accurately predict their customers' future buying behavior.
2. Salespeople will provide an honest forecast to their management.
3. Improving customer-level forecasts improves company performance.

While sales force involvement is sometimes advocated as a best practice in the forecasting process, closer inspection reveals that such engagement may not be necessary or even advisable in many situations. I learned this from a humbling experience early in my forecasting career.

EXAMPLE

While managing the forecasting process for a large, processed-meats manufacturer, we generated weekly forecasts for approximately 500 finished items shipped through 10 distribution centers (DCs). After much persuasion, the VP of Sales reluctantly agreed to require forecasting input from his sales force.

Sales reps were provided with computer-generated customer/item forecasts for the larger customer/item combinations (those that constituted 80% of total sales volume at the DC). Reps were required to pencil in any changes from what was provided.

Within a few months we realized that the customer/item forecast adjustments coming from the sales reps were having no effect on accuracy of the DC/item forecast (which is the forecast we cared about for planning purposes). The time they spent on forecasting was wasted. A few months later, we (embarrassingly) pulled the plug on the sales rep forecasting experiment.

While this one failure doesn't damn sales force engagement to the heap of "worst practices" in forecasting, the circumstances of the experiment are not unique. This article examines common methods for obtaining sales force input to the forecasting process, the use of incentives for motivating sales rep forecasting performance, and whether improved customer/item forecasts provide any benefit.

Gathering Sales Force Input

Two main ways of soliciting sales force input are to ask sales for their forecasts, or to have them adjust forecasts that have been provided. One study argues for the latter method:

> *. . . we have found that salespeople generally do a poor job of taking their previous experience and turning that into an initial*

> *sales forecast. However, these same people are generally quite good at taking an initial quantitative sales forecast and qualitatively adjusting it to improve overall accuracy (Mentzer and Moon, 2005, p. 321).*

Other studies question the value of many types of judgmental adjustments to the statistical forecasts and find them often overused and ineffective (Fildes and Goodwin, 2007, and Fildes and colleagues, 2009). For example, at the manufacturer cited above, we found that 60% of adjustments to the initial statistical forecast actually made it worse! Mercifully, only about half of the statistical forecasts were adjusted.

Eric Wilson of Tempur Sealy dealt with this issue by appealing to the competitive nature of salespeople, urging them to "beat the nerd in the corner" and make adjustments only when certain they will improve the nerd's statistical forecast (Wilson, 2008). This procedure not only limited the adjustments being made to those forecasts the reps were confident they could improve upon but also provided the data to determine the effectiveness of their adjustments through use of the forecast value added (FVA) concept (Gilliland, 2013).

Recognizing that time spent forecasting is time taken away from selling, Stefan de Kok of ToolsGroup has suggested another way of gathering sales force input:

> *. . . there is huge value in getting input from humans, sales reps included. That input however should be market intelligence, not adjustments to quantities. For example, let the sales rep input that their account is running a promotion and then let the system determine what the quantity impact is. Not only will the uplift become more accurate quickly, but also the baseline will improve. Ultimately it becomes a lower effort (but not zero) for the sales people and their forecasts become much more reliable.*

Under this approach, salespeople would no longer provide (or adjust) specific numerical forecasts. Instead, they provide information (promotional plans, new store openings (or store closings), more (or less) shelf space, etc.) that can be put into the statistical forecasting models. Implementation, of course, requires software that can incorporate these inputs and assess their effectiveness in improving forecast accuracy. On the negative side, there is the risk of disenfranchising salespeople by removing their direct control of a specific numerical forecast.

Can Salespeople Forecast Their Customers' Behavior?

Don't salespeople have the closest contact with customers, and know their customers' future behavior better than anyone else in the organization? That is the common understanding:

> *Firms rely on their salespeople to stay in touch with customers. Good salespeople know what customers need and want and the sales prospects of the market they serve (Chen, 2005, p. 60).*
>
> *. . . experienced salespeople are likely to have more precise information about sales prospects in their own territories than central planners who are not close to the market (Mantrala and Raman, 1990, p. 189).*

But does this superior knowledge of their customers allow salespeople to accurately predict their customers' future buying behavior?

The value of sales force involvement is predicated upon their ability to provide better forecasts, or to provide information that can be used for better forecasts. But salespeople are employed because of their ability to sell—to execute the marching orders of sales management, to find and nurture prospective customers, and to achieve a revenue target. Knowledge of time-series modeling techniques, or demonstrated talent for predicting the future, are at best secondary or tertiary job requirements.

While implausible to believe that all salespeople have exceptional ability to predict the future buying behavior of their customers, let's assume this is true. Is this reason enough to engage them in the forecasting process?

Can You Trust the Forecast from a Salesperson?

It has long been recognized that biases and personal agendas influence the input from participants in the forecasting process. For example, from a 1976 article in the *Journal of Marketing*,

> *. . . asking a sales force for future sales estimates and using these inputs in any fashion requires a degree of caution and a concern for just how to interpret that information (Wotruba and Thurlow, 1976, p. 11).*

Even if we grant that salespeople can predict their customers' future buying behavior, is there reason to believe they will share this information? What is their motivation to provide an honest forecast?

Forecasts are used to make business decisions. Forecasts of future demand drive all sorts of important supply chain decisions regarding procurement, production, inventory, and distribution. Demand forecasts also assist decisions in finance (projecting cash flow and profit), marketing (how much promotional support is required?), and sales (quotas and compensation plans).

These decisions are not made in a vacuum, but in an intense political environment. Any participant in the forecasting process can have a personal agenda—some interest or incentive that outweighs the incentive for an unbiased forecast. Any time there is asymmetry in the personal cost of missing a forecast too high versus too low, there is the opportunity for intentional bias. Two obvious scenarios potentially biasing the sales force are:

1. **Quota Setting**: There may be a natural (and well justified) inclination for salespeople to lower expectations and argue that demand is going to tenuous, to help keep their quotas as low as possible. We often refer to this gaming as sandbagging.
2. **Maintaining Service**: A necessary condition for avoiding service issues is to have available inventory. While inventory planners might not be keen on keeping excess inventory (something contrary to their own incentives), the sales force can help assure an excess by purposely over forecasting future demand. (Note that this is opposite the behavior exhibited during quota-setting time.)

John Mello's earlier article in *Foresight* offers a comprehensive description of the "sales force game playing" and its impact on the firm and its supply chain (Mello, 2009).

So even if salespeople can accurately forecast their customers' future demand, there may be more personal benefit to bias the forecast than to give an honest answer.

Compensation as an Incentive for Honesty

In a basic compensation system, commissions are paid for achievement of a quota. It is perfectly reasonable to set the quota based on the potential of a sales territory, so as to reward each salesperson for their selling effort. (Note that selling effort is not necessarily proportional to sales volume, since some territories will have more potential than others.) However, "Inducing salespeople to disclose what they know about the market and providing incentives for them to work hard can sometimes be conflicting goals" (Chen, 2005, p. 60). In other words, there is every reason for the salespeople to turn in the lowest possible forecast.

The Gonik System

One way to address intentional bias is to make forecast accuracy itself a performance objective (along with meeting the quota and other objectives). To have any impact on behavior, the incentives for good forecasting would have to be large enough to overcome incentives for biasing the forecast. Gonik (1978) published a frequently-cited compensation program developed for IBM Brazil that purports to do just this.

In the Gonik system, the company provides an initial objective or quota (Q) for each salesperson. The salesperson then provides his or her forecast (F), and the F/Q ratio provides the horizontal axis on the bonus payout grid (a small section of which is shown in Table 4.3). The ratio of actual sales (A) to quota provides the vertical axis of the grid.

At period end, when actual sales are known, bonus payout can be determined from the grid. In Gonik's example, if John is given a quota of $Q = 500$, forecasts 500, and then sells 500, his bonus payout is 120% (since $F/Q = 1.0$ and $A/Q = 1.0$); that is, he received a 20% premium for his accurate forecasting.

If John had sold 750 (150% of his quota), while still having forecasted 500, his bonus payout would be 150%. So he was properly awarded for his hard work (exceeding his quota), even though his forecast was off.

However, if John had upped his forecast to 750 and then sold 750, this would have awarded him a 180% bonus payout (an additional 30% premium for his hard work and accurate forecasting).

In the other direction, if John sold only 250 (on a quota of 500 and forecast of 500), payout would have been just 30%. But if he had forecast 250, payout would be 60%.

Note that Gonik's system does not appear to protect against bias in the quota setting by management. (This was pointed out by Len Tashman.) Since Q is in the denominator, management has an incentive to set higher quotas than they would have otherwise, as a higher Q reduces payouts at all levels of Forecast and Actual.

Menu of Contracts

A somewhat more complicated alternative to the Gonik scheme is to offer a menu of contracts (alternative bonus plans) to each salesperson.

Table 4.3 Gonik Bonus Payout Grid

		F/Q (Forecast/Quota)				
		0.0	**0.5**	**1.0**	**1.5**	**2.0**
A/Q (Actual/Quota)	**0.0**	0%	0%	0%	0%	0%
	0.5	30%	60%	30%	0%	0%
	1.0	60%	90%	120%	90%	60%
	1.5	90%	120%	150%	180%	150%
	2.0	120%	150%	180%	210%	240%

A menu of contracts system assumes that each salesperson has special knowledge about the market (for example, potential sales volume) that is unknown to central planners. The salesperson does not want to reveal this information because it could be used to set a higher quota. However, the very process of choosing a particular contract (presumably the one likely to maximize his or her bonus payout) reveals market information to the central planners.

We want the sales force to work hard, sell as much as possible, and to accurately forecast future sales. Both the menu of contracts and the Gonik approach show that it may be possible to motivate this desired behavior. But then the effort spent evaluating contracts or generating forecasts is effort that could be spent building relationships with customers and making sales. This is an unspoken opportunity cost.

Does Improving Customer Level Forecasts Always Matter?

Let's continue to assume that our sales force can accurately forecast customer buying behavior and also that our sales force is honest, willingly providing accurate, unbiased forecasts for each customer. We must now ask: Is engaging the sales force worth the effort? Will better customer-level forecasts improve overall company performance?

Many (perhaps most) companies do not need customer-level forecasts for planning purposes. To maintain appropriate inventory and customer service (order fill) levels, they find it sufficient to have a good forecast for each item at each point of distribution (which we'll refer to as the DC). Therefore, it doesn't matter whether individual customer/item forecasts are good or bad as long as they aggregate to a reasonably good forecast at DC/item (or other intermediate level).

When customer level forecasts are unbiased, then positive and negative errors in the customer/item forecasts will tend to cancel out when aggregated to intermediate levels. In this situation, improved customer-level forecasts will likely have little effect improving DC/item forecasts, so such effort would be a waste.

However, when customer-level forecasts are biased (as we suspect they sometimes may be when coming from the sales force), then improving their forecasts (reducing bias) would translate directly to more accurate DC/item forecasts. In such circumstances, the focus should be on efficiently gathering forecasts for the biggest customers who dominate demand for the item at the DC. (It is probably not worth the effort to solicit forecasts for the many small customers that have little impact on total DC demand.)

It is true that some organizations utilize customer level forecasts for account planning, setting sales quotas, etc. So there can be other direct applications of customer level forecasting. But improving supply chain operations and demand fulfillment, in many situations, is not one of them.

A related issue, not covered in this article, is the appropriate level of aggregation from which to reconcile the hierarchy of forecasts. It may be that a top-down or middle-out approach is more effective than a bottom-up approach (which starts with customer/item forecasts).

Commitments Are Not Forecasts

In response to a blog post in which I questioned the value of sales force input to forecasting (Gilliland 2014), John Hughes of software vendor Silvon presented a counter-argument in favor of engaging the sales force.

> *Sales people have a responsibility to themselves and their company to try and predict sales for many good reasons, mostly to help balance company assets (inventory) that drive customer service. Engaging sales people directly with an on line tool ensures their commitment to the numbers and publicly displays the results for all to see and grade them. . . . [T]hey have the same responsibility as the rest of us to commit to a task and then complete it.*[1]

While engaging the sales force for their commitment to a number is a legitimate objective, this is not the same as providing a forecast. Presumably, there is a reward for beating the commitment (or at least a penalty for failing to achieve it), naturally biasing the commitment toward the low side. Empirical evidence of bias could easily be found by seeing whether actuals are historically below, above (what we might expect), or about the same as the commitment.

There is nothing wrong with having quotas, stretch targets, budgets, commitments, and any other numbers that float around the organization for informational and motivational use—as long as we recognize their different purposes. These are not the same as an "unbiased best guess at what is really going to happen" which is what the forecast represents. The fatal flaw of "one number forecasting" (aka "a single version of the truth") is that it reduces quotas, targets, budgets, commitments, and forecasts to a single number—when they are meant to be different!

Conclusions

It is good to be wary of any inputs into the forecasting process, and this naturally includes inputs from sales. Forecasting process participants have personal agendas, and when we ask someone for a forecast, we shouldn't expect an honest answer.

There can be good reasons to engage the sales force in forecasting; we just can't assume this is always the case. In the spirit of "economy of process," unless there is solid evidence that input from the sales force has improved the forecast (to a degree commensurate with the cost of engaging them), we are wasting their time—and squandering company resources that could better be spent generating revenue.

On a personal note, if you find that your salespeople are not improving the forecast, then you'll make them very happy—and give them more time to sell—by no longer requiring their forecasting input. Going back to the original question that started this discussion, rather than implementing new software to gather sales input, it may be simpler, cheaper, and ultimately more beneficial, to not pursue their input.

Notes

1 Engaging the sales force: Forecasts vs. commitments. *The Business Forecasting Deal* March 19, 2014. http://blogs.sas.com/content/forecasting/2014/03/19/engaging-the-sales-force-forecasts-vs-commitments/.

REFERENCES

Chen, F. (2005). Salesforce incentives, market information, and production / inventory planning. *Management Science* 51 (1) (January), 60–75.

Fildes, R., and P. Goodwin (2007). Good and bad judgment in forecasting. *Foresight: International Journal of Applied Forecasting 8* (Fall), 5–10.

Fildes, R., P., Goodwin, M., Lawrence, and K. Nikolopoulos (2009). Effective forecasting and judgmental adjustments: An empirical evaluation and strategies for improvement in supply-chain planning. *International Journal of Forecasting* 25 (1), 3–23.

Gilliland, M. (2013). Forecast value added: A reality check on forecasting practices. *Foresight: International Journal of Applied Forecasting* 29 (Spring), 14–18.

Gilliland, M. (2014). To gather forecasting input from the sales force—or not? *The Business Forecasting Deal* March 14. http://blogs.sas.com/content/forecasting/.

Gonik, J. (1978). Tie salesmen's bonuses to their forecasts. *Harvard Business Review* (May–June), 116–122.

Mantrala, M. K., and K. Raman (1990). Analysis of sales force incentive plan for accurate sales forecasting and performance. *International Journal of Research in Marketing* 7, 189–202.

Mello, J. (2009). The impact of sales forecast game playing on supply chains. *Foresight: International Journal of Applied Forecasting* 13 (Spring 2009), 13–22.

Mentzer, J. T., and M. Moon (2005). *Sales Forecasting Management* (2nd ed.). Thousand Oaks, CA: Sage Publications.

Wilson, J. E. (2008). How to speak sales. IBF Supply Chain Forecasting Conference. Phoenix, AZ, February 2008.

Wotruba, T. R., and M. L. Thurlow (1976). Sales force participation in quota setting and sales forecasting. *Journal of Marketing* 40(2) (April), 11–16.

4.10 GOOD AND BAD JUDGMENT IN FORECASTING: LESSONS FROM FOUR COMPANIES*

Robert Fildes and Paul Goodwin

In their investigation into corporate forecasting practices, Robert Fildes and Paul Goodwin uncover evidence of excessive use of judgmental adjustment to statistical forecasts. From an examination of more than 60,000 forecasts in four supply chain companies, they found that making judgmental adjustments to statistical forecasts is not only a popular activity (75% of the forecasts were adjusted) but one that is far too popular for the good of the companies.

Fildes and Goodwin explore the motivations that lead business forecasters to this sometimes counterproductive behavior and offer recommendations to ensure that forecast adjustments are made for the right reasons. They find that forecasters usually feel they have good justifications for making adjustments, but in reality are overly confident and biased toward *recency*—putting more emphasis on recent history while treating the more distant past as less relevant.

Since making a large adjustment takes some nerve, the authors speculate that larger adjustments will be made only for very good reasons. And, sure enough only these larger adjustments were found to be worth making. Interestingly, large negative (downward) adjustments were more likely to improve forecast accuracy than large positive adjustments.

Introduction

If you are a forecaster in a supply chain company, you probably spend a lot of your working life adjusting the statistical demand forecasts that roll down your computer screen. Like most forecasters, your aim is to improve accuracy. Perhaps your gut feeling is that a statistical forecast just doesn't look right. Or maybe you have good reason to make an adjustment because a product is being promoted next month and you know that the statistical forecast has taken no account of this.

But if you are spending hours trying to explain the latest twist in every sales graph or agonizing over the possible impact of Wal-Mart's forthcoming price cut,

* This article originally appeared in *Foresight: The International Journal of Applied Forecasting* (Fall 2007), and appears here courtesy of the International Institute of Forecasters.

is this time well spent? Would it make any difference to forecast accuracy if you halved the number of adjustments you made and spent your newly found free time chatting with colleagues at the water cooler about the Broncos' latest signing, Wayne Rooney's soccer injury, or the best beaches in the Caribbean?

To answer this question, we have carried out an in-depth study of four British-based supply chain companies:

1. A nationwide retailer
2. A leading international food company
3. A subsidiary of a U.S. pharmaceutical company
4. A manufacturer of own-label domestic cleaning products

We collected data on over 60,000 forecasts, interviewed the companies' forecasters, and observed forecast review meetings where managers discussed and approved any adjustments that they thought were necessary. The results allowed us to identify which types of adjustments tend to improve accuracy substantially, which make the forecasts worse, and which make little difference, but simply waste management time. We supplemented this data with survey evidence of 149 (mostly U.S.) forecasters.

Adjustments Galore

Adjusting forecasts is certainly a popular activity in all our companies, as shown in Figure 4.11. In fact, the forecasters spend so much time making adjustments that they are probably making a significant contribution to world demand for headache tablets.

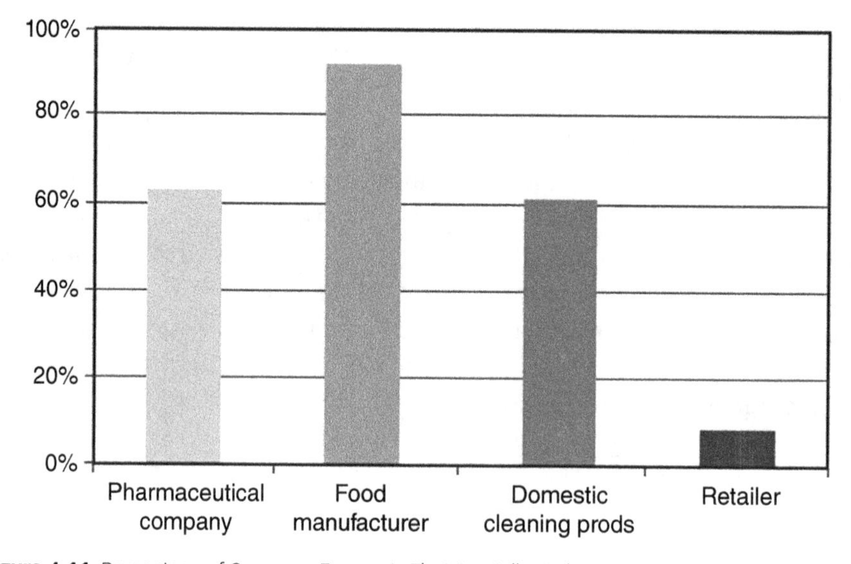

Figure 4.11 Percentage of Company Forecasts That Are Adjusted

Those working for the food manufacturer adjusted 91% of the forecasts that had been generated by their expensive and sophisticated forecasting software. The four forecasters employed by the retailer adjusted only about 8% of their forecasts, but then they had over 26,000 forecasts to make each week, so there probably wasn't enough time to put their mark on each forecast. The pharmaceutical company held 17 forecast review meetings every month, tying up about 80 person hours of valuable management time. On average 75% of the statistical forecasts in our companies were adjusted. Our survey of forecasters (Fildes and Goodwin, 2007) tells much the same story, with just 25% of the forecasts based only on a statistical method. Judgment, either used exclusively (25%) or combined with a statistical forecast (50%), was regarded as important or very important by most of the respondents.

What sort of adjustments did the forecasters make? Many of the adjustments were small, and in some cases very small. It was as if forecasters sometimes simply wanted to put their calling card on forecasts by tweaking them slightly to show that they were still doing their job. Indeed, we received anecdotal evidence from a consultant that people at review meetings tend to adjust more of the forecasts that are presented earlier in the meetings, rather than later on. As the meeting progresses they tire and feel that they have already done enough to justify the meeting, so later forecasts are simply waved through.

TIP

Review the important A-class first.

Of course, showing that they were still alive was not the only reason the forecasters made adjustments. They usually felt that they had good justifications for making them and we found that often this was the case. The problem is that people have a tendency to find a ready explanation for every movement in the sales graphs, including those swings which are really random. And this makes them overconfident that their adjustments will increase accuracy.

> *Our customers were stocking up two months ago because they were anticipating a price increase so our sales swung upwards.*
>
> *Okay, they didn't stock up in the previous year when they knew there was going to be a price increase because interest rates were high and there was a lot of uncertainty about.*

We are brilliant at inventing theories for everything we observe. Scott Armstrong (1985, p. 54) discusses a case where a Nobel laureate published a hypothesis to explain an oddity in the graph of a macroeconomic variable. Later, it was shown that the anomaly was the result of an arithmetic error. At 13:01 on a December day in 2003 after Saddam Hussein had been captured, the price of U.S. Treasuries rose. Half an hour later, the price fell. Taleb (2007, p. 74) reports that the Bloomberg News channel used the capture of Saddam to explain both price movements. The unfortunate, dull statistical forecast can offer no competition to these colorful, but often groundless, tales and so it gets adjusted.

The Illusion of Control

All this adjustment behavior can have some odd consequences, according to psychologists. When we engage in activities that involve skill and effort, we normally believe that we have more control over what we are doing. For example, if you develop your skills and invest effort in learning to play a musical instrument, you will make fewer mistakes. The same applies to controlling the ball in a sport like football. But many of the swings in a sales graph are beyond the forecaster's control. They are the result of random, unpredictable events. Yet, because forecasters see making adjustment as a skillful activity, they can develop the false belief that they have control over the demand that they are trying to forecast and hence that they can predict the movements in the sales graph. The phenomenon is called the illusion of control. It's likely to motivate you to make even more adjustments. After all, the more you adjust, the more control you think you have.

Don't adjust without an explicit, recorded reason.

When Do Adjustments Improve Accuracy and When Do They Not?

Despite these concerns, judgmental adjustments to statistical forecasts can still play a useful role in improving accuracy. Our study found that on average they lowered the average percentage error (MAPE) by 3.6 percentage points for all companies except the retailer. But this modest improvement masks considerable variation in the effectiveness of the adjustments. Is it possible to filter out the type of adjustments that are likely to be useless or even damaging to accuracy?

We first examined how the direction of adjustments affected forecast accuracy. We contrasted adjustments that increased the forecast (positive adjustments) with those that lowered it (negative adjustments). For one of our four companies, Figure 4.12 shows the extent to which these adjustments led to improvements. The results are typical of our three non-retail companies.

The graph breaks the size of the adjustments into quartiles: Quartile 25% represents the smallest 25% of the adjustments while quartile 100% represents the largest quarter of the adjustments. Two results are immediately apparent: (1) larger adjustments tend to improve accuracy and (2) negative adjustments tend to be much more beneficial than positive.

Why are larger adjustments more likely to improve accuracy? To make a large adjustment takes some nerve. Senior managers may be on to you if you make a big adjustment and then things go badly wrong. This means that the larger adjustments are likely to be made for very good reasons. You are likely to have reliable information about some important future events that will cause the statistical forecast to have a large error. In contrast, the smaller adjustments are the tweaks that we mentioned earlier or the result of a forecaster hedging his or her bets because information about a future event is unreliable. The lesson is clear: While small adjustments, by definition, can do relatively little harm to accuracy, they are generally a waste of time. Doodling in your notepad is likely to be more productive and certainly more therapeutic.

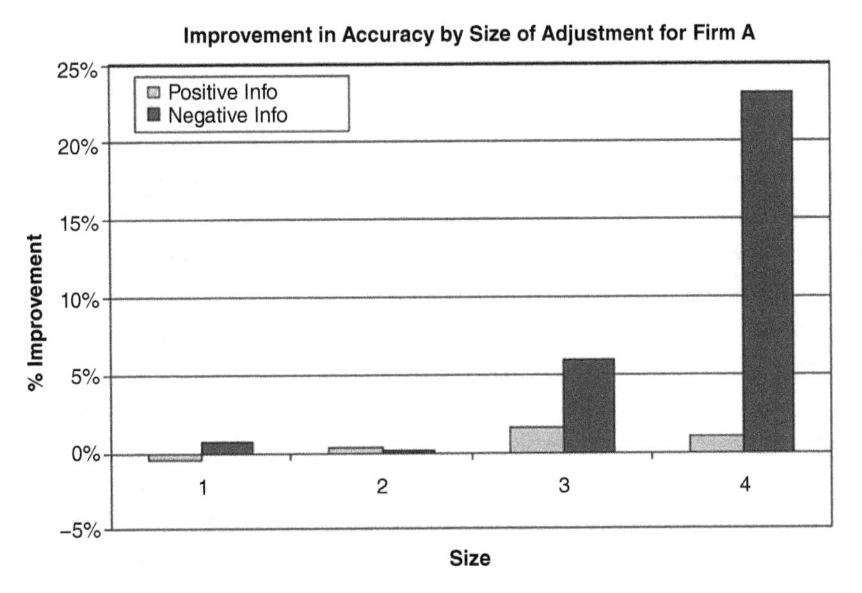

Figure 4.12 Effect of Adjustments by Size and Direction (% improvement measures the reduction in Median APE, so higher is better)

Why do the positive adjustments fare so much worse than the negative? Psychologists tell us that people have an innate bias toward optimism. For example, most construction projects usually take longer to complete and cost far more than was originally predicted. Some of this may be a result of deliberate misrepresentation (see Flyvbjerg et al., 2005) to gain contracts, but there is evidence that optimism bias still plays a significant role in these poor estimates. It seems, therefore, that when our company forecasters are asked to estimate the effects of a sales promotion campaign or a price reduction, they cannot resist being overly optimistic. And of course this reflects the enthusiasm of their colleagues in sales or marketing. In contrast, when they make a negative adjustment they are much more realistic in their expectations.

A particularly damaging intervention is called a wrong-sided adjustment. For example, this occurs when you adjust the forecast upward but should have made a negative adjustment. Suppose that the statistical forecast was for 600 units and you adjusted upward to make a forecast of 650 units. When actual sales turn out to be 580, you'll realize that your adjustment was in the wrong direction. Any wrong-sided adjustment is bound to reduce accuracy. Yet surprisingly, our companies made a large number of these adjustments, particularly when the direction of adjustment was positive. More than a third of the positive adjustments made by the nonretailers were in the wrong direction. If we could remove even 50% of the wrong-sided positive adjustments, accuracy would be improved by 7 percentage points. For negative adjustments the effects were much more limited.

TIP

Beware the enthusiasm of your marketing and sales colleagues!

We investigated whether the wrong-sided adjustments might be a result of misjudging the timing of promotion effects (e.g., expecting an immediate uplift in sales when the actual increase is delayed) but found no evidence of this. Once again, misplaced optimism seems to be the most likely explanation.

But how can forecasters make fewer wrong-direction mistakes? We've explored some possible solutions. We believe that the first stage in eliminating wrong-sided adjustments is to catalogue the reasons behind each and every adjustment. In our survey 69% of companies claimed to do this. But of the companies we observed, none collected this information effectively. Second, when large errors have occurred, a post-mortem on the reasons has the potential to help the next time similar incidents threaten. And this should be done as part of a forecast quality improvement program rather than in an atmosphere of blame. An effective forecasting support system can help by encouraging the compilation of the historical record to make life easy for the forecaster to look back at past events (such as promotions) and to reflect on how today's circumstances match with the past record. In our research we showed just how this can be done through the design of effective software that lets the forecaster examine the past record of similar analogous promotions (Lee et al., 2007).

TIP

Collect information on key drivers, learn from large errors.

The Importance of Definitions

So far, we have not mentioned the retailer. When we analyzed the accuracy of the retailer's adjustments, they looked awful. The positive adjustments its forecasters made more than doubled the MAPE from 32% to 65%. Moreover, 83% of these adjustments were either too large or in the wrong direction. Something odd was going on. Why would the forecasters of a major national company be spending so much time and effort making mediocre statistical forecasts so much worse?

Most people would probably consider a forecast to be an estimate of the most likely level of future demand. It turned out that the retail forecasters were estimating a different quantity. Often they were trying to determine the levels of demand that only had a small chance of being exceeded—that is, the level that would limit stockouts. Determining this level would tell them how much inventory they needed to hold. For example, their statistical forecasting system might provide a demand forecast of 500 units but they would adjust this upwards to 550 units, reasoning that this level of inventory would be sufficient to cover anything but the most extreme level of demand. In an informal way they were forecasting fractiles, as discussed by Goodwin in the Hot New Research Column in *Foresight,* Summer 2007. So our MAPEs were unfairly measuring the effectiveness of the forecasters' adjustment because they were not trying to predict the actual demand.

However, there were still serious problems with the retail forecasters' approach. First, they had never clearly defined what they were forecasting. They simply referred to their adjusted figures as "forecasts," posing the obvious danger that other managers would wrongly interpret these as estimates of the most likely level of demand and then make decisions based on this assumption. Second, their approach was informal. They had never determined what probability of a stockout was appropriate in order to balance inventory-holding costs against the costs of disappointing customers (see Catt, 2007). Nor had they done any analysis to see whether their adjustments were leading to over- or understocking for the many products they sold.

Finally, the forecasters were trying to do two jobs at once. They were adjusting the statistical forecasts for special events like promotions and, at the same time, adjusting them to estimate inventory requirements. They may have been taking on too much. The evidence from psychologists is that humans have limited information-processing capacity and that better judgments can be obtained by breaking judgmental estimation down into simpler and easier tasks—a process called decomposition.

TIP

Make your forecast your estimate of most-likely future demand. Then adjust to account for the relative costs of under- and overforecasting.

History Is Not Bunk

Henry Ford is alleged to have said that history is more or less bunk. Many of the forecasters in our companies had the same philosophy. In review meetings they examined most recent movements in sales graphs with forensic intensity while they often ignored earlier data. In one company, the forecasters told us that they never fit their statistical methods to demand data that are more than three years old because "back then, the trends were different." Sometimes the software they had bought seemed to share the same attitude—the active data base only went back three years!

There was no evidence that they had tested this claim. So great was the bias toward recency that sometimes statistical methods were only fitted to the last six months' data. This did not give these methods much of a chance. As Rob Hyndman and Andrey Kostenko wrote in the Spring 2007 issue of *Foresight,* statistical methods can require quite lengthy periods of data to detect underlying patterns, even when the demand data is well behaved and the level of randomness in the series is relatively low. Moreover, the methods commonly found in business forecasting software are designed so they can adapt to changes in trends or seasonal patterns if these occur. If you restrict the data available to your statistical methods, then you are unlikely to be making judgmental adjustments from a reliable baseline.

TIP

Use all the data you can lay your hands on. Discard data only with good reason.

Conclusions

Judgmental adjustment of statistical forecasts is a crucial part of the forecasting process in most companies. It is often not practical to use statistical methods to model the effect of forthcoming events that you know are likely to have a big impact on demand. Management judgment then has to step in to bridge this gap and, if applied correctly, it can bring great benefits to forecasts. However, our study has shown that these potential benefits are largely negated by excessive intervention and overoptimism. Indeed, had our nonretail forecasters been banned from making positive adjustments to their forecasts, but still been allowed to make negative adjustments, their judgmental adjustments would have improved the MAPE by over 20 percentage points, rather than the mediocre 3.6 points that we reported earlier.

In most companies, however, banning all positive adjustments would not be a realistic strategy. The answer is to make these adjustments with more care and only on the basis of better market information. In the long run, software enhancements might be helpful here.

Our study also emphasizes the importance of having a clear definition of what you are forecasting. It's not good for morale when a colleague complains you've overforecasted demand by 40% when that's not what you were trying to predict.

Finally, we leave you with these recommendations on your adjustment policy.

- Accept that many of the movements in your sales graph are random. You have no control over them and they cannot be predicted.
- Small adjustments are likely to waste time and effort and may damage accuracy.
- Positive adjustments (moving the statistical forecast upwards) should only be made with care. Be especially cautious about being too optimistic.
- Give statistical forecasting methods a chance; they need plenty of data to detect underlying patterns in demand.
- Define clearly what you are forecasting.

REFERENCES

Armstrong, J. S. (1985). *Long-Range Forecasting* (2nd ed.). New York: John Wiley & Sons.

Catt, P. M. (2007). Assessing the cost of forecast error: A practical example. *Foresight: International Journal of Applied Forecasting* 7, 5–10.

Fildes, R., and P. Goodwin (2007). Against your better judgment? How organizations can improve their use of management judgment in forecasting. *Interfaces* 37 (6), 570–576.

Flyvbjerg, B., M. K. Skamris Holm, and S. L. Buhl (2005). How (in)accurate are demand forecasts in public works projects? The case of transportation. *Journal of the American Planning Association* 71 (2), 131–146.

Goodwin, P. (2007). Supermarket forecasting: Check out three new approaches. *Foresight: International Journal of Applied Forecasting* 7, 53–55.

Hyndman, R. J., and A. V. Kostenko (2007). Minimum sample size requirements for seasonal forecasting models. *Foresight: International Journal of Applied Forecasting* 6, 12–15.

Lee, W. Y., P. Goodwin, R. Fildes, K. Nikolopoulos, and M. Lawrence (2007). Providing support for the use of analogies in demand forecasting tasks. *International Journal of Forecasting* 23, 377–390.

Taleb, N. N. (2007). *The Black Swan.* London: Allen Lane.

Acknowledgments: This research was supported by Engineering and Physical Sciences Research Council (EPSRC) grants GR/60198/01 and GR/60181/01. Michael Lawrence, Kostantinos Nikolopoulos, and Alastair Robertson contributed substantially to the data analysis.

4.11 WORST PRACTICES IN NEW PRODUCT FORECASTING*

Michael Gilliland

Organizations commit significant resources to new product development and release, often basing the "go/no-go" decisions on the favorability of demand forecasts. But how trustworthy and reliable are new product forecasts? Are they based on any sales history or other quantifiable information?

Common practices, Michael Gilliland argues, cast doubt on the trustworthiness and reliability of new product forecasts. Forecasting by analogy is a popular approach, basing the new product's forecast on sales of similar products from the past. But selection of the analogs is subject to *cherry picking*—choosing only successful previous products, and ignoring past failures.

Other worst practices include reverse engineering the forecast (to meet organizational hurdles on volume or revenue), the "hold-and-roll" for pushing forecast misses into future periods, and ignoring a new product's impact on the overall product portfolio (i.e., the potential for cannibalization). Gilliland observes that any of these worst practices also apply to forecasting of existing products, not just new products.

New product forecasting (NPF) is perhaps the most difficult and thankless of all forecasting endeavors. Organizations commit significant resources

---

* This article originally appeared in *Journal of Business Forecasting* (Winter 2012–2013), and appears here courtesy of Dr. Chaman Jain, editor in chief.

to new product development and release, and sometimes even "bet the company" on promising new ideas. Yet the foundation on which such decisions are made—the forecast of unit sales and revenue—may be very shaky, ill-conceived, and implausible. This article identifies several of the "worst practices" that can plague new product forecasting.

Unrealistic Accuracy Expectations

Perhaps the most fundamental worst practice of new product forecasting, like any kind of forecasting, is to have unrealistic expectations for the accuracy of the forecasts.

Forecasting is about knowing the future, something humans (and organizations) are not necessarily very good at accomplishing. Consistently accurate forecasting is possible when three conditions are met:

1. The behavior we are forecasting (e.g., demand for a product) is guided by a structure or rule (known as the data generating process [DGP]).
2. There is not too much randomness in the behavior (i.e., demand follows the DGP quite closely).
3. The DGP does not change within our forecasting horizon (i.e., demand follows the DGP in all future time periods we are forecasting).

When these conditions are met, along with the assumption that we understand the DGP and have it correctly expressed in our forecasting model, then we can generate accurate forecasts. If any of these conditions don't hold, or if we fail to correctly express the DGP in our model, then accurate forecasting is much less likely.

In new product forecasting, we of course have no prior demand behavior to analyze. Even using the method of *forecasting by analogy* (where we look to the prior introduction of similar products), determination of the DGP is still highly speculative. It would seem reasonable, therefore, to temper our faith in the accuracy of new product forecasts.

What we want to avoid is making huge, dangerous bets based on the assumption of accurate new product forecasts. If the above argument isn't convincing, then take a look at your history of past new product introductions. Look at the forecasts prior to the product releases, and look at the actuals as they rolled in after the release. How accurate were your forecasts? Some perhaps were reasonably good, but most were poor to awful. Each new product is released with an expectation for success in the marketplace, even though we know most new products fail. Looking at your organization's history of forecasting new products gives you the hard evidence of your new product forecasting capability.

Reverse Engineering the Forecast

Well before a new product is released, there has usually been a management review of the new product idea so that it can be "approved" and funded for development. As part of the review process, product management (or whoever is pitching the new product idea) is expected to provide estimates of product cost and demand, so that the financial implications of the new product can be assessed.

The review board may set a minimum units or revenue hurdle that must be met to obtain approval for the new product idea. Not surprisingly, those proposing the new product idea will provide a forecast high enough to meet the hurdle. Generating such a forecast is not an objective and dispassionate process, seeking an "unbiased best guess" at what demand is really going to be. Rather, generating that forecast was an application of reverse engineering, starting with the forecast that was needed for management approval, and then figuring out some justification for why that forecast is correct.

Reverse engineering the new-product forecast is just a special case of the worst practice of *evangelical forecasting*, where the "forecast" (which should be an unbiased best guess of what is really going to happen) gets contaminated by the "target" (what management wants to see happen). Such an environment can be quite disheartening to the professional forecaster, whose role becomes not to objectively guess the future but to generate numbers that management will approve.

Cherry-Picking Analogies

Forecasting by analogy is a commonly used method for generating new product forecasts. In this approach, we start by identifying similar (analogous) products that have been introduced in the past. Analogs are selected by what we believe are relevant attributes, such as type of product or its function (e.g., smart phone or men's dress shirt), features, size, color, intended market, etc. As Ken Kahn (2006) stated in his book, *New Product Forecasting: An Applied Approach*, "Looks-like analysis (i.e., forecasting by analogy) is a popular technique applied to line extensions by using sales of previous product line introductions to profile sales of the new product."

The use of analogies is not, in itself, an unreasonable approach to NPF. What better way to gain perspective on what might happen with a new product than to look at the history of prior introductions of similar products? The worst practice comes into play, however, when the analogs are "cherry picked" to favor the desired outcome.

Figure 4.13 shows the first 20 weeks of sales for a group of analogous DVDs (all sharing the two attributes Rating [= R] and Genre [= Horror]). While they all share a similar profile (biggest sales in the first week of release, and rapidly falling thereafter), the actual units sold in the release week range from around

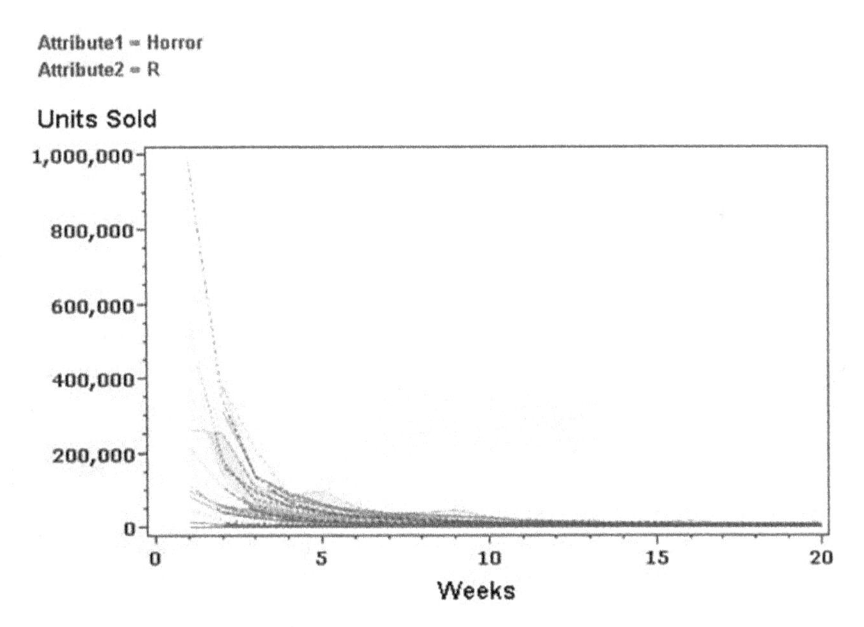

Figure 4.13 Ignoring the Uncertainty
Source: Gilliland and Guseman (2009)

one thousand to nearly one million. (A three-orders-of-magnitude range is not very helpful for supply planning!) It might be possible to narrow this range by using additional attributes (e.g., movie director or starring actors) to reduce the set of analogous DVDs; but is there any justification for this? It is easy for the unscrupulous forecaster to limit the set of analogs to those that were successful in the marketplace to have the desired amount of sales, while ignoring other perfectly analogous products that failed.

Forecasts are usually expressed as a single point (e.g., sales forecast = 500 units), but a better approach is to also provide a range (prediction interval) about that single point where the actual is likely to fall. This range is an important consideration in decision-making, as we may select an entirely different course of action when the forecast is 500 ± 50 units compared to when the forecast is 500 ± 500 units.

For ongoing products with lots of available history, you can get a reasonable sense of the prediction interval. (Note: The prediction interval may be much wider than you wish it would be!) However, for NPF when there is no history, how would we determine this? Here, forecasting by analogy shows its main value. The history of analogous products (as we saw in Figure 4.13) can give you a sense of the range of likely outcomes.

Insisting on a Wiggle

A time series of historical sales is almost invariably "wiggly." There are not only the major ups and downs of trend, seasonality, and long-term cycles, but there is randomness or noise. When we release a new product to the marketplace, we would expect its sales to be wiggly as well. So, is our forecasting model wrong if it doesn't wiggle?

A good statistical model removes the noise and expresses the underlying data generating process. This model will generate forecasts with the major ups and downs of trend, seasonality, long-term cycles, and *event*-related impacts, but will not reintroduce the randomness and noise that caused all the little wiggles in history. Forecasts are sometimes criticized because they are not wiggly enough (they do not look enough like history), but this criticism is misguided. It is actually a bad practice (overfitting) to try to model the noise.

The Hold-and-Roll

It is not unreasonable to expect forecasts to become more accurate as we get nearer the period being forecast. However, if you find your forecasts get worse the closer you get to the period being forecast, this may be a very bad sign. But how can such a thing happen?

Organizations are fond of making all sorts of plans, such as the annual operating plan. A technique favored by some management teams is the *hold-and-roll,* where plan misses are rolled into future periods to maintain ("hold") the annual plan. Thus, if we miss January sales by 10%, that miss would be added to the sales forecasts for February (or spread across February through December), so the total for the year would be unchanged. Several months of downside misses, added to the forecasts of remaining future months, could lead to even greater forecast errors in those months.

In his book *Demand-Driven Forecasting,* Charlie Chase (2009) points out a comical example of dealing with the Sales Department:

> *A common response to the question "What makes you think you can make up last month's missed demand next month?" is that "The sales organization will be more focused." "But weren't they focused last month?" "Yes, but they will be more focused next month."*

Would such a response give anyone more confidence in Sales' ability to hit the numbers?

Ignoring the Product Portfolio

New products are not released in isolation; rather, they are part of a portfolio of all the company's offerings. Sometimes the new product is completely new to the world (an invention), or part of a product category that the company previously didn't offer. In such cases, it may be reasonable to assume that all new sales are incremental to the sales of existing company offerings. Also, an existing product may be released into a new market (e.g., into additional countries), and again the new volume would likely be incremental to existing volume.

In the case of new products that are simply improvements or extensions of existing product offerings, it is unlikely that sales of the new product will be entirely incremental. It would be wrong to model the new product's demand as a distinct, independent entity and not part of an integrated portfolio. Cannibalization and halo effects are likely, as are phase-in/phase-out effects when the new product is intended to replace its predecessor.

Using Inappropriate Methods

As with any other forecasting exercise, it is important to fit the method used to the problem being solved. NPF problems include new to the world inventions, product improvements or line extensions, and new categories or markets. Also, new products can be intended to have short (e.g., fashion items or magazine issues) or long life cycles. Forecasting in these different situations will require different approaches, including both judgment and statistical modeling, although not necessarily traditional time-series modeling. A worst practice is to expect one method to work well across all of these types of NPF situations, and not be open to creative new approaches to this vexing business problem.

(Thanks to Andrew Christian, Snurre Jensen, Michael Leonard, Charlie Chase, Peter Dillman, Priya Sarathy, Udo Sglavo, Tammy Jackson, Diana McHenry, David Hardoon, and Gerhard Svolba, who contributed suggestions for this article.)

REFERENCES

Chase, C. (2009). *Demand-Driven Forecasting: A Structured Approach to Forecasting.* Hoboken, NJ: John Wiley & Sons.

Gilliland, M., and S. Gusman (2009). Forecasting new products by structured analogy. *Journal of Business Forecasting* (Winter), 12–15.

Kahn, K. (2006). *New Product Forecasting: An Applied Approach.* Armonk, NY: M.E. Sharpe.

4.12 SALES AND OPERATIONS PLANNING IN THE RETAIL INDUSTRY*

Jack Harwell

We conclude this chapter with two articles on the widespread implementations of sales and operations planning (S&OP). Although S&OP has more traditionally been used by manufacturers, Jack Harwell's article shows how it should be applied in retailing.

* This article originally appeared in *Journal of Business Forecasting* (Fall 2006), and appears here courtesy of Dr. Chaman Jain, editor-in-chief.

After providing a brief history of retailing in the United States, Harwell notes that retailers have looked to manufacturers to learn how to improve operations including *assortment planning*, *promotion planning*, and *sales and inventory planning*. For S&OP to succeed in retail, Harwell argues, there must be a sequence of escalation and filtering between three basic levels of organization: execution, executive, and C-level. Through S&OP, effective coordination can be achieved among the levels, resulting in consensus on sales plans, delineation of activities required to achieve these plans, and management of constraints.

As the postwar industrial revolution in Japan reshaped the economy, Japanese manufacturers adopted practices that enabled them to threaten the existence of American manufacturers. This threat came in the last few decades of the 20th century in the form of customer preferences. American customers recognized the superior quality and better value of Japanese goods and began to express their preferences by consuming these foreign goods.

To avoid extinction, manufacturers in the United States responded to this threat by aggressively improving the quality of their products, their production processes, and the supply chains. Retailers are facing pressures similar to those that American manufacturers felt in the last century.

Challenges facing retailers in the United States have increased dramatically. The proliferation of stock-keeping units (SKUs), growth in retail space, and increased pricing competition are forcing retailers to recognize that successful retailing requires more than just exceptional merchandising. Improving the supply chain is emerging as a key competitive weapon in the retail industry.

Historically, a small assortment of basic products in most categories was sufficient to meet the needs of the consumer. There were relatively few items, and the dominant store format was the inner-city department store. In the last half of the 20th century, fashion merchandise became the primary driver of revenues and profits. Specialty stores became more popular as shopping centers moved to the suburbs and the product choices within virtually every category exploded. As retailers began to source more products from overseas, consumer expectations for lower prices resulted in extended supply chains. Demand for a particular SKU became less predictable as the abundance of choice tempted consumers to vary their buying habits.

As these market changes occurred, retailers struggled to keep up with outdated supply chain capabilities. Historically, fashion products were bought in bulk and kept in a warehouse or the backroom of each store until it was time to display them for sale. This often resulted in overstocks or lost sales, and costly product markdowns became a strategy to not only increase sales and profits, but also to maintain cash and inventory flow.

Successful retailers have looked to manufacturing to learn how to improve their operations. They are learning how to apply the techniques developed and proven in the manufacturing industry to upgrade their retail planning and distribution processes. Quick response and lean distribution are based on putting lean manufacturing concepts into operation along the retail supply chain. More and more retailers are applying lean and Six Sigma methodologies to keep up with consumer demands and with those competitors who have become early adopters of these techniques.

Sales and Operations Planning

One discipline that has been very successful in improving the planning capabilities in manufacturing is sales and operations planning (S&OP). S&OP was developed in manufacturing in the late 1980s as an extension of MRP II. The concept of S&OP is simple: It is a structure of internal collaboration to resolve the natural tensions between supply and demand, to reach consensus on a single sales plan that every department in the company will support, and to coordinate and communicate operational plans required to achieve the sales plan.

Planning in retail also involves natural tensions that must be resolved. The availability of products, both in larger assortments and quantities, supports more sales. However, this comes with the cost of carrying inventory, reduced cash, obsolete merchandise, and severe markdowns. In retail, the balance of supply and demand can be viewed as optimizing two constraints—cash and space—while capitalizing on demand. Productivity of cash and space are essential to success in retail.

Three Plans

There are three plans that are critical in any retail organization. These are the assortment/life cycle plan, the promotion plan, and the sales and inventory plan. These plans address the opportunities in the marketplace while optimizing results. If a retail organization can organize an S&OP process around these plans, there is a high probability this process will add value to the organization.

Assortment/Life Cycle Planning

Planning assortments, a key activity of the retail merchant, is typically performed in two stages: long-term assortment planning and detailed assortment planning. Long-term assortment planning involves determining which categories of products best represent the brand image of the company, serve the needs of its customers, and attract new customers in support of the corporate strategy. Once it is determined that a category fits the overall assortment strategy, the merchant must perform detailed assortment planning.

Detailed assortment planning consists of choosing the items that will be sold by the retailer in the assortment. Before selecting the items, certain constraints must be considered. These constraints include:

- Cash available for purchasing the merchandise and the related inventory budget

- Display space in the store
- Marketing funds
- Required profits

Within these constraints, a selection of items must be chosen to meet customer expectations, which may include color, size, features, and quality. Typically, the customer wants to have multiple options when they make a purchase. However, the ideal assortment rarely involves providing all available options known to man. To do this would probably violate one or more constraints. In fact, the essence of assortment planning is to select the ideal number and variety of items within a category that optimizes the demand with space and cash availability. This also includes the pricing of items to achieve certain profit goals and to guide the consumer to purchase those items that maximize the profit.

Many activities of the retail organization depend on the assortment decisions. Where to put merchandise, how to display it, how much to purchase of each item, and other questions are answered by the assortment.

A related activity that is critical to assortment planning is life cycle planning. Because of changing technology, the customers' demand for variety, and the need to extend the brand to remain relevant to an ever-changing marketplace, many products offered by today's retailer have a limited life cycle. The typical consumer product goes through five major life cycle phases: (1) product introduction, (2) sales growth, (3) maturity, (4) decline and markdown, and (5) liquidation. Within a category, there may be many items at each life cycle phase.

Shepherding products through their product life cycles requires considerable planning and coordination. Decisions made through each stage include pricing, quantities forecasted and purchased, marketing strategies, and discount strategies to minimize product costs and maximize profits over the entire life cycle.

Promotion Planning

Since promotional events are designed to increase sales volumes, draw traffic into stores to purchase other products, and increase brand awareness, they are the staple of most retailers. These events typically take the form of product advertising in various media and in-store. Promotional planning addresses media, store operations, product selection and pricing, merchandise deliveries, and other activities required to successfully maximize profits and customer satisfaction during a promotional event.

Planning media that supports a promotion starts with choosing the geographic and socioeconomic markets that will yield the best results. The media type (newspaper insert, direct mail, broadcast, etc.) is then identified.

Product planning is also critical to the success of a promotional event. Products are selected because they are expected to attract customer interest. Typically, this is based on seasonal preferences, technological innovations, and current fads. These time-based attributes imply that the retailer must be able to make quick decisions, respond to changes in market conditions, and change direction in a coordinated manner.

Product availability, inventory budgets, and advertising budgets are all constraints that must be managed in a promotion. S&OP is an ideal structure to facilitate decisions to optimize profits from promotional activities.

Sales and Inventory Planning

Sales planning is fundamental to establishing the company goals and it serves as a basis to measure success in reaching these goals. Sales and the associated gross profits must be planned on both a financial and a unit basis.

Financial sales plans are referred to as top-down planning. Corporate goals are established, supporting activities such as staffing, financing, and inventory budgeting. Typically, financial sales plans are managed at levels of the product hierarchy above the item level and in monthly or quarterly periods.

Unit sales plans, on the other hand, are required to execute the financial sales plans and to identify which items must be purchased, displayed, and promoted. These unit sales plans are defined by item and by weeks or days.

Additionally, inventory planning is required at the financial level as well as at the unit level. The financial inventory plans help formulate the inventory budget and purchasing plan—typically referred to as *open to buy.* Unit inventory plans are used to identify which items to purchase, in what quantities, and when. Inventory flows from suppliers through distribution centers to the points of sales are determined from the unit inventory plans.

Sales and inventory planning is the process of reconciling the financial and unit sales plans, both for sales and inventory. Without this reconciliation, the company goals are at considerable risk. Sales will not materialize and inventory will be short or in excess.

Three Levels

When considering S&OP, one should view the organization as having three basic levels of structure: the execution level, the executive level, and the C-level. The execution level participants include individuals and managers that develop and execute the three plans. The executive level consists of those mid-level managers, directors, and vice presidents who are charged with setting policy, approving plans, and resolving issues among departments. The C-level is made up of senior executives who are accountable for establishing and meeting the expectations of the company's stakeholders.

Execution Level

The amount of coordination and communication required in a retail company to successfully execute the three plans is enormous. The S&OP process is a structure that can greatly enhance the company's ability to formulate and execute these plans across multiple functions.

Organizations vary from one retail company to another. However, there are five basic functions that are involved in developing and executing the three plans of retailing. These are merchandising, marketing, finance, supply chain, and store operations. Though organizational strategies combine different functions into various roles, the descriptions of these functions follow.

- **Merchandising** determines the assortment, approves the product, establishes pricing policies, and is accountable for the sales, gross profit, and inventory plans. The merchant owns the product plans and is responsible for obtaining financial results for their assigned product categories. This is a key function in the S&OP process.
- **Marketing** sets the advertising and brand strategy, manages the advertising budget, determines how to display products, defines store formats, and plans media and other events.
- **Finance** reconciles the sales, gross profit, and inventory plans with the corporate financial strategy.
- **Supply chain** activities include planning and executing the distribution of merchandise through the supply chain.
- **Store operations** manage the execution of displays, formats, and inventory control at the store level, interfacing with the customers, and making the sale.

The individuals working at the execution level determine assortments; plan promotions; project sales, margin, and inventory; place purchase orders with suppliers; plan and execute distribution to stores; and evaluate the financial impact of these plans. They work together on a daily basis to review and analyze results and take action to respond to the unfolding dynamics of the market, making minor corrections as required to achieve their goals.

In the S&OP structure, participants working at the execution level manage both item plans (SKUs and quantities) and financial plans (sales, gross profits, and inventory dollars aggregated at various levels of product hierarchy). Teams are formed to align with product categories or subcategories, enabling everyone to focus on the same strategies and results.

Once detailed plans are formulated, actual results are evaluated and corrective actions are developed. These must then be translated into an overall picture of where the company is going and what is required to get there. This picture must be painted at the summary level, with only the amount of detail required to clarify significant issues. Decisions that can be made at the execution level are filtered out, leaving only those requiring support from senior management. The purpose of this translation is to effectively communicate with and request assistance from the executive staff involved. Typically, the discussion at the executive level is kept at the category or department level.

Executive Level

The responsibilities of the executive level in S&OP include resolving conflicts between organizations, approving major decisions made at the execution level, and ensuring that the plans and results coming out of the execution level meet the corporate objectives.

Representatives of the execution level participants meet with those of the executive level to review the plans, results, issues, and results for their assigned products. Decisions that can be made at this level are documented and communicated to the rest of the execution team.

C-Level

As leaders of the organizations involved in sales and operations planning, the C-level executives must be kept informed of progress with regard to plans and goals, major actions required to remain on track, and opportunities that have developed in the market. This is done by combining the information from the various categories into one consolidated view of the business. This high-level view is used to communicate results and future expectations to the company owners.

Sales and Operations Planning Escalation Process

The interaction among the execution, executive, and C-level staff is a sequence of escalation and filtering, as described above. Plans, issues, and decisions required are filtered up through the organization, while decisions are cascaded down. This process of escalation and filtering is an efficient way to keep senior executives involved in the S&OP process.

Figure 4.14 is an illustration of how the various levels interact, significant issues and information are escalated, and decisions are cascaded.

Other Keys to S&OP Success

One important aspect of an S&OP structure is the frequency of meetings. In most cases, it is sufficient to review and discuss the three plans mentioned above monthly. However, when designing the meeting structures at the execution level, it is advised that a separate meeting be held for each plan. This allows sufficient time on the agenda to adequately cover all topics.

The timing of sales and operations planning meetings should consider when the financial plans must be developed. In a public company, this is usually

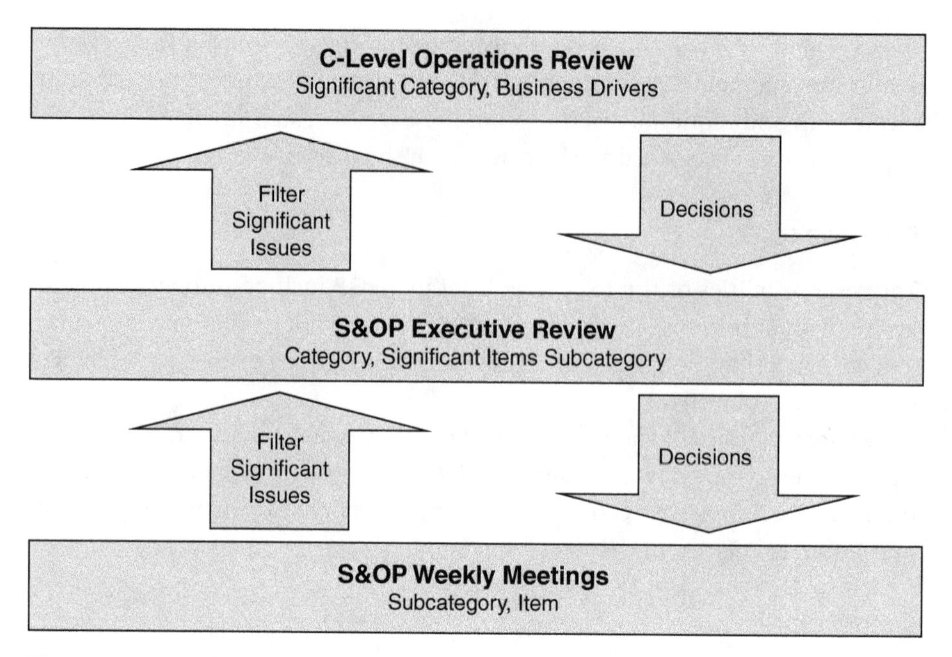

Figure 4.14 S&OP Escalation Process

dictated by the schedule set by a board of directors to support announcements and disclosure to stockholders and the Securities and Exchange Commission. Even though not accountable to the public, private companies also require periodic review and resetting of financial plans. Most companies—public and private—have adopted a monthly financial review.

It is also important to structure the timing of the meeting levels so that the executive level and C-level meetings follow the execution level. This allows the execution level participants to identify issues, develop actions to resolve them, and reset plans.

Adequate time must be available to articulate a comprehensive view of the business to senior management. In addition, those larger issues and changes to the plan that the execution team cannot resolve or approve must be communicated to the next level for approval. Figure 4.15 is an example of a meeting cadence that can be used for S&OP.

	Week 1	Week 2	Week 3	Week 4
Financial Planning Cadence			Sales Plan	Inventory Plan
Weekly S&OP Cadence	Sales/Inventory Plan		Assortment/Life Cycle Plan	Promotional Plan
Monthly S&OP Cadence		Executive Review	C-Level Operations Review	

Figure 4.15 Meeting Cadence

Goals and Key Performance Indicators

It is critical that metrics, or key performance indicators (KPIs), are defined to establish goals and measure success. These KPIs should take into account the objectives of the company and measure the ability to manage the constraints.

In a retail environment, there are two main constraints to consider: display space and inventory levels. Gross profit return on space (GPROS) and gross profit return on inventory (GPROI) are effective in measuring the ability to optimize profits within these constraints. Because these KPIs reflect the efforts of all participants and the cross-functional nature of the S&OP process, putting an emphasis on them will keep everyone involved focused on success. GPROS and GPROI are measured as follows:

$$\text{GPROS} = \text{Gross profit} / \text{Display space}$$
$$\text{GPROI} = \text{Gross profit} / \text{Average inventory}$$

Top-Level Support

S&OP is a highly cross-functional activity. Because of this, top level support of the process is critical to success. However, it is not sufficient for senior leadership to simply express their support in words. It is great to have a powerful cheerleader on your side, but more is required. Senior managers must define KPIs, agree on reporting format, establish expectations for information flow and decision making, require participation from all, and expect actions to be completed on time.

As mentioned before, KPIs must be designed to measure the performance of everyone involved in S&OP. When top management identifies KPIs and sets goals using these metrics, a definition of success emerges. The organization will more likely make the right decisions if they focus on these KPIs, and will share both the successes and failures.

It is typical for different organizations within a company to use various report formats to support their unique activities. The cross-functional nature of S&OP requires that a standard format for reports is used to communicate plans and record results. To keep everyone on the same page—literally—the report formats must be the same. Because top management ultimately needs to understand the information communicated to their level, it is a good idea for senior managers to define how the information will appear to them. Of course, the actual work in defining the reports will probably be performed by one or more subordinates; however, top level agreement is critical.

Information flow defines how and when information about plans, results, issues, and decisions are communicated up and down the organization. Top management must define when issues are to be communicated, the degree of granularity, and the rules regarding who must be informed of an issue or make a decision. This will make sure there is consistency among organizations and provide the necessary structure for delegating planning authority at each level.

S&OP demands involvement of all the functions to build and execute effective plans. Senior leaders of the organization must make it clear that there has to be participation at all levels, including attendance at all meetings and the timely completion of assigned tasks. A standard format for action logs, including a record of attendance, will assist management in supporting the process.

If effectively communicated, formats, expectations, and discipline will cascade from the top. It is more likely that everyone will fall in line with top management guidance if this communication is clear and consistent.

Conclusion

U.S. manufacturers have responded to competitive pressures by aggressively reducing costs and improving quality. Among the many processes developed to achieve these goals, sales and operations planning is used to gain consensus on a sales plan, to coordinate activities required to achieve these plans, and to manage constraints.

Like other manufacturing methods, this process can be adapted successfully to the retail environment. Addressing the three plans of retailing—assortment/life cycle, sales and inventory, and promotion—the key functions of retail reach a consensus on common goals and the means to achieve them. Once established at the execution level, these plans should be reviewed with the executive level and C-level leaders. Significant issues and required decisions are filtered upward; direction and support are cascaded downward. The process of working together both horizontally and vertically ensures that the entire organization is working toward common goals and is successfully meeting the challenges that retailers face today.

4.13 SALES AND OPERATIONS PLANNING: WHERE IS IT GOING?*

Tom Wallace

Tom Wallace, along with co-author Bob Stahl, has contributed much of the key thinking on sales and operations planning over the last 20 years. In this article, Wallace reflects on a series of frequently asked questions about the S&OP process and its future direction.

* This article originally appeared in *Journal of Business Forecasting* (Summer 2013), and appears here courtesy of Dr. Chaman Jain, editor in chief.

Although "invented" over 20 years ago, S&OP is currently in a stage of wide popularity and rapid adoption, which Wallace points out is consistent with the adoption curves for other business processes like TQM/Six Sigma, JIT/Lean, and MRP/ERP. With the proliferation of products and distribution channels, as well as shorter product lifecycles and longer lead times, specialized S&OP software will continue to replace Excel for managing the process.

Wallace distinguishes S&OP (which operates with aggregated data such as product families) from weekly scheduling meetings that focus on individual products. He also considers the need for global S&OP as well as the use of S&OP for new product launches. He concludes with brief examples from three companies featured in his 2011 book, *Sales & Operations Planning: Beyond the Basics.*

Sales and operations planning (S&OP) or executive S&OP has emerged as a highly effective process for managing a business. As a result, it's quite popular, just about everyone is either "doing S&OP" or implementing it. Contained in this thought is good news and bad news. The good news is that S&OP is robust.

When done properly, a company can generate enormous benefits, which we divide into two categories: hard benefits and soft benefits. Hard benefits are those that can be quantified, including among others:

- Higher levels of on-time shipments
- Lower inventories
- Shorter customer lead times
- Reduced time to launch new products
- Improved plant productivity

Soft benefits can't be quantified, but in many successful S&OP-using companies, they're considered of equal importance or nearly so. Soft benefits include:

- Enhanced teamwork
- Improved communications—institutionalized
- Better decisions with less effort and time
- Better $$$ plans with less effort and time
- Greater accountability
- Greater control
- Window into the future

Today some companies are receiving all of these benefits, and more. But now for the bad news: Not all companies are getting all or most of the benefits; some are receiving less than half, some are near zero, and there are some that haven't yet started. The reason for this sub-par performance is that, in almost all cases, S&OP was not implemented properly. However, when people see more than a few companies are not being successful with the process, the tendency is to blame the process, and not the people who implemented it. This, of course, is too bad because it may lead them to think that, since the process is not working, it should be discontinued. I get a fair amount of questions along these lines, and here's a sample of the more common ones:

Q. How long will S&OP stay popular?

A. If by popular we mean red hot, as it's been for the past roughly half dozen years, my guess is another six years or so. On the other hand, if by popular we mean widely used in businesses around the world, I believe strongly that it's here to stay. As long as there are businesses, manufacturing and otherwise, it'll be here even long after we're all gone. (Double entry bookkeeping, one of the important foundations for Generally Accepted Accounting Practices, was invented in the 15th century in Italy, and it's still widely used.)

The Adoption Curve, as shown in Figure 4.16, states that there is roughly a 20-year lag between the initial creation of a process and its widespread adoption (Inflection Point A). After a period of intense implementation of the process, its growth levels off and the growth rate of the process becomes that of industry in general (Inflection Point B). We can see that S&OP is following the same curve as Six Sigma, Lean, and ERP.

Q. Will S&OP change and evolve?

A. This is virtually certain. What's equally certain is that it will change less than it stays the same. The changes will be primarily peripheral rather

There is a 15–25-year lag between the development of a new process and its widespread adoption.

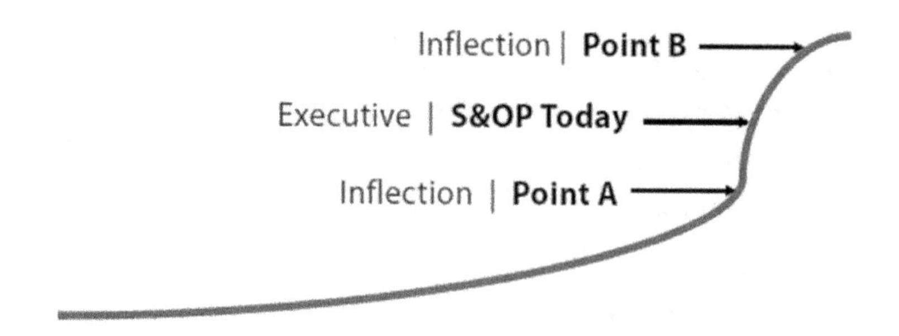

Examples: TQM/6SIGMA, JIT/LEAN, MRP/ERP

Figure 4.16 The Adoption Curve

than being in the heart of the process . . . in extensions and enhancements, but not in fundamentals. A good example is MRP. Back in its heyday, a frequently asked question was will it change a lot and will it maybe go away? Today, we see it stronger than ever: evolving into ERP, more widely used beyond manufacturing but with the same basic capabilities that were present in the 1970s.

Q. Will the S&OP software affect its growth?

A. Yes it will, and for the better. The world is becoming a far more complex place, and the level of complexity that is prevalent today didn't exist a dozen of years ago. Back in those days, we were saying, "You don't need software to be successful with S&OP; you can get by with Excel." Today we have proliferation of products and channels of distribution as well as shorter life cycles and longer lead-times. One can say, "You don't need software to be successful if your business is relatively small and simple." As shown in Figure 4.17, if you're at the lower end of the diagonal—a simple business with few products and materials, short lead times, highly cooperative customers, and so on—you may need S&OP but won't need S&OP software.

Figure 4.18 shows that as you move up the diagonal toward more and more complexity and change, your need for first-rate S&OP software increases right along with it. Complexity increases as a result of doing business globally; lengthy, fragile, and non-agile supply chain; need to respond quickly to changes in market dynamics; demand for higher and higher customer service level; and availability of large amount of data. For most companies now, the days of "Blood, Sweat, and Excel" are over.

Q. Will S&OP become a real-time process?

A. In one sense, it already is. For example, in an Executive Meeting, when data is needed to support a given decision, it often can be gathered, synthesized, and presented in the meeting on the fly. However, I don't believe that real

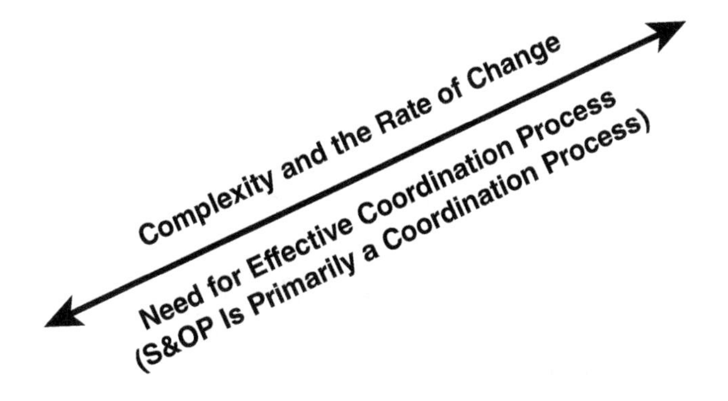

Figure 4.17 Complexity, Change, and Coordination

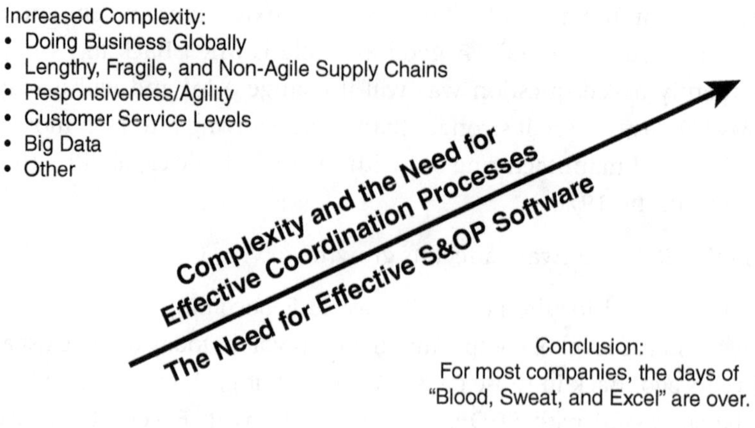
Increased Complexity:
• Doing Business Globally
• Lengthy, Fragile, and Non-Agile Supply Chains
• Responsiveness/Agility
• Customer Service Levels
• Big Data
• Other
Complexity and the Need for
Effective Coordination Processes
The Need for Effective S&OP Software
Conclusion:
For most companies, the days of
"Blood, Sweat, and Excel" are over.

Figure 4.18 Complexity, Change, and Coordination

time in the true sense of the word will ever play much of a role. If S&OP becomes truly real time, it will no longer be S&OP and the job that S&OP does today will almost certainly not be done. Why? Because S&OP is not a short-term scheduling and optimizing tool; rather it's a medium-to-long-term planning process, directed by executive management, and it sets the conditions for success when the medium and long terms move into the near term. Using short-term, real-time tools to address medium and long-term issues is the managerial equivalent of using a saw to hammer nails. Does it make sense to try to use in real time the tool that has monthly time buckets and operates on a monthly basis? I think not.

Q. But what about companies that do weekly S&OP?

A. I've seen some of these and they do not qualify as S&OP. Rather they look more like a type of Master Scheduling. S&OP operates with aggregated data such as product families; Master Scheduling focuses on individual products and stock keeping units (SKUs). I have nothing against a weekly meeting, in addition to S&OP. That way, you'll be using a saw to cut wood and a hammer to drive nails. That works. A weekly meeting to address next week's schedules and other issues can be very helpful (as it was for me back in the old days).

Q. One of the factors that adds complexity is globalization. Since most companies today do business globally, don't most companies need to do global S&OP?

A. Not necessarily. Let's take the case of the Superior Widgets Company, a manufacturer of widgets for home and industry. Its only plant is located in Nebraska serving its four sales regions around the world. Guess what? Superior does not need Global S&OP; it can make S&OP work very well

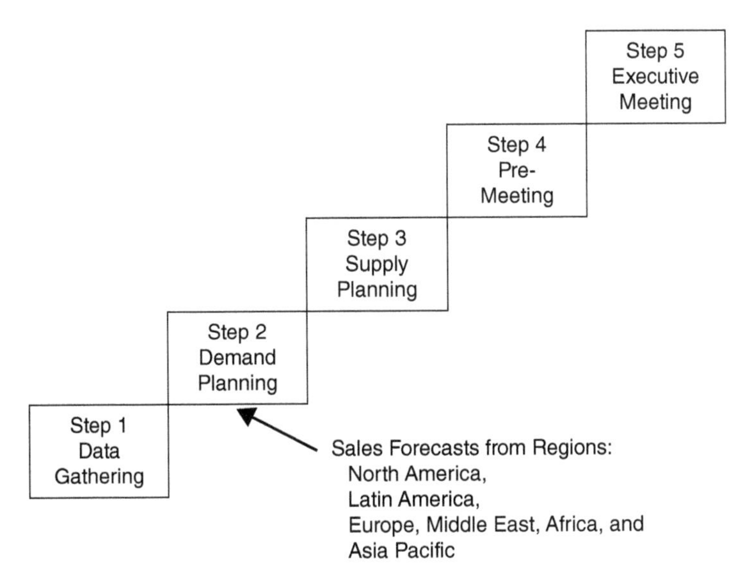

Figure 4.19 The Executive S&OP Process for Superior Widgets, Inc.

with the standard Five-Step Process. (See Figure 4.19.) The plant has to get the demand planning picture from all of the regions before it can complete its supply planning. How could it do otherwise? If Superior at some point adds a plant outside of North America making the same products, then they would need Global S&OP because they have two separate demand/supply streams.

Q. New product launch (NPL) is, for many companies, the most difficult thing to do. Can S&OP help in launching new products?

A. Yes, it can help and has been helping for many years, for decades even. Some of the early adopters of S&OP saw that it was a natural to support the introduction of new products. Why is it a natural? Because NPL is replete with opportunities for things to go wrong: quality and performance issues, production problems, supplier shortfalls, and so forth. As mentioned earlier, S&OP is fundamentally a coordination tool; when things go wrong, S&OP can be very helpful in realigning priorities and creating a new plan. This will help keep the NPL on schedule and to be more "sure-footed" during the entire launch.

A disclaimer: It's likely that most or all of your existing NPL processes will still be needed, e.g., stage-gate decision making. S&OP's job is to blend the specific new product plans into the company's sales and supply plans.

Q. Is S&OP strategic or tactical?

A. The answer is yes; it's actually both. It was developed as a tactical planning tool and has filled that role extremely well. However, a first-rate S&OP

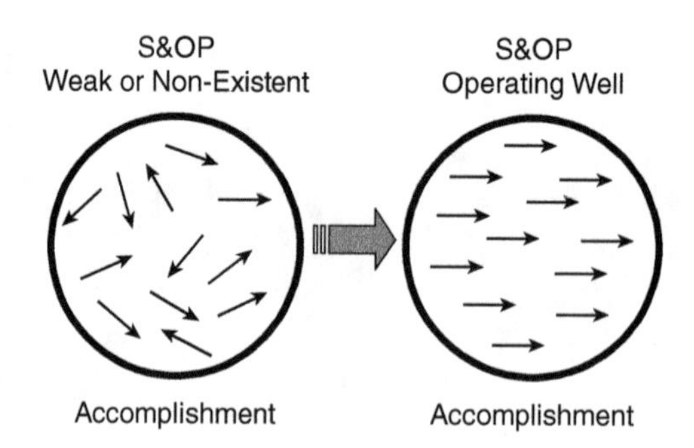

Figure 4.20 Energy Alignment

process can greatly enhance a company's ability to execute its strategic plans. Here, coordination is the key. A somewhat tongue-in-cheek statement about the CEO's mission is: Keep the Herd Moving Roughly West. We call it energy alignment. S&OP will work well, if all are moving in the same direction. (See Figure 4.20.)

Here are three examples of companies that use S&OP to enhance and execute their strategic plans (Wallace, 2011).

1. **BASF**: Around the year 2000, the company set a strategic goal to become No. 1 in the chemical business worldwide. It achieved that goal before the end of the decade, and they credit S&OP with providing substantial help in that regard. How? By optimizing its production plans globally based on gross profit, and used the additional profit to fund the necessary growth.
2. **Cisco Systems**: It created an entirely new business from scratch, with products quite different from their traditional ones. Cisco people state that S&OP played a major role in enabling them to launch on schedule, ship 98% on time from day one, and keep order fulfillment lead times to less than five days. It is now No. 1 globally in this business.
3. **Dow Chemical**: The acquisition of Rohm and Haas was a key element in Dow's long-term strategy of moving more heavily into specialty chemicals. S&OP is credited with playing a significant role in helping to integrate the two companies—on time and ahead of budget—and was a driving force for generating cost and growth synergies.

There is a relationship between the strategic/tactical issue and the time frame. In the short term, S&OP is almost totally tactical; medium term it becomes somewhat more strategic; long term, it's focused heavily on strategic issues.

Summary

Here's a recap of the issues we focused on:

1. How long will S&OP be popular? Longer than any of us will be around.
2. Will it change and evolve? Yes, but the fundamentals will stay the same.
3. Will S&OP software affect its growth? Yes, and on balance for the better.
4. Will S&OP become a real-time process? Perhaps partially, but not fully.
5. What about the companies that do weekly S&OP? Weekly S&OP is not S&OP except in periods when there is extreme seasonality.
6. Don't most companies need to do global S&OP? No. Only those with global sources of supply in addition to global demand.
7. Can S&OP help with launching new products? Absolutely. It has been helping for years, decades.
8. Is S&OP strategic or tactical? It's both.

My concluding comment: S&OP is here to stay; it'll get better and better; and will, at some point in the future, be widely accepted as the standard set of processes with which to run a business. Neglect it at your peril.

REFERENCE

Wallace, T. (2011). *Sales and Operations Planning: Beyond the Basics*. Montgomery, OH: T. F. Wallace & Company.

About the Editors

Michael Gilliland is the marketing manager for SAS forecasting software, editor of the Forecasting Practice section of *Foresight: The International Journal of Applied Forecasting*, and author of *The Business Forecasting Deal*. He has published articles in *Supply Chain Management Review*, *Journal of Business Forecasting*, *Analytics*, *Supply Chain Forecasting Digest*, *APICS Magazine*, *Swiss Analytics Magazine*, and *Foresight*. Mike holds a BA in philosophy from Michigan State University, and master's degrees in philosophy and mathematical sciences from Johns Hopkins University. Follow his blog *The Business Forecasting Deal* at blogs.sas.com/content/forecasting.

* * *

Len Tashman is the founding editor of *Foresight: The International Journal of Applied Forecasting*, now in its 10th year of publication. He serves on the board of directors of the International Institute of Forecasters and is organizer and chair of the Forecasting in Practice Track at the annual International Symposium on Forecasting. Len is an emeritus professor of business administration at the University of Vermont and Director of the Center for Business Forecasting.

* * *

Udo Sglavo is the senior director of predictive modeling R&D at SAS Institute. His team develops industry-leading and award-winning software for data mining, machine learning, and large-scale automatic forecasting. He has published articles in *Analytics* and is a contributor to *The Business Forecasting Deal* blog. Udo has served on the practitioner advisory board of *Foresight* and holds a diploma in mathematics from the University of Applied Sciences, Darmstadt, Germany.

Index

Printed in the USA
CPSIA information can be obtained
at www.ICGtesting.com
LVHW080900101123
763411LV00029B/32